MOBILIZING THE COMMUNITY

URBAN AFFAIRS ANNUAL REVIEW

A semiannual series of reference volumes discussing programs, policies, and current developments in all areas of concern to urban specialists.

The **Urban Affairs Annual Review** presents original theoretical, normative, and empirical work on urban issues and problems in volumes published on an annual or bi-annual basis. The objective is to encourage critical thinking and effective practice by bringing together interdisciplinary perspectives on a common urban theme. Research that links theoretical, empirical, and policy approaches and that draws on comparative analyses offers the most promise for bridging disciplinary boundaries and contributing to these broad objectives. With the help of an international advisory board, the editors will invite and review proposals for **Urban Affairs Annual Review** volumes that incorporate these objectives. The aim is to ensure that the **Urban Affairs Annual Review** remains in the forefront of urban research and practice by providing thoughtful, timely analyses of cross-cutting issues for an audience of scholars, students, and practitioners working on urban concerns throughout the world.

RECENT VOLUMES

MOBILIZING THE COMMUNITY

◆

Local Politics in the Era of the Global City

edited by
ROBERT FISHER
JOSEPH KLING

**URBAN
AFFAIRS
ANNUAL
REVIEW
41**

SAGE Publications
International Educational and Professional Publisher
Newbury Park   London   New Delhi

For information address:

SAGE Publications, Inc.
2455 Teller Road
Newbury Park, California 91320

SAGE Publications Ltd.
6 Bonhill Street
London EC2A 4PU
United Kingdom

SAGE Publications India Pvt. Ltd.
M-32 Market
Greater Kailash I
New Delhi 110 048 India

Printed in the United States of America

ISSN 0083-4688

ISBN 0-8039-4247-8 (cl).

ISBN 0-8039-4248-6 (pb)

93 94 95 96 10 9 8 7 6 5 4 3 2 1

Sage Production Editor: Diane S. Foster

Contents

Acknowledgments

There are so many people, directly and indirectly, who make a volume such as this possible. We would like to acknowledge our debt and thanks to those most directly involved. Dennis Judd had the initial idea for the book; his enthusiasm about the importance of community mobilization was the spark behind our work. The series editors, Dennis Judd and Susan Clarke read all the contributions and their comments were always insightful, challenging, and demanding. Prudence Posner must be given credit as a silent editor. She read many of the articles, made meticulous suggestions, and helped sharpen many of the debates. Whatever the volume's strengths, much is owed to her support and help. We would also like to acknowledge the support of St. Lawrence University and the University of Houston, especially the latter's small grant to finish this project. Finally, we want to thank the contributors themselves who put up with our constraints, criticisms, requests for revisions, and deadlines. Their willingness to engage in debate has resulted in what we believe are a compelling set of essays on an issue that continues to be a central one for our time—the possibility of community action and local change in an era where power is becoming more and more concentrated globally.

Introduction: The Continued Vitality of Community Mobilization

ROBERT FISHER
JOSEPH KLING

The world is in dramatic flux. Global concerns force themselves on people's everyday lives at the same time that local events, with unprecedented speed and frequency, become global matters. Political upheaval, environmental degradation, cultural images, international summits, and multinational corporate decisions travel worldwide, as fast as the speed of electronic informational systems, and directly and indirectly affect the lives of people next door as well as those thousands of miles away.

The idea of the global village was a once fashionable description of the ways in which the connections between people and nations across the globe have intensified and increased in the modern era. But it is, at the same time, a cliché that fails to capture how these global processes have disordered people's conceptions of who they are and to whom they are related and have undermined their bearings as to the nature of the social spaces in which their daily lives are grounded.

Village signifies a place where there are few disruptions of the routines of living, few surprises, few threats. In the village, strangers are rare, and, if everyone does not quite know everyone else, people at least recognize most of the faces they pass in the street. It is a metaphor for the closeness of people and for the reassuring familiarity and durability of the day to day.

Life in the "global village" is a bit more complicated. People are indeed connected to one another, but the connections remain, for many, mysterious and poorly understood. They are generally experienced as forms of intrusion and imposition rather than ones of support and community. If the world is a village, then it is one without security, constancy, predictability. Of course, there is another side to all of this: Global restructuring also brings new fluidity, openness, and possibilities. Indeed, the opportunities offered by the current changes and transformation of global society make up one of the central theses of this volume. While in response to what is variously called the shift to late capitalism, postindustrialism, post-Fordism, postmodernism, or complex society, some people and institutions seek innovation, most desire more control.

Some seek control to halt the changes, preferring to return to a more traditional past, usually mythical and conservative, of laissez-faire capitalism and fundamentalist values. Others seek control to empower themselves and their communities to be able to affect change to promote a more peaceful and equitable society. Those with the most concentrated power—the forces of capital—affect the process with disproportionate and greatest success, influencing global politics and economics, dominating the lives of communities, villages, and cities, determining through the flow of investments which shall live or die, which shall prosper or decline. Those with the least concentrated resources—ordinary, relatively powerless citizens, and especially the poor—seek at the grass roots to promote their interests, protect their communities, resist the ravages of the new world order, and, at their best, to stimulate the egalitarian, democratic potentials of our current time through a multitude of types of grass-roots citizen action. It is grass-roots organizing, the primary form of popular resistance and direct political participation in the new world order, that is the subject of the chapters in this volume.

Efforts to mobilize communities are a global phenomenon. "In villages, neighborhoods, and shantytowns around the world," Durning (1989, p. 5) writes, "people are coming together to strike back at the forces of environmental and economic decline that endanger our communities and our planet." In the United States the growth of grass-roots activism in the 1970s, including more than 20 million Americans, seemed like a "backyard revolution" (Boyte, 1981). The United Kingdom experienced a similar "upsurge of urban social movement activity" (Lowe, 1986, p. 4). Throughout Europe in the late 1970s, citizen action efforts expanded constantly, leading one commentator to declare "no apparent end in sight" (Susskind et al., 1983, p. 22). And while grass-roots organizing and urban protest have been key elements of political life in the West in the last quarter of a century, this phenomenon is not limited to "modern states" (Katznelson, 1981; see also Corbridge, 1991, for a review of recent literature on Third World grass-roots oppositional movements). Seen from a global perspective, community movements, numbering membership in the hundreds of millions, proliferated throughout the West and South and, with extraordinary and as yet uncertain results, in the East (Boyte, 1981; Durning, 1989; Frank & Fuentes, 1990, p. 163).

By the late 1970s almost all social scientists studying Western politics agreed that "the idea of unconventional political participation as a legitimate source of democratic citizenship ha[d] spread out into the wider political community" (Sharpe, 1979, p. 59). But the significance of such activity remains ambiguous and hotly debated. Ceccarelli (1982) sees urban social movements as a powerful force in Europe in the late 1960s and early 1970s, but as a temporary, brief episode before elites forged a new political consensus in the late 1970s. For him, community-based organizing persists, but its heyday was the 1970s when the struggles of the 1960s were still unresolved. Gottdiener, writing about efforts in the United States, despairs about the future and potential of grass-roots movements, which he finds powerless to challenge the massive structural changes of the 1980s. "No mechanisms currently exist that can aggregate neighborhood mobilization of needs into a viable public discourse on the future state of the metropolis," he wrote. "Today one can speak realistically only of the decline of political culture, not its prospects for rebirth at some time" (1987, p. 285). Such frankly stated pessimism is at the least bracing.

On the other hand, neopopulists like Durning (1989) and Boyte (1981) argue that a grass-roots revolution is occurring both worldwide and in the United States. New social movement theorists like Touraine (1985) and Castells (1983), not to mention world systems theorists such as Wallerstein (1990), see these grass-roots social movements as the best hope for a progressive future. For them, grass-roots mobilization is the most effective, if flawed, means to develop progressive urban policy, empower citizens, and foster the emergence of a dynamic and democratic public life.

Thus analysis regarding contemporary community-based organizing has been highly theoretical and sharply divided, reflecting the recent reemergence and unpredictable impact of grass-roots citizen action. This volume's importance lies in its attempt to bring both empirically based case studies and theoretical clarity to the issues at hand. The chapters demonstrate that, in spite of the fragmentation of the traditional Left, efforts to mobilize communities go on worldwide. They convey a sense of the tremendous variety of these movements as well as their continued vitality. And, finally, the work offers to both analysts and practitioners some theoretical ways out of the maze of debate about the meaning of contemporary activism and some suggestions for the direction of practice.

The volume seeks to be as inclusive as possible, comprising efforts as distinct as citizen initiatives, ethnic self-help organizations, community-based development and service delivery programs, political lobbying and advocacy efforts, political party building, and direct action protest groups. Chapters address, for example, oppositional efforts of middle-class suburbanites, the poor, women, gay men and lesbian women, communists, neopopulists, workers, immigrants, Hispanics, and blacks. The tendency here is to focus on the more oppositional, more resistance-oriented aspects of the grass-roots phenomenon; for us, they represent the vanguard of citizen action. The volume is necessarily global in perspective, including chapters on efforts in the United States, the United Kingdom, Western Europe (France and Germany), Latin America (Brazil), and Asia (India). Much is missing, particularly movements in the formerly state socialist sector of Eastern Europe, but these efforts require both more attention and more time to develop than we have available.

■ Theoretical Debates

The shift from industrial to postindustrial, or complex, society has profoundly affected the makeup and organization of social movements and challenged all received notions about their functioning. The old ways of thinking about social movements are not commensurate with the realities of today's complex society, and new ways of imagining the workings, forms, and ends of collective struggle have not yet been established or stabilized. While social movements, as the case studies in this volume demonstrate, continue to exist and to revitalize themselves, there are a number of ways in which they simply do not fit older categories of understanding.

The central theoretical tensions in the literature cohere around competing models of structuralism, the force of contingent and local political realities, and human agency. Simply put, structuralists emphasize the existence of a global political economy that determines the nature and potential of grass-roots mobilization worldwide. For those emphasizing the structural base of the international economy and the global restructuring of cities, urban forms and responses are increasingly converging, even as the particular urban form of the central city disaggregates into the postindustrial metropolitan complex. The transformation of urban centers like New York and London into corporate headquarter cities reverberates in semiperipheral cities like São Paulo and Bombay and peripheral ones like Nairobi and Manila. Regionally grounded social movements draw from differential placement in relation to the use and mobility of capital investment: They are at different points in a connected but fluid process. The movements that, in American communities threatened by pollution and gentrification, resist continued economic growth are responding to the same forces that lead the residents of Brazilian *favelas* to organize their own health clinics and set up their own schools. Thus the central argument that structuralists make is about the ways in which grass-roots mobilizations worldwide are linked, despite their different histories, politics, and locations in the varied geographic and cultural spaces, in an overall world capitalist system.

Local political process proponents emphasize that local and national political contexts, not the primacy of some sort of global political-economic structures, are critical to understanding urban developments, especially grass-roots mobilization. Most participants in a recent comparative study of urban restructuring argue strongly, for example, that national and local context, especially political power relations, should be the focus of urban analysis (Logan & Swanstrom, 1990). These authors find suspect any lumping together of developments across nations and cities and doubt neo-Marxist arguments about how the hypermobility of capital in the current global economy locks cities and citizens into specific political and economic forms. For them, the global political economy is mediated through local and national politics, resulting in diverse urban cultures, political structures, everyday policies, and, for our purposes, grass-roots resistance. "The determinism to be wary of these days," Harvey Molotch (1990, p. 177) warns, "is the notion that the globalism of production patterns translates into uniform spatial and social consequences at the urban level." Pickvance and Preteceille (1991, p. 222) concur, arguing for "variation-seeking" models of local political processes because, based on their research, comparative analysis does not support "convergence theory." For Ceccarelli (1982, p. 275), "Differences instead of similarities ought to be stressed and better analyzed."

Human agency proponents emphasize that the nature and potential of citizen action is determined at the grass roots. In the everyday interactions of people, in the meetings of organizers and activists, consciousness is raised through discourse and experience. Here strategies and tactics are planned; here people react to and initiate change. As M. P. Smith (1989, p. 355) notes, impersonal conditions constitute the historical context within which people act but "people are not merely passive recipients of these structural economic and political conditions. They are creators of meaning, which is also a wellspring of human action and historic change." "Within the boundaries of certain structures," Melucci (1989, p. 197) adds, "people participate in cognitive, affective, and interactive relationships and creatively transform their own social action." The emphasis here is on the organizers and the organized, on the microscopic level where people live their lives and choose how to resist domination. The foundation of this literature is a wide array of work by social workers, social historians, and activists, all of whom focus on the question of organizing from the perspective of the organizer and the organized. Postmodernist texts, especially in anthropology and literature, now join this side, emphasizing that it is the inclusion of the lives of those formerly disregarded—the polyvocal voices of diverse peoples—not the macro (global political economy) or mezzo (national/local) forces of history, that best represents the true state of domination and resistance.

One of the points this volume demonstrates is that, to an extent, all three of these approaches are correct. The mezzoanalysis of diverse political realities is right: Different local contexts do spawn profound differences in citizen action. Community mobilization is shaped by past and current conditions, from the larger contexts of national political culture to more specific ones regarding current political regimes and power relationships, oppositional groupings and leadership within and outside a city, and local assumptions about the legitimacy of direct action. All of these help explain why activism in one nation, city, or community might differ from another (Kaase, 1990; Susskind et al., 1983). Organizing in Munich, London, New York, Houston, and Bombay, to state the obvious, is deeply affected by the widely different "structural potentials for collective action," including the political opportunities and indigenous organizations, found there (McAdam, 1982; C. Smith, 1991).

But models emphasizing the diverse political realities of community mobilization across space and time do not account for the common conditions that have helped produce the global proliferation of grassroots citizen action in the past 25 years. Sassen (1990, p. 237), for example, disagrees with most of the other authors in the Logan and

Swanstrom volume, concluding that "these chapters mostly show that larger translocal economic forces have far more weight than local policies in shaping urban economies." While dramatic change occurs from place to place as well as over time, cities are now caught up in the webs of a global political economy. The keen desire of Houston, Texas, to be a "world class city" is instructive (Feagin, 1988). The shared characteristics of grass-roots organizing throughout the globe are startling. Molotch's warning heeded, transnational factors, such as the mobility, velocity, and needs of global capital, do profoundly affect city form and function and the nature of grass-roots resistance.

It is painfully obvious that both the macro and the mezzo levels influence and are influenced by the people involved at the grass roots. Of course, not all resistance is organized, and not all institutions are formal. In living rooms, bars, beauty parlors, and basketball courts, people find and create free spaces. Here they make collective choices about whether and how to advance their claims and address their grievances. In more formal grass-roots resistance, people make decisions about leadership, organization, ideology, goals, strategy, tactics, and so forth, none of which are predetermined at the macro or mezzo level. Nevertheless, the focus on free spaces, human agency, and the day-to-day lives of people frequently forgets or does not see, as is too often true with the citizenry itself, the larger systems, institutions, and processes that shape their lives, choices, and organizing efforts (Fisher, 1984).

This volume offers a synthesis of the competing analyses and claims. We think grass-roots mobilizations are the product of and are deeply affected by the international transformation of the global economic base *and* its mediation through national/local political contexts *and* people's everyday actions and activism. Each chapter in the volume does not necessarily incorporate all these elements, though it is impressive how much use of different approaches does occur. But the goal here is for the sum of the chapters to yield a synthetic framework, so that, finally, the volume will argue for a fuller, more inclusive treatment and understanding of grass-roots resistance.

■ The Chapters

We are convinced that a conceptual synthesis of the way the three factors of the global political economy, local politics, and activist responses conjoin in the world of action is critical to any understanding of the way subordinate groups and classes might become empowered and create conditions under which they begin to exercise meaningful control over their lives. To contribute to the development of a new synthesis is never easy, particularly in an edited collection, and especially on a topic as broad and current as the status of worldwide community mobilization. Yet we believe that the chapters have enough common threads to weave a broadly diverse, fluid, and powerful understanding of the subject. The chapters blend theory with a multitude of suggestions regarding strategy, tactics, ideology, and leadership to enhance the potential and help fulfill the prospects of grass-roots mobilization. We offer a brief description of each chapter to show how it fits with the larger empirical and theoretical synthesis suggested by the volume as a whole.

The first three chapters attempt to place contemporary mobilization in historical and theoretical context. Robert Fisher's opening chapter examines the subtle ways in which the three arenas of the global political economy, local/national politics, and the efforts and consciousness of organizers and the organized intertwine to yield grass-roots initiatives. The chapter emphasizes the shared characteristics and heritage of grass-roots resistance worldwide and argues that in our contemporary global context efforts must focus not only on empowering citizens and communities but also on challenging the local/national state.

Joseph Kling's chapter examines the phenomena of the new social movements. It offers a theory of how the complexities of postindustrial and postmodern societies, as well as the restructuring of urban space in the disaggregated cities of our time, have helped reshape social movement forms. Because, while class structures continue to inform the experience of everyday life, and the new social movements are, in many ways, part of a continuum grounded in the community mobilizations that were common features of the industrial era, the oppositional efforts that emerge in complex society are not simple extensions of prior activist structures. The centrality of issues of identity, the presence of new modes of cultural resistance, and concern with questions of personal liberation and empowerment differentiate them sharply from both the class- and the community-based mobilizations of earlier periods.

Susan and Norman Fainstein's chapter focuses on the issue of the globalization of the economy and its impact on urban restructuring. It applies this issue to the dual question of the relationship among capitalism, democracy, and participation, on the one hand, and between national and local levels of government, on the other. Their comparative analysis of the structures of community participation in New York and London clearly echoes the notion of the political process proponents that local/national politics matters, but the Fainsteins emphasize that these processes occur within a context of common global pressures on the politics of local economic development. Thus both British and U.S. leadership are committed to neoconservative and free market responses to the fiscal crises wrought by global capital mobility. But British leaders attempt to maintain neoconservative policies by centralizing political institutional power, while those in the United States seek to reinforce control through a strategy and philosophy of political decentralization. Still, for the Fainsteins, participation issues are heavily determined by forces far beyond community borders, and the challenges they recognize are the constraints these forces place on urban-based social movements.

We have divided the case studies into two parts. The first group of case studies, in Part II of the volume, consists of chapters that have as their subject more traditional community-based mobilizations. The second group, in Part III, however, looks at collective action that is shaped as much, if not more, by concerns with identity and personal empowerment as it is by institutional and distributional politics. There are overlaps, of course, because one of the findings that emerges from an overall reading of these chapters is the remarkable complexity of contemporary social movements as well as the difficulty of constructing any clear-cut and stable typologies to categorize them.

In the first of the case studies, Sallie Marston and George Towers accept that the restructuring of cities by global capitalism has a generalized impact on urban social movements but argue that, while structural forces form the basis for grass-roots mobilization, they do not determine the nature of political action. Grass-roots mobilization is seen as a contingent process shaped by the varying organizational and institutional resources of local communities. Their chapter analyzes how the diversified urban contexts of Tucson and El Paso led to differently grounded popular countermovements to development and restructuring.

In a study of grass-roots organizing in Oakland, California, around health care for poor people of color, Gary Delgado emphasizes that grass-roots success is affected primarily by the consciousness and skill level of organizers. Written from an organizer's vantage point, the chapter recognizes how the organizing process is influenced by local political factors external to the organizing effort, chief among them, in this case, the shifts to a more conservative political climate and the shrinking availability of resources for organizing. But Delgado finds that the perspective and abilities of grass-roots leadership, especially those who seek to build multiracial organizations tied to both cultural and class concerns, is of utmost importance.

Organizing poor people of color in a conservative political context is the basis as well for Betty Reid Mandell and Ann Withorn's chapter on the welfare rights claimants' movement in Massachusetts since the 1970s. Here the political structure of privatization, the ascendancy of neoconservative theories and politicians, and the dismantling of the state in Massachusetts shaped the movement's history and strategies. Welfare rights organizing is important to our study because it blends organizing around class (poor), gender (women), and race (disproportionately African American) identities in a movement tied to making claims on the state. The dilemma is that in the past 15 years contemporary organizing more easily focused on gender and race but retreated from class and, equally important, avoided theories and strategies that sought to make demands on the increasingly delegitimized state.

The chapter by Margit Mayer looks to community mobilization efforts in Western Europe. Mayer, in a study of the recent historical "career" of urban social movement formation in West Germany, focuses on the interrelationship between local/national political opportunity structures and social movement opposition to the Fordist modernization process. Mayer's longitudinal analysis illustrates how waves of opposition movements have changed over time in response primarily to shifting economic and political contexts. This dialectical process of grass-roots resistance and state co-optation has ultimately resulted in the structured consolidation of a movement sector in German politics that has a most unclear and uncertain future.

Mathew Zachariah's chapter discusses community organizing in the province of Kerala in India, in an underdeveloped area seemingly removed from the reaches of postindustrial capitalism and the cultural politics of postmodernism. Here the organizing project is opposed to the building of a hydroelectric dam, which traditionally in the Third World represents economic growth and improved living standards. For the environmentalist in Kerala, however, the dam embodies the coming of increasing development, the intervention of the global economy, and the devastation of the pristine environment. Focusing on the heritage as well as the tensions in the ideologies of communism and Sarvodaya that were available to people in Kerala, Zachariah concludes that credible leadership, people's heightened consciousness, and a tradition of resistance are critical factors in popular mobilization. In Kerala their presence contributed significantly to the defeat of the dam project.

Sonia Alvarez's richly textured piece about national/local politics in Brazil and its relationship to social movement formation and development provides a splendid conclusion to the first set of case studies. Her study of the Workers Party in Brazil at the grass-roots level is simultaneously about tensions between new social movement and more institutional actors and also about tensions within new social movements among activists. It reminds us that urban social movements need not be extrapolitical and that the struggle for state political power and the grounding of political power in grass-roots organizations is more than an abstract ideal. It is the essence of grass-roots efforts in Brazil and perhaps in much of Latin America.

Judith Allen's study of the Paddington Federation, a community-based tenants and residents association in London, opens the second group of case studies, in Part III of the volume. It stands as a transition piece between the study of community-based and identity-based mobilization and probes the ways in which subjectivity, agency, structure, and local politics intermesh in people's lives at the level of everyday life. Her chapter is especially sensitive to power as both institutional and intersubjective. Drawing on Foucault's notion of knowledge as power, Allen seeks to show how, despite increasing economic and political domination, people resist through organizations that allow them to discuss openly their situation, define themselves in terms different than those set by the authorities, and name their own strategies. In independently derived language and discourses and the free exchange of ideas among peers and leaders, there is the ability to demystify power and legitimize resistance.

Valerie Lehr's study of gay and lesbian activism around AIDS extends the discussion of identity-based political groupings. Following a central theme of the volume, she insists that organizers go beyond self-referential cultural bases to include alliances that respect difference and open the possibility of increased organizational power. Human agency and the deliberations of grass-roots resistance are the essence here. AIDS, especially, becomes an issue that can force organizers beyond the limits of a narrowly defined identity politics. As Lehr emphasizes, the problems in dealing with AIDS involve the polity as a whole. Grass-roots organizers therefore are in position to develop forms that affect not only community needs but larger institutional politics and policies.

Sophie Body-Gendrot, in her study of immigrant Moslem women in France, continues the focus of this section on those aspects of resistance that are most immediate and personal, not necessarily formal and institutional. She expands traditional definitions of how people resist and pushes us to understand that human agency comes in many forms. She grounds agency in the specificity of difference and voice by looking at the responses of Arab women—the "other" in French society—to political and cultural domination. Body-Gendrot demonstrates how these women, by working organizationally to become locally based entrepreneurs, seek power over their lives and in their communities.

Finally, Barbara Epstein's chapter on local protest against the Gulf War in the Bay Area warns us of the dangers of an identity politics that fails to transcend narrow self-definitions and interests. She looks at grass-roots responses to a global international event and emphasizes what is problematic in the strategies, consciousness, and cultural politics/identities of the local participants. Agency, Epstein reminds us, is ambiguous; it is neither constructive nor destructive, inclusive nor exclusive, good nor bad. While grounding her work, as do many of the authors, in participant-observation research, she offers a personalized analysis of grass-roots opposition to the war and comes away impressed by the level of resistance but critical of the limits of an agency without ideology or a larger political program.

The volume will inevitably pose more questions than it answers because the emergence of new models and paradigms for citizen action is very much an ongoing exploration. But this collection is meant for both academics and activists. Its authors are all students of community mobilization, as well as participants. While they write from different theoretical and political perspectives, they do so with the same dual objective in mind: to enhance praxis as well as knowledge. We hope readers find their efforts worthwhile.

REFERENCES

Boyte, H. (1981). *The backyard revolution.* Philadelphia: Temple University Press.
Castells, M. (1983). *The city and the grassroots.* Berkeley: University of California Press.

Ceccarelli, P. (1982). Politics, parties, and urban movements: Western Europe. In N. Fainstein & S. Fainstein (Eds.), *Urban policy under capitalism* (pp. 261-276). Beverly Hills, CA: Sage.

Corbridge, S. (1991). Third World development. *Progress in Human Geography, 15,* 311-321.

Durning, A. B. (1989, January). Action at the grassroots: Fighting poverty and environmental decline. *Worldwatch Paper, 88,* 1-70.

Feagin, J. R. (1988). *Free enterprise city.* New Brunswick, NJ: Rutgers University Press.

Fisher, R. (1984). *Let the people decide: Neighborhood organizing in America.* Boston: Twayne.

Frank, A. G., & Fuentes, M. (1990). Civil democracy: Social movements in recent world history. In S. Amin et al. (Eds.), *Transforming the revolution: Social movements and the world-system* (pp. 139-180). New York: Monthly Review Press.

Gottdiener, M. (1987). *The decline of urban politics.* Newbury Park, CA: Sage.

Kaase, M. (1990). Mass participation. In M. K. Jennings & J. VanDeth (Eds.), *Continuities in political action* (pp. 23-64). Berlin: Walter de Gruter.

Katznelson, I. (1981). *City trenches: Urban politics and the patterning of class in the United States.* Chicago: University of Chicago Press.

Logan, J., & Swanstrom, T. (Eds.). (1990). *Beyond the city limits: Urban policy and restructuring in comparative perspective.* Philadelphia: Temple University Press.

Lowe, S. (1986). *Urban social movements: The city after Castells.* London: Macmillan.

McAdam, D. (1982). *Political process and the development of black insurgency, 1930-1970.* Chicago: University of Chicago Press.

Melucci, A. (1989). *Nomads of the present: Social movements and individual needs in contemporary society.* Philadelphia: Temple University Press.

Molotch, H. (1990). Urban deals in comparative perspective. In J. Logan & T. Swanstrom (Eds.), *Beyond the city limits: Urban policy and restructuring in comparative perspective.* Philadelphia: Temple University Press.

Pickvance, C., & Preteceille, E. (1991). *State restructuring and local power: A comparative perspective.* London: Pinter.

Sassen, S. (1990). Beyond the city limits: A commentary. In J. Logan & T. Swanstrom (Eds.), *Beyond the city limits: Urban policy and restructuring in comparative perspective.* Philadelphia: Temple University Press.

Sharpe, L. (1979). Decentralist trends in Western democracies: A first appraisal. In L. J. Sharpe (Ed.), *Decentralist trends in Western democracies.* London: Sage.

Smith, C. (1991). *The emergence of liberation theology: Radical religion and social movement theory.* Chicago: University of Chicago Press.

Smith, M. P. (1989). Urbanism: Medium or outcome of human agency. *Urban Affairs Quarterly, 24*(3), 353-358.

Susskind, L., Elliott, M., et al. (1983). *Paternalism, conflict, and coproduction: Learning from citizen action and citizen participation in Western Europe.* New York: Plenum.

Touraine, A. (1985). An introduction to the study of social movements. *Social Research, 52,* 749-787.

Wallerstein, I. (1990). Antisystemic movements: History and dilemmas. In S. Amin et al. (Eds.), *Transforming the revolution: Social movements and the world-system* (pp. 15-23). New York: Monthly Review Press.

Part I

Historical and Theoretical Contexts

1 Grass-Roots Organizing Worldwide: Common Ground, Historical Roots, and the Tension Between Democracy and the State

ROBERT FISHER

The last decade of the twentieth century promises to be a time of social conflict and political struggle over who will benefit from the "epochal" global transformation under way (Jacques, 1990, p. 16). Currently, liberation struggles and democratic experiments occur alongside worldwide militarism, ethnocentrism, repression, and privatization. While it is easy to be pessimistic about the prospects for progressive change, grass-roots mobilization seems to many activists and commentators worldwide to hold the greatest potential (Greider, 1992). This chapter seeks to contribute to the debate about the significance of grass-roots organizing by arguing that, despite current intellectual emphasis on diversity and difference, any effective understanding of community mobilization must recognize its global proliferation, common origins, and similar content as well as its differentiated local basis.

It argues, furthermore, that the history of community mobilization, when combined with a critique of contemporary efforts, reveals a serious, inherent tension. The populist vision of a more democratic public life conflicts with the antistatist ideology, goals, strategies, and tactics of community mobilization efforts, especially among more affluent groups in the West. Such antistatist oppositional movements, though they practice democratic process and seek the restoration of a truly democratic and public life, may too readily, albeit unintentionally,

AUTHOR'S NOTE: I would like to thank Susan Clarke, Joe Kling, George Lipsitz, and Bruce Palmer for their invaluable comments on an earlier draft of this chapter.

replicate the antipublic, antidemocratic global trends under way. Accordingly, this chapter argues, oppositional grass-roots efforts must build both democratic, empowered communities *and* recognize the state as, if not a site of support, then at least a central arena and critical target for oppositional demands.

■ **Global Phenomena with Common Origins and Form**

A global lens reveals the common heritage, origin, structure, strategy, ideology, and objectives of grass-roots organizing. The diversity and differences in community mobilization worldwide should be expected given widely different local conditions, political opportunities, heritage of resistance, and indigenous organizations (Fisher, 1984; Kaase, 1990; Logan & Swanstrom, 1990; Pickvance & Preteceille, 1991; Susskind et al., 1983). But when seen in global perspective, most arresting is the *similarity* of community action worldwide (Aronowitz, 1992; Cnann, 1991; Corbridge, 1991; Durning, 1989; Fisher & Kling, 1991; Laclau & Mouffe, 1985; Lowe, 1986; McCormick, 1989). These mobilizations are fundamentally alike and appear almost everywhere, regardless of the local political context, because they are rooted in the historical and contemporary social development of the global capitalist economy (Sassen, 1990; Slater, 1985; Smith & Feagin, 1987). Grass-roots resistance has adopted worldwide what some see as a "new social movement" form (Brand, 1990; Offe, 1987).

Grass-roots mobilization, of course, is not new (Calhoun, 1983; Evans & Boyte, 1986). Each historical era produces its own, most salient and appropriate, forms of popular resistance (Fisher, 1984). A widespread, republican voluntarism, for example, characterized preindustrial capitalism, occurring in sites as disparate as Denmark and the United States in the nineteenth century (Gundelach, 1984; de Tocqueville, 1969). In the early twentieth century social-democratic movements and regimes in Western Europe and the United States arose to control both the inefficient competition and the labor exploitation of industrial capitalism. These "old social movements" were grounded in the labor insurgency organized in response to industrial capitalism. Recognizing that the "old" versus "new" social movement paradigm is too simple and too rigidly time-bound to do justice to the complexities of both history and social movements, the old social movements in the West nevertheless share critical similarities (Epstein, 1990; Fisher, 1992; Scott, 1990). Primarily workplace based, union organizing in the industrial factory was their most common form. In the unions they organized around class issues and were consciously ideological, that is, they offered a critique of the existing system and an alternative vision of the future, usually tied to Marxist or Keynesian ideas. Further, they targeted the private sector, their employers, at the same time that they connected local workplace efforts to a larger agenda of winning state power. Their victories became the basis of post-World War II politics in the West. In all sites, these "old" social movements, when they won state power, as they often did, used the state as a "top-down" means of ordering and reforming existing conditions. They created between 1946 and the late 1960s virtually unchallenged regimes built on the liberal-democratic consensus of welfare state expenditures and U.S. military dominance and focused on economic growth, distribution, and security, especially for the heretofore disregarded white, indigenous working class (Offe, 1987). But this political economy produced its own opposition as well, in the form of more state services and public intervention (Mayer, 1987).

Numerous factors led to the decline of the old social movements. Most profound was the increasing globalization of the world economy, which undermined and continues to undermine the ability of the old social movements and their mass parties to use the state to redistribute resources to constituents. As capital flow increasingly supersedes state control in the global economy, the welfare state faces increasing fiscal crises. The social-democratic state loses support and those associated with it lose credibility. Moreover, the pressures of a new postindustrial global economy complicated two inherent problems in the old social movements. First, those in power developed an increasingly parochial and self-serving agenda. Second, while the old social movements achieved power as the voice for disadvantaged workers, they also perpetuated the silence of others such as minorities, women, and the least skilled. Growing centralization and bureaucratization made change through "the system" to the mounting urban problems more and more difficult. Increasingly, the once silent groups mobilized, challenging the social-democratic leaders and parties that excluded them last. The opposition emerged in insurgent grass-roots associations over issues of democratic participation, personal liberty, civil rights, and quality of life. The heirs of the old social movements, hamstrung by a global economy and under attack from the right and segments of the new social movements for their "statist" politics, seemed to devolve into anachronisms in the generation between 1960 and 1990 (Flacks, 1990).

In Western Europe and the United States, the challenges of the new social movements to the postwar political economy, while somewhat different in each region and locality and emerging at different times, took a common form. Five elements distinguish them from the old social movements.

First, they are community based, that is, around communities of interest or geography, not organized necessarily at the site of production or against the principal owners of capital (Offe, 1987).

Second, they are transclass groupings of constituencies and cultural identities such as blacks, ethnics, women, gay men, students, ecologists, and peace activists. Labor becomes one, not *the*, constituency group. Class becomes part of, not *the primary*, identity. Moreover, for labor to be truly effective, it must, like other groups, unite with constituencies outside its own domain (Brecher & Costello, 1990; Fisher, 1992).

Third, the ideological glue is democratic politics. They reject authoritarianism not only in the state but also in leadership, in the party, in ideology, in organizational structure, and in relationships (Amin, 1990). Their organizational form is sufficiently small, loose, and open to be able to "tap local knowledge and resources, to respond to problems rapidly and creatively, and to maintain the flexibility needed in changing circumstances" (Durning, 1989, pp. 6-7). Some see the new social movement forms as presenting themselves as "nonideological," that is, as overtly rejecting the old ideologies of capitalism, communism, and nationalism and tending to play down a critique of the dominant system. Recent commentators argue that ideological congruence is the essence of the new social movements; their "neopopulist" principles and beliefs are one of the things that make them new (Boyte, Booth, & Max, 1986; Boyte & Riessman, 1986; Dalton & Kuechler, 1990; Fisher & Kling, 1988; Offe, 1987).

Fourth, struggle over culture and social identity play a greater role in community-based movements than in workplace-based efforts of the past. "After the great working class parties surrendered their remaining sense of radical political purpose with the onset of the cold war," Bronner (1990, p. 161) writes, "new social movements emerged to reformulate the spirit of resistance in broader cultural terms": feminism, Black Power, sexual identity, ethnic nationalism, victim's rights. Of course, culture and identity—grounded in historical experience, values, social networks, and collective solidarity—have always been central to all social movement formation (Gutman, 1977; Thompson, 1963). But as class becomes increasingly fragmented in the postindustrial city and as the locus of workplace organizing declines in significance, resistances that emerge increasingly do so around cultural and identity bases (Fisher & Kling, 1991; Touraine, 1985).

Fifth, strategies focus on community self-help and empowerment, though the most effective efforts go beyond community capacity building to target the public sector. Most community-based organizing seeks independence from the state rather than state power. They rely on a "unitary" conception of democracy, which is used within the community and assumes a predominant concern to promote the common interest; they deemphasize "adversarial" democracy, which challenges national, state, and local politics and presupposes conflicting interests (Mansbridge, 1980, p. 3). As Midgley (1986, p. 4) points out, central to the rationale of community participation

> is a reaction against the centralization, bureaucratization, rigidity, and remoteness of the state. The ideology of community participation is sustained by the belief that the power of the state has extended too far, diminishing the freedoms of ordinary people and their rights to control their own affairs.

Community capacity building becomes the natural focus of new social movement efforts, reflecting antistatist sympathies and decentralization trends of the postindustrial political economy. The most effective new social movement efforts, however, target the public sector, understanding, at least implicitly, that the sites of production cannot be leveraged as easily or effectively by the new social movements as they could by the old social movements and, equally important, that the state is the entity potentially most responsible and vulnerable to new social movement claims and constituencies (Fisher, 1992; Piven & Cloward, 1982).

This argument of a common new social movement form plays out a bit differently in other parts of the world. One key difference is that the old social movements in the Third World (South) and Second World (East) were nationalistic and communistic, respectively, not social democratic as in the West (Wallerstein, 1990). In the southern hemisphere the debilitating heritage of colonialism modified the common form of community mobilization. Nations such as India shared with the West the centralization and homogenization of politics of the postwar political economy. But these regimes resulted from the anti-imperialist struggles led by national bourgeois elements, not social-democratic movements. Peripheral to and dependent on Western capital, the old social movements in the South could not deliver material security or political liberty. Most became a new hierarchical, antidemocratic arm of Western imperial control. In response, community movements "mushroomed" all over the South. Similar in form to counterparts in the West, their often different objectives and social base reflect local conditions and their subordinate position in the global economy. As in the West, they are community based, constituency or identity oriented, neopopulist in ideology, and focused on self-help strategies. But in the South, community movements emphasize material needs—survival itself (Frank & Fuentes, 1990). In India, for example, Bonner (1990, p. 2) writes, community activists seek immediately realizable benefits, such as more food, improved health care, housing, and nurseries for children. "The social movement is concerned entirely with the poor."

This is an important difference, one relevant not just to the South. Where old social movements achieved distributional victories only for a few, as in the southern hemisphere, or where such victories did not include significant minority segments, as in the United States, grassroots efforts struggled to achieve a minimal standard of living and get basic services like housing and health care. Where material victories have been won, primarily among the more affluent in the West, the new democratic struggle is mostly over "postmaterialist" concerns "in which needs for belonging, esteem, and intellectual and aesthetic satisfaction become more prominent" (Inglehart, 1990, p. 69).

In the West the social base tends to be the educated middle class (Merkl, 1987). But where basic material needs still remain to be won in the South and among the oppressed and disenfranchised in the West, the new social movement form of resistance includes the poor and powerless and interweaves struggle over postmaterial and material objectives. For example, workplace organizing is certainly not an anachronism in the industrializing nations of the southern hemisphere, but neither is it the central site of struggle as it was with the old social movements in the West. Community-based identity and constituency movements abound, but in the South and wherever oppressed people find themselves without basic needs met, these efforts, unlike more affluent counterparts in the West, are tied to distributional objectives and focus not only on community development but on targeting the local and/or national state (Corbridge, 1991). Nevertheless, in contemporary grass-roots resistance, the central focus is on empowerment, shedding identities of oppression such as, in India, the caste system and the belief in "karma," ending hierarchies, and including all in the decision-making process. Moreover, in India, as is true worldwide, a major characteristic of the new social movement form is "the high percentage of women as members and leaders. With their criticism of patriarchal oppression, women heighten the suspicion of hierarchy" (Bronner, 1990, p. 2).

Of course, basic survival concerns are important even in those groups in the West professing to hold to "postmaterialist" values. Survival is tied to ridding the world of nuclear weapons, toxic wastes, domestic violence, or AIDS, all of which cut across class lines. Relatedly, the politics of identity, concern for personal and political freedom, and desire to belong to a supportive and habitable community are of concern to new social movement efforts worldwide. Democratic self-help, community empowerment, is their essence. Predictably, new social movements develop easily among the affluent and around postmaterialist issues. But they succeed better as agents of transformative social change when they combine both distributional and postmaterialist objectives. The distributional demands ground identity in a class politics that understands, at least implicitly, the need in a postindustrial global economy to target the public sector and struggle for state power as well as to develop democratic alternatives at the grass roots.

■ Contemporary Bases of Local Insurgency

While the common form of new social movement activism evident in community mobilization today emerged in response to the postwar political economy and the limits of the old social movements, grassroots activists and organizers fashioned them at the local level. Impersonal, macro conditions constitute the historical context within which people act but, as Lipsitz (1988, p. 68) notes, "structural forces do not create movements for social change—people do."

Effective organizing, McAdam (1982) suggests, requires three elements: expanding political opportunities, indigenous organizations, and insurgent consciousness. The first two combine to offer structural potentials for collective action, but they require the third to be transformed into actual insurgency. Insurgent consciousness includes the understanding that the problem is structurally or intentionally caused, the cause is identifiable, the conditions are undeserved and unjust, organized action is legitimate and necessary, and, if risks are taken to organize insurgency, there is a reasonable chance of success. Individual and collective grievances—people's daily experiences—combine with the perspective and leadership of organizers to form the basis of an "oppositional imagination" (Cocks, 1989; Fisher & Kling, 1988; C. Smith, 1991). The assumption of a "new" social movement form seems at first glance to detach it from a heritage of resistance. But this chapter argues the opposite. The ideology and experience of prior efforts help provide a *common* basis for contemporary insurgent consciousness. Of course, prior collective insurgency is not the only source of a "collective memory of resistance" upon which an insurgent consciousness can build (Lipsitz, 1988). But organizing efforts succeed best when they use ideas generated by and tested in prior community mobilization. As Rude (1980) concludes, effective organizing demands a gentle mix of inherited (local and traditional) and derived (external and insurgent) ideology, and the most available source of derived ideology is recent activism (Evans, 1979).

What follows in this section therefore is a brief discussion of post-World War II mobilization efforts that provide the essential shared antecedents of contemporary insurgent consciousness. They include the (a) community-based resistance of Saul Alinsky, (b) liberation struggles of people of color, (c) urban decentralization and citizen participation programs, (d) new left movements, and (e) new social movements. Of course, this is not to suggest that the heritage of community resistance does not include efforts prior to 1945 (Fisher, 1984, 1992). Nor is it to suggest that all contemporary community mobilization efforts build on each of these antecedents. Rather, it identifies key elements in the formation of a shared new social movement consciousness. And it seeks to highlight another aspect of this chapter's argument, that the shared heritage of resistance includes the tension between grass-roots democracy and the state.

Community-Based Resistance of Saul Alinsky

While the organizing projects of Saul Alinsky during his lifetime never amounted to much in terms of material victories and while his projects only took off when the southern civil rights movement shifted to northern cities in the 1960s, the community-based, constituency-oriented, urban populist, confrontational politics developed by Alinsky in the United States provides one of the earliest models of the new social movement form and one of the best examples of the transition from old to new social movements (Fisher & Kling, 1988). Beginning just before World War II, Alinsky's work in Chicago built on the old social movement models of the Congress of Industrial Organizations and Communist Party United States of America (Fisher, 1984; Horwitt, 1989). From these it drew its labor organizing style, conflict strategies, direct action politics, and idea of grounding organizing in the everyday lives and traditions of working people. But Alinsky's model added something new: a kind of labor organizing in the social factory (Boyte, 1981). The community organizer was the catalyst for change. The task was to build democratic community-based organizations. The goal was to empower neighborhood residents by teaching them basic political and organizing skills and getting them or their representatives to the urban bargaining table (Boyte, 1981; Fisher, 1984). Both the site of production (supporting labor demands) and the public sector (making city hall more accountable) served as the primary targets of Alinsky organizing.

This was an insurgent consciousness of "urban populism," based in neighborhood "people's organizations," oriented to building community power, discovering indigenous leaders, providing training in democratic participation, and proving that ordinary people could challenge and beat city hall (Boyte, 1981; Fisher, 1984; Horwitt, 1989; Swanstrom, 1985). At their weakest, Alinsky efforts sought to replace the political program and ideology of the old social movements with the skills of democratic grass-roots participation, the abilities of professionally trained organizers, a faith in the democratic tendencies of working people to guide organizations toward progressive ends, and a reformist vision of grass-roots pluralistic politics. At their best, however, Alinsky efforts continue to empower lower- and working-class, black and Latino community residents and to demand expanded public sector accountability and public participation in an increasingly privatized political context (Delgado, 1986; Fisher, 1984; Horwitt, 1989; Kahn, 1970; Rogers, 1990). As an important transitionary form of community organizing and as an exemplary case of the growth in popularity during the past generation in this type of political participation, the efforts of Alinsky and his heirs have widespread importance today, especially in the United States but also throughout the world, though most organizations do not know they are borrowing from Alinsky and his successors. But in the United States among community organizers, Alinsky is seen as the father of contemporary community mobilization (Boyte, 1981).

Liberation Struggles of People of Color

Much more significant in terms of impact are the liberation struggles of people of color throughout the world since the 1950s. The civil rights movement in the United States and the national liberation struggles in the southern hemisphere served as important models for a community-based, ethnic/nationalist politics oriented to self-determination and sharing the political liberties and material affluence of the societies that exploited people of color. As a model for grass-roots direct action and insurgent consciousness, the southern civil rights movement spawned most of what was to follow in the United States and established important precedents for others throughout the world (Branch, 1988; Morris, 1984; Reagon, 1979). The liberation struggles in Africa, Asia, Latin America, and the Middle East, specifically early efforts in Ghana, Vietnam, Iran, Guatemala, and Cuba, not only provided models for people worldwide, including activists in the civil rights movement in the United States, but symbolized the mobilization of a worldwide liberation struggle of people of color. The demand for national self-determination for all people, not just those of European descent; the opposition to policies of racism and imperialism; and the plea of the civil rights movement for "beloved community" helped pierce the consensus politics of the 1950s and early 1960s. More recent liberation struggles in Nicaragua, El Salvador, and South Africa, to name but a few, continue to challenge conservative, racist, and imperialist paradigms in the 1980s and 1990s.

The continuous liberation struggles of people of color emphasize three other lessons critical to the insurgent consciousness of contemporary community activism. First, citizen insurgency and social movements are not political aberrations. They are legitimate and important, informal parts of the political process to which all those without access to power can turn. Second, if oppressed people, often illiterate, rural peasants with few resources, could mobilize, take risks, and make history, then people of other oppressed or threatened constituencies can with sufficient organization and leadership do the same. Third, strategy must include both community self-help and constituency empowerment, on the one hand, and the struggle for state power, or at least the targeting of the public sector as the site of grievances and as a potential source of support, on the other. This dual quality of building community capacity and targeting the state, though not always in equal balance and often in tension, as exemplified in struggles between the Southern

Christian Leadership Conference (SCLC) and the Student Nonviolent Coordinating Committee (SNCC), was as true for the civil rights movement in the United States as it was for the liberation struggles in the Third World (Carson, 1982).

Urban Decentralization and Community Participation

The struggles of people in the southern hemisphere dramatized the exploitative nature of the imperial postwar political economy at the very moment in the 1960s that some progressive capitalists, political leaders, and planners in both the public and the voluntary sectors found themselves unable to address mounting urban problems at home. From 1960 onward, as liberal leaders such as Presidents Kennedy and Johnson in the United States advocated for modest social reforms and a more democratized public sector, pressure mounted for urban decentralization and citizen participation. The Community Action Program of the 1960s in the United States and the Urban Programme of the late 1960s in Britain were among the most noted of public projects seeking "maximum feasible participation" at the grass-roots level. But such programs proliferated widely, making state-sponsored municipal decentralization and community participation an international phenomenon (Chekki, 1979; Kjellberg, 1979; Midgley, 1986).

Of course, such postwar programs differ dramatically from Alinsky and liberation movement efforts in their origins and problem analysis. They are initiated largely by reformers in the public and voluntary sectors, professionals such as urban planners and social workers, who either seek modest structural change or find themselves too constrained on the job to do much more in their agencies than deliver needed services at the grass-roots level. As such, these initiatives represent a more institutionalized, more formalized wing of the grass-roots mobilization phenomenon. They tend, as well, to implement decentralized structure and democratic participation in public agencies without a sense of the contradictions inherent in doing so but with a knowledge of the importance of linking the state and grass-roots activism. The state becomes not the target of democratic insurgency but the employer and supporter of citizen initiatives (Merkl, 1985). At their worst, these measures defuse and co-opt insurgency. But contemporary organizing draws from this legacy a commitment to serving the people, to advocacy, and to citizen participation. For, at its best, this is a legacy about the delivery of services at a grass-roots level, where people will have better access; about the inclusion of more people, even lay people, in the decision-making process at a more decentralized level; about making sure they have real power to make decisions and control resources. It is a heritage entailing struggle from within the state bureaucracies and agencies to achieve economic and participatory democracy for the greatest number of urban dwellers.

The New Left Movement

Despite the efforts noted so far, urban problems and tensions continued to escalate in the 1960s. In response, direct action movements mounted, especially in the United States. Early SDS (Students for a Democratic Society) and SNCC (Student Nonviolent Coordinating Committee) community organizing projects focused on "participatory democracy" and "letting the people decide," seeking not only to pressure local and national policy but to create "prefigurative," that is, alternative, social groups (Breines, 1982; Evans, 1979). They also developed a critique of American policy abroad and the liberal consensus at home. They built a movement in opposition to the politics of both corporate capital and the old social movements. After 1965 organizing adopted more nationalist and Marxist perspectives; Black Power efforts, for example, were less concerned with participatory democracy and more interested in challenging imperialism abroad and at home, winning "community control," and building black identity (Jennings, 1990).

Such efforts in the United States were part of an insurgent trend in the West. Massive peace protests in the United Kingdom registered strong disapproval of cold war policies, directly challenging social-democratic regimes. These early efforts, among others, initiated a widespread "new left" movement throughout the West, one that was soon to expand beyond university sites and student constituencies to develop, according to Ceccarelli (1982, p. 263), into "an unprecedented outburst of urban movements": Paris and West German cities in the spring of 1968; Prague, Chicago, and Monterrey, Mexico, during that summer; in Italy the "Hot Autumn" of 1969 and the urban conflicts of the early 1970s; squatters in Portuguese cities after the April Revolution; urban social movements in Madrid and other Spanish cities after Franco. All testify to a massive grass-roots mobilization that developed rapidly, and perhaps even in an unprecedented way, throughout Europe, the United States, and parts of the Third World (Ceccarelli, 1982; Teodori, 1969).

Concern for and experimentation with participatory democracy, nonhierarchical decision making, prefigurative cultural politics, linking the personal with the political, direct action tactics, and constituency-based organizing (students, the poor, and so on) characterized new left insurgent consciousness (Breines, 1982; Jacobs & Landau, 1966). Unlike most new social movement resistance to follow, the new left emphasized the formation of coalitions or political parties tied to national revolutionary/emancipatory struggles. There was a sense in the late 1960s, in cities as disparate as Paris, Berlin, Berkeley, and Monterrey, that "successful and autonomous urban movements are not a real alternative outside the context of a revolutionary national movement" (Walton, 1979, p. 12). The struggle over state power, over who should make public policy, fueled local organizing efforts. Grass-roots organizing was for most activists a democratic means to larger objectives that transcended the local community. This strategy persists, in a more reformist form, in certain notable efforts since then, such as the Green parties in Europe, the Workers party in Brazil, and the Rainbow Coalition idea in the United States (Alvarez, in this volume; Collins, 1986; Spretnak & Capra, 1985).

Grass-roots efforts that followed tended to borrow more heavily from the "newer" side of the new left. These activists saw community organizing, alternative groupings, and grass-roots efforts as at least the primary focus if not the sole end. They emphasized democratic organizational structure, the politics of identity and culture, existential values of personal freedom and authenticity, and the development of "free spaces" where people could learn the theory and practice of political insurgency while engaging in it. So did much of the new left, but the other, more Marxist segments, closer in style and politics to the old social movements, adhered strongly to old social movement concerns with public policy and winning state power (Carson, 1982; Evans, 1979; Evans & Boyte, 1986).

One of the major contributions of the diverse and ambiguous new left movement of the late 1960s was its helping to birth later efforts by assailing the promise and practice of the old social movements and advancing new forms of organization and values as potential models for future activists. As Wallerstein (1990, p. 41) sums it up,

Thus, when in 1968, amidst a continuing war in Vietnam, Black Power movements, a growing "counterculture" raging against a consumer society side by side with the "growing gap" between North and South, the rebellious students and workers in the West could turn neither to the Social-Democrats nor to the Communists as ways of expressing their angers and their commitments. *Instead, they created a new movement. Its beginnings were so vague that at first it was often called merely* "the movement." By the 1970s one began to speak in the plural of "new social movements."

But the new left's insurgent consciousness, steadfast in its opposition to the largely undemocratic, often inhumane, and essentially alienating politics of the cold war era, offered an ambiguous legacy to later community organizing regarding the relation between grass-roots democracy and the state.

New Social Movements

Despite a marked backlash worldwide against the radical activism of the late 1960s, the 1970s and 1980s witnessed not the end of community-based activism but the proliferation of grass-roots activism and insurgency into highly diversified, single issue or identity-oriented, community-based efforts. These efforts, the subject of this volume, include women's shelters and feminist organizations, efforts in defense of the rights and the communities of oppressed people of color, struggles around housing, ecology, and peace issues, gay and lesbian rights and identity groups, and thousands of neighborhood- and issue-based citizen initiatives, complete with organizer training centers. While these organizing efforts vary from one national and local context to another, they share a common form and movement heritage. Based in geographic communities or communities of interest, decentralized according to constituencies and identity groups, democratic in process and goals, and funded most often by voluntary sources, they serve as the archetype for the new social movement model.

The roots of their insurgent consciousness, while not always direct, can be found in the movement ideals discussed thus far: (a) that ordinary and previously oppressed people should have a voice and can make history; (b) that citizen and community participation, which gives "voice" to people previously silent in public discourse, is needed to improve decision making, address a wide range of problems, and democratize society; (c) that "by any means necessary" covers the gamut of strategies and tactics from revolutionary to interest group politics; (d) that culture, whether it is found in a traditional ethnic neighborhood, battered women's shelter, counterculture collective, or gay men's organization, must be blended with the quest for "empowerment" into an identity- or constituency-oriented politics; and (e) that "the personal is political," articulated first by radical feminists in the late 1960s, guides people to organize around aspects of daily life most central and dear to them, while keeping in mind that struggles over personal issues and relationships—personal choice, autonomy, commitment, and fulfillment—are inextricably tied to collective ones of the constituency group and the larger society.

Most commentators tend to see the focus on democracy as the essence of new social movement insurgent consciousness and the source of its potential. As Frank and Fuentes (1990, p. 142) put it, the new social movements "are the most important agents of social transformation in that their praxis promotes participatory democracy in civil society." Pitkin and Shumer (1982, p. 43) go further, declaring that "of all the dangerous thoughts and explosive ideas abroad in the world today, by far the most subversive is that of democracy. . . . [It] is the cutting edge of radical criticism, the best inspiration for change toward a more humane world, the revolutionary idea of our time." And these democratic projects have had profound impact: empowering participants, teaching democratic skills, transforming notions of political life, expanding political boundaries, returning politics to civic self-activity, strengthening a sense of public activism, raising new social and political issues, struggling against new forms of subordination and oppression, and even advancing agendas of the middle class to which formal, institutional politics remain closed (Roth, 1991; Slater, 1985).

But, while the emphasis on democracy unites these efforts, it also helps detach them in the West from the material needs of the poor and it contributes to their fragmentation into a plethora of diverse, decentralized community mobilizations. The pursuit in the West of democracy, without sufficient concern for equality, has resulted in the failure of the new social movements to address the material needs of the most disadvantaged (Flacks, 1990, p. 46). Moreover, the new social movement efforts are too fragmented and too exclusive to be effective social change agents. Despite their obvious shared characteristics and their affinity for other new social movement groups and causes, they tend to parallel rather than interact with each other (Fisher & Kling, 1991). For example, the diversity and flexibility that theorists of postmodernity attribute to contemporary society are nowhere more evident than in the variety of new social movement efforts that emerged, grew, declined, disappeared, and reemerged in different groups since the 1970s. A commitment to diversity embodies their emphasis on democratic politics. It encourages each constituency or identity group to identify its own struggles, develop its own voice, and engage in its own empowerment. This may be the future of politics, a "postmodernization of public life," with its "proliferation of multiple publics [and] breaking down of rigid barriers between political and private life" (Kaufmann, 1990, p. 10). But the central challenges to these efforts require more immediate and realistic strategies. How do they encourage diversity *and* counteract fragmentation? How do they influence or get power at levels—the city, state, and nation—beyond their own limited universes *and* at the same time build community capacity?

■ Community Mobilization and the State In A Postindustrial Context

The challenge to influence or hold power has been made more difficult by recent trends in the global political economy. Calling for privatization to solve the economic crises of the 1970s, "free market" regimes now hold power across the globe (Barnekov, Boyle, & Rich, 1989; Fisher, 1992). They have dismantled the welfare state and promoted decentralized, private forms of organization and service delivery as alternatives to centralized public programs. They have sought not only to promote conservative proponents of the new social movement form but to undermine the state, whose legitimacy this chapter argues is critical to citizen insurgency in a postindustrial context. From the neoconservative vantage point, the true proponents of "the community revolution" of the 1960s and 1970s were not the new left and new social movements but rather conservatives calling for privatization (Schambra, 1985). Such neoconservatives assert that privatization not only solves urban problems better than public programs but, equally significant, empowers people at the grass roots. Community-based efforts, they proclaim, give "power back to the people" by "allowing local people and organizations to take the lead in tackling their own problems and opportunities—with the minimum of outside interference" (Butler, 1982, p. 4; Fitzgerald, 1988).

Of course, conservative proponents of citizen action are not unique to the 1980s; there is a long history of community organizing designed to protect property and conservative traditions and oppose social change

(Fisher, 1984). And there is a long history of reactionary as well as left populism (Boyte & Riessman, 1986; Brinkley, 1983; Goodwyn, 1978; Khoros, 1980; Palmer, 1980). But even the reactionary and conservative forms in the past tended to be indigenous efforts, grounded in the understandable, if unjust and parochial, claims of peasants and workers who sought to protect what little they had (Calhoun, 1983). Now elites initiate neoconservative programs from above to undermine oppositional movements and demonstrate the advantage of private sector over public sector initiatives.

The ramifications of such policies are obvious. The public sphere, people's opportunities for democratic public discourse, shrinks daily as people's lives become increasingly private and privatized. Moreover, the voluntary sector, especially at the local and community level, has grown, actually been forced to grow, to try to meet the decline in social and public services (Wolch, 1990). But the worsening of urban conditions under privatization policies, for everyone but the most affluent, occurs worldwide. In addition, privatization, by undermining government legitimacy and responsibility, results not only in a declining public life and fewer public services but in loss of access to a potentially accountable and responsible pubic sector, *the* major victory of the old social movements and a crucial target of most earlier forms of new social movement organizing (Fisher, 1988, 1992; Piven & Cloward, 1982). As neoconservative ideology increasingly makes the public sector synonymous with bureaucratic inefficiency and encroachment on political liberties (a critique offered earlier by both decentralizers and the new left) and as the private "marketplace" of individual competition and consumption is touted, along with other private institutions, as the best if not the only arena for human interaction, the public sector disappears as the source of grievances or solutions. Citizen action is undercut.

Citizen insurgency in a postindustrial global political economy requires a prominent public sector. While the new social movement form of contemporary resistance focuses its attention on community-based self-help and empowerment, it does so partly because the state—one of the primary arenas and targets for antecedents such as Alinsky, the civil rights movement, national liberation efforts, and the new left—has been delegitimized. Community organizations require a public sector arena and target because, unlike the old social movements that had some power at the site of production, in our current era of high velocity global capital and declining labor activism, where it is much more difficult for workers and citizens to affect the private sector, the community- and constituency-based new social movements have the state as the entity most responsible and vulnerable to their constituencies (Fisher, 1992; Piven & Cloward, 1982). To the extent that privatization proceeds worldwide, it not only worsens social conditions but undermines the prospects of citizen action.

The prospects for grass-roots mobilization are definitely unclear and ambiguous, especially given the wide variety of politics, issues, and programs included in these efforts and the transitionary stage of the world political economy. Much remains to be done if the conservative manipulation is to be successfully countered and if contemporary organizing is to be more than the busy reproduction of fragmented collective behavior. The two strategies emphasized throughout this volume are coalition formation among deeply fragmented groupings and mobilization around a political program that can unite grass-roots constituencies. What is also required is a more significant understanding of the relationship between citizen action, democracy, and the state (Midgley, 1986).

The prodemocracy, antistatist elements of contemporary organizing are stark. Touraine warns that the new social movements, if left totally to their own devices, could open the way for a reactionary retreat into the politics of culture. "The main risk," he has written (Touraine, 1985, p. 780),

> is no longer to see social movements absorbed by political parties, as in Communist regimes, but a complete separation between social movements and the State. In such a situation, social movements can easily become segmented, transform themselves into defense of minorities or search for identity, while public life becomes dominated by pro- or anti-State movements.

Kaufmann (1990, p. 10) sees a similar trend, noting that "practitioners of identity politics attribute great importance to the exploration and articulation of individual and collective identities, and tend to focus more heavily on individual and group self-transformation than on engaging with the state." Lehmann (1990, p. 64) argues against a withdrawal into civil society "to get around the problem of the state and its biases." For community- and constituency-based struggles to avoid collapse into antimovements, their democratic vision and practice must extend beyond the immediate and self-referential.

Contemporary mobilization demonstrates the weaknesses of decentralized democratic ideology: too small to be effective, too few resources to sustain much of an effort, too parochial to build a larger movement, too fragmented and identity focused to build coalitions necessary for achieving fundamental change, too self-oriented to see collective problems and solutions, too occupied with issues of democratic process to address critical concerns of equity and equality, and too antistate to understand the important dialectic that exists in the late twentieth century between the government and popular mobilization. For at the same time that the democratic impulse of these efforts seeks autonomy from the state itself—opposing large bureaucracies and recoiling against a legacy of state coercion, oppression, and disenfranchisement—these movements both need the state and need to control it. Contrary to the direction of much grass-roots organizing in the 1980s and 1990s, the future may call for the state to be revived as a site of dialectical struggle and, despite the obvious contradictions, reconceptualized as a source of support for citizen action and grass-roots initiatives.

As Palmer (1990) shows for agrarian populism in the late nineteenth century in the United States, the failure of "democratic localism" led to a national solution: Reform the state to support local needs. If the struggle to save communities and promote the interests of the powerless does not occur at both the community and the state level, it is doomed to the inherent parochialism and limits of democratic localism. Accordingly, the democratic struggle succeeds best when it is waged not only in alternative settings engaged in empowerment and building community capacity but also in public settings, through protest and negotiation, opposition and coproduction, in the public sector. For example, organize voluntary social service programs *and* engage in conflict and negotiation with public service bureaucracies. Build domestic violence-free spaces *and* challenge the sexism of the state and its manipulation of women and disregard of children. Counsel against AIDS, nurture the sick, *and* fight for national health care and state support of access to alternative medical care providers. Recycle the by-products of industrialization *and* oppose the wanton destruction of the land by international capital and state policies that fail to regulate it. Build coalitions and a political party whose individual members organize communities and constituencies *and* fight for state power. This is one of the central lessons of Alinsky organizing, the civil rights movement, national liberation struggles, and the new left that much of contemporary citizen action forgets or rejects. The power to make sufficient change does not rest within individuals and their communities. Organizers who primarily organize the poor around material needs know this well. As Ernesto Cortes (cited in Rips, 1986, p. 13) put it at a strategy meeting of an Alinsky-style organization in Houston, Texas:

> The reason you were created is to hold public officials accountable. That whole philosophy is being challenged at the local level, the state level, and the national level. . . . There has to be a public sector. It has to be more effective. It won't be unless you hold them accountable.

As Flacks (1990) and others suggest, part of the oppositional project of the near future includes reforming the state. A strong state is more often the oppressive arm of private capital than it is the political battleground between oppositional and mainstream forces. Flacks (1990, pp. 48-49) calls for the "reinvention" of the state not as the source of control and initiative or the solution to problems but "principally as the potential source of capital and law that would enable people to solve their problems at the level of the community." There are precedents for such a reconceptualized state, but most significantly the government as a source of capital for communities may be the best function left for the state in a context "that is both globalizing and decentering." Lehmann (1990), in his study of social movements in Latin America, agrees that movements not so much capture the state as see it as a target, something to "challenge" and begin to "colonize . . . in order to put into practice a commitment to due process and to civil and human rights" (Corbridge, 1991, p. 314). Current grass-roots mobilizations obviously seek to return politics to the realm of society and civic self-activity, broadening the definition of political life to include more than occasional electoral participation or state policies. Nevertheless, this chapter argues, as do others, that citizen action needs to broaden its program, and this expansion needs to include a critical, if altered, role for the state (Roth, 1991).

At any given historical moment, community mobilization efforts represent the state of conflict over the large and small contradictions in urban life. Currently that conflict does not go well. Some think it succeeds better in the South and East than in the West; others argue the opposite (Brand, 1990; Ceccarelli, 1982; Durning, 1989; Melucci, 1984; Wallerstein, 1990). Nevertheless, progressive grass-roots efforts represent more than any other form of social change the major contradictions in contemporary society: an economy that is "hierarchical, nonassociative, and nonegalitarian" versus movements that at their best and most often are nonhierarchical, egalitarian, and highly associative (Rankin, 1991, p. 75). Advanced capitalist society leaves most social institutions with only capitalist functions; the means of selfish individualism produces the divided, contentious, consumerist society as its end (Wolin, 1981). Grass-roots mobilizations worldwide pose an alternative. Despite diverse objectives, at their best they seek to fulfill the modernist project of material equality, political and personal liberty, and supportive community *and* they seek to use democratic and humane means to do so. The odds have always been stacked against such projects. This volume is devoted to addressing both the limits and the potential of contemporary organizing to remedy the former and enhance the latter. And this chapter suggests three important bases: a fuller recognition of the common ground and potential solidarity among efforts worldwide, a better understanding of movement history, and an increased appreciation of the complex relationship between democratic community organizing and the state.

REFERENCES

Amin, S. (1990). The social movements in the periphery. In S. Amin et al. (Eds.), *Transforming the revolution: Social movements and the world-system.* New York: Monthly Review Press.

Aronowitz, S. (1992). *The politics of identity: Class, culture, social movements.* New York: Routledge.

Barnekov, T., Boyle, R., & Rich, D. (1989). *Privatism and urban policy in Britain and the United States.* Oxford, UK: Oxford University Press.

Bonner, A. (1990). *Averting the apocalypse: Social movements in India today.* Durham, NC: Duke University Press.

Boyte, H. (1981). *The backyard revolution.* Philadelphia: Temple University Press.

Boyte, H., Booth, H., & Max, S. (1986). *Citizen action and the new American populism.* Philadelphia: Temple University Press.

Boyte, H., & Riessman, F. (1986). *The new populism.* Philadelphia: Temple University Press.

Branch, T. (1988). *Parting the waters: America in the King years, 1954-1963.* New York: Simon & Schuster.

Brand, K. (1990). Cyclical aspects of new social movements: Waves of cultural criticism and mobilization cycles of new middle-class radicalism. In R. Dalton & M. Kuechler (Eds.), *Challenging the political order.* New York: Oxford University Press.

Brecher, J., & Costello, T. (1990). *Building bridges: The emerging grassroots coalition of labor and community.* New York: Monthly Review Press.

Breines, W. (1982). *Community and organization in the new left, 1962-1968: The great refusal.* New York: Praeger.

Brinkley, A. (1983). *Huey Long, Father Coughlin, and the Great Depression.* New York: Vintage.

Bronner, S. E. (1990). *Socialism unbound.* New York: Routledge.

Butler, S. (1982). *The enterprise zone: Capitalism in the inner city* (Special Report 21). Grove City, PA: Public Policy Education Fund, Inc.

Calhoun, C. J. (1983). The radicalism of tradition: Community strength or venerable disguise and borrowed language? *American Journal of Sociology, 88,* 886-914.

Carson, C., Jr. (1982). *In struggle: SNCC and the black awakening of the 1960s.* Cambridge, MA: Harvard University Press.

Ceccarelli, P. (1982). Politics, parties, and urban movements: Western Europe. In N. Fainstein & S. Fainstein (Eds.), *Urban policy under capitalism.* Beverly Hills, CA: Sage.

Chekki, D. (1979). *Community development: Theory and method of planned change.* New Delhi, India: Vikas.

Cnann, R. (1991). Neighborhood organizations and social development in Israel. *Social Development Issues, 13,* 44-54.

Cocks, J. (1989). *The oppositional imagination.* London: Routledge.

Collins, S. (1986). *The rainbow challenge.* New York: Monthly Review Press.

Corbridge, S. (1991). Third World development. *Progress in Human Geography, 15,* 311-321.

Dalton, R., & Kuechler, M. (Eds.). (1990). *Challenging the political order: New social and political movements in Western democracies.* New York: Oxford University Press.

Delgado, G. (1986). *Organizing the movement: The roots and growth of ACORN.* Philadelphia: Temple University Press.

de Tocqueville, A. (1969). *Democracy in America.* New York: Doubleday, Anchor.

Durning, A. B. (1989). Action at the grassroots: Fighting poverty and environmental decline. *Worldwatch Paper, 88,* 1-70.

Epstein, B. (1990). Rethinking social movement theory. *Socialist Review, 20,* 35-65.

Evans, S. (1979). *Personal politics: The roots of women's liberation in the civil rights movements and the new left.* New York: Vintage.

Evans, S., & Boyte, H. (1986). *Free spaces: The sources of democratic change in America.* New York: Harper & Row.

Fisher, R. (1984). *Let the people decide: Neighborhood organizing in America.* Boston: Twayne.

Fisher, R. (1988). Where seldom is heard a discouraging word: The political economy of Houston, Texas. *Amerikastudien, 33,* 73-91.

Fisher, R. (1992). Organizing in the modern metropolis. *Journal of Urban History, 18,* 222-237.

Fisher, R., & Kling, J. (1988). Leading the people: Two approaches to the role of ideology in community organizing. *Radical America, 21*(1), 31-46.

Fisher, R., & Kling, J. (1991). Popular mobilization in the 1990s: Prospects for the new social movements. *New Politics, 3,* 71-84.

Fitzgerald, R. (1988). *When government goes private: Successful alternatives to public services.* New York: Universe.

Flacks, D. (1990). The revolution of citizenship. *Social Policy, 21,* 37-50.

Frank, A. G., & Fuentes, M. (1990). Civil democracy: Social movements in recent world history. In S. Amin et al. (Eds.), *Transforming the revolution: Social movements and the world-system.* New York: Monthly Review Press.

Goodwyn, L. (1978). *The populist moment: A short history of the agrarian revolt in America.* New York: Oxford University Press.

Greider, W. (1992). *Who will tell the people: The betrayal of American democracy.* New York: Simon & Schuster.

Gundelach, P. (1984). Social transformation and new forms of voluntary associations. *Social Science Information, 23,* 1049-1081.

Gutman, H. G. (1977). *Work, culture, and society in industrializing America.* New York: Vintage.

Horwitt, S. (1989). *Let them call me rebel: Saul Alinsky, his life and legacy.* New York: Knopf.

Inglehart, R. (1990). Political value orientations. In M. K. Jennings & J. VanDeth (Eds.), *Continuities in political action.* Berlin: Walter de Gruter.

Jacobs, P., & Landau, S. (1966). *The new radicals: A report with documents.* New York: Vintage.

Jacques, M. (1990). After capitalization: What now? *Social Policy, 21,* 12-16.

Jennings, J. (1990). The politics of black empowerment in urban America: Reflections on race, class, and community. In J. Kling & P. Posner (Eds.), *The dilemmas of activism: Class, community, and the politics of local mobilization.* Philadelphia: Temple University Press.

Kaase, M. (1990). Mass participation. In M. K. Jennings & J. VanDeth (Eds.), *Continuities in political action.* Berlin: Walter de Gruter.

Kahn, S. (1970). *How people get power: Organizing oppressed communities for action.* New York: McGraw-Hill.

Kaufmann, L. A. (1990, Fall). *Democracy in a postmodern world. Social Policy,* pp. 6-11.

Khoros, V. (1980). *Populism: Its past, present, and future.* Moscow: Progress.

Kjellberg, F. (1979). A comparative view of municipal decentralization: Neighborhood democracy in Oslo and Bologna. In L. J. Sharpe (Ed.), *Decentralist trends in Western democracies.* London: Sage.

Laclau, E., & Mouffe, C. (1985). *Hegemony and socialist strategy: Towards a radical democratic politics.* London: Verso.

Lehmann, D. (1990). *Democracy and development in Latin America: Economics, politics, and religion in the postwar period.* Cambridge, UK: Polity.

Lipsitz, G. (1988). *A life in the struggle: Ivory Perry and the culture of opposition.* Philadelphia: Temple University Press.

Logan, J., & Swanstrom, T. (1990). Urban restructuring: A critical view. In J. Logan & T. Swanstrom (Eds.), *Beyond the city limits: Urban policy and restructuring in comparative perspective.* Philadelphia: Temple University Press.

Lowe, S. (1986). *Urban social movements: The city after Castells.* London: Macmillan.

Mansbridge, J. (1980). *Beyond adversary democracy.* New York: Basic Books.

Mayer, M. (1987). Restructuring and opposition in West German cities. In M. P. Smith & J. Feagin (Eds.), *Global cities.* New York: Basil Blackwell.

McAdam, D. (1982). *Political process and the development of black insurgency, 1930-1970.* Chicago: University of Chicago Press.

McCormick, J. (1989). *The global environmental movement: Reclaiming paradise.* London: Belhaven.

Melucci, A. (1984). An end to social movements? *Social Science Information, 23,* 819-135.

Merkl, P. (1985). *New local centers in centralized states.* Berkeley: University Press of America.

Merkl, P. (1987). How new the brave new world: New social movements in West Germany. *German Studies Review, 10,* 125-147.

Midgley, J. (1986). *Community participation, social development, and the state.* London: Methuen.

Morris, A. (1984). *The origins of the civil rights movement: Black communities organizing for change.* New York: Free Press.

Offe, C. (1987). Challenging the boundaries of institutional politics: Social movements since the 1960s. In C. Maier (Ed.), *Changing boundaries of the political: Essays on the evolving balance between the state and society, public and private in Europe.* Cambridge, UK: Cambridge University Press.

Palmer, B. (1980). *Man over money: The southern populist critique of American capitalism.* Chapel Hill: University of North Carolina Press.

Palmer, B. (1990). New wine in old bottles: Southern populism and the dilemmas of class, ideology, and state power. In J. Kling & P. Posner (Eds.), *The dilemmas of activism: Class, community, and the politics of local mobilization.* Philadelphia: Temple University Press.

Pickvance, C., & Preteceille, E. (1991). *State restructuring and local power: A comparative perspective.* London: Pinter.

Pitkin, H., & Shumer, S. (1982). On participation. *Democracy, 2,* 43-54.

Piven, F., & Cloward, R. (1982). *The new class war: Reagan's attack on the welfare state and its consequences.* New York: Pantheon.

Rankin, M. (1991, July/August). Roundtable reply. *Z Magazine,* p. 75.

Reagon, B. (1979). The borning struggle: The civil rights movement. In D. Cutler (Ed.), *They should have served that cup of coffee.* Boston: South End.

Rips, G. (1986, February 21). Privatization: The next big lucha. *The Texas Observer,* p. 13.

Rogers, M. B. (1990). *Cold anger: A story of faith and power politics.* Denton: University of North Texas Press.

Roth, R. (1991). Local Green politics in West German Cities. *International Journal of Urban and Regional Research, 15,* 75-89.

Rude, G. (1980). *Ideology and popular protest.* New York: Pantheon.

Sassen, S. (1990). Beyond the city limits: A commentary. In J. Logan & T. Swanstrom (Eds.), *Beyond the city limits: Urban policy and restructuring in comparative perspective.* Philadelphia: Temple University Press.

Schambra, W. A. (1985). Progressive liberalism and American community. *The Public Interest, 80,* 31-48.

Scott, A. (1990). *Ideology and the new social movements.* London: Unwin Hyman.

Slater, D. (Ed.). (1985). *Social movements and the state in Latin America.* Holland: Foris.

Smith, C. (1991). *The emergence of liberation theology: Radical religion and social movement theory.* Chicago: University of Chicago Press.

Smith, M. P., & Feagin, J. (1987). *The capitalist city: Global restructuring and community politics.* Oxford: Basil Blackwell.

Spretnak, C., & Capra, F. (1985). *Green politics*. London: Grafton.

Susskind, L., Elliott, M., et al. (1983). *Paternalism, conflict, and coproduction: Learning from citizen action and citizen participation in Western Europe*. New York: Plenum.

Swanstrom, T. (1985). *The crisis of growth politics: Cleveland, Kucinich, and the challenge of urban populism*. Philadelphia: Temple University Press.

Teodori, M. (1969). *The new left: A documentary history*. New York: Bobbs-Merrill.

Thompson, E. P. (1963). *The making of the English working class*. New York: Vintage.

Touraine, A. (1985). An introduction to the study of social movements. *Social Research, 52*, 749-787.

Wallerstein, I. (1990). Antisystemic movements: History and dilemmas. In S. Amin et al. (Eds.), *Transforming the revolution: Social movements and the world-system*. New York: Monthly Review Press.

Walton, J. (1979). Urban political movements and revolutionary change in the Third World. *Urban Affairs Quarterly, 15*, 3-22.

Wolch, J. (1990). *The shadow state: Government and voluntary sector in transition*. New York: Foundation Center.

Wolin, S. (1981). Why democracy. *Democracy, 1*, 3.

2 Complex Society/Complex Cities: New Social Movements and the Restructuring of Urban Space

JOSEPH KLING

■ New Social Movements, New Urban Spaces

The issue explored in this chapter is whether the emergence of new social movements in the West can be conceptually and empirically connected to the splintered urban spaces that seem to structure and inform the corporate cities of the late twentieth century. I will tentatively answer this question in the affirmative and suggest that the new movements, as well as the turbulent cities in which many of them have been fostered, represent two facets of a single but multifaceted process: the global transformations that have occurred in the shift from industrial to complex society. New social movements, I will argue, can be understood, at least in part, as societal forms through which the tensions created by the contemporary fracturing of people's urban life spaces get played out.

A theory of social movements always presupposes a theory of society. In a period as technologically and culturally volatile as our own, however, this has led to serious definitional, conceptual, and practical problems. Marxist theories of collective action, for example, which

AUTHOR'S NOTE: Earlier versions of this chapter were presented at the meeting of the American Political Science Association, Washington, DC (September 1991) and at a conference sponsored by the International Sociological Association, Committee 21, University of California, Los Angeles, "A New Urban and Regional Hierarchy?" (April 1992). I would like to thank Marshall Berman, and Michael Peter Smith and Edward Soja, for their helpful comments and criticisms at these meetings.

view social movements as essentially class based, have become outworn. As Barbara Epstein points out, Marxism "has no way of accounting for movements that center around the defense and construction of identity (as in the gay and lesbian movements), the critique of personal life and gender (as in the women's movement) or the effort to realize a utopian vision of community (as in the direct action movement)" (Epstein, 1990, p. 45). At the same time, the notion of a long-term historical project, to which all forms of progressive mobilization might at least loosely attach themselves, and culminate in the realization of some sort of global socialism, is no longer credible.

Few challenge the argument that new modes of sociocultural production and reproduction have eclipsed the class-oriented structures of the once familiar industrial society. But there is little consensus as to how the new society, and the decentered urban nodes through which its energies are exercised, shall be named, understood, influenced. To articulate these notions, we need a fuller understanding of the *complexity* not only of the contemporary urban experience but of the society that has produced and structured that experience. This chapter, generally, will examine the character of the complex city and attempt to understand how it connects to the appearance and functioning of the new social movements that have generated so much discussion over the past few years.

The analysis first traces some elements of the idea of a complex society back to French new left thought of the 1960s and then looks at Albert Melucci's recent exposition of the construct. The next part of the chapter suggests how complexity is played out in the everyday spaces of the corporate city and how these spaces might affect the formation of political identities.

The discussion of the spatial character of the complex city is followed by a brief historical section. Here, the chapter explores the way the class-oriented cultures and institutions of the industrial city were, over the course of the twentieth century, displaced by the rise of a fragmented, privatizing, and service-oriented urban polity. It attempts to probe the meanings of these spaces created by the disjunctions between older, disappearing urban political forms and newly salient, particularist ones. It is through these fragmenting spaces of everyday life that identity politics, I argue, become merged into the flow of social energies in contemporary urban arenas.

The chapter closes with a discussion of what sorts of understandings and strategies might enhance public control over the new sociospatial processes that are having such powerful political impacts on people's lives. My concluding thesis will be that new social movements, to fully realize their promise, do need to ground themselves in the particularity of identity politics. At the same time, however, unless they relate to a generalized political space that connects them across difference, their effectiveness will be severely curtailed.

■ The Idea of Complex Society

The "city," as that social formation has come traditionally to be understood, is no longer with us. To the typology of the ancient city, the medieval city, the mercantile city, the industrial city, urban theory now adds the corporate city and grounds it in the notion of a world hierarchy of cities. For the functions and population distributions that once defined a central city have become too spatially extended and delocalized, and the global interplay of cities too prevalent a sociohistorical force, for the old categories to work anymore.

The emergence of this new city is inseparable from the conditions that have shaped what is variously referred to as "late capitalist/postindustrial/post-Fordist/postmodern" society. These seemingly competing classifications look to and describe different aspects of a common set of disordered and unruly social processes. While different analysts use different terms, and there is constant argument and controversy over which formulation is the more fruitful, these varying theoretical frameworks, I suggest, run more on parallel tracks than competing ones. In fact, because there is a larger agreement as to the general empirical conditions that describe the character of this society, it would be helpful to have a discourse rich enough to move between the available terms and frameworks for talking about it.

Let me suggest that Alberto Melucci's remarkably direct and deceptively simple formulation of "complex society" most effectively captures many of the tangled elements that characterize contemporary social systems: their mode of production (late capitalist), their technological organization (postindustrial/post-Fordist), their predominant forms of cultural expression (modern/postmodern; Melucci, 1989). It allows us to move back and forth between these varied facets of present-day society and conceptually relate them to one another. Melucci's language also places discussion of social movements well within the growing body of literature that recognizes systemic turbulence as central to the epistemological and scientific frameworks of our time (Briggs & Peat, 1989; Gleick, 1987; Hardison, 1989; Morley & Shachar, 1986; Pagels, 1989; Poundstone, 1988; Rosenau, 1990). Melucci's concept of complex society has a firm historical grounding. Its roots trace back to the attempt of French new left thinkers, in the early 1960s, to understand the changes in working-class and social movement formation that were then becoming visible. The ideas of these writers and activists were inseparably tied to the theory of "the new working class." "Automated industry," Serge Mallet wrote in 1965, "creates a new type of skill highly remote from the knowledge of the traditional *metier*, but which requires a much greater cultural and technological knowledge: it begins the progressive elimination of the distinction between manual and intellectual labor" (Mallet, 1975, p. 41).

Here were some of the first recognitions by radical theorists of the significance of information- and computer-based technologies for traditional Marxist understandings of class and class conflict. While perhaps somewhat naive, the theorists of the new working class saw automation as opening up possibilities for a truly democratic and collective organization of production, one that, for the first time, would make workers' self-management a viable technopolitical option. Computerized processes of production demanding high levels of knowledge and skill could eliminate the domination of the worker by both the capitalist owners of the means of production in the West and the bureaucratic regulators and controllers of production in the East. "The technician working class, strongly integrated into the production process, is led to demand, beyond its immediate needs, the possession of certain instruments of control over the economic activity which makes it live" (Mallet, 1975, p. 42). The theory of "postindustrial society" began to be developed and appropriated by young European radicals disaffected with the Soviet Union, Stalinism, and the Communist parties. "Self-management" became a key slogan of this emerging new left. It was a left that was anti-Leninist in its suspicion of hierarchical organization, established leadership structures, and received ideologies from above.

During the 1960s the consequences of the technological shifts that had been occurring in the West since the end of World War II built to a critical mass. People began, for the first time, to directly experience their impact. A society based for more than 150 years on the class conflicts generated by industrial forces of production was undergoing transition. Structures of capitalist exploitation and surplus extraction continued in place. But, at the same time, social processes were coming to be shaped by group conflicts over the purposes and ends of production, the meanings of personal, gendered, and cultural identities, and the control of local space and the building of community. This transition literally exploded into collective awareness in the aftermath of the student rebellions of 1968. "Let us begin with a very simple idea: a new type of society is taking shape," Alain Touraine wrote in his study of the student upheavals of that year.

> Growth and power are no longer generated simply by economic activities and relations; society as a whole and every aspect of human life are involved in comprehensive change. The social struggles over this change are also comprehensive. . . . New class struggles are emerging and being organized in areas which a short time ago were considered outside the sphere of "productive" activities: urban life, the management of needs and resources, education. (Touraine, 1971, p. 23; see also Lefebvre, 1969)

Touraine became one of the leading, and most prescient, theorists of post-Marxist society (Touraine, 1971, 1981, 1988; Touraine, Wieviorka, & Dubet, 1987). Class, and the system of production, never disappeared from his purview while, at the same time, he provided a richly developed framework for identifying the conflicts and struggles that surfaced with the displacement of the factory as the prime locus of social control.

Touraine called this new society "programmed" because its primary form of accumulation is not material wealth "but the capacity to produce production, the very principle of creative work, which is to say *knowledge*" (1977, p. 93).

For Touraine, the grounding of society in information and communication processes, and in the realms of consumption and personal life, created the conditions for ordinary people to set in motion their own cultural agendas against those of technocratic elites. In Touraine's terms, the new social movements represented conflicts over the control of *historicity*, that is, over control of the very models of knowledge, accumulation, and culture that shape people's fundamental relation to their world.

Alberto Melucci—who was Touraine's student in the early 1970s and who wrote his dissertation under Touraine's direction—built upon the ideas of his mentor. There are significant differences between the two regarding the stability and meaning of the impact of new social movements, but they agree about the directions that contemporary society opens up for collective action.[1] For both these theorists, the political economy of developed societies is at least as much about the production, management, and control of information as it is about the extraction of surplus value from direct producers. This leads to new possibilities for social struggle.

In postindustrial society, according to Melucci, the access of working people to knowledge- and data-based technologies provides them with increased levels of control over production of the social codes and norms that traditionally shape consciousness and belief. "In complex societies," Melucci writes,

> material production is increasingly replaced by the production of signs and social relations. Systemic conflicts center on the ability of groups and individuals to control the conditions of their own action. Complex societies are networks of high density information and are dependent on a degree of autonomy for their constituent elements. (Melucci, 1989, p. 45)

Under these conditions, struggle at the workplace—class conflict—does not disappear but expands to include struggles over the control and direction of culture and cultural models and over the meanings of social and personal identity. Thus a second consequence of complex society is that oppositional struggles spill out of the workplace and into everyday life itself, broadening the fields of social conflict.

> In recent years, these developments have initiated much debate, especially about the concept of identity. . . . Why has the theme of identity become such a central issue? The probable reason is that it reflects the capacity of contemporary action to go beyond modifying and transforming the natural environment. Action on "outer" nature was the binding nucleus of industrial society. . . . In contemporary systems we find an emerging awareness of the capacity to act upon human action itself. (Melucci, 1989, p. 46)

A technology based on information processes, as well as on direct material production, expands the locus of social movements from the site of production, the realm of traditional class conflict, into the sites of consumption and reproduction. Thus it is within the context of complex society that what have been called the new social movements come to prominence. It is not that such movements were ever absent from industrial society but that, within the context of postindustrialism, they take on a new centrality and meaning.

The idea of complexity also permits theory to move beyond the confines of Western social systems. For if the developed nations may be understood in "postindustrial/postmodern" terms, certainly this is not true for Third World nations in precisely the same way. Ulf Hannerz, for example, charges that the information society is just another Occidentalist idea, probably fully shared only with Japan. "The organized large-scale production of knowledge new to the combined cultural inventory of humankind . . . remain[s] as much more the features of the center than of the periphery," Hannerz writes (1992, p. 33). Indeed, raw class conflict, and the dynamics of primary and secondary production, continue to play much more direct roles in the Third World than they do in the developed capitalist economies.

Still, there is no escaping the far-reaching impact of information technologies. These same technologies, which have led to consumer societies in the North, have made it possible to export manufacturing and assembly functions to the countries of the South, leading to the emergence of a world political economy and the gradual building of a complex global culture, one with both convergent and contradictory strands. Indeed, the idea of complexity gives us a much better idea of how the developed and underdeveloped worlds connect, interpenetrate, and oppose one another. At the same time, the notion of complexity affirms the double insight that capitalist modes of surplus extraction and control are still essential to the everyday workings of the information society, while postmodern cultural forms increasingly mix with and reshape daily life in the Third World.

What concerns us in the remainder of this chapter is the relation between urban spaces and complex society. For the social processes that define the postindustrial world do not take place in a spatial vacuum. The city—despite its decline, despite its divisions and conflicts, and despite its collapse as a coherent cultural, political, and economic form—remains a kind of social crucible, in which the factors building to various forms of resistance collect, heat, thicken, and slowly come to boil.

■ Urban Formation in Complex Society: The Disaggregated City

The mobility of capital, made possible by the electronics and computer technologies developed during and after World War II, leads to a global web of cities. The multilayered, service-based cities of late capitalism come to serve as loci from which transnational corporations, orchestrating technological capacity and accumulated wealth on a global scale, shape the character of semiperipheral and peripheral cities in the Third World; these, in turn, by drawing away jobs and factories, and exporting their assembled products to the consuming nations, react back upon and destabilize the quality of life in the urban centers of the core (Cohen, 1981; Frobel, Heinrichs, & Kreye, 1980; Hymer, 1979; Smith & Feagin, 1987). The new space of a world capitalist system, Manuel Castells writes,

> is a space of variable geometry, formed by locations hierarchically or-
> dered in a continuously changing network of flows: flows of capital, labor,
> elements of production, commodities, information, decisions, and sig-
> nals. . . . Space is dissolved into flows: cities become shadows that ex-
> plode or disappear according to decisions that their dwellers will always
> ignore. The outer experience is cut off from the inner. (Castells, 1983,
> p. 314)

There is a shattering of the notion of the city as a public, as a delimited sphere in which persons are accountable and connected to one another. The urban begins to be experienced as a setting without order, meaning, coherence: a region of flows.

It is important to recognize the way these shifts in the organization of space alter our most fundamental encounters with the world and hence our basic conceptions of ourselves and the way we are related to others. Indeed, over the course of the 1970s, theorists like Castells came to understand the urban as *sociospatial* in nature, that is, as a material form that resonates between economic, political, and cultural processes, on the one hand, and the way in which people experience, and act back upon, the intrusion of those processes into their everyday lives, on the other.

"*Spatiality situates social life*," Edward Soja has written. His prem-ises are that spatiality is shaped both by structural social forces and by human consciousness and that space and consciousness reciprocally affect and reshape each other. Space is not the mere and abstract extension of physics and classical epistemology. It is, according to Soja, "an active arena where purposeful human agency jostles problemati-cally with tendential social determinations to shape everyday activity, particularize social change, and etch into place the course of time and the making of history" (Soja, 1985, p. 90). Soja's formulation goes a long way in helping us understand the politics and quality of life of the complex city as well as the resistances that form within it.

A spatial theory of urbanization, of course, had always been fundamental to Marxist readings of the industrial revolution and the formation of the working class.[2] But "space" was not conceptualized as an independent political factor in Marxist analysis until the impact of the new technologies on the global urban network, and on the reordering of the internal structure of advanced industrial cities, became starkly apparent. Castells's *The Urban Question* (1972/1979), Henri Lefebvre's *The Production of Space* (1974/1991), and David Harvey's *Social Justice and the City* (1973), were distillations and recombinations of ideas that had been developing throughout the postwar decades.

Castells and Harvey, in their early work, were heavily influenced by Althuserian structuralism. Lefebvre, on the other hand, had long been a critic of structuralism and the way it seemed to minimize the power of agency (Gottdiener, 1984, p. 199; see also Gottdiener, 1985). "Spatial practice is neither determined by an existing system, be it urban or ecological, nor adapted to a system, be it economic or political," Lefebvre (1991) wrote.

> On the contrary, thanks to the potential energies of a variety of groups capable of diverting homogenized space to their own purposes, a theatricalized or dramatized space is likely to arise. . . . An unequal struggle, sometimes furious, sometimes more low-key, takes place between the Logos and the anti-Logos. . . . On the side of the Logos . . . are ranged the forces that aspire to dominate and control space: business and the state, institutions, the family . . . corporate and constituted bodies of all kinds. In the opposite camp are the forces that seek to appropriate space: various forms of self-management or workers' control of territorial and industrial entities, communities and communes, elite groups striving to change life and transcend political institutions and parties. (p. 391)

Lefebvre's insistence upon agency over structure is clear. Still, the two schools were linked by their agreement that spatial politics were an essential element of everyday life in urban arenas.[3] The appropriation and use of space were now assumed to be matters of political struggle that, like struggles at the workplace and over state policy, had direct and primary effect upon the differential distribution of the social product.

The theory of the postindustrial city built upon this new approach to the political character of space. The character of the industrial city, for example, is familiar: majority working-class population; ethnically focused but class-rooted ward politics; powerful labor unions; cohesive and supportive neighborhoods, where, in the regional cities, everybody knows somebody who works in the Industry or the Mill or one of the Plants or, where, in the national cities, there is a sense of centering, downtown public spaces that promote the mingling of residentially segregated racial and economic groups. But, with postindustrialism, this city begins to unravel. It evolves into a chaotic form characterized by layers that, as one descends through them, become increasingly disordered.

Critical masses of people who once lived and worked within the formal political boundaries of cities leave for surrounding regions, earning their livings outside the reach of the central city's legislative and taxing powers and entering its jurisdiction only occasionally, on shopping and leisure excursions. As a recent textbook in urban geography points out, over half the commuting work trips in metropolitan areas today are suburb to suburb rather than suburb to central city (Hartshorn, 1992, p. 178). Yet these same people remain well within the center's sphere of influence, profoundly shaped by, as well as shaping, the feedback loops that characterize the way it draws in, uses, and expels natural, economic, and social resources. The ecological effects of these loops—of the need of cities to concentrate energy and heat use, for example, and the dissemination of the resulting wastes—extend as far as the Arctic and Antarctic and as high as the ozone layer.

In this disaggregated, complex city, the professional services essential to technologically advanced economies replace manufacturing and direct production as the primary sources of employment and wealth.[4] Huge financial, banking, and corporate centers come to characterize the downtown built environment. Cities attempt to make up for the loss of revenue associated with the decline in manufacturing employment by emphasizing tourism and building convention centers, sports arenas, and upscale shopping malls presented as urban spectacle (Baltimore's Harbor Place, Atlanta's Underground and Peachtree Center, New York's South Street Seaport; see Harvey, 1989, pp. 256-278; also Boyer, 1992).

Government services, "concerned with the maintenance and reproduction of the world city, as well as the provision of certain items of collective consumption," such as health, public housing, basic utilities, local transportation, and sanitation, constitute another layer of employment. Then there is the "informal," "floating," or street economy—day

laborers, illegal aliens in sweat shops, street vendors, household workers, and modest artisans, selling earrings on street corners. Much of this
work is done by women and children. Finally, the informal economy
includes those who have given up looking for work—the full-time
unemployed, the homeless, the indigent—as well as those who have
entered the world of illegal commerce: hustlers, pimps, prostitutes,
petty criminals, drug dealers, enforcers (Friedmann & Wolff, 1982, pp.
320-321).

Margit Mayer describes this as the post-Fordist, or dual, city. The
class structure in the post-Fordist city, she writes, "is determined by two
equally dynamic sectors: the advanced services and high-tech sector and
the unregulated, labor-intensive sector" (Mayer, 1991, p. 109; see also
Storper & Walker, 1984). My own argument is that the new division of
labor is complex rather than dual—indeed, Mayer herself points out that
some researchers have begun to talk of an "eight-milieu society"—but
it is the sense of fragmentation and disparate lives and experiences that
is essential here.

The separation of work and residence imposed originally by industrial capitalism, and the global flight of productive capital to the periphery, is multiplied and reproduced in ways so disorderly at the core that
complex cities become analogous to turbulent systems (Gleick, 1987;
Remy, 1989). Within the spaces of the day to day, little is assured, fixed,
predictable. Infrastructures decay. Elevated highways collapse. Pieces
fall off buildings, while giant, glass-faced towers in fanciful geometri-
cal shapes spring up in new commercial centers that, at night, become
empty underground malls and deserted urban canyons. Familiar land-
marks are torn down. Local shops and family stores disappear. Homeless people materialize, on street corners, in parks and rail terminals,
huddled in storefront entrances. Chemical spills poison the air, defile
wetlands, pollute harbors, menace the drinking supply. There is random
violence: muggings, racial assaults, drug wars, aimless gunfire, mur-
dered children.

The collapse of the ordered city does not mean the end of collective
action. Within the context of their communities, people *do* organize
against the depredations of a corporate-controlled global economy. As
the chapters in this volume confirm, people organize to bring social
services to their communities, to assert tenant entitlements, to resist
commercial and industrial development, to assert and empower themselves culturally. Cities remain the key sites through which nationally

oriented movements emerge for racial equality, women's rights, gay liberation, environmental protection. This is a crucial fact in understanding both the history of mobilizations within the urban complex and the potential for its future directions. What has happened is that, as industrial production is exported, first to the suburbs, then to less developed internal and bordering regions, and finally to the Third World, both the urban proletariat and the city, as in some sense *a center of working-class* life, fade. For with the postindustrial reshaping of capitalist space, the structural bases for class-oriented mobilizations literally move out from under organized labor. Pockets of industrially based organization remain, but they no longer possess the political salience they had when manufacturing was the determining economic activity of core urban regions. In the next section, I want to trace the nature of this transition, so that, in the conclusion, we can take a closer look at some of the contradictions engendered by the social movements of our time and propose strategies for moving beyond them.

■ From Public to Disaggregated City: Corporate Capitalism, and the Rise of New Social Movements

It is important, in this discussion, to be clear about my argument. I am *not* saying that, once upon a time, there was a unified, public, class-oriented industrial city, which, in face of the electronics revolution precipitated by World War II, began to fall apart. I am not saying that, before our very eyes, it metamorphosed into the fragmented, privatizing, service-oriented, postmodern city with which we are all so familiar. The dichotomy was never so hard and fast, and the transition, never so abrupt. In the classic industrial city, forces existed that *both* divided people *and*, at the same time, drew them to a sense of a shared cultural and political world. My argument is that, over an extended period, the beginnings of which can be traced to before World War I, a slow process of transition and displacement undermined the centripetal forces of this primarily working-class city. Eventually its citizens were left without the economic, political, and spatial experiences necessary to the building of a strong, common public life and culture. In the complex city, the forces of division and fragmentation came to prevail.

Admittedly, this transition is not easily captured, especially for the American city, because its politics and culture were never totally structured in terms of class. Ira Katznelson, for example, has convincingly demonstrated that the distinction between workplace and neighborhood identities, which has done so much to reinforce racial and ethnic consciousness in America, as well as undermine consciousness of class, dates back to the city of the pre-Civil War era. His concept of a system of "city trenches"—a system whereby the politics of work and community are structurally and ideologically disjoined—provides a powerful framework for explaining the phenomenon peculiar to the United States of worker militancy at the workplace but political privatism in the community (Katznelson, 1981).

Katznelson is correct when he insists that political parties at the neighborhood level organized their working-class constituents, "not as workers, but as residents of this or that ward, as members of this or that ethnic group; and they did not intrude on workplace concerns" (Katznelson, 1981, p. 57). And his theory of the divided industrial city is given support by Martin Shefter. For Shefter, even as he demonstrates the ways in which trade unions, political parties, and local machines mitigated the potential for disruption in the industrial city, reminds us of the centrality of class, race, and ethnic conflicts to its everyday life. The middle class, he writes, established a full set of institutions enabling them to shop, pray, play, and educate their children without ever, outside work, having to come into contact with members of the working classes. Neighborhoods were segregated along the class, ethnic, and racial divisions that are still familiar today. And though workers in the cities often united across craft and ethnic lines in times of labor crisis, when such episodes passed the old cleavages reemerged to divide them (Shefter, 1986, p. 240). And one would do well, when considering the issue of the strength of an urban public culture in the industrial city, to keep in mind the image of New York society during the Progressive Era drawn by E. L. Doctorow in *Ragtime* (1976), with its class conflicts, patriarchal oppression, sexual exploitation, ethnic tensions, and racial violence. The emergence of a shared public life and culture in the classic industrial cities was hardly a given.

Nevertheless, a strong case can be made that, in the era of industrialization, urban-based social movements remained tied to a politics of labor and class. A centralizing urban culture did evolve, one existing in uneasy relationship to forces for separation and narrow group identity. If the ward machines of the time, for example, were able to appease their working-class constituents in terms of a politics of accommodation, ethnicity, turf, individual payoff, and personalism, they were still constrained to represent themselves to the larger community as spokesmen for "the working man" and the "lower classes." It was the "middle-class" and "good government" people ("goo-goos") who were seen as the enemy—even if the machine bosses did cooperate with the latter when it suited them (Judd, 1988, chaps. 3-4).

Other students of the period make similar observations. Greenstone and Peterson point out how both machine and reform politics worked symbiotically to reinforce the idea of a public weal. The ward politicians repeatedly justified their "side payments and willingness to compromise" as necessary techniques for bringing immigrant populations into the fold of American public life; while, in response, reformers emphasized the generalized authority structures and regime principles that the machine violated (Greenstone & Peterson, 1976). The issue was not the private-regarding working class versus the public-regarding upper and middle classes but different notions—drawn from different class positions—of how the public good could best be realized for opposed constituencies within a liberal democracy.

Herbert Gutmann, in his study of the late-nineteenth-century city, also discovered a salient urban working-class subculture, one deeply rooted in people's experience of their neighborhood and community. "Gilded age workers," Gutmann writes,

had distinct ways of work and leisure, habits, aspirations, conceptions of America and Christianity, notions of right and wrong, and traditions of protest and acquiescence that *were linked together in neighborhoods by extensive voluntary associations and other community institutions* . . . these strands wove together in ways that shaped a particular subculture. (1977, p. 277; italics added)

And as immigration flooded the industrial city of the early twentieth century, this working-class subculture did not dissipate but opened itself to the more overt socialist orientation of the European worker. During the periodic business depressions of these years, Madeleine Adamson and Seth Borgos tell us, demonstrations by thousands of unemployed workers in cities like New York, Philadelphia, and Chicago linked demands for work and cash relief with community calls for lower rents and food prices (Adamson & Borgos, 1984, p. 101).

The era of the industrial city also saw the deskilling and mechanization of the labor process. This led to the widespread creation of a class of semiskilled factory operatives who required virtually no skills to perform their jobs (Gordon, Edwards, & Riech, 1982, p. 118). One's community politics may have been organized in terms of ethnicity and ward, but the experience of being a semi- or unskilled wage earner was shared with one's neighbors in the city at large. It is easy to imagine how, across compartmentalized working-class neighborhoods and wards, this sense of a common work experience, a common relationship to the productive plant, and a common sense of exploitation could spill over into the politics of the larger society and replicate itself as a relatively homogeneous, class-influenced outlook on social policy.

The depression further manifested the politics of class. The Communist party established Unemployed Councils in local neighborhoods in Chicago and New York, while the CIO became the center of organizing across the urban and industrialized northern states. The politics of the New Deal were liberal and Keynesian, in that they believed opposing class interests could be reconciled within the context of capitalism, but they nevertheless came out of a welfare state philosophy that saw class as the centrally shaping element of public policy. Finally, while race was a factor that the politics of class could overcome only under the most exceptional of circumstances, one needs to recall that the earliest stirrings of the civil rights movement came from the CIO organizing drives of the 1930s. The impetus toward an interracial labor movement was further sparked by the militance of black labor leaders like A. Philip Randolph, Bayard Rustin, and James Farmer. It was these men who, in the early 1940s, came up with the first idea for a March on Washington (Adamson & Borgos, 1984; Buhle & Dawley, 1985; Fisher & Kling, 1988).

Only after World War II do identity- and culturally based movements come to dominate the politics of protest and direct action. But it is essential to recognize that *the conditions that lead to their ascendance take shape much earlier.* Theirs is not a sudden appearance, the marking of a historical disjuncture, a qualitative leap into a new, postmodern epoch. One of the things that the new social history has certainly taught us is that, grand theories aside, history simply does not move that way. First, as Katznelson and others demonstrated, race and ethnicity were always part of the urban political structure in the United States. But, second, corporate and small-scale production were fragmenting along urban/suburban lines in the years before World War I. By the turn of the century the corporations were beginning to site themselves in the suburbs, setting the stage for a restructuring of the urban economy and using the impact of such spatial separation to undermine the salient, but always precarious, sense of unity among urban-based American workers.[5]

The Great Depression, and then the war, interfere with this economic and political reorganization of industrial space. But it starts again with a vengeance once the war is over. For the American corporate sector has increased and concentrated its wealth, developed new industries—such as electronics, aerospace, and defense—and come out of the war years with revolutionary technologies in satellite and telecommunications, information processing, and high speed transportation. World War II intensified the development of what is now generally described as postindustrial capitalism, with its core and peripheral industries, primary and secondary markets, headquarter cities, and suburban production sites.

The complex city begins to emerge, with its new and dizzying division of labor. The new, fractured structures of workplace life intersect with the spaces of residential life to overwhelm the experience of a common working-class culture and politics. Higher paid blue-collar workers tend less and less to live in predominantly "working-class neighborhoods" but next to white-collar workers in communities that are best described as "occupationally mixed" (Halle, 1984, pp. 18-19). Many of these workers have long since left the city for the suburbs, but, if they remain within the residential neighborhoods under central city jurisdiction, their communities, again, represent a spectrum of middle-income employment and reflect middle-class, often ethnically based, political identities.

What is most telling is that the long legacy of racial separation and tension in the United States is then reinforced by the different economic and residential patterns that follow the segmented labor markets. "There are larger social and cultural differences between midtown Manhattan and the South Bronx than between Manhattan and Frankfurt," Mayer (1991, p. 110) asserts. This certainly overstates the case, given that language, mass media, educational systems, and the forces of cultural and national assimilation continue to do their work. Living in America—even for an Asian immigrant in an uptown sweatshop—carries with it a whole different set of meanings and experiences than living in Germany. But the fact remains that racial and ethnic differences at the workplace are reproduced in the residential community. "It is division by race, into black and white areas, that dominates the residential setting far more than division by occupation," Halle writes. And, today, it is a segregation "accompanied by a mutual fear, for many whites and blacks are clearly wary of straying, at least on foot, into each other's strongholds" (Halle, 1984, p. 26). And though Asians were not part of the industrial plant in central New Jersey that Halle studied, his picture needs to be completed by the terrible conflicts that have erupted between African American and Korean communities.

* * *

There is another side to all of this, of course. As the core industries export manufacturing jobs to the countries of Asia and Latin America, where wages are lower, unions often illegal, and benefits nonexistent, the American worker suddenly discovers his or her own vulnerability to class forces. Unemployment drops at first, as it did in the Reagan years, but the new jobs are either in low-paying periphery manufacturing and service sectors or require the kind of graduate professional training few workers can afford for their children. There is little aid for education available, as the export of manufacturing inevitably precipitates a fiscal crisis, and a sharp cutback in the social wage. Meanwhile, wages rise more slowly, and workers find that, in the context of an expanding economy, they have less disposable income. Housing and health costs soar beyond the reach of even the highly skilled primary sector laborer. At the same time, working people find their homes and communities threatened by growth coalitions and environmental pollution. The system, workers discover, has its contradictions.

The point is that class structures do not disappear within the context of postindustrial capitalism but become inextricably intermingled with other sources of identity, division, and conflict. If the analysis proposed in this chapter is correct, however, the resistance of subaltern groups, as these resistances become manifest in the spaces of everyday life—the spaces where people reside and consume, as opposed to those where they work—will not again be formulated in terms of a politics of class. The localized mobilizations that emerge within the context of complex society, while circumscribed by the logic of accumulation, will nevertheless be based on identity issues such as race, gender, and community and on cultural resistances to those values of state and corporate bureaucracies that affirm growth for its own sake and the regulation of everyday life. The final issue I want to explore, therefore, is whether, and in what ways, the politics of identity, constituency, and culture can influence the larger structures of social policy.

■ The New Narratives of Collective Action

The postmodern city tends to neglect or dismantle the public spaces and public sensibilities that nurture the formation of an extended collective consciousness. Identities based on the commonalities of class, or on the sense of a shared urban culture, weaken. They are overtaken by new, particularist identities tied to community, race, ethnicity, and gender. These give salience and voice to experiences and cultural realities not sufficiently marked in the more generalized politics of the classic central city. The ability of people to come to power over the quotidian, however, turns upon their capacity to imagine and name not only the immediately experienced elements of their lives but those elements, as well, that structurally connect them to distant others. This means that the reconstruction of any sort of mutually supportive, redistributive politics must look to the building of new public forms.

Certain trends emerge. First, the logic of capital accumulation creates, across identity politics, common grievances and experiences of domination and control. These compel some sort of search for connection. The threat to the environment is one such aggregating issue. The needs for day care, for a nationally legislated family leave policy, and for more comprehensive support of the elderly are others. In the United States, the devastation wrought by the absence of a national health care system becomes more and more evident. Indeed, it is clear that the salience of many of these issues significantly contributed to the election of Bill Clinton as president of the United States.

The new social movements that emerged out of the 1960s, and that have informed the theory and practice of collective action in the closing decades of the twentieth century, offer the primary possibility of re-creating a public life for working people in the current era. This is not to dismiss a class-based politics as irrelevant or archaic: Industrial production continues in the developed economies of the West, and the labor movement remains the most potent force for combatting global corporate power. In this country, for example, there is a whole spectrum of coalition activities related to the labor movement, from local support of striking workers to labor-community coalitions such as the Tri-State Conference on Steel in the Pittsburgh area (Brecher & Costello, 1990). Nevertheless, in a society in which the sphere of consumption plays as significant a role in shaping social life as that of production, class identity serves as only one form of political resistance among many. The erosion of class as a primary and overarching form of social identity leaves no alternatives to the new cultural movements as major vehicles for contemporary struggle. But to the extent that this sort of identity politics opens for people the opportunity to affirm themselves, name the particularities that inform their lives, and mold challenges to the conditions that restrict and control them, it is positive and liberatory.

Still, it will not do to romanticize the grass roots: In itself, action on community levels can reflect a wide variety of political values. Its use to exclude unwanted economic and racial groups is a staple of local politics. The story of Canarsie, for example, a once liberal, labor-oriented community retreating into a politics of racism, privatism, and conservative exclusion, captures the double-edged meanings of the spaces and politics of urban restructuring (Rieder, 1985). In a slightly different vein, "not in my backyard" strategies pit community against community over the issue of where new landfills or incinerators are to be placed. They are grounded therefore in acceptance of the existing structures of waste disposal and weaken the effort to unite groups to challenge prevailing policy in the fields of energy use, recycling, and waste creation. The values at stake in political mobilization have to be assessed in each particular case.

For publics commensurate with the conditions of social complexity to emerge, identity- and community-focused groups will have to come together, eventually, in larger alliance and coalition structures. The identity groups of a postmodern politics will still have to tackle the shaping of state policy, contest privatization, seek representatives for public office, and name an ideology—or set of explicitly acknowledged values and theoretical understandings—that justify a shared struggle for social justice and human freedom (Fisher & Kling, 1991).

Whether social movements will be able to nurture a sense of connection to larger political spaces is an open question. For contemporary movements do not offer the neat and hopeful narratives that Marxism once promised. If there are to be new narratives through which people come to understand the meaning of collective action, then they will have to be less unified, less visionary, less assuring. Melucci's language captures the sense of flow, instability, and resurgence that such movements express. Collective action in the 1980s came to be based on "movement areas," Melucci wrote,

> networks composed of a multiplicity of groups that are dispersed, fragmented and submerged in everyday life and which act as cultural laboratories. . . . The latent movement areas create new cultural codes and enable individuals to put them into practice. When small groups emerge in order to visibly confront the political authorities on specific issues, they indicate to the rest of society the existence of a systemic problem and the possibility of meaningful alternatives. (Melucci, 1989, p. 60)

The constituent elements of these networks are not political parties, or national umbrella groups, or ideologically unified organizations. They are grass-roots movements, informal social circles, community and ad hoc associations, subcultures, and life-style groupings. They will not replicate the structural continuity of the social movements of earlier times, such as the labor or civil rights movements. The actors and groupings of complex publics will come together over broadly oriented issues, find themselves in conflict over others, break apart, realign—and then begin again.[6] They form, I suggest, the base for a set of complex, postmodern publics, but only a base.

The narratives that people develop to account for these realities will need to incorporate a sense of the importance of connection to difference and to a world of publics. As frameworks of understanding, they will need to value a spectrum of social movements that are variegated, diverse, multicolored. At the same time, these narratives must leave room for the recognition that, in the future, the constituent elements of collective action will be more insular and close to self, more present oriented, more grounded in the immediacies of place.

Such narratives have not yet surfaced. And some postmodern thinkers predict the permanent extinction of all social narratives, the stories we tell ourselves to give coherence to, and make sense of, life (Lyotard, 1979). But narratives, like all human constructions, are made of historical stuff. They change. Old ones erode and disappear, new ones grow and emerge, as people seek to gain control over their communities, their livelihoods, and their cities; as they challenge bureaucratic domination of everyday life; as they struggle to build a world of dignity and meaning for themselves. The new publics of the complex city, when they condense, will tie people to the immediacy of lived cultural spaces but,

at the same time, join them to the larger networks of the social fabric.
"I risk a general proposition," Kevin Lynch writes, "a good place is one
which, in some way appropriate to the person and her culture, makes
her aware of her community, her past, the web of life, and the universe
of time and space in which those are contained" (Lynch, 1984, p. 142).
At this time, the built environment of cities works against this placement of persons in physical and cultural settings that attach them to
realities beyond themselves. The issue then becomes whether, and in
what ways, public understandings, public institutions, public spaces,
and public politics can be rebuilt.

NOTES

1. "While acknowledging my debt to Alain Touraine's theoretical work, my analysis
has progressively taken me a critical distance away from his hypothesis that in 'post-in-
dustrial society' *a* central movement is likely to replace the working-class movement"
(Melucci, 1989, p. 80). Touraine saw the general impact of bureaucratic technocracy as
eventually providing the spate of new social movement formations with a unifying
project: opposition to the bureaucratic control of everyday life. Melucci isn't so sure.

2. The analysis is familiar. The productive capacity of the steam-driven factory
displaces artisans and family producers from their cottages in and around the rural village.
The new social forces compel them to locate in the concentrated regions that become the
classic industrial era cities. These are characterized by their extremes of wealth and
poverty, their overcrowding, disease, and crime, their use of force to maintain "public
order." As central as such processes were to a Marxist theory of urbanization, however,
it continued to understand struggles over space as secondary and dependent variables in
the dynamics of social change (see Katznelson, 1992).

3. See Soja (1989) for an extended history of the emergence of the role of space in
contemporary critical thought.

4. Friedmann and Wolff list these as management, banking and finance, legal services,
accounting, technical consulting, telecommunication and computing, transportation, research, and education. Then come the support services for this primary sector: real estate,
construction, hotels, restaurants, luxury shopping, entertainment, private security forces,
and domestic services (Friedmann & Wolff, 1982, p. 320).

5. David Halle, in his study of the workers in an oil refining plant in Linden, New
Jersey, refers to this history. For, in the late nineteenth and early twentieth centuries, the
Jersey marsh and port areas were developed precisely as such early industrial suburbs.
Industrial suburbs were a common feature of the economic growth of the period, Halle
writes. "They were typically on the outskirts of existing urban areas, for only there
were. . . available the large amounts of space required for new industries such as steel,
oil, chemicals, automobiles" (Halle, 1984, p. 10). Other, perhaps better known examples
of such classic industrial suburbs are Pullman and Gary, outside Chicago, and Homestead,
near Pittsburgh (Halle, 1984, p. 308).

6. For an insightful study of "direct action movements" as inheritors of the tattered mantle of collective action passed on by the new left, see Epstein (1991). Epstein recognizes both the liberating and the democratic sides of these movements as well as their unstable and self-destructive ones.

REFERENCES

Adamson, M., & Borgos, S. (1984). *This mighty dream: Social protest movements in the United States.* Boston: Routledge & Kegan Paul.

Boyer, C. (1992). Cities for sale: Merchandizing history at South Street Seaport. In M. Sorkin (Ed.), *Variations on a theme park: The New American city and the end of public space.* New York: Noonday.

Brecher, J., & Costello, T. (1990). *Building bridges: The emerging grassroots coalition of labor and community.* New York: Monthly Review Press.

Briggs, J., & Peat, F. D. (1989). *Turbulent mirror.* New York: Harper & Row.

Buhle, P., & Dawley, A. (1985). *Working for democracy.* Urbana: University of Illinois Press.

Castells, M. (1979). *The urban question.* Cambridge: MIT Press. (Original work published in French, 1972, Maspero)

Castells, M. (1983). *The city and the grassroots.* Berkeley: University of California Press.

Cohen, R. B. (1981). The new international division of labor, multinational corporations, and urban hierarchy. In M. Dear & A. J. Scott (Eds.), *Urbanization and planning in capitalist society.* London: Methuen.

Doctorow, E. L. (1976). *Ragtime.* New York: Bantam.

Epstein, B. (1990). Rethinking social movements. *Socialist Review, 20*(1), 35-65.

Epstein, B. (1991). *Political protest and cultural revolution.* Berkeley: University of California Press.

Fisher, R., & Kling, J. (1988). Leading the people: Two approaches to the role of ideology in community organizing. *Radical America, 21*(1), 31-46.

Fisher, R., & Kling, J. (1991). Prospects for new social movements. *New Politics, 3*(2), 71-85.

Friedmann, J., & Wolff, G. (1982). World city formation: An agenda for research and action. *International Journal of Urban and Regional Research, 6*(3), 309-344.

Frobel, F. Heinrichs, J., & Kreye, O. (1980). *The new international division of labor: Structural unemployment in industrialized countries and industrialization in developing countries.* Cambridge, UK: Cambridge University Press.

Gleick, J. (1987). *Chaos: Making a new science.* New York: Penguin.

Gordon, D. H., Edwards, R., & Reich, M. (1982). *Segmented work, divided workers: The historical transformation of labor in the United States.* Cambridge, UK: Cambridge University Press.

Gottdiener, M. (1984). Debate on the theory of space: Towards an urban praxis. In M. Smith (Ed.), *Cities in transformation* (Urban Affairs Annual Review 26). Beverly Hills, CA: Sage.

Gottdiener, M. (1985). *The social production of urban space.* Austin: University of Texas Press.

Greenstone, J. D., & Peterson, P. E. (1976). *Race and authority in urban politics: Community participation and the war on poverty.* Chicago: University of Chicago Press.

Gutmann, H. G. (1977). *Work, culture, and society in industrializing America.* New York: Vintage.

Halle, D. (1984). *America's working man.* Chicago: University of Chicago Press.

Hannerz, U. (1992). *Cultural complexity: Studies in the social organization of meaning.* New York: Columbia University Press.

Hardison, O. B., Jr. (1989). *Disappearing through the skylight.* New York: Penguin.

Hartshorn, T. A. (1992). *Interpreting the city: An urban geography* (2nd ed.). New York: John Wiley.

Harvey, D. (1973). *Social justice and the city.* Baltimore: Johns Hopkins University Press.

Harvey, D. (1989). *The condition of postmodernity.* Cambridge, MA: Basil Blackwell.

Hymer, S. (1979). *The multinational corporation: A radical approach.* Cambridge, UK: Cambridge University Press.

Judd, D. (1988). *The politics of American cities: Private power and public policy* (3rd ed.). Boston: Scott, Foresman.

Katznelson, I. (1981). *City trenches, urban politics and the patterning of class in the United States.* Chicago: University of Chicago Press.

Katznelson, I. (1992). *Marxism and the city.* Oxford: Clarendon Press.

Lefebvre, H. (1969). *The explosion: Marxism and the French upheaval.* New York: Monthly Review Books.

Lefebvre, H. (1991). *The production of space.* Cambridge, MA: Basil Blackwell.

Lynch, K. (1984). *Good city form.* Cambridge: MIT Press.

Lyotard, J. (1979). *The post-modern condition: A report on knowledge.* Minneapolis: University of Minnesota Press.

Mallet, S. (1975). *Essays on the new working class* (D. Howard & D. Savage, Eds.). St. Louis: Telos.

Mayer, M. (1991). Politics in the post-Fordist city. *Socialist Review, 21*(1), 105-124.

Melucci, A. (1989). *Nomads of the present.* Philadelphia: Temple University Press.

Morley, D., & Shachar, A. (Eds.). (1986). *Planning in turbulence.* Jerusalem: Magnes Press, Jerusalem University.

Pagels, H. R. (1989). *The dreams of reason: The computer and the rise of the sciences of complexity.* New York: Bantam.

Poundstone, W. (1988). *Labyrinths of reason.* New York: Doubleday.

Remy, D. (1989, March 15-18). *Notes toward a theory of urban studies.* Paper presented at the Urban Affairs Association meeting, Baltimore, MD.

Rieder, J. (1985). *Canarsie: The Jews and Italians of Brooklyn against liberalism.* Cambridge, MA: Harvard University Press.

Rosenau, J. (1990). *Turbulence in world politics.* Princeton, NJ: Princeton University Press.

Shefter, M. (1986). Trade unions and political machines: The organization and disorganization of the American working class in the late nineteenth century. In I. Katznelson & A. Zolberg (Eds.), *Working class formation.* Princeton, NJ: Princeton University Press.

Smith, M. P., & Feagin, J. (Eds.). (1987). *The capitalist city: Global restructuring and community politics.* New York: Basil Blackwell.

Soja, E. W. (1985). The spatiality of social life: Towards a transformative retheorisation. In D. Gregory & J. Urry (Eds.), *Social relations and spatial structures.* New York: St. Martin's.

Soja, E. W. (1989). *Postmodern geographies.* New York: Verso.

Storper, M., & Walker, R. (1984). The spatial division of labor: Labor and the location of industries. In L. Sawers & W. K. Tabb (Eds.), *Sunbelt/Snowbelt: Urban development and regional restructuring.* New York: Oxford University Press.

Touraine, A. (1971). *The May movement: Revolt and reform.* New York: Random House.

Touraine, A. (1977). *The self-production of society.* Chicago: University of Chicago Press.

Touraine, A. (1981). *The voice and the eye: An analysis of social movements.* Cambridge, UK: Cambridge University Press.

Touraine, A. (1988). *Return of the actor: Social theory in postindustrial society.* Minneapolis: University of Minnesota Press.

Touraine, A., Wieviorka, M., & Dubet, F. (1987). *The workers' movement.* Cambridge, UK: Cambridge University Press.

3   Participation in New York and London: Community and Market Under Capitalism

NORMAN FAINSTEIN
SUSAN S. FAiNSTEIN

The political ferment in Eastern Europe and the Soviet Union manifests in a new context two themes that have long been of interest in Western political theory and that have been of considerable importance in the practical politics of the United States and Western Europe over the last quarter century. The first centers on the uneasy relationship among capitalism, democracy, and participation. The second concerns the connections between the national and local levels of government, and the opportunities for participation and control inherent in each.

With the organization of nation-states and of capitalism simultaneously in flux as the century ends, predictions about the possibilities of more *effective* democratic participation are especially unreliable. The development of an integrated, world-level capitalism in the face of disaggregation of nation-states seems to suggest that democratic forces will have reduced opportunities for employing political power to overcome economic inequality and hierarchy. Yet this world capitalism is itself flexible and decentralized in many respects, thereby raising the hope that political and economic power might be fused in some parts of the world, creating for the first time communal democracies that enter into the world political economy as effective players—a profusion of democratized Singapores. The size and organization of such democratic "communities" cannot be fully specified in the abstract, much less in terms of a realistic historical path of transition. Still, democratic theory does shed some light on the pitfalls and possibilities of a new integration of community and market under capitalism. It is to this discussion that we now turn.

■ Capitalism, Democracy, and Participation

Despite the historical correlation between democratic process and capitalist economy, each contains elements that undermine the other. When popular forces press for social protection and regulation of industries, they threaten to destroy the self-regulating markets at the core of capitalism. Polanyi (1944, p. 234) states the basic contradiction between market discipline and democratic control succinctly:

> Socialism is essentially, the tendency inherent in an industrial civilization to transcend the self-regulating market by consciously subordinating it to a democratic society. . . . [But] the mere possibility that they [democratically elected socialist parties] might decide to do so undermines that type of confidence which in liberal economy is vital, namely, absolute confidence in the continuity of the titles to property. . . . [Such] assurance of formal continuity is essential to the functioning of the market system.[1]

The aggregation of individual choices rather than conscious collective decision making comprises the essence of market rationality; according to the market paradigm, actions in line with communal sentiment produce market distortion.

Within the historical context of the destruction of feudalism, capitalism, by destroying traditional hierarchies based on birth, does in fact constitute a move toward egalitarianism and social power based on talent. At the same time, however, it generates a class structure in which disproportionate social and political power normally rests with the capital-owning class even when formally democratic institutions rule (Lindblom, 1977). Liberal theorists have disputed that the state is inevitably the creature of upper-class interests, contending that the political sphere possesses genuine autonomy within liberal democracies and that numerous social groupings hold political resources enabling them to participate effectively in policymaking (Dahl, 1956). The separation between state and economy intrinsic to capitalism, however, has a double-edged quality. Although it limits political domination by a wealthy minority, it simultaneously insulates economic decisions from popular oversight. On the one hand, the power of the state over society and the power of capital over the polity are restricted. On the other, democracy in the polis is contravened by authoritarianism in the workplace, and the well-being of communities depends on the investment strategies of remote executives with no economic interest in the localities where production takes place (Smith, 1988). Thus the inequalities generated by capitalist work incentives, private control of labor and investment markets, and monopolistic tendencies inherent in unregulated economies contradict the egalitarian norms that underlie democratic citizenship.

The conservative resurgence of recent years has based its ideological defense of the compatibility of capitalism and democracy on the ideal of the free market. Conservative defenders of capitalism maintain that the separation of state from economy protects citizens from authoritarianism, furnishes equality of opportunity if not condition, and offers free choice within the marketplace. Consumer choice, it is contended, is as much a mode of democratic participation in economic decision making as is state or worker control. Further, the rapid economic growth fostered by unfettered capitalism provides the majority of the population with a consensual value even when its benefits are not equally distributed.[2]

If one wing of a historic debate hinges on democracy and capitalism, the other hinges on democracy and participation. Many have argued that democracy only requires the right to hold rulers accountable through periodic elections, not ongoing involvement by ordinary people in day-to-day decision making (Berelson, Lazarsfeld, & McPhee, 1954). Such a view, however, assumes that representatives will act in the interests of broad constituencies based on their voting strength rather than narrow ones with access and financial power. By now, centuries of practical experience with representative democracy show that such an expectation is overly sanguine.

To be sure, deficiencies exist in the principle of direct participation from the viewpoint of the participants themselves and the public at large. For participants, the process can be time-consuming, co-optative, and nonproductive. If they do not have the power to command additional resources, their efforts are unlikely to make a significant difference in the quality of their lives (Pateman, 1979, chap. 8). For the public as a whole, the use of participatory mechanisms as blocking and delaying devices can increase program costs and halt desirable investments. Despite these arguments, however, only participatory democracy can truly approach the ideal of enlightened, collective self-governance inherent in the concept of government by the people. We list below the arguments that justify widespread political participation rather than consumer choice among candidates and goods as necessary for achievement of the democratic ideal.

First, representatives necessarily act in their own interests. Regardless of their intentions, they in fact project their personal needs onto their conceptions of the public good. Rousseau (1950) long ago asserted that only the person affected by an action can be a legitimate judge of his (or her)[3] own interests. Other theorists have sought to solve the problem of representation through the devising of mechanisms for ensuring accountability of elected officials. Only Rousseau's formulation, however, does away with the tension between individual and public good.

Second, participation is the school of citizenship. Rousseau, and the Greeks before him, contended that democratic citizenship required active involvement rather than passive acquiescence. Within the modern age of media manipulation, information overload, and breakdown of community bonds, intelligent oversight by voters participating only in periodic elections seems impossible.

Third, hierarchical bureaucracies charged with the implementation of public policy subvert the intentions of legislation. They displace goals onto processes and fail to respond to their publics, who are transformed from citizens into clients. Unless bureaucratic clients can directly control appointed officials, even the nominal power of the electorate becomes only symbolic as civil servants carry on the real business of government.

Finally, direct interchange is often essential to rational action. Many of the most pertinent issues of modern societies cannot be satisfactorily addressed by formal institutional devices. Questions of the uses of open space, the relationships between parents and children, the contents of educational curricula, cultural standards, the bonds between men and women are increasingly politicized but are not susceptible to resolution within the programs of political parties or the deliberations of legislatures (Offe, 1987). Only a process of negotiation within particular contexts can produce outcomes acceptable to all actors.

Decentralization, Participation, and Control

Democracy in its essential form runs headlong into conflict not only with the particular requirements of capitalist economies but with the more general processes of all large-scale organizations, not the least of which are nation-states themselves. Within the latter context, issues of democracy and participation frequently get translated into questions of decentralization and control. These issues constitute a second analytic dimension that cuts across—and entangles—the debate about capitalism and democracy, because increasing participation requires the development of institutional mechanisms allowing groups of people to interact directly with government.

Beginning in the 1960s with the rise of urban social movements in the United States and Western Europe, controversy concerning political versus market modes of participation in economic decision making has been centered at the urban level. On the left, there have been varying emphases regarding the decentralization of political power but universal acceptance of the notion that market forces must be constrained through strong government, with the most vocal activists in recent years arguing for community decision-making powers.

For this reason, proponents of popular empowerment, not least the "left" in Eastern Europe, argue for decentralization of authority within the liberal state and for the political empowerment of citizens at the communal level. This has been adopted as more or less official political theory by the reform government in Poland, which is not only establishing a decentralized state but sending its officials to the United States for internships in local governance. The contradictions have not yet become apparent to Eastern Europeans between decentralization of political power and its disaggregation to the urban or communal level, on the one hand, and the centralization of economic power and its organization at the world level. In other words, if centralized nation-states have difficulty controlling the forces of international capital, how can disaggregated political systems be more effective? (On this point, see Lake & Regulska, 1990.)

Within cities, the focus of leftist activists has been on the physical character of economic development and the allocation of social services. Mobilizations in opposition to business domination of such investment decisions as what type of physical structures will be developed (i.e., manufacturing, commercial, residential), where development will occur, the social and environmental impacts of development, and the tax consequences of social welfare expenditures seek to overcome the dependence of urban populations on business choices. Clearly the position of urban residents as consumers of corporate products gives them no control over production decisions concerning where and how commodities will be produced, decisions that are frequently crucial to their livelihood, even if in aggregate they do affect what product will be offered in what quantity. Hence only political activity affords them an opportunity to affect these kinds of business decisions.

Defenders of the market, however, have a parallel argument at the urban level to that at the national: even though the mass of people do not influence allocations within factor markets, they may choose their own location, thus optimizing their individual situation (Tiebout, 1956). The market in places equates with the market in goods. Personal mobility thereby becomes a form of participation that potentially affords the participant more individual satisfaction than he or she could achieve through a collective form of control and further does not impede economic efficiency.[4]

Whatever its intellectual merits, the conservative, promarket argument has prevailed within the national electoral systems of the United States and the United Kingdom. Since 1980 the governments of both nations have enacted programs of privatization, deregulation, tax incentives to capital accumulation, and cutbacks in social welfare expenditures. The United Kingdom went even further than the United States by stifling local political efforts to implement redistributive measures: The Thatcher Government eliminated the metropolitan level of government, introduced a regressive poll tax in place of the wealth-related rate, and sharply restricted local expenditures.

The remainder of this chapter addresses the relationship between economic development, the welfare state, and popular participation at different levels of aggregation. We examine the experience of London and New York in the last decade to provide insights into the impact of a shift from welfarism to market incentives on participation and individual choice in those cities. Our aim is to analyze the relationship between urban restructuring, democracy, and equality and the possibilities for participation in the current ideological and economic climate.

■ Urban Democracy and the Welfare State

In twentieth-century Britain and the United States, the fears of nineteenth-century opponents of universal suffrage that the electorate would use its franchise to expropriate property never came to pass. The seeming contradiction between formal political equality and economic inequality was reconciled through the national welfare state. While the two welfare states were differently organized—with the British earlier and more fully developed—each contributed substantially to the political loyalty of its citizenry.

Simultaneous with the postwar burgeoning of the welfare state, central cities in both countries increasingly became the repositories of concentrations of low-income people. In New York and London, which continued to house their nations' financial and cultural elites, material inequality became more and more glaring despite enlarged governmental programs. By the 1960s the effects of development on the environment brought quality-of-life issues to the fore, while racial and ethnic antagonisms exacerbated divisions over claims to territory and relationships between service providers and recipients. Urban social movements arose demanding power for communities and bureaucratic clients over the public programs and agencies that provided collective benefits and services (Fainstein & Fainstein, 1974; Magnusson, 1979).[5]

At the same time, political leaders began to acknowledge that neither growing national wealth nor welfare state measures had succeeded in ending poverty, environmental degradation, and ethnic hostility. Politicians and community leaders increasingly blamed unresponsive bureaucracies for the failure of social programs, while scholarly analysts identified a self-perpetuating cycle of poverty and despair that they partly attributed to feelings of powerlessness in poor communities (Clark, 1965; Cloward & Ohlin, 1960; Marris, 1987). Thus community elements demanding power, benefits, and changes in regulatory policies combined with policymakers who believed that according them some degree of participation might prove therapeutic (Moynihan, 1969). Direct participation by bureaucratic clients was seen as a way both to improve the quality of governmental outputs and to legitimate decision making without requiring a large increment in governmental expenditures; the conflict between democracy and inequality within cities was to be solved by extending democracy beyond the realm of purely electoral politics into program implementation, although not into the economy.[6]

By the early 1970s the growth in the scope of the political, along with rising expectations by nonelite groups who believed themselves entitled to make specific demands on public bodies, led conservatives to assert that the state was overburdened. Whether or not an objective limit on the state's capacity to respond to claims had in fact been reached cannot be proved. The perception, however, was sufficiently widespread as to legitimize retrenchment from earlier welfare commitments and the dismantling or diminution of programs mandating citizen participation. Welfare and participation ceased quickly to be the formula for coping with the contradiction of democracy and inequality. As economic restructuring and its ensuing social disruptions and insecurities accelerated after 1975, a marked switch took place in ideology and policy. Unemployment, reduction in the social wage, privatization of social service provision and development planning, and population displacement became identified as necessary costs of economic advance. Old criticisms of community participation were revived. As well as being attacked for encouraging excessive claims upon the state, participation was blamed for fostering parochialism and governmental paralysis because of the enhanced veto power of particularistic interests. Indeed, the NIMBY ("not in my backyard") phenomenon had become endemic to urban politics as neighborhoods blocked undesired uses such as homeless shelters, garbage disposal facilities, highways, and large commercial structures. While communities could not command desired investments within their borders from either the private or the public sectors, neighborhood and environmental groups could employ a variety of legal devices ranging from court suits to environmental reviews as a bulwark against construction. Opposition to projects that were generally wanted but only somewhere else frequently resulted in underinvestment in infrastructure and service facilities and encouraged the tendencies of businesses to flee highly politicized large cities.

In addition to undermining the ideological support for citizen participation, economic restructuring, as various scholars have observed (Fisher, 1991; Lake & Regulska, 1990), objectively limited its potential by augmenting the magnitude of decisions made outside the geographic boundaries of localities. The restructuring process involved decisions made by corporations that were not tied to particular geographic areas. Thus, even though some participatory mechanisms developed during the 1960s and 1970s continued to exist after these decades, participants found that there was less and less that they could affect.[7] Part of the reason that neighborhoods became so obsessed with vetoing projects within their midst was that they had no influence over the larger decisional arena that, for example, fostered homelessness or the growth of solid waste. Community groups could only address the consequences of reductions in housing subsidies or of modern packaging rather than the processes that generated them. An examination of the principal cities of the United States and Britain reveals these national and urban dynamics under specific local conditions.

■ Economic Restructuring and Democracy in New York and London

Between 1960 and 1990 New York City and Greater London followed rather similar economic paths. They both experienced the sharp decline of manufacturing and port-related activities, along with a substantial expansion of service production, led by financial industries and advanced corporate services (Fainstein & Fainstein, 1987; Fainstein, Fainstein, & Swartz, 1989; Fainstein, Harloe, & Gordon, 1992; Parkinson, Foley, & Judd, 1988). The political and social correlates of these changes were, however, quite different during the first two thirds of the period, with London exhibiting a much greater commitment to a social-democratic model of urban development.

Indeed, we and other commentators pointed frequently to the superiority of the British model in representing working-class interests (S. Fainstein, 1979; Fainstein & Fainstein, 1978). The British commitment to the public provision of housing, to town planning, and to health care and income support programs all testified to this superiority. While private capitalist corporations largely determined the character of production and its location in both metropolitan areas, the British governmental system, although offering few vehicles for community participation, mitigated the spatial impact of economic growth for the lower classes and significantly counterbalanced market-determined inequalities in wealth and income.

London Before Thatcher

Even with strong national urban and welfare policies, however, London began to experience two "inner-city" problems well known to New York. The first stemmed from black and Asian migrants concentrated in a few central London boroughs. While never amounting to more than a quarter of the population of the most "nonwhite" boroughs, the new migrants suffered from housing and employment discrimination, were the targets of racial attacks, and began to make "racial" claims for political participation. The Labour party, however, strongly resisted racial and ethnic bases for group membership and policy intervention. It responded with an underfunded Community Development Program and with community councils aimed at reducing racial tensions through citizen participation. On the whole, these efforts were successful mainly in keeping race off national and municipal political agendas until the

Thatcher regime ended immigration to Britain from the Caribbean and the Indian subcontinent.

The second inner-city problem lay in the increasing obsolescence of large urban sites vacated as a consequence of the decline of shipping and rail transport and the out-migration of manufacturing. The biggest of these obsolete areas was the London docklands, a tract of some 5,000 acres extending east from the city of London (i.e., the central financial district) along both sides of the Thames. Once the busiest port in the world, it was by now almost entirely abandoned, except for the remaining residents of five working-class neighborhoods, and constituted the largest developable central urban site in Europe.

From the start, the future of the docklands engendered a fundamental debate, on the one hand, between working-class and business interests and, on the other, between central government planners advancing "rational" solutions and community residents seeking democratic participation and local control (Marris, 1987). Put in the starkest terms, the strategic debate centered on whether the docklands should be appended onto the city of London office district and become a center for finance capital and upper-income professionals or whether it should be rebuilt primarily with light industry and council housing. Facing strong opposition from mobilized residents and the borough councils to what they viewed as a "balanced" plan for redevelopment, the national Labour government and the Greater London Council (GLC)[8] responded by establishing an advisory council and an elaborate process of participatory planning. Its proposals, however, failed to attract private investment, and a fiscally constrained public sector refused to make available the resources necessary for its public component. As a result, the docklands remained largely empty. The impasse showed that the old postwar accommodations between the British working class and capital were disintegrating. The representation of the British working class in a centralized governmental system that made planning possible was being threatened by the failures of extant national policy and, to some extent as well, by the demands of local communities for greater direct representation in government programs[9]—demands that had come a decade earlier in New York.

New York Before Reagan

The contrasts with London were sharply evident throughout the 1960s and 1970s, even though New York was the most European of U.S.

cities in the size of its governmental sector and the extent of its redistributive programs. With limited national governmental resources to deal with a massive influx of low-income black and Hispanic people and with no ability to act outside of its municipal boundaries, New York City's liberal mayoral regimes in the 1960s and early 1970s attempted to balance the objectives of social welfare, political stability, and capital accumulation (Fainstein & Fainstein, 1988).

One element involved the targeting of benefits to poor blacks and Hispanics, who had mobilized politically through urban social movements, riots, and electoral strength. A wide range of programs were established to provide housing, income maintenance, employment training, and neighborhood development through "community action." While expanded benefits for the minority poor were often dispensed grudgingly, there was nonetheless a sense among political and business leaders that the new urban poor had to be incorporated into the economic and political mainstream if political stability were to be maintained.[10] To achieve this aim, new decentralized institutions were developed that made public agencies more responsive to their clienteles by facilitating direct communal participation in government administration. Most important in this regard was the establishment of about 60 community boards with limited authority to affect planning decisions and service delivery and about 30 local school boards with considerable authority over primary schools. In part because of the unwillingness of the national government to fund the kind of direct public supply of housing and social benefits that characterized London, and in part because of much more grass-roots participatory and self-help activity in New York, the city also witnessed a proliferation of community-based housing, economic development, and service-providing organizations. Together with the various boards and a city council of some 40 members, they offered multiple bases and channels for interest group mobilization and communal participation.

At the same time, the city pursued an active program of restructuring the built environment, initially in a fashion oblivious to neighborhood concerns, becoming later much more responsive. The highway system was substantially enlarged, resulting in considerable displacement and neighborhood dismemberment, but ultimately community opposition halted further expansion. Urban redevelopment projects, which at first had proceeded with no citizen input, came to involve elaborate requirements for public hearings, participation by project area citizens' committees in the planning process, and several layers of governmental review, most of it public.

By the 1970s, then, in New York a racially divided citizenry enjoyed multiple routes of political participation under a well-defined unitary municipal government. This government functioned within a metropolitan region it could not control and within a national context of feeble urban policy. In London at the same time, the unified municipal government (the GLC) was relatively weak and popular routes to participation were less developed, yet the city's working-class interests were much better represented through a national party system in a strong central government with highly developed housing and welfare programs.

Political Convergence in the 1980s

The decade-long downturn in parts of the capitalist world economy following the Arab oil embargo of 1973 facilitated electoral success for conservative politicians in a number of countries, including Sweden, France, and Germany, in addition to, of course, Britain and the United States. In U.S. cities and especially in New York, the shift to the right was under way by 1975, at just the time when the British Labour government was experimenting with various forms of community action and 3 years before its fall to the Thatcherite Conservatives.[11]

During the 1970s economic restructuring in New York was accompanied by a sharp contraction in the overall economy and tax base, resulting in budgetary shortfalls. When bankers refused to roll over the city's short-term notes, they not only created more than 3 years of fiscal crisis, they also signaled a general counterattack by capital in the United States against "excessive" government expenditures, union power, and economic inefficiency. Whereas barely a decade earlier, political stability was threatened by minority groups demanding enfranchisement, now a legitimacy crisis was produced by business interests demanding a reordering of public priorities.

New York Mayor Edward Koch had formulated an ideological and programmatic package quite similar to Ronald Reagan's. He offered the minority poor neither new programs nor old symbols. He continued to emphasize economic development over social welfare, even when economic growth began to accelerate after 1982, providing subsidies to large corporations in the name of expanding the tax base and employment. New York under Koch, perhaps more than other cities, exemplified the redefinition of U.S. urban goals from social and political democracy to economic competitiveness and growth.

In Britain a milder form of white working-class "backlash" against urban minority groups helped bring Margaret Thatcher to office in 1979. More important in explaining her triumph, however, elements of the middle class and entrepreneurial capitalists revolted against the power of the trade unions and against the comfortable accommodation between the Labour and Conservative establishments that lay at the core of the British welfare state. Once in power, without ever attaining a majority of the popular vote, the Thatcher regime massively transformed the political situation in London and other big cities.

Britain's centralized party and governmental institutions permitted rapid adoption of a succession of measures that limited working-class power, changed the system of taxation and benefits, and reconstructed the system of municipal governance, in particular in Greater London. Andy Thornley (1991, p. 2) termed the effort "authoritarian decentralism," which he defined as

> the process by which the authoritarian strand is employed to concentrate power in the hands of central government. However, the motivation for seizing this power is not to directly formulate and implement new central government policy. Instead the power is used to set up the conditions whereby the decision making can be devolved to market processes.

In the United States Reagan reduced federal aid to localities but allowed them considerable programmatic autonomy, thereby continuing a trend that began during the 1970s. The Thatcher government, by capping local spending and introducing a poll tax, attempted directly to restrict tax progressivity and local spending on social services and housing. It also eliminated the metropolitan level of government that had been used as a vehicle for enhancing citizen participation and enforcing redistributive measures at the local level.

These national differences were reflected in the politics and governmental operations of New York and London. New York under Koch maintained its strong local government and elaborate institutions for political representation. While the municipal boundaries encompassed only about half the population of the metropolitan area, they nonetheless contained the richest territory in the United States—Manhattan. The city therefore could raise sufficient revenue to continue internally redistributive programs even with the curtailment of federal support, if it so chose. But Greater London by the late 1980s ceased to exist as a political unit, or rather it became nothing more than 33 boroughs forced increasingly to rely on their own fiscal bases to finance services. In this sense, the privatized mode of urban development in London, which was otherwise quite similar to that in New York, functioned without even the possibility of majority control at the municipal level offered by the New York City government.

The strategies of both urban regimes were based on justifications rooted in the language of democracy. In the case of Thatcher's London, the emphasis was on the participatory opportunities extended by the market; in Edward Koch's New York, it was on majoritarian sentiment and the moral requirement that rewards be provided to those who are self-supporting.[12] The stress on market determinations and citywide rather than group-specific benefits in both places replaced an earlier ideological thrust toward community decision making.

While the two world cities entered the 1980s from quite different political positions, privatized development became the common overarching strategy in both. Its central institutional vehicle was the development corporation, an organization created by government and endowed with public authority to take property, implement urban plans, and sell debt, but otherwise designed to behave like a capitalist developer. Corporations like the London Docklands Development Corporation and the New York Public Development Corporation were almost completely insulated from popular participation and recruited their cadres from private developers. They operated autonomously from the regularly elected government and offered no channels for citizen participation. They largely usurped the role of the formal city planning agencies, making land use determinations on the basis of economic return rather popular decision.

As a result, the mode of citizen input changed in both places. Rather than community groups operating through officially designated project area committees or community boards, they increasingly used court suits, environmental reviews, political pressure, protests, and threats of delay as tactics to force developers to negotiate the content of their projects. Because, even if the developer could prevail in the end, lost time cost him or her substantial money, so developers found it in their interest to offer concessions to community groups. Called "exactions" in the United States and "planning gain" in the United Kingdom, these offerings could consist of public facilities, affordable housing, job training programs, or neighborhood amenities. Local planning officials were frequently the intermediaries who made the deals between developers and neighborhood groups.

Examples of this form of bargaining over neighborhood development in New York can be seen in the 42nd Street Redevelopment project and in the construction of Worldwide Plaza on the midtown West Side. In the former case, vehement protests from the adjacent Clinton neighborhood to the threat of secondary displacement presented by office construction in Times Square resulted in the allocation of $25 million to the community to spend on affordable housing and community improvements. The developer of Worldwide Plaza, on a long-vacant urban-renewal site, contributed a number of units of low-income housing on a nearby site. In London, planning for huge developments on the former rail yards at King's Cross in central London and at the Spitalfields market in the east end has accrued enormous potential gains for the neighborhoods involved, including housing, recreational facilities, and employment programs to be financed by the developer.

In these cases, however, as well as in the similar compromise plan for Donald Trump's West Side development in Manhattan, the actual implementation of the projects awaits the revival of the real estate markets in their respective cities. Thus community groups have learned to deal directly with the private sector, but they can only do so in situations where there is private sector interest in development, and they are likely to see their programs carried out only in periods of high real estate demand. Isolated low-income neighborhoods, into which private developers have no inclination to go, have no real leverage in the current system of privatized bargaining.

As the decade of the 1990s opened, the prospects for popular participation dimmed further in both world cities. National regimes led by Bush and Major remained as uninterested as their predecessors in policy interventions that might improve the economic situation of lower income urban residents or in any mechanisms that might enhance these residents' political power. Both cities were harshly affected by the recessionary period that commenced in 1989, with their real estate industries hard hit. The restructuring of the banking industry in particular resulted in extreme caution in lending policies and sharply reduced demand by financial institutions for new office space. Consequently, what little control local communities had when investors wanted their contested land now largely evaporated.

In New York the promise of enhanced popular democracy offered by the election of the city's first black mayor, David Dinkins, turned to recrimination under the economic downturn and ensuing fiscal crisis. The 1989 Dinkins campaign had repudiated the strong business orientation of the Koch administration and purported to represent lower income people, especially minorities. Its constituency was heavily based in the civil service unions, whose support was essential in electing Dinkins and who had the most to lose from budgetary retrenchment. With New York State in its own fiscal crisis, and the Bush administration utterly uninterested, the city produced a budget in June 1991 that involved a patchwork quilt of stop-gap measures, significant tax increases, and severe cuts in basic services. The mayor was widely blamed for his vacillation and was left with little leeway in policymaking. Absent a turnaround in the local economy, it is impossible to know at this point whether Mayor Dinkins would actually act differently than Mayor Koch on matters of development and popular participation.

■ Obstacles to Urban Participation

The recent history of New York and London does not make the observer sanguine that, whatever the theoretical merits of citizen participation, it is a practical strategy within a political economy subject to severe market constraints. Although community residents desired enhanced governmental programs and regulation of growth, the resources to pay for programs were not theirs to command and the businesses subject to regulation threatened to leave the cities' boundaries. Consequently, fiscal crisis, taxpayers' revolts, and crises of business confidence underpinned a conservative ideological counterattack on decentralized programs. The experience we have within these two metropolises of direct, local public ownership, autonomous cultural institutions, and development by community not-for-profits does indicate potential directions for greater democratization. The scale and stability of these efforts, however, have been insufficient to allow great confidence concerning their promise.

The current trend toward privatization of services and physical development insulates producers ever further from democratic control even while it may increase choices for a proportion of the population. If most enterprises are responsible only to their stockholders, or even only to their employees, then democratic control by the community in which they are located must be severely circumscribed. The dilemma is particularly acute if the market for the product or service offered resides largely outside the geographic confines of the host community. No ideal institutional arrangement can be found that will provide influence over decisions to the community, the owners, and the consumers if these are all different groups. Housing cooperatives, where the three constituencies are unified, provide the best model for small-scale, participatory democracy. The more equity control a community can acquire in other kinds of enterprises, the greater the possibilities for community democracy. Short of full public ownership, with its potential for bureaucratization, stifling of innovation, and inefficiency, we can imagine a greater variety of mixed corporations, with public funds used to obtain partial ownership and representation on corporate boards. Given the enormous disjuncture between the scale of communities of residence and the scale of modern production, however, our expectations for community participation must remain modest.

Democracy has normally been justified as both an end in itself through the opportunities it provides for self-actualization and as a means to achieving the public interest. Criticisms of participation as co-optive and ineffectual do not undermine the arguments made in its favor; rather, they point to the difficulties of attaining democracy as either end or means. Within large cities like London and New York, where government is remote, society is extremely heterogeneous, the contrast between privilege and deprivation is distinctively evident, and the local economy is strongly tied to the international one, the difficulties are particularly stringent even as the needs are especially great (see Titmuss, 1969, chap. 11).

NOTES

1. Polanyi's rooting of the difficulty in the dependence of the state on business confidence presages later structuralist analyses of the capitalist state (see, e.g., Jessop, 1982).

2. See Peterson's (1981) defense and Goldthorpe's (1987) critique.

3. Rousseau, like all the contract theorists, excluded women from the negotiation (see Pateman, 1988).

4. Hobbes (1950) long ago identified physical mobility as the fundamental freedom. See Markusen (1978) for a critique of the argument that citizens can express their public service preferences through mobility.

5. Significantly, however, these movements did not seek public ownership of economic enterprises. Some limited efforts were made at community ownership of businesses and housing, but their dependence on outside financing restricted the ambitions of their proponents.

6. There are five categories of decision making that broadly affect urban residents; each involves a different mix of political and private components. They are (a) the location of productive investment, (b) allocation and delivery of goods and services among groups,

(c) regulation of activities ranging from land use to gambling, (d) allocation of tax dollars among governmental functions, and (e) allocation of tax levies among groups.

Within the political arena, decisions can be made solely by representatives account-able only at the next election, by centralized or decentralized bureaucrats subject to oversight by elected officials but insulated by civil service protection, or by either of these two types of officials in consultation with citizens' groups. Even under the most radical decentralization programs of the 1960s and 1970s, citizens' groups in New York and London never had authoritative decision-making power.

Private business normally chooses the location of industrial and commercial ventures based on economic rather than social criteria. Britain differed from the United States during the period of Labour rule in having nationalized a number of key industries. In the case of nationalized industries, locational decisions are removed from the private to the public sphere. Most analysts of decision making by such industries, however, argue that market constraints cause them to make such decisions according to the same market indicators as privately held companies. Nevertheless, even though such concerns must maintain a competitive cost structure and therefore may also choose to operate in low-wage areas or close uneconomical plants, they are not subject to the locational pressures caused by mergers or the preferences of chief executives.

7. See the prescient essay by Robert Dahl (1967), in which he stressed the trade-off between jurisdictional size and scope of control. We also discussed the subject a few years later (Fainstein & Fainstein, 1976a, 1976b). Obviously, the increasing internationaliza-tion of economic decision making since then has further reduced the effectiveness of communal participation and control.

8. The Greater London Council (GLC) then constituted a metropolitan government for Greater London. Although its powers were relatively weak compared with the national government and the boroughs, it provided an important political platform for the Labour party, which controlled it.

9. Thus the national Community Development Program in the late 1970s as well as the docklands project both came under attack for insufficient direct citizen participation.

10. There was much less consensus on how to respond to the white working and middle classes, who increasingly resented the proliferation of governmental programs aimed at the minority poor. In retrospect, we can see that a series of policies and reforms helped to represent the interests and stabilize the communal situations of these groups, even though their origins and rationales hardly reflected their ultimate function. Despite strong attacks from the real estate industry, the city maintained its complex system of price controls on rental housing. It also subsidized middle-income households overtly through new construction programs and covertly through lower rates of taxation on owner-occupied houses. Expanded public employment and higher education visibly benefited minority households but disproportionately provided jobs and schooling to the white working class.

11. In the United States, Jimmy Carter, a conservative Democrat—and a centrist in the overall spectrum—was elected president in 1976. His victory over Gerald Ford, a weak candidate, provided an inertial force in U.S. urban policy. Carter emphasized local initiative and economic development programs and believed that the national government should not intervene in the regional restructuring then under way—the so-called rise of the Sunbelt states of the South and West. But he also maintained a variety of federal housing programs and targeted, with some ambiguity, the major program of intergovern-mental aid (Community Development Block Grants) to low-income neighborhoods.

12. Moon (1988, p. 33) explains that redistributional policies lack a moral basis in contemporary society, that the value of altruism clashes with individualistic concepts of self-respect: "Self-respect is an achievement earned by living in a way that is worthy or honorable, not a good that one can have simply by virtue of being a person."

REFERENCES

Berelson, B., Lazarsfeld, P. F., & McPhee, W. N. (1954). *Voting*. Chicago: University of Chicago Press.

Clark, K. (1965). *Dark ghetto*. New York: Harper & Row.

Cloward, R., & Ohlin, L. (1960). *Delinquency and opportunity*. New York: Free Press.

Dahl, R. (1956). *A preface to democratic theory*. Chicago: University of Chicago Press.

Dahl, R. (1967). The city in the future of democracy. *American Political Science Review, 61*, 953-970.

Fainstein, N., & Fainstein, S. S. (1974). *Urban political movements*. Englewood Cliffs, NJ: Prentice-Hall.

Fainstein, N., & Fainstein, S. S. (1976a). The future of community control. *American Political Science Review, 70*, 905-923.

Fainstein, N., & Fainstein, S. S. (1976b). Local control as social reform: Planning for big cities in the seventies. *Journal of the American Institute of Planners, 44*, 275-285.

Fainstein, N., & Fainstein, S. S. (1978). National policy and urban development. *Social Problems, 26*, 125-146.

Fainstein, N., & Fainstein, S. S. (1987). The politics of land use planning in New York City. *Journal of the American Planning Association, 53*, 237-248.

Fainstein, N., & Fainstein, S. S. (1988). Governing regimes and the political economy of redevelopment. In J. H. Mollenkopf (Ed.), *Power, culture, and place: Essays on New York City* (pp. 161-199). New York: Russell Sage.

Fainstein, N., Fainstein, S. S., & Schwartz, A. (1989). Economic shifts and land use in the global city: New York, 1940-1987. In R. Beauregard (Ed.), *Atop the urban hierarchy* (pp. 45-85). Totowa, NJ: Roman & Littlefield.

Fainstein, S. S. (1979). American policy for housing and community development: A comparative analysis. *Policy Studies Journal, 8*(2), 231-245.

Fainstein, S. S., Harloe, M., & Gordon, I. (1992). *Divided cities*. Oxford, UK: Basil Blackwell.

Fisher, R. (1991). Organizing in the private city: The case of Houston Texas. In H. Beeth & C. D. Wintz (Eds.), *Black Dixie*. College Station: Texas A&M University Press.

Goldthorpe, J. H. (1987). Problems of political economy after the postwar period. In C. S. Maier (Ed.), *Changing boundaries of the political* (pp. 363-407). Cambridge, UK: Cambridge University Press.

Hobbes, T. (1950). *Leviathan*. New York: Dutton.

Jessop, B. (1982). *The capitalist state*. New York: New York University Press.

Lake, R., & Regulska, J. (1990). Political decentralization and capital mobility in planned and market societies: Local autonomy in Poland and the United States. *Policy Studies Journal, 18*(3), 702-720.

Lindblom, C. E. (1977). *Politics and markets*. New York: Basic Books.

Magnusson, W. (1979). The new neighborhood democracy: Anglo-American experience in historical perspective. In L. J. Sharpe (Ed.), *Decentralist trends in Western democracies* (pp. 119-156). Beverly Hills, CA: Sage.

Markusen, A. R. (1978). Class and urban social expenditure: A Marxist theory of metropolitan government. In W. K. Tabb & L. Sawers (Eds.), *Marxism and the metropolis* (pp. 90-112). New York: Oxford University Press.

Marris, P. (1987). *Meaning and action.* London: Routledge & Kegan Paul.

Moon, J. D. (1988). The moral basis of the democratic welfare state. In A. Gutmann (Ed.), *Democracy and the welfare state* (pp. 27-52). Princeton, NJ: Princeton University Press.

Moynihan, D. P. (1969). *Maximum feasible misunderstanding.* New York: Free Press.

Offe, C. (1987). Challenging the boundaries of institutional politics: Social movements since the 1960s. In C. S. Maier (Ed.), *Changing boundaries of the political* (pp. 63-106). Cambridge, UK: Cambridge University Press.

Parkinson, M., Foley, B., & Judd, D. (1988). *Regenerating the cities: The UK crisis and the US experience.* Manchester, UK: Manchester University Press.

Pateman, C. (1979). *The problem of political obligation.* Chichester, UK: John Wiley.

Pateman, C. (1988). *The sexual contract.* Stanford, CA: Stanford University Press.

Peterson, P. E. (1981). *City limits.* Chicago: University of Chicago Press.

Polanyi, K. (1944). *The great transformation.* Boston: Beacon.

Rousseau, J. (1950). *The social contract.* New York: Dutton.

Smith, M. P. (1988). *City, state, and market.* Oxford, UK: Basil Blackwell.

Thornley, A. (1991, July). *Thatcherism and the Swedish "model": Centre/local relationships in urban planning.* Paper presented at the joint meeting of the American Collegiate Schools of Planning and the Association of European Schools of Planning, Oxford, UK.

Tiebout, C. (1956, October). A pure theory of local expenditures. *Journal of Political Economy, 64,* 416-424.

Titmuss, R. M. (1969). *Essays on the welfare state.* Boston: Beacon.

Part II

Community-Based Mobilizations

4 Private Spaces and the Politics of Places: Spatioeconomic Restructuring and Community Organizing in Tucson and El Paso

SALLIE A. MARSTON
GEORGE TOWERS

The American Sunbelt has experienced dramatic transformations over the last several decades. Riding the tide of economic restructuring, the region has been the setting for the growth and development of high-technology and related industries, low-wage traditional manufacturing industries, corporate and consumer services as well as expansion of government and government-related activities. The transformation has resulted in an intensely uneven pattern of spatial development that is articulated at both the regional and the urban scale. In this chapter we explore the ways in which two communities have responded to uneven growth and change. In Tucson and El Paso, political action, directed at restructured urban landscapes, has taken very different forms. In the former, middle-class citizens have used their neighborhoods as a platform for organizing to contain uncontrolled growth. In El Paso, ethnicity, class, religion, and geography have shaped the activism that has developed to challenge the intransigence of the local state. Through a comparison of the forms taken by community activism in Tucson and El Paso, we can trace how popular political responses to the impact of restructuring are shaped by local economic, political, and cultural contexts.

AUTHORS' NOTE: Sallie Marston would like to thank Cindi Katz and Andrew Kirby for their helpful comments on the first draft of the Tucson case study and also those Tucson activists who participated in interviews.

Our theoretical framework draws on the work of Castells (1983), who argues that the contradictions generated by the capitalist political economy find physical expression in urban space, which provides the empirical basis for political action. Yet this assertion hardly ends the matter. For it is impossible to read off from any given set of economic structures or their spatial manifestations the particular shape that political action will take. As Katznelson (1981) suggests, we must look, additionally, at the way people actually live their lives, lives shaped by such factors as race, gender, ethnicity, nationality, and even geography, and the "dispositions," or the interpretations of society, that they construct from those daily experiences. We regard political action as a process contingent upon the scope and content of economic restructuring as well as upon the organizational and institutional resources of the local community.

In the case studies that follow, we explore how and why the two Sunbelt cities of Tucson and El Paso have experienced such very different popular political responses to restructuring. We highlight the uneven development of the Sunbelt in an attempt to debunk the myth of a homogeneous region uniformly reflecting the positive impacts of contemporary global economic restructuring. We investigate the importance of the history and key actors at the local level who negotiate the impact of restructuring on the urban landscape (Fainstein & Fainstein, 1985). We also examine institutional agents—especially local (city and county) government bureaucracies—that have been responsible for executing federal as well as local policies, land development interests, and local corporations and small business groups (Logan & Molotch, 1987; Stone & Sanders, 1987). Finally, we look closely at the popular organizations that have emerged as a response to restructuring in both cities providing insights into their histories, organizational structures, leaders, objectives, and impacts.

As elsewhere, restructuring in the Sunbelt has initiated and reinforced formal and functional differentiation among (and sometimes within) cities due to its predication on a sharply bifurcated labor market (Abbott, 1987; Noyelle & Stanback, 1984). On the one hand, research and development activities and high-level service functions require skilled, well-educated, and highly paid workers (Saxenian, 1984). This end of service and goods production is typically conducted in places offering support from local government and universities as well as the climatic and recreational amenities desired by its relatively scarce labor force. On the other hand, labor-intensive assembly operations search for pools of low-wage workers in an attempt to reduce labor costs—the most expensive component of the production process. The high end of the restructuring has contributed to the growth of Tucson while the low end has significantly advanced recent growth and development in El Paso. The two cities, proceeding on divergent economic paths, converge to present a rather comprehensive perspective on uneven Sunbelt growth and change, particularly for medium-sized cities. Furthermore, the different economic roles of the two cities are reflected in their social composition and spatial form. Tucson is largely a middle-class metropolitan area characterized by low-density, attractive, suburban-style neighborhoods. El Paso is a city of poor Mexican Americans and Mexican immigrants ringed by substandard housing in inadequately serviced neighborhoods.

Castells's observations are particularly germane to the two cities: In each, political activists have organized around issues of a changing space economy. In Tucson urban space reflects the tensions produced by "growth machine" politics (Logan & Molotch, 1987). Growth machines, an important force in American urban politics, typically comprise business and real estate interests and local governments seeking to realize the income potential of land development and commercial/industrial growth. These powerful coalitions evaluate urban space for its profitability; their development projects often alter the content of existing residential neighborhoods and peripheral undisturbed tracts. For the most part, Tucson community organizations have formed to protect and preserve neighborhood values and unique desert landscapes. Activists originate from hundreds of different Tucson neighborhoods resulting in, what Castells (1983) has termed, a "citizen action" effort that is for the most part fragmented and reactive. In El Paso the contradictions embodied in urban space reflect the city's role as a production site utilizing cheap immigrant Mexican and Mexican American labor. Much of this population lives at or below the poverty line in pockets of deprivation, unable to afford adequate housing or services. The crowded, unsanitary tenements of South El Paso and the unserviced or underserviced, ramshackle ring of immigrant *colonias* surrounding the city expose the ways in which the conjunction of class and ethnicity is central to the city's economy.

The best example of community organization in El Paso is EPISO, the El Paso Interreligious Sponsoring Organization, which formed to organize El Paso's working poor and improve their quality of life. EPISO was initiated by organizers from San Antonio belonging to a larger national network of the Industrial Areas Foundation. EPISO's efforts are citywide and its organizational centralization is complemented by the shared experiences of its constituency. Most live in slum neighborhoods and are subjected to class and ethnic discrimination. EPISO organizes these neighborhoods around the failure of government to provide basic services to Mexican American neighborhoods and seeks to translate neighborhood activism into the permanent empowerment of El Paso's poor Mexican American community. EPISO has approached neighborhood organizing not only toward gaining the Mexican poor a voice in local politics but also toward bringing the growth model responsible for El Paso's oppressive social geography into question.

In the section that follows, we examine the case of Tucson, Arizona, a city whose growth has been predicated on burgeoning military spending in high-tech-based defense research and development as well as service sector and tourism activity. With this growth has emerged a sustained and multivoiced chorus of neighborhood groups that has mounted, often successfully, a variety of challenges to the local growth machine. We look at this homegrown movement, explore its origins, organization, institutional support, and impacts on local politics and policy. Following the discussion of Tucson's largely fragmented social movement, we consider El Paso's more solidary one and describe its very different inception, distinctive organizational structure and leadership, and impacts. Through our discussion of Tucson and El Paso, we argue that the traditional private spaces of social life are both the generative sites and the focus of these new struggles for political power (de Certeau, 1984; Touraine, 1988). Yet, while both social movements emanate from the same type of territorial base, they differ dramatically with respect to group identity, cohesion, institutional structure, leadership, and immediate objectives. What unites them is not only geography but the attempts to enhance the role of citizens in realizing a more fully participatory democratic politics.

■ Restructuring and Neighborhood Politics in Tucson

Growth in Tucson and Pima County, 1940-1990

During the New Deal the federal government, through the financing, upgrading, and expansion of Davis-Monthan, Tucson's municipal airport, initially set the small city of about 30,000 people on the path to rapid economic and physical expansion. When national defense activities were accelerated with America's entrance into World War II, the federal government decided to acquire and convert the municipal airport into a major military installation and air base. Following the war, Davis-Monthan Air Force Base continued to act as a magnet for funding attention, which translated into increases in employment and the physical development of the southeastern section of the city.

Private aviation-related defense industries, the largest of which was Hughes Aircraft, accompanied the growth of Davis-Monthan. While a group of citizens raised objections to the location of industrial firms in the Tucson basin, manufacturing output in terms of value added increased from $1,120,000 in 1940 to $84,423,000 by 1963 (Luckingham, 1982, p. 82). Though it did not maintain a pace of growth similar to Phoenix, by the early 1970s Tucson had established itself as a military and high-technology defense center—having attracted Gates-Learjet, IBM, and National Semiconductor—while expanding its role as a regional service center for mining, ranching, and farming (Luckingham, 1982; Waterstone & Kirby, 1991). From the late 1960s until the late 1980s, Tucson experienced rapid development, exceeding the national growth rate during this period (Abbott, 1987). Between the war years and the current time, Tucson's population expanded nearly 10 times from 36,818 in 1940 to approximately 400,000 at the beginning of 1990 (Tucson Economic Development Corporation, 1990). In addition, its incorporated area increased from a small town of 7 square miles in 1930 to a classic sprawling Sunbelt city of 156 square miles—though the metropolitan area is far larger.

During the postwar boom, the Tucson 30—composed of bank presidents, car dealers, land developers, and other "captains of industry" backed by the local media and powerful public utility companies—determined the political and economic direction of the Tucson Basin (Fleagle, 1966; Luckingham, 1982; Vonier, 1986). In both the city and the county, a very close relationship existed between business and government, which joined together to foster and promote economic and physical growth. In the 1960s and 1970s, in addition to promoting economic development along the city/county border through retail mall projects, residential and resort developments, and industrial and office parks, local officials also undertook downtown renewal projects—mostly high-rise office complexes. In 1971 the city completed the Tucson Community and Convention Center aimed at "revitalizing" the inner city. The downtown has also been the focus of a limited amount of redevelopment efforts with a few state and local banks building headquarter offices there. At this time, the downtown is dominated primarily by city and county government buildings with much of the remainder of corporate development occurring in office parks in scattered locations around the city. While an organization of downtown business interests, the Downtown Business Association (DBA), does exist, the downtown is not the spatial heart of the metropolitan area's business interests. Indeed, there is no particular location that can claim that distinction. Instead, land interests and other related business interests in the city often use the Southern Arizona Homebuilders Association (SAHBA) or the Tucson Business Coalition (TBC) as their organizational mouthpieces. The former is a coalition of representatives of the development and construction industry while the latter is an organization of small business owners.

Serious problems have resulted from the rapid physical and population growth of Tucson. Its location in the Sonoran Desert and total dependence on groundwater has made water conservation an issue upon which political careers rise or fall.[1] In addition, the physiographic positioning of the metropolitan area in a broad basin has combined with air subsidence and the widespread use of private automobiles to create alarming air pollution problems. At the same time, many citizens complain that the amount and rate of movement of rush hour traffic on city streets is unacceptable. While environmental problems such as air and water quality and supply have been important political issues in Tucson (Martin et al., 1984), a more widespread activism has emerged in Tucson's neighborhoods around multidimensional land use changes.

The history of neighborhood activism since 1966. Neighborhood activism in Tucson occurs both formally and informally. Formally, the city has set up an agency to facilitate neighborhoods organizing. Neighborhoods that wish to be officially recognized by the city register with the Citizen Participation Office (CPO) and can receive support for the printing and mailing of newsletters and other neighborhood literature. The CPO also has an advisory capacity. Previous to the city's funding of a CPO in 1980, neighborhood organization occurred around a number of federally funded programs, from the Office of Economic Opportunity's citizen action programs and later Model Cities to the Community Development programs promoted under President Carter in the late 1970s (Marston, 1993). Neighborhood and homeowner organizing also occurs in the unincorporated county area, where no formal mechanism for neighborhood formation has been or is provided. Neighborhood and homeowner associations in the county can register with the County Planning and Zoning Department—though the county provides no administrative and only limited advisory services to the neighborhoods. Currently, there are over 250 neighborhood and homeowner associations registered with either the city of Tucson CPO or Pima County Planning and Zoning.

The most important influence on neighborhood activism occurred in the metropolitan area over two decades ago in the form of the federally mandated programs for public participation. In 1966 Tucson was one of the many communities across the country selected to host the Office of Economic Opportunity's citizen action program (see Marston, 1993, for a fuller discussion of the War on Poverty in Tucson). Inner-city residents elected representatives to nine different neighborhood councils representing the poorest neighborhoods in the city. Neighbors and OEO staff established a central administrative board, the Committee on Economic Opportunity, which included members from the different councils as well as from city departments and service agencies. The participation program sought to improve social service delivery, such as education and health care, by getting input from the receiving groups.

By 1969 Model Cities replaced OEO and, in addition to the same goal of improving community services, especially to lower income areas of the city, sought to bring disenfranchised groups into the political process by informing them how the local political process worked and how they could become more involved in local decision making. Model Cities eventually expanded the number of participating neighborhoods and continued to work on issues as diverse as economic development, transportation, drug abuse prevention, and services to the elderly (F. Acosta, former administrator, Tucson's Citizen Participation Office, personal communication, March 14, 1991; Sharon Maxwell, administrator, Tucson's Citizen Participation Office, personal communication, March 14, 1991).

Increases in neighborhood activism have most often coincided with the accelerated growth that has occurred in the metropolitan area. While Model Cities organizers emphasized social programs and service delivery to low-income neighborhoods, neighborhoods have been more commonly concerned with changing land use issues such as transportation projects, resort and residential development, the siting of human service facilities, and preserving Tucson's unique desert environment. Indeed, there appear to be significant decade-by-decade differences in the activism that has characterized Tucson's neighborhoods. In the 1950s residents outside of the formal city limits mounted sustained though inevitably unsuccessful opposition to annexations as well as to changes to zoning ordinances and city and county plans (Logan, 1990). These county residents, mostly Anglo and middle class, outnumbered the city residents nearly 2 to 1, and, as Logan points out, the opposition was "more than simply a 'no growth' reaction, the resistance targeted both the physical size of the city and the increasingly arbitrary nature of the city government" (1990, p. 8). Opposition to the physical expansion persisted through the 1960s and accelerated in the 1970s and 1980s with resistance to large-scale development still high on the agenda of current county residents. By the late 1960s, however, a new influence on neighborhood activism stimulated inner-city low-income minorities to join in agitating for the attention of local government officials. While residents on the fringes of the city argued for "controlled growth," residents of the inner city began demanding improved service delivery, greater control over their schools, and increased access to the political process. This bifurcated expression of neighborhood activism continued to characterize popular politics in the metropolitan area through the 1970s. With the advent of the 1980s and the redirection of federal funding to private economic development initiatives, activism in the inner-city neighborhoods subsided significantly though certainly not completely.

Since the late 1970s, middle-class neighborhoods, largely Anglo, have dominated popular politics in both the city and the county. They learned to incorporate the tactics and use the institutions of Model Cities activism, becoming increasingly organized and vocal in the process. Access to the electronic and print media has been high and group organization has been facilitated by the city's CPO, an agency whose roots derive directly from the 1960s citizen action programs of the federal War on Poverty. Through neighborhood and homeowner associations, citizens have raised objections to the "growth as usual" practices that have dominated the agenda of the local governing coalition since World War II. In the 1987 citywide election, neighborhood issues were particularly prominent. A mayor and several council members sympathetic to neighborhood concerns were elected despite the efforts of the Southern Arizona Homebuilders Association, which plastered billboards across the city with the worried query: "Does Your Job

Depend on Growth?" In the November 1989 elections, two more "neighborhood candidates" were added to the city council. Neighborhoods have been less successful in maintaining a presence on the County Board of Supervisors with only one of the five current supervisors rated acceptable by the Neighborhood Coalition of Greater Tucson (NCGT), a political action committee organized by leaders of several city and county neighborhood associations, that promotes "neighborhood candidates" in local elections.

The focus and impact of neighborhood activism. In 1993 neighborhoods continue to be active in both the city and the county[2] and can be categorized as either proactive or reactive. Reactive neighborhoods are those that lie dormant until threatening issues present themselves. Proactive neighborhoods are highly organized and vigilant and usually able to anticipate threats. While reactive neighborhood associations do exist in the Tucson area, more common and formidable are the proactive ones. Proactive neighborhood organizations in Tucson run the socioeconomic gamut from high to low income, contain renters and homeowners (and even mixes of both), and include different ethnic groups, particularly Anglos, Hispanics, and African Americans (again, as well as mixes of some or all of these; Marston & Meadows, 1988). Often, neighborhood associations organize initially around the preparation of the state-mandated neighborhood plan.[3] They may also organize around a specific threat, most often a land use conflict, though, in low-income neighborhoods, the possibility for federal CDBG monies or demands for improved public services are also important stimulants.

Examples include Tucson Mountain Association, a middle-class largely Anglo neighborhood west of downtown, which has been in existence for over 20 years and, in coalition with other neighborhoods in the area, has been an important force in the shape and content of development on Tucson's western side. Armory Park, an inner-city neighborhood of mixed income, ethnic, and tenure groups, was formed in 1978 and continues to be highly active in issues that range from downtown development and historic preservation to the location of homeless shelters. Pueblo Gardens Neighborhood Association is a lower-middle-income central city neighborhood with a high percentage of African Americans and Hispanics. It was organized during the Model Cities era and continues to be active, most recently around issues of crime and gang activity. Neighborhood leaders trained via the citizen action programs of the War on Poverty are still important in keeping Pueblo Gardens active and organized. Generally speaking, central city neighborhood issues cover the gamut from land use (especially transportation) to service delivery conflicts, though concerns with the latter are most prominent and common. Peripheral neighborhoods are almost exclusively concerned with land development issues as they relate both to the physical and to the built environment.

The over 250 associations in the metropolitan area represent a wide range of organizational structures. Most associations, at one time or another, elect governing boards with agenda and meeting schedules that vary from association to association. Some associations meet monthly, bringing together both board and general members. Sometimes the associations are dealing with immediate issues; at other times they are simply maintaining group cohesion. Other associations conduct meetings of board members on a routine basis and have general membership meeting only once or twice annually. Some associations raise operational funds through dues, house tours, rummage and recycling drives, and so on, while others have no operating budgets whatsoever. Some associations have charismatic leaders with citywide reputations. These individuals will oftentimes sit on city and county task forces or citizen boards. Other leaders are, by comparison, low profile and go about their business strictly within the confines of their neighborhood. Occasionally, geographically contiguous neighborhoods as well as neighborhoods experiencing similar kinds of threats will coalesce for a time and work jointly on pressuring the parties involved in the issue. There have even been coalitions of neighborhoods and business interests such as the Inner City Neighborhood Coalition, which joined together with the Fourth Avenue Merchants Association and the Downtown Business Association to address "downtown issues."

Most often, neighborhood leaders are the members of their neighborhood's governing board, though this is not always the case. There are numerous longtime activists who no longer work strictly within the context of their neighborhoods and have long since held every possible position within their own associations. Many of these leaders are actively involved with community politics at large and some produce their own general circulation newsletters like *Point of Contact*, which has metropolitanwide coverage and is produced by a well-known activist who unsuccessfully made a bid for an elected position in the late 1980s. Another of these high profile leaders has become influential in a citizen advisory capacity, in the development of the Pima County Comprehensive Plan. This activist also ran unsuccessfully for elected office—a seat on the county board of supervisors. These two, and some who have been successful in their electoral bids, are characteristic of a cohort of neighborhood leaders who have moved beyond the confines of their neighborhood into the larger metropolitan political arena. In addition to attempting elected office, these high profile activists have been important forces behind numerous local propositions that have appeared on city and county ballots over the years advocating or opposing a range of issues from the comprehensive planning process to greenbelts, parkways, and underpasses, to returning local runoff elections to a ward rather than a citywide basis, among many others. Through these extra-neighborhood activities as well as within their own residential areas, neighborhood activism has and continues to be a powerful current in local politics in Tucson.

The persistence and continuing emergence of active neighbors is suggestive of a high level of civic commitment by hundreds of Tucson citizens. When asked why she gave so much of her free time to community issues, one activist stated that "in a democracy citizens have the right and the responsibility to participate directly in policymaking and planning." Another prominent activist, recognized as a powerful figure in the metropolitan area by both business and government, states that the widespread system of neighborhood associations and coalitions in Tucson "parallels the formal government system." He explains that this "underground government is building up because the existing government cannot represent the average citizen." Still another activist, formerly on the governing board of the NCGT, feels that it and other neighborhood associations formed because of citizen frustration with "elected officials who were not doing their jobs as representatives of the people who put them into office." Other activists have identified changing relations within the household, particularly women's greater participation in the paid labor force, as having an important influence on neighborhood organization. Several of Tucson's leading women activists have pointed to a number of gendered reasons for their involvement. They have indicated that their activism with respect to the negative externalities of urban restructuring emanates from their everyday experiences and is fundamentally tied to seeing neighborhood and community as complex extensions of themselves and their families. They also perceive that neighborhoods have an important role to play in emphasizing the emotional, spiritual, and personal value of place in contrast to more powerful market-oriented considerations. A third factor is the belief that community and the environment (both natural and built) are critical elements in a satisfactory quality of life. Finally, some women see their own activism as reflecting traditional women's concerns with their family's (and by extension the larger community's) health and welfare (Leavitt & Saegert, 1988; Marston, in press; Marston & Saint-Germain, 1991). As the above activists have indicated, people organize against state ineptitude and irresponsibility, on the one hand, and out of a desire for community and empowerment, on the other.

The neighborhoods' effectiveness record with respect to both challenging and negotiating some of the negative externalities of rapid economic and spatial restructuring has been checkered at best. At one level, neighborhoods have been extremely successful in making their presence felt and having their demands considered. The Neighborhood Protection Amendment, the Notification Requirement, electoral victories, and any number of successes with respect to halting or modifying both public and private development proposals are testimony to their power.[4] Additionally, the success of neighborhood groups in facilitating the election of high-level government officials has enabled them to have some influence over politicians and policymaking.

Existing contextual factors have been critically important to their success. First, at least for city neighborhood associations, is the existence of a public agency dedicated to neighborhood concerns. The Citizen Participation Office is immeasurably important to nurturing and maintaining active neighbors. Second is the extensive spatial development of the city. With a classic Sunbelt spatial structure, the built-up area sprawls for 156 square miles; the official metropolitan planning area is nearly 500 square miles. Within that extensive geographic context, there is no one group of business people or land entrepreneurs who speak with a single voice for the business community. Indeed, the DBA, which represents only one of the city's spatially concentrated business communities, is often at odds with the sentiments of the SAHBA, whose focus of attention is frequently occupied in fringe locations of the metropolitan area. Furthermore, both of the major daily newspapers are owned by national syndicates and the power of the press in supporting the local business community has been diluted as homegrown weeklies and monthlies have frequently championed residents' concerns over economic development.

While neighborhoods have had a significant measure of success, there have been many defeats as well. Arguably the single most important factor has been the absence of a completed and enforceable comprehensive plan. While efforts at producing such a plan began over 40 years ago, and various area plans have been in existence for decades, an overarching comprehensive plan was only recently adopted in October 1992 and went into effect the following month. Despite the existence of an impressive set of legally enforceable land use regulations, many observers are skeptical that the newly elected Pima County Board of Supervisors will vigorously enforce the plan. Indeed, in the month between adoption and when the plan actually went into effect, the board of supervisors approved plans for the development of a large-scale and very controversial resort, which—though legally allowable as the plan was not yet in effect—is in direct violation of the Natural Habitat Element of the Comprehensive Plan.

In the aggregate, the "neighborhood movement" in the Tucson metropolitan area is seldom a coherent and unified political force. Differences in the location and socioeconomic characteristics of neighborhoods as well as simple geographic distances have routinely hindered sustained interaction and the pursuit of common objectives. Indeed, the predominant focus of neighborhood activism in the metropolitan area appears to shift and respond to the macro-political and economic structural changes that are expressed on the local landscape. In the late 1950s "suburban neighbors" became active around the issue of urban annexation. By the late 1960s, as the national state experienced fiscal and legitimation crises, this middle-class activism was overshadowed by activism among inner-city low-income residents. As the 1970s witnessed the onset of rapid growth, both of these groups made demands on the local state. By the 1980s, middle-class, geographically peripheral groups' concerns managed to dominate the "neighborhood agenda," though by the end of the decade and even more so recently, some of the previously quiescent inner-city low-income minority populations have begun successfully to reshape the so-called neighborhood movement. This past summer, an offshoot of the Texas branch of the Industrial Areas Foundation announced that it has been training and organizing citizen groups and evaluating local problems in the Tucson metropolitan area through the Pima County Interfaith Council (PCIC). The council is a multidenominational, cross-class, cross-race, and cross-ethnicity, transmetropolitan coalition of local church parishioners and clergy (Johnson, 1991). Having gone "public" only this past August, it is too soon to tell whether the PCIC will have the impact on Tucson's poor and minority communities that it has had in El Paso.

■ Restructuring and Community Politics in El Paso

Growth and Immigration in the El Paso Space Economy

In El Paso, Texas, the First World meets the Third. The pressures generated by global economic restructuring are felt quite immediately along the border. In recent years, the restructuring of U.S. and Mexican political economies has effected profound changes upon the El Paso space economy. One such transformation, the emergence of a suburban ring of *colonias*, unserviced, irregular, poverty-stricken subdivisions inhabited largely by recent Mexican immigrants, has brought new actors and new themes to El Paso politics.

El Paso's colonias would not exist in the absence of a large and steady flow of migrants from Mexico's interior to the U.S. border. Mexican migration is an element in the reshaping of the world economy. As First World and Third World economies are restructured, Third World workers are dislocated and are pulled to North America and Western Europe. In Mexico the capitalization of agriculture has displaced labor. Mexico's economy, staggered by debt and devaluation crises, and Mexican industry, long subjected to capital-intensive development strategies, have failed to absorb the country's rapidly growing labor force. Migrants stream north, drawn by the promise of employment, however menial, and by the elusive hope of sharing in the First World's standard of living. This immigration flow has greatly contributed to the growth of El Paso and its Mexican counterpart, Ciudad Juarez.

From 1950 to 1990 the population of the border cities exploded. The population of El Paso tripled during these four decades, from approximately 195,000 in 1950 to over 600,000 in 1990. In the same period, the population of Ciudad Juarez increased by nearly a factor of 10, from slightly more than 130,000 people to almost 1,300,000.[5] Much of El Paso's growth was in the city's Mexican-origin population: Of the 301,840 people added to El Paso's population from 1960 to 1990, 253,789, or 84%, were of Spanish origin. Furthermore, El Paso's Mexican-born population increased by 240% between 1960 and 1980 and constitutes roughly 20% of the city's total.[6] The cities' rapid growth is the undeniable result of Mexican migration.

Mexican immigrants to the United States typically find work in America's secondary labor market, which comprises unskilled jobs in agriculture, services, and labor-intensive industry. The arrival of Mexi-

TABLE 4.1. Industrial Employment in El Paso: High- and Low-Wage Industries (1950-1985)[a]

Year	High-Wage Industries (percentage)	Low-Wage Industries[b] (percentage)
1950	34.0	29.0
1960	27.8	38.1
1970	14.4	65.1
1980	9.1	62.2
1985	11.0	55.9

SOURCE: U.S. Bureau of the Census, Department of Commerce (1952, 1961, 1970, 1972, 1980, 1982, 1985, 1987), Reschenthaler (1968), and U.S. Bureau of the Census (1960).

a. Figures indicate percentages of El Paso industrial employment.

b. High-wage and low-wage industrial categories were determined from national wage data listed in the *Statistical Abstract of the United States*. Hourly wages in high-wage industries are 115% or more of the national average manufacturing wage; hourly wages in low-wage industries are 85% or less of the national average manufacturing wage. Primary metals and petroleum and coal account for most of El Paso's high-wage industry. Apparel, electronics, and leather account for most of El Paso's low-wage industry. Electronics does not fall into the low-wage category as defined here on a national level; however, electronics is a low-wage industry in El Paso.

can immigrants to the border has been matched by the arrival of labor-intensive, low-wage industries to El Paso. As discussed in the first section of this chapter, the industrial production process has undergone increasing technological separation and concomitant spatial dispersion during the current round of restructuring.

El Paso, a First World city providing immediate access to a rapidly growing supply of Third World labor, has attracted modern industry's assembly operations. The factories that have come to characterize El Paso industry offer unskilled jobs to workers willing to accept low wages. Since 1950 low-wage manufacturing has claimed the majority of industrial jobs in El Paso while higher paying industries have lost two thirds of their share of El Paso's industrial labor force (see Table 4.1). The two industries most involved in this transformation are apparel and electronics. While these industries are on different trajectories on a national level, their El Paso branches have much in common.

The apparel industry is a mature industry. Technological innovation in the production process is no longer important, and manufacturing is highly routinized. Low fixed capital expenses make wages the largest production cost (U.S. Congress, Office of Technology Assessment,

1987, p. 69). Accordingly, the industry employs unskilled labor at low pay. Having moved south and west from their northeastern core area, U.S. apparel manufacturers recruit the most vulnerable segments of the American labor force: women, minorities, and aliens (Arpan, de la Torre, & Toyne, 1982, pp. 3, 10; Maram, 1980, pp. 5, 10). The growth of El Paso's apparel industry is a part of these dynamics. Mexican women, many of them Ciudad Juarez residents, are the garment industry's work force. Throughout the history of El Paso apparel manufacturing, these workers have been paid at or below the federal minimum wage and have been granted few benefits and little job security (La Mujer Obrera, n.d.-a, n.d.-b; Mitchell, 1955; Rungeling, 1969; van de Ende & Haring, 1983, pp. 48, 51).

The electronic semiconductor industry, after an initial period of rapid innovation in the 1950s and 1960s, began to separate unskilled assembly operations from the rest of the production process in the 1970s. Assembly has been dispersed to peripheral locations harboring supplies of low-cost labor (Markusen, 1985, p. 115; Saxenian, 1984, p. 173; Scott & Storper, 1987, p. 227). El Paso is one such assembly site. In El Paso electronics assembly, as in the city's apparel manufacturing, Mexican women make up most of the labor force and work for low wages and few benefits in poor working conditions (Hardesty, Holmes, & Williams, 1988, p. 483; van de Ende & Haring, 1983, p. 48). In recent decades, El Paso has undergone significant change. Mexican migration has contributed to the explosive growth of El Paso and Ciudad Juarez. Concomitantly, El Paso's industrial economy has been oriented toward low-wage manufacturing as decentralizing industries arrive to engage the cities' growing population of unskilled workers. This restructuring has lowered El Paso's standard of living, making the city one of the poorest of its size in the nation.[7]

The formation of colonias on the city's outskirts is one of the ways in which El Paso is being redefined. Empty quarter- and half-acre lots in outlying subdivisions are sold on $150 monthly payment contracts to poor Mexican immigrants and Mexican Americans. Colonia residents live in makeshift housing without water or sewer service and in neighborhoods without paved roads or street lights. Because residents use well water contaminated by nearby septic tanks and outhouses and by agricultural chemicals, waterborne diseases such as shigellosis, salmonella, and hepatitis have reached epidemic proportions in the colonias. An average colonia subdivision covers 25 acres; since 1960 and with increasing speed since 1975, an estimated 250 such subdivisions have been developed in El Paso County. Government estimates put the colonia population at 70,000 (U.S. General Accounting Office, 1990, p. 22).

The Politics of Colonia Growth

The unsettling conditions of colonia life have, however, been the basis for the emergence of a new group of actors onto El Paso's political stage. El Paso Interreligious Sponsoring Organization (EPISO) has organized colonias residents' efforts to improve their lot. EPISO belongs to the Industrial Areas Foundation (IAF), a consortium of activist organizations that are tied to Saul Alinsky's model of community organizing.

Alinsky-style organizing is based on two principles. First, the neighborhood is assumed to be the most important scale for political activity in modern society. To Alinsky, the neighborhood is "the unit of social structure small enough to be sensitive to individual needs but large enough, if sufficiently organized, to meaningfully attack shared problems" (Reitzes & Reitzes, 1987, p. 271). Second, Alinsky believed that citizen participation is the strength and salvation of the American political system. Organizations based on his ideas aim to increase political participation, particularly among America's poor, to effect a more perfect functioning of democratic government and a more equitable distribution of power and resources. These two basic principles are united in neighborhood-based political activism. Alinsky groups typically organize around neighborhood social and infrastructural service dilemmas.[8] Typical issues include neighborhood redevelopment, absentee landlordism, and the quality of local schools (Bailey, 1974; Finks, 1984, pp. 136-156; Ortiz, 1984, p. 571). These issues appeal to people's self-interest and to community preservation and improvement and are used by Alinsky organizations to generate political participation.[9]

Consistent with this emphasis on cultivating neighborhood associations, Alinsky's methods prove more productive in ethnically homogeneous neighborhoods (Castells, 1983, p. 64). El Paso's colonias, with their entirely Mexican American population and catastrophic service shortfalls, are exactly the sort of community in which Alinsky organizers are most successful. EPISO was founded in 1977 and modeled after San Antonio's IAF organization: Communities Organized for Public Service (COPS; Villarreal, 1988, p. 84). EPISO's goals and efforts draw upon the examples provided by COPS and other Alinsky groups. Like other IAF groups, EPISO's ultimate objective is increasing the poor's political participation and gaining a voice for the poor in local politics.

Sister Mary Beth Larkin, an EPISO director, defines the group's mission as teaching the poor to engage the political system (Sister Mary Beth Larkin, personal communication, December 13, 1989). Just as COPS organized around issues affecting San Antonio's Mexican American south side to encourage citizen activism, EPISO targets immediate neighborhood goals such as gaining public water and sewer service for the colonias (Boyte, 1984, p. 135). Like COPS and many other successful Alinsky organizations, EPISO has organized through existing community institutions, the most important of which is the Catholic church. EPISO's early efforts, however, were resisted by the church and the surrounding community. Many within the church saw EPISO as outsiders with "radical" intentions (Rogers, 1990, pp. 162-163). Before EPISO was able to use church associations to organize the colonias' Catholic Mexican American population, the leadership, many of whom were clergy themselves, had to convince the local church of their commitment to help El Paso's poor. The Catholic church then proved crucial in EPISO's growth, coordinating $130,000 in annual funding for EPISO in the early 1980s (Villarreal, 1988, p. 84). Like the church, much of the larger El Paso community and media initially thought of EPISO as a group of troublesome outsiders (Villarreal, 1988, p. 85). As EPISO proved its loyalty to its constituency and enlisted the support of many prominent local and state politicians, the group has gained public acceptance. Since attaining political legitimacy in the eyes of the community, EPISO has made three types of organizing efforts to gain services for the colonias and impel El Paso's poor to take political action.

First, EPISO has mobilized the Mexican American community for local and state elections. EPISO has undertaken voter registration drives and endorsed candidates sympathetic to the colonias' plight and to ballot issues that would bring funds to the colonias. Elections in 1984 and 1989 are representative of this first type of organizing effort. In 1984 500 EPISO volunteers helped register over 20,000 Mexican American voters in El Paso County (Navarro, 1986). These additional voters significantly increased the political might of El Paso's Hispanic community. In 1980, 39% of registered voters in El Paso County were Hispanic; the 1984 registration drive increased this share to 46% (Villarreal, 1988, p. 85). Furthermore, EPISO translated this electoral potential into results. Before the 1984 congressional election, EPISO held an "accountability night" attended by the candidates and 600 EPISO members. The candidates' responses to questions about government's role in servicing the colonias, controlling utility rates, and revitalizing neighborhoods led to EPISO's tacit endorsement of Ronald Coleman. Coleman's victory owed much to the overwhelming majorities he received in areas targeted by EPISO's registration drive (Villarreal, 1988, pp. 85-86). On the county level, EPISO's accountability nights and subsequent endorsements aided the 1984 elections of County Judge Luther Jones and County Attorney Joe Lucas, both of whom advocated public funding for colonia services ("El Paso's Perimeter," 1987, p. A9).

In 1988 and 1989, EPISO strenuously campaigned for the passage of Proposition 2, a state ballot issue that would provide colonia residents with $100 million over 4 years for hookups to public water systems. Colonia residents would borrow the state money through counties, cities, and water districts. The loans would then be repaid by residents and by a combination of federal, state, and private funds. EPISO was involved in developing Proposition 2 as well as in ensuring its ultimate passage. In the fall of 1988, a year before the measure would come before the electorate, EPISO worked with state comptroller Bob Bullock to craft the bill ("State Bill," 1988, p. A4). The following April, EPISO and its sister IAF organization, Valley Interfaith of South Texas's Rio Grande Valley, brought 1,000 colonia residents to the state capitol to encourage lawmakers to put Proposition 2 on the November ballot ("Utility Lines," 1989, p. A1). Before the election, EPISO enlisted 200 volunteers to conduct door-to-door sweeps in El Paso to increase voter turnout and held a rally for Proposition 2 attended by state officials Ann Richards and Jim Hightower ("EPISO Works," 1989, pp. A1, A2; "Richards Urges," 1989, p. B1; "Water Development," 1989, p. B2). The ballot measure won 60% of the vote statewide and 65% in El Paso.

A second set of organizing strategies through which EPISO works involves pressuring officeholders to speed service delivery to the colonias. EPISO brings its members, sometimes numbering in the hundreds, to attend city council, county commissioners' court, El Paso Public Service Board, and Lower Valley Water District Authority meetings that touch on colonia water issues. In addition to busing colonia residents en masse to public meetings, EPISO's more provocative actions include presenting local officials with jars of the fetid water colonia residents must use while waiting for public water service and with petitions calling for policy revisions. Through these steady efforts, EPISO has forced colonia issues before local government and into the local media.

The 1989 Water Summit provides a good example of EPISO's success in these areas. In August 1989, EPISO organized a meeting of 25 officials representing seven government agencies to discuss the status of plans to get water for the colonias. Specifically, EPISO members

wanted a forum to vent their frustration with the El Paso Lower Valley
Water District Authority's slow pace in connecting colonia homes to
public water pipelines. The authority had promised to hook up 600
homes in 1989 but had connected only 5 by late August. Although the
El Paso Times reported that "finger pointing" and "confusion" characterized the Water Summit, the meeting succeeded in keeping the colonias before the public and making local government attend to colonia
issues ("Loan Could Help," 1989, pp. B1, B2).
    Occasionally, EPISO has made a third type of organizing effort:
developing electoral campaigns. The 1985-1986 Socorro annexation
election is EPISO's most prominent colonia campaign. Socorro is a
community containing a large colonia population and adjoins the city
of El Paso to the southeast. EPISO wanted Socorro to agree to be
annexed by El Paso so that Socorro's colonias would receive El Paso
city services. Presumably, annexation would speed service delivery. In
November 1985, EPISO submitted a 1,200-signature petition to El
Paso's city council to annex Socorro. Socorro, however, would have to
vote to disincorporate before annexation could proceed. A disincorporation election was scheduled for April 1986 ("Annexation of Socorro,"
1985, p. B1; "Socorro Ponders," 1985, p. B5; "Socorro to Vote," 1985,
p. B1). EPISO's efforts were opposed by a group of longtime, noncolo-
nia Socorro residents who organized as Concerned Citizens of Socorro
(CCOS). CCOS argued that annexation would bring higher taxes to
Socorro, that a Socorro government would be more responsive to
Socorro's needs, and that annexation would not reduce the cost of water
hookups for those in Socorro's colonias. While EPISO portrayed CCOS
as affluent and self-interested, CCOS warned that annexation would
only make Socorro a poor, neglected part of El Paso (Joe Carrasco,
mayor of Socorro, personal communication, May 14, 1990; "Socorro
Factions," 1986, p. B1; " 'Us' vs. 'Them,' " p. A7). Ultimately, Socorro
residents found CCOS's arguments more persuasive and voted against
disincorporation by a 3 to 2 margin ("Socorro to Remain," 1986, p. A1).

The Limits of EPISO

    Industrial restructuring and immigration have given rise to the colo-
nias, a spatial manifestation of the conflation of class with ethnicity so
fundamental to the El Paso economy. EPISO has seized upon this
inequitable social geography, converting it to a platform for community
organizing. EPISO forced colonia residents' long ignored problems
before El Paso's attention and gave formerly silent colonia residents a

voice in local politics. Among its many successes, EPISO contributed to the election of candidates supportive of colonia residents' struggle for water and sewer service, the passage of Proposition 2, the creation of the Lower Valley Water District Authority, and a greatly increased city and county commitment to regulating subdivision development. Even in its failures—the Socorro annexation campaign, for example— EPISO has demonstrated the potential of colonia residents to effect political change. EPISO is a success by the standards of Alinskyism. EPISO's neighborhood-based organizing has not only contributed to resolving the colonias' water problems but has also encouraged El Paso's poor to take a part in local politics. What remains to be determined, however, is whether EPISO can or will compel the Mexican American community to use its increasing political voice to articulate challenges to the exploitative type of industrialization generating El Paso's spatial injustices and driving the city's growth.

It is likely that EPISO will go no further than neighborhood politics. As an Alinsky organization, its ultimate goal is to increase participation in American democracy, not to challenge the relationships underlying American capitalism. According to former EPISO director Sister Pearl Caesar, "We're only giving the people the tools to act—like learning to read" ("Fighting for Water," 1988, p. 12). Father Ed Roden of EPISO agrees that, "EPISO has survived because it has been consistent and persistent in its basic philosophy of helping people to help themselves" ("Priest's Passion," 1989, p. B1). Ironically, EPISO's myopic focus on neighborhood issues fails to bring the larger processes generating the colonias and their grinding poverty into view. An instructive example is EPISO's search for new issues following the apparent resolution of the colonias' water problems in 1990. EPISO did not move on to engage issues central to the future of the Mexican American community such as the nature of economic development along the border or immigration legislation but instead initiated a campaign to secure air-conditioning for South El Paso tenements. EPISO's version of neighborhood politics excludes issues that carry a challenge to the American political and economic system.

■ Conclusion

We began this chapter with the argument that in Tucson and El Paso uneven economic and spatial restructuring is engendering new forms of local popular action based on concerns about protecting neighborhoods and the community's sense of place as well as maintaining at acceptable levels the health and welfare of residents. At the theoretical level, we remain uncertain about the ultimate structural challenges that neighbors and colonia residents pose for contemporary society. What is clear, however, is that the very different contexts of the two cities—their political capacities, market extensions, demographic characteristics, and local histories—have differently shaped the form and the content of two popular countermovements to restructuring. Most important has been the scope and content of restructuring and the history and organizational resources of each city. It will be useful at this point to summarize how, in each place, these two factors have been played out.

The regional political economy of the Sunbelt, particularly in terms of the impacts of postwar restructuring, has affected each of the two cities in distinctive ways. While Tucson experienced growth across economic sectors, the leading sectoral growth has taken place in research and development and related manufacturing, tourism, nonprofit government services, and retail activity. Immigrants into the metropolitan area have been a mix of middle, lower middle, and working classes. New residential development has been aimed primarily at the middle-income, single-family owner market and the lower-middle-income renter market. In contrast, El Paso has been the site for low-end restructuring, most clearly expressed by the decline in higher wage manufacturing employment while lower wage manufacturing employment has increased. At the same time that tens of thousands of poor Mexican immigrants have been streaming in from across the U.S.-Mexican border, El Paso has experienced a net loss in low-income housing. In both cities, particular popular responses to the negative impacts of restructuring have emerged.

Middle-class, home-owning, Anglo residents of Tucson have used common geography with their neighbors as the basis upon which to challenge the physical manifestations of restructuring in their city. The institutional structures that have lent support to this response have been relatively weak. The CPO has limited funds and a small staff and, as part of the local state apparatus, is constrained in the kinds of support it can provide to citizen-neighbors. Homegrown institutions like the Neighborhood Coalition of Greater Tucson are intermittent in their influence and difficult to sustain except at election time or when specific threats occur. Overall, the "neighborhood movement" is fragmented along class, race/ethnicity, and geographic lines. The greatest cleavages reflect class reinforced by location. Confronted with irregular threats, and confounded by competing identities, the citizen action movement in Tucson is highly fragmented, though not necessarily ineffective. In contrast, El Paso's collective consumption movement displays a high degree of homogeneity. EPISO's strength is a direct result of its strong institutional supports: IAF and its strategy of engaging stable and enduring community institutions in its organizing, in this case, the Catholic church. Although initially reluctant to take on the colonias' cause (Rogers, 1990), the Catholic church eventually provided a base upon which to wage the struggle for decent service provision in the colonias. Furthermore, colonia residents, in addition to geographic proximity, are also linked by a common ethnicity, class, and religion and thus share important meaning systems that give shape and content to their grievances. EPISO has helped to demystify the local political process and provide colonia residents with improved access to the political and policy process.

While EPISO is a single unifying organization with the weight of the locally formidable Catholic church behind it, there is, in Tucson, no single institution that shapes neighborhood activism. Certainly there are charismatic, high profile leaders, but there is no one person or entity that channels the grievances of the over 250 homeowner/neighborhood associations in the Tucson metropolitan area. Furthermore, while the colonias lie exclusively within the jurisdiction of El Paso County (the regulations of which are largely responsible for enabling the growth of colonias in the first place), neighborhoods in Tucson are divided by different, sometimes contradictory, city and county regulatory structures.

Yet, while different contexts have resulted in different forms of activism, there are two very important similarities between the two cases. First, our case studies support the work of theorists like Castells and Touraine who argue that the new urban politics appears very much centered upon domestic spaces. In both Tucson and El Paso, community organizing has been launched from neighborhoods and is centered upon the communal issues of private life that occur there. Even though the popular movements in each place are substantially different in terms of form, leadership, composition, and institutional resources and support, both are consistent in their aims to improve the quality of private/domestic spaces by exerting a greater measure of control over the forces that shape them. This emphasis upon the affairs of everyday life in Tucson and El Paso, as well as in many cities across the United States, signals an ideological and practical shift away from the more traditional concerns surrounding industrial era shop-floor militancy and unionization and certainly requires continued research attention (several of the case studies in Logan & Swanstrom, 1990, further illustrate this point). A second commonality is that citizens in both Tucson and El Paso have come to recognize the key targets of their discontent in local political and economic actors. In both cities, residents have organized and been organized with the explicit intention of creating greater access to the local political system. Their efforts have been to curb some of the more extreme manifestations of the contemporary restructuring regime. Not surprising, the official local political leadership has attempted to discount or ignore their opinions and inputs and to shunt them aside. In response, citizens in Tucson have attempted to make their voices heard more directly, bypassing their elected representatives. EPISO, too, organizes around the objective of making democracy "more democratic" by helping formerly powerless citizens to participate more directly in the local democratic process.

Of interest, a recent study funded by the Kettering Foundation found that Americans across the country are disillusioned and frustrated with their representatives and are increasingly discounting the ballot box as an effective mechanism for voicing their views (Kettering Foundation, 1991). These same Americans are becoming politically active at the local level, where they feel their efforts can most tangibly be realized. We would like to suggest that community activism in Tucson and El Paso may be part of a much larger trend toward more direct forms of citizen engagement with, at the very least, the local political process. Indeed, just as democratic movements in Eastern Europe and the former Soviet Union are signaling dramatic political transformations in those places, it appears that Americans in Tucson, El Paso, and cities across the country are engaged in a quiet revolution of their own as they bypass many of the conventional mechanisms of representative democracy and construct a more participatory one.

NOTES

1. In the fall of 1992, the Central Arizona project (CAP) began delivery of surface water, diverted from the Colorado River, to parts of metropolitan Tucson. The final portion of the urban area will be brought into the CAP delivery system sometime in 1993. Most of the population will then be using a combination of both groundwater and highly salinated and expensively treated surface water.

2. The Tucson metropolitan area includes eastern Pima County as well as the incorporated city of Tucson. There are several additional jurisdictions within this 495-square-

mile area including the city of South Tucson, a 1-square-mile city completely surrounded by Tucson, the Tohono O'odham Indian reservation, and the independent towns of Marana and Oro Valley.

3. The state of Arizona's Urban Environment Management Act requires all jurisdictions to prepare general plans. Neighborhood plans constitute the most detailed level of planning effort and are combined with the city's area plan into a general plan. The city and county general plans are combined and coordinated to constitute the comprehensive plan.

4. The Neighborhood Protection Amendment, championed by one of the leading community activists in the early 1980s, is an addition to the city charter that provides for major road improvements to be put before a vote of the electorate. Individual projects proposals are entered on the ballot and the entire city decides whether to approve or reject them. The Notification Requirement is an important policy innovation, created through pressures from various neighborhood associations, which mandates that the city council meeting agenda be sent to all registered neighborhood associations (as well as other registered interest groups) 2 weeks before the meeting is to be held.

5. Data are from the University of Texas at El Paso (1989) and the U.S. Bureau of the Census (1950, 1960, 1970, 1980).

6. Data are from the City of El Paso (1989) and the U.S. Bureau of the Census (1960, 1970, 1980).

7. Data are from the U.S. Bureau of the Census (1960), U.S. Bureau of the Census, Department of Commerce (1970, 1980, 1985), and Reschenthaler (1968).

8. Data are from Rand McNally (1990), the University of Texas at Austin (1989), and the U.S. Bureau of the Census (1950, 1960, 1970, 1980).

9. There is a large literature on Alinsky and Alinsky community organizations. Sources include Bailey (1974), Boyte (1980, 1984), Castells (1983), Finks (1984), Ortiz (1984), and Reitzes and Reitzes (1987) as well as Alinsky's own works.

REFERENCES

Abbott, C. (1987). *The new urban America: Growth and politics in Sunbelt cities.* Chapel Hill: University of North Carolina Press.

Annexation of Socorro snags on legal question. (1985, October 1). El Paso Times, pp. B1, B3.

Arpan, J. S., de la Torre, J., & Toyne, B. (1982). *The U.S. apparel industry: International challenge, domestic response.* Atlanta: Georgia State University.

Bailey, R., Jr. (1974). *Radicals in urban politics: The Alinsky approach.* Chicago: University of Chicago Press.

Boyte, H. C. (1980). *The backyard revolution.* Philadelphia: Temple University Press.

Boyte, H. C. (1984). *Community is possible.* New York: Harper & Row.

Boyte, H. C. (1989). *CommonWealth: A return to citizen politics.* New York: Free Press.

Castells, M. (1983). *The city and the grassroots.* Berkeley: University of California.

City of El Paso, Department of Planning, Research and Development. (1989). *El Paso population and housing trends 1980-1988.* El Paso, TX: Author.

de Certeau, M. (1984). *The practice of everyday life.* Berkeley: University of California Press.

El Paso's perimeter of poverty. (1987, August 17). *Washington Post*, pp. A1, A9.

EPISO works all out to pass water measure. (1989, November 7). *El Paso Times*, pp. A1, A2.

Fainstein, S., & Fainstein, N. (1985). Economic restructuring and the rise of urban social movements. *Urban Affairs Quarterly, 21*(2), 185-206.

Fighting for water in the colonias. (1988, October 17). *Time*, pp. 12-13.

Finks, P. D. (1984). *The radical vision of Saul Alinsky*. New York: Paulist Press.

Fleagle, R. K. (1966). *Politics and planning: Tucson metropolitan area*. Unpublished master's thesis, University of Arizona, Tucson, Department of Government.

Hardesty, S. G., Holmes, M. D., & Williams, J. D. (1988). Economic segmentation and worker earnings in a U.S.-Mexico border enclave. *Sociological Perspectives, 31,* 466-489.

Herr, J. (1991, November 21). Hughes to cut 1,600 jobs. *The Arizona Daily Star*, pp. 1-2.

Johnson, J. (1991, August 7-13). New movers and shakers. *The Tucson Weekly*, pp. 5-7, 25-28.

Katznelson, I. (1981). *City trenches: Urban politics and the patterning of class in the United States*. Chicago: University of Chicago Press.

Kettering Foundation. (1991). *Citizens and politicians: A view from Main Street*. Bethesda, MD: Author.

La Mujer Obrera. (n.d.-a). *A brief history of the El Paso garment industry*. El Paso, TX: Author.

La Mujer Obrera. (n.d.-b). *The garment industry in El Paso*. El Paso, TX: Author.

Leavitt, J., & Saegert, S. (1988, Autumn). The community-household: Responding to housing abandonment in New York City. *Journal of the American Planning Association*, pp. 489-500.

Loan could help colonia water flow. (1989, August 25). *El Paso Times*, pp. B1, B2.

Logan, J., & Molotch, H. (1987). *Urban fortunes: The political economy of place*. Berkeley: University of California Press.

Logan, J., & Swanstrom, T. (Eds.). (1990). *Beyond the city limits: Urban policy and economic restructuring in comparative perspective*. Philadelphia: Temple University Press.

Logan, M. (1990). Fighting city hall: Contested growth in Tucson, 1950-1960. *Locus, 3,* 16.

Luckingham, B. (1982). *The urban Southwest: A profile of Albuquerque, El Paso, Phoenix, and Tucson*. El Paso: Texas Western Press.

Maram, S. L. (1980). *Hispanic workers in the garment and restaurant industries in Los Angeles County* (Working Papers in U.S.-Mexican Studies 12). San Diego: University of California, Program in United States-Mexican Studies.

Markusen, A. R. (1985). *Profit cycles, oligopoly, and regional development*. Cambridge: MIT Press.

Marston, S. (1993). Lose the war, change the terrain: Federal War on Poverty programs and citizen participation in Tucson, 1966-1991. In H. Ingram & S. R. Smith (Eds.), *Public policy for democracy*. Washington, DC: Brookings Institution.

Marston, S. (in press). *The people and the public sphere: The space and culture of democracy in an American city, 1966-1991*. Tucson: University of Arizona Press.

Marston, S., & Meadows, R. (1988). Citizens in conflict: Neighborhood politics and urban growth in Tucson. In M. Philak (Ed.), *The city in the twenty-first century* (pp. 265-276). Tempe: Arizona State University.

Bureau of the Census. (1960). *U.S. population census: Characteristics of the population*. Washington, DC: Government Printing Office.

Bureau of the Census. (1970). *U.S. population census: Characteristics of the population*. Washington, DC: Government Printing Office.

Bureau of the Census. (1980). *U.S. census of population: General social and economic characteristics*. Washington, DC: Government Printing Office.

Bureau of the Census, Department of Commerce. (1952). *Statistical abstract of the United States*. Washington, DC: Government Printing Office.

Bureau of the Census, Department of Commerce. (1961). *Statistical abstract of the United States*. Washington, DC: Government Printing Office.

Bureau of the Census, Department of Commerce. (1970). *County business patterns*. Washington, DC: Government Printing Office.

Bureau of the Census, Department of Commerce. (1972). *Statistical abstract of the United States*. Washington, DC: Government Printing Office.

Bureau of the Census, Department of Commerce. (1980). *County business patterns*. Washington, DC: Government Printing Office.

Bureau of the Census, Department of Commerce. (1982). *Statistical abstract of the United States*. Washington, DC: Government Printing Office.

Bureau of the Census, Department of Commerce. (1985). *County business patterns*. Washington, DC: Government Printing Office.

Bureau of the Census, Department of Commerce. (1987). *Statistical abstract of the United States*. Washington, DC: Government Printing Office.

Congress, Office of Technology Assessment. (1987). *The U.S. textile and apparel industry: A revolution in progress—special report*. Washington, DC: Government Printing Office.

General Accounting Office. (1990). *Rural development: Problems and progress of colonia subdivisions near Mexico border*. Washington, DC: Government Printing Office.

versity of Texas at Austin, Bureau of Business Research. (1989). *Texas fact book*. Austin: Author.

versity of Texas at El Paso, Bureau of Business and Economic Research. (1989). *Statistical abstract of El Paso, Texas*. El Paso: Author.

" vs. "them." (1985, November 12). *El Paso Times*, pp. A7, A9.

ity lines long overdue, residents say. (1989, April 13). *El Paso Times*, pp. A1, A2.

de Ende, A., & Haring, H. A. (1983). *Sunbelt frontier and border economy: A fieldwork study of El Paso*. El Paso: Center for Inter-American and Border Studies, UTEP.

arreal, R. (1988). EPISO and political empowerment: Organizational politics in a border city. *Journal of Borderlands Study, 3*(2), 81-95.

ier, R. (1986, November/December). The big one. *City Magazine*, pp. 23-29.

er development proposal includes $100 million in aid for Texas colonias. (1989, October 18). *El Paso Times*, pp. B1, B2.

erstone, M., & Kirby, A. (1991). Escaping the conceptual box: Ideological and economic conversion. In A. Kirby (Ed.), *The Pentagon and the cities* (pp. 171-187). Newbury Park, CA: Sage.

Marston, S., & Saint-Germain, M. (1991). Urban restructuring and political groupings: Women and neighborhood activism in ? *Geoforum, 22,* 223-236.

Martin, W., et al. (1984). *Saving water in a desert city.* Washingto the Future.

Mitchell, E. I. M. (1955). *The clothing industry of El Paso from* Unpublished master's thesis, Texas Western College.

Navarro, A. C. (1986). *Understanding the Mexican American voter: of the Mexican American community in El Paso.* Unpublis University of Texas, El Paso.

Noyelle, T., & Stanback, T. (1984). *The economic transformation* Totowa, NJ: Rowman & Allanheld.

Ortiz, I. D. (1984). Chicano urban politics and the politics of refo *Social Science Journal, 19,* 101-119.

Priest's passion inspires others to help the poor. (1989, March 19). B1, B2.

Rand McNally and Company. (1990). *1990 commercial atlas and ma? ed.).* Chicago: Author.

Reitzes, D. C., & Reitzes, D. C. (1987). Alinsky in the 1980s: Two con organizations. *Sociological Quarterly, 28,* 265-283.

Reschenthaler, P. (1968). Postwar readjustment in El Paso, 1945-1 *Studies, 21.*

Richards urges voters to OK aid for colonias. (1989, October 27). *El*

Rogers, M. (1990). *Cold anger.* Denton: North Texas University.

Rungeling, B. S. (1969). *Impact of the Mexican alien commuter on th of El Paso, Texas.* Unpublished doctoral dissertation, Universit

Saxenian, A. (1984). The urban contradictions of Silicon Valley: Regio restructuring of the semiconductor industry. In L. Sawers & V *Sunbelt/Snowbelt: Urban development and regional restructuri* New York: Oxford University Press.

Scott, A. J., & Storper, M. (1987). High technology industry and regio A theoretical critique and reconstruction. *International Social Sc?* 215-232.

Socorro factions war over annexation. (1986, January 27). *El Paso Her*

Socorro ponders annexation and incorporation. (1985, September 25) p. B5.

Socorro to remain a town; 2nd election to follow. (1986, April 6). *El* A1, A4.

Socorro to vote on annexation. (1985, November 13). *El Paso Times,* p.

State bill would aid "colonias." (1988, October 24). *El Paso Herald Po?*

Stone, C., & Sanders, H. (1987). *The politics of urban development.* Lawr? of Kansas Press.

Touraine, A. (1988). *Return of the actor: Social theory in postindustrial s* polis: University of Minnesota Press.

Tucson Economic Development Corporation. (1990). [Community audit]. ?

U.S. Bureau of the Census. (1950). *U.S. population census: Charac? population.* Washington, DC: Government Printing Office.

5 Building Multiracial Alliances: The Case of People United for a Better Oakland

GARY DELGADO

On June 11, 1991, 32 members of People United for a Better Oakland (PUEBLO) watched as the city council voted to pass the organization's lead abatement and screening plan, over the vociferous objections of the County Apartment Owners and Taxpayer's Associations. How was this group able to force local government to mobilize additional financial and personnel resources in an era of fiscal cutbacks? What secondary and third party forces were mobilized to support the primary constituency? How were resources developed and deployed to achieve the organization's objectives and what is the significance of the organization's work? These are the questions that the case study in this chapter explores.

Epstein (1990) emphasizes the stark need for case studies to test new social movement theory. Case studies as a research approach have the unique ability to examine the actual process and pressing concerns of organizing: issue identification, the recruitment and development of leadership, the role of the organizer, and the formation and implementation of mobilization strategies. Case studies are also useful in an analysis of the effects of developing both new theories and improved action. In terms of the theoretical issues raised in this volume, the case study of PUEBLO underscores the increasing complexity that comes from both an increasing diversity of inner-city neighborhoods and a decrease in the availability of fiscal resources. Despite new social movement theory, which suggests that class has receded in salience as a basis for mobilization and that people are lost in a fragmented politics of identity, this case study demonstrates that organizing in low-income, multilingual, multicultural, and multiracial communities requires an approach grounded in both an awareness of class and material concerns *and* a politics of inclusion that seeks as a priority unity among culturally diverse constituencies.

■ Shifting Demographics: A New Political Context

The 1990 census revealed important shifts in the demographic characteristics of the U.S. population. Nowhere is this shift more pronounced than in California, which boasts both the largest state population and an economy that, if separated from the rest of the country, would rank seventh in the world. The most important of California demographic characteristics, however, is not the sheer growth in the state's population (from 23 million to almost 29 million between 1980 and 1990) but the significant growth of populations in communities of color ("Bay Area's Racial," 1992).

The census documents the decade's growth in the number of people of color relative to "non-Hispanic whites," revealing that the Asian American population has grown the fastest, up 127%. Latinos are next, up 69.2%, while the increases have been 21.4% for African Americans and 20.3% for American Indians, in comparison with a 13.8% growth in the white population. The total population growth rate for the state from 1980 to 1990 was 25.7%. High birthrates and a flood of immigrants are reported to have been the reasons for the record 793,000 new residents in 1990 alone, resulting in a total 1991 population for the state of 30,351,000. These figures only begin to explain the magnitude of change that the state and its major institutions are facing. The Department of Finance estimates that by the year 2003 over 50% of California's population will be people of color (*The New York Times,* February 26, 1991; *The San Francisco Chronicle,* June 5, 1991).

Currently, California is home to almost 6 million foreign-born residents, and nearly half of the state's new residents are recent immigrants. One third of all Latino children and two fifths of all Asian children in the United States live in California. Unfortunately, this population growth rate is matched by increasingly high child poverty rates, especially for children of color. Between 1979 and 1989, for example, there was a 123% increase in the number of Asian American children living below the poverty line.

What are the implications of these statistics? To begin with, the state's major institutions will have to adapt to these new populations and cultures. In the field of education, for instance, a majority of schools have been affected by immigration and rapidly changing demographic characteristics. In many elementary schools and most secondary schools, students and teachers face complex and diverse classrooms in terms of culture and language. Consequently, there is a strong need for a host of new understandings, skills, institutional arrangements, and support to ensure that diversity is positive and equitable. Addressing diversity is not always easy.

As Leticia Quezada, the first Latina member of the California School Board, notes, "The system is designed to educate middle-class families in the '40s and '50s when mothers stayed home and it was assumed they were high school graduates who would help their children with school work and get involved with the PTA . . . that is simply not our situation." A similar situation exists in the arena of health care. Few health service providers have the linguistic or cultural capacity to address the needs of California's new immigrant communities.

PUEBLO was formed in response to this need for an infrastructure accountable to communities reflected in the changing demographic landscape. Based in Oakland, California, PUEBLO was founded in the spring of 1989 as a project of the Center for Third World Organizing (CTWO). The center had developed a successful record in training young organizers of color and had an organizational interest in developing an Oakland-based project that would "directly address the concerns of people of color in Oakland and train organizers who would be more able to meet the challenge of building multicultural organizations" (Center for Third World Organizing, 1988).

Twenty-six year old Francis Calpotura was named director of the project and given 3 months to develop an initial plan. Calpotura himself was an example of a new breed of organizer. Born in the Philippines, Francis immigrated to the United States in 1977. Recruited as a student leader from the University of California, Berkeley, Francis was accepted into CTWO's first organizer training class in the fall of 1984. Through CTWO, he worked as an organizer with the Farm Labor Organizing Committee (FLOC) in Ohio and as lead organizer with the Coalition Against the Marcos Dictatorship before developing the Oakland-based campaign. Soft-spoken and introspective, with a wry sense of humor, Calpotura brought to the project a strong commitment to the development of a campaign that would meet the needs of immigrant communities.

■ Developing the Initial Campaign

In classic community organizing, a direct action organizing campaign is a series of escalating organizational activities through which human, financial, and communicative resources are focused on a target or targets to win specific demands. The purposes of conducting a campaign are to develop the capacity of the organization's indigenous leadership, to win specific benefits for the organization's membership and constituency, and to build the power of the organization. These general notions of campaign development are most workable in an expanding economy with a liberal state (given that the majority of the targets are governmental) and with a constituency that has certain political rights that are protected by law and custom.

The composition of Oakland's population, however, suggested that this classical model be modified to work successfully in a multicultural environment. Reflecting the demographic characteristics of the state, Oakland's 360,000 population comprises approximately 65% people of color. The largest percentage growth was in the Asian community, which went from 4% of the city's population in 1970 to almost 20% in 1990. Because there are many established immigrant communities in Oakland, the city is a locus for secondary migration, with many new immigrants coming to Oakland from other communities. Over 50 languages are spoken in the Oakland public schools and 1 of every 4 children is classified as "limited English proficient" (LEP).

Economically, the city suffers from many of the problems that plague larger urban centers. Between 1981 and 1986 the private sector lost 1.3% of its work force, or 2,000 jobs; manufacturing lost 3,200 jobs, or 11.1%; and transportation and public utilities lost 26% of their work force, or 4,900 jobs. Of the 14 cities in Alameda County, only 2 had lower per capita incomes than Oakland's $12,215.

Looking at business development in the city, the picture is equally bleak. Unable to develop a significant number of anchor tenants for the city's downtown shopping development, Oakland also has the highest number of office vacancies in the Bay Area (18.8%). In addition, both city hall and a block of downtown businesses are still closed because of damage from the 1989 earthquake.

The city also has massive social problems. One fourth of the children fail to graduate from high school. Less than 50% of African American workers laid off during the city's 1981-1986 recession have been able to get new jobs. And, while infant mortality for non-African Americans in the county declined by 26% between 1978 and 1988, it increased for African Americans by 22% ("Economy Makes," 1991; "Oakland Leads," 1991; "Oakland: New," 1991; "Retail Jobs," 1991).

Given this diversity and the need for the Oakland project to be successful, Calpotura had to develop an organizing approach that was culturally inclusive, delivered real benefits, and would not be competitive with existing organizations. Before making a decision on the form, structure, or approach of the project, Calpotura spent 6 months laying the groundwork. Beginning in September 1988, he began an exhaustive 4-month interviewing process with 40 key leaders in community, labor, church, and social service organizations. Borrowing from the "commitment building" interview process used by the Industrial Areas Foundation (IAF), the Alinsky adherents of an institutional or church-based approach, the campaign identified and interviewed key leaders to identify issues and build support from the established social service agency and church infrastructure. There were two objectives of this interviewing process. First, the interviews could identify key issues that the new group might address. Second, potential opposition to the project could be identified and either neutralized or avoided.

The interviews were helpful in achieving both of the initial organizational objectives. They were particularly useful in helping Calpotura zero in on three health-related issues affecting Oakland's communities of color: first, the closing of Oakland Hospital, a facility that served the low-income community; second, the long waits and poor service at Highland Hospital, the county's primary public facility; and, third, the trauma caused by the closing down of Maxicare, a private health maintenance organization (HMO) that had serviced 40,000 Oakland residents.

It was not only the interviews that pointed Calpotura toward an investigation of health care availability, however. Information gleaned from an article published in CTWO's *Minority Trendsletter* suggested that one of the results of the Reagan-initiated health care cutbacks was a decrease in childhood immunizations and an increase in reported cases of vaccine-preventable diseases (Adamson & Delgado, 1988). Calpotura had a hunch that Oakland had low immunization rates and that it probably wasn't rich kids who weren't getting their shots.

To test the waters, the project formed a planning committee composed of community residents in late January 1989 to develop the second stage of organizational activity—the expansion of the constituent base—by launching a massive, eight-language, door-to-door, community health survey. Recruiting community volunteers from six social service agencies, local ethnic churches, and students from the Social Work Department at San Francisco State University and the Ethnic Studies Department at UC Berkeley, over 1,000 families were surveyed in a 4-month period. "The survey," recalls Calpotura, "was our first organizing tool. Not only did we involve over 80 multilingual volunteers, we were also able to get key leaders in a number of communities invested in the survey results" (personal communication, November 1991). Both the initial interviews and the community surveys, a tactic borrowed from tenant organizers, served as effective contact and assessment tools and were important in gauging the potential of the group's initial campaign.

The survey results were relatively predictable. They pointed to inadequate health services, lack of transportation to health facilities, massive underinsurance, a lack of trained multilingual personnel, and a 24% underimmunization rate. In a planning meeting that assessed the survey's results, the third stage of the project began when committee members decided to launch a campaign to force the county to increase the number of multilingual personnel in county facilities and make free immunizations available to county residents—the Campaign for Accessible Healthcare.

Campaign members released the survey results in a press conference just prior to California State Assembly health care hearings held in Oakland in early May 1989. The mobilization of 60 families involved in the survey and 25 of the survey volunteers to testify at and disrupt the hearings gave the campaign an almost immediate victory in their effort to force the county hospital to hire Vietnamese and Spanish translators. When campaign members pointed to the immunization gap, however, David Kears, the county health administrator, balked. Ridiculing the campaign's assertion that large numbers of low-income Asian, African American, and Latino children were underimmunized, Kears claimed that immunizations were available free to low-income people at county clinics. He also pointed out that children would not be able to attend school "without their shots."

Kear's recalcitrance moved the campaign's efforts up a notch. The campaign's steering committee had to validate their research findings concerning immunization levels as well as find out why the available clinics weren't being used.

Assistance in proving the group's case came from unexpected sources. First, a meeting with school nurses in the district confirmed that many children were not immunized until they were forced to, right before entering school. This left a gap of several years between when they were supposed to have received their immunizations and when they actually did receive them—a window of opportunity for the rapid spread of these diseases.

Kear's point about the underuse of public clinics for immunizations also had an answer: Only two of the clinics offered free immunizations—once a month each, on a weekday. The clinics did not even publicize these times in English, much less in any of the languages spoken in the immigrant communities. In the words of Dr. Loring Dales, immunization unit chief of the California State Department of Health in Berkeley, "If a clinic only immunizes once a week and you have five children and no baby sitter and no car, it's not easy" (interview in the *Oakland Tribune,* March 8, 1990). An additional factor in weakening the county's position was the discovery that the county had returned monies to the state's Child Health and Disability Prevention Program (a health care program for low-income children) without conducting any outreach in poor communities.

Even the uncovering of these facts, however, may not have made a difference in the county's policies were it not for another development predicted by the campaign: a tremendous increase in the number of reported cases of measles and whooping cough between September 1989 and February 1990. In a press conference in early November 1989, campaign members once again presented their survey statistics and demanded multilingual outreach and Saturday immunization clinic hours. Citing reports of measles epidemics and deaths in Houston, Los Angeles, and Boston, and bolstered by a statement from the American Academy of Pediatrics that second immunizations should be made available to all people under 32 years of age, the campaign argued that the conditions in Oakland represented "an outbreak just waiting to happen." Health officials replied that the proposal for massive outreach was "premature and unaffordable" ("Health Officials," 1989).

By February 1990, however, it was clear that the county had a serious problem, with 30 reported cases of measles for the month of January, compared with only 31 reported for the whole previous year. When the reported numbers shot up to 103 in February and 206 in March, the county was forced to declare a state of emergency.

In a banner headline, the *Oakland Tribune* declared a "Measles Alert" and cited sources in the department of public health who declared, "It's out of control . . .!" Finally acceding to the campaign's demands in mid-March, the county health department agreed to initiate a massive, multilingual outreach program and to allocate funds for county health clinics to offer immunizations on Saturdays and evenings ("County Declares," 1990; "Measles Alert," 1990). The first weekend, 2,000 children were inoculated. In a 4-month period, campaign organizers estimated that 30,000 children were immunized. By June 1990 the number of reported measles cases was down to under 10. The time line for winning the campaign: 11 months.

At this juncture, the only difference between the campaign and the hundreds of other ad hoc committees, or single issue mobilizations (SIMS), that come together in communities of color all over the country was that this campaign's efforts had been successful in raising an issue and delivering concrete benefits to their constituency. The campaign had conducted significant research, built relationships among people from a number of communities, and mobilized hundreds of community residents and volunteers. The effort, however, had neither changed relations of power nor built a permanent organization. To build an organization, organizers and community leaders had to make a long-range commitment. In addition, they had to develop a plan to generate financial resources and to transform loose-knit, issue-based agreements into organizational commitment and temporary multilingual affiliations into permanent multicultural alliances.

Could such an organization be built in Oakland? In a daylong retreat in the late spring of 1990, a nine-person organizing committee decided to "build a permanent, multi-issue organization, representing the interests of low-income people." Enthused by their recent success in the immunization campaign, the committee decided to call the new organization People United for a Better Oakland, later shortened to "People United" in English and "PUEBLO" in Spanish.

■ Cutting the Issue

Conventional wisdom in community organizing dictates that organizational issues are developed carefully, reflective of the interest of the organization's base constituency, and have, in the Alinsky tradition, "specific, immediate, and realizable" solutions. Additional criteria for selecting an issue include the visibility of the problem, the ability of the issue to open opportunities for the group to forge alliances, and clear "handles" (e.g., regulations, conflicts of interest, or precedents) through which decision makers can be pressured. By the early summer of 1990, PUEBLO members had chosen to work on an issue that met almost none of these criteria: lead poisoning.

Following up on a tip from a health care worker in the state department of public health, PUEBLO's leadership was able to unearth a copy of a 1988 state-financed study conducted in the San Antonio and Fruitvale neighborhoods of Oakland. The study indicated that as many as 20% of the 551 children tested in those neighborhoods had high levels of lead in their blood and that 75% of the interior paint and 91% of the exterior paint of the homes contained dangerous levels of lead ("Get the Lead," 1989; "State's Kids," 1990).

The report had been released and then quietly buried. While "executive summaries" of the report were available to the public, it took PUEBLO members over 2 months to get copies of the full report. The difficulty that the PUEBLO leadership had in securing copies of the state report only served to reflect the group's opinion of public health officials—"that they didn't give a damn about poor people." As organizing committee member and later group chair Gwen Hardy recounts,

> The lead study just reinforced our idea that the county health officials didn't care about our communities. When we found out that the state had tested kids in the neighborhood, found high levels of problems and then decided not to tell people about the test results or of the dangers of the exposure, we were completely outraged and we were determined not to let them get away with it. (personal communication, November 1991)

Even though the results cited in the report could have devastating effects on the children in two Oakland neighborhoods, the ability of the organization to move forward on the issue was still hampered by two factors: First, the issue was not "deeply felt" by neighborhood residents because they didn't know the results of the study. Second, even though the Centers for Disease Control had issued a report in 1985 ("Lead Poses," 1990) estimating that as many as 8 million children in the United States might be affected by lead poisoning, the public was less likely to support PUEBLO's efforts because there was a general sense that lead poisoning, like vaccine-preventable diseases, had largely been eliminated.

The issue, while vitally important, was invisible. To address the problem of lead contamination, PUEBLO members would have to heighten the visibility of the issue not only to the general public but also to the communities directly affected.

■ Creating Issue Visibility

Concerned that lead poisoning could cause brain damage, mental retardation, and behavioral problems (Rabin, 1985; "U.S. Opens," 1990; "Why Young," 1990), PUEBLO members requested that state researchers release the names of the families who participated in the research so that the children affected could be treated. State researchers refused to release the names on the grounds that the families involved were part of a confidential study. Stymied by the state's refusal, PUEBLO's organizing committee decided to replicate the outreach efforts of the measles campaign, focusing on the two neighborhoods cited in the state's report.

The measles campaign had used three methods to reach people in the community. The first method was to convince the staff of key community agencies of the importance of the survey and to have the staff assist survey volunteers in reaching the agency's client base. The second method was to contact a tier of traditional leadership in Oakland's communities of color and convince them of the importance of the inoculations. This tier included indigenous community leaders and ranged from ministers to the community organizing notion of the "block mayor," the person in the neighborhood that everybody respects, as well as the leaders of ethnic organizations having their origins in traditionally structured societies (for example, in the Mien community, the major contact was a tribal chief). The third method was direct contact: one-on-one door knocking and either neighborhood, or language group, house meetings. It was this third method, door knocking the neighborhoods, that PUEBLO first employed to get the word out about lead.

Targeting the neighborhoods cited in the study, volunteers from the group's organizing committee went from door to door with two purposes in mind: (a) informing people about the symptoms of lead poisoning and (b) finding the families who had been contacted in the state's initial study. In an intensive door knocking effort, committee members were only able to identify 8 children who were tested in the state's study. One of their parents, however, was hopping mad. Karleen Lloyd's children were tested and she was told that "she didn't need to worry." After conducting some of her own research, Ms. Lloyd became convinced that the learning disability of one of her children was due to lead poisoning. In addition to finding a small number of children who had been tested in the first study, and almost 30 homes that had been tested, the door knocking effort uncovered a different set of problems related to soil contamination. Because the Fruitvale community was bordered by two major freeways, much of the topsoil was exposed to the by-products of leaded gas. And because parts of both communities were zoned for light industry, there was evidence of waste dumping from a number of small factories.

Given the complexity of the issue, and the fact that lead poisoning was still not a "hot issue" in the neighborhoods, simple one-on-one door knocking was not an approach that could develop group cohesion. The organizers had to develop an approach that would reach neighborhood residents in a nonthreatening atmosphere, develop a group consciousness of the issue, and allow residents to discuss both the potential problem caused by lead poisoning and the options they had for action on the issue. The initial technique of door knocking was useful to identify families and homes that had been tested. To explain the implications of the lead problem, however, PUEBLO organizers took a page from the UFW boycott organizer's book and used house meetings for discussions among people in the neighborhood. The house meetings had the advantage of being small (4 to 12 people), intimate, and interactive. They also tapped different networks for participation, because they are based on personal connections. Thus the house meetings would often include extended families or friendship networks as well as neighbors.

After conducting almost 50 house meetings with residents from over 300 families, PUEBLO called a meeting with Lynn Goldman, chief of the California State Department of Environmental Epidemiology and Toxicology, and Rafat Shahid, director of Alameda County's Waste Management and Hazardous Materials Division. The meeting, which included 45 community residents, was conducted in English, Cantonese, and Spanish. While Goldman still refused the group's repeated request for the list of families tested in the initial study, she and Shahid did agree to release a map of areas with "known contamination" and to test 30 soil samples for lead contamination.

Initially, the response from county and state agencies appeared to be positive. The *Oakland Tribune* (July 18, 1990) wrote an article about the meeting: "A health group that correctly predicted Alameda County's measles epidemic is now pushing the county on a new front: lead poisoning." Between June and August 1990, organizing interns from CTWO's Minority Activist Apprenticeship Program (MAAP) worked with PUEBLO to conduct 23 Community Lead Action and Information Meetings (CLAIMS), reaching 472 people in four languages and mobilizing 35 community residents to picket Kears's office chanting, "David Kears, you can't hide, lead poisoning is genocide!"

The response from the state agencies, however, was more symbolic than real. Although the group's old nemesis David Kears promised to make free lead tests available, there was no place to conduct them and demands for lead tests at the local Children's Hospital brought bills of $60.00 per test for group members, despite federal regulations that required such tests be given free to low-income children under the Early Preventive Screening Diagnosis and Treatment Program (EPSDT).

In a similar vein, Shahid dragged his feet on the soil contamination tests, claiming that he didn't have the facilities. PUEBLO was forced to have the soil tested in facilities provided by the National Toxics Coalition (NTC) in Boston. Finally, in September 1990, city and county officials appeared to be sympathetic and agreed to meet with PUEBLO members to draft a plan for lead abatement.

The process was slow, however, and PUEBLO members were suspicious of the motivations of the elected officials. Organizer Susan Goetz recalls,

> On the one hand, the county was actually moving on the immunization outreach. They had continued the program, complete with bilingual billboards, and claimed credit for designing a proactive health care program. But in terms of doing anything about lead, they were completely lame. There were lots of meetings, but the county refused to *do* anything. It became clear to the members of the negotiating team that the lead abatement meetings were just set up to keep us quiet. (personal communication, January 1992)

■ Developing Internal Organization

Probably the most important events in PUEBLO's development between June 1990 and February 1991 were internal. First, Francis Calpotura was voted into the codirectorship of the Center for Third World Organizing and Sandra Davis was chosen by the PUEBLO organizing committee to replace him as lead organizer of PUEBLO. Like Calpotura, Davis was a new kind of organizer. A graduate of the MAAP program, Davis had spent a good deal of her upbringing in Germany, as 1 of 4 children in a black-white, biracial family. A graduate of Evergreen College and an ardent feminist, Davis brought to the organizing process a strong sense of the potential role of women as well as the conviction that a major component of community organizing should be the development of political consciousness.

When she took the PUEBLO lead organizer position in September 1990, Davis's perception of the main tasks for the months ahead was twofold: On the one hand, she had to develop the capacity of the organization to successfully address the issue of lead contamination, while, on the other, she had to develop the leadership and structure of the group. While external development would focus on the organization's ability to "cut the issue" and present a viable solution, exploiting the weaknesses of state and local governmental agencies, the internal development would include building relationships among people from the same ethnic groups and between different language groups. In addition, the organization needed to develop a decision-making process that represented the broad range of concerns of all of the various constituencies.

At times, these two objectives ran at cross-purposes. For example, meetings of neighborhood committees of the group would often be conducted in the predominant language of the committee: Spanish, English, Vietnamese, and Mien, while leadership council meetings were often translated from English. Therefore, while the separate meetings would often result in strategic agreements for members of a particular language group, each group's position had to be renegotiated at the leadership council meetings. On the other hand, when decisions were made by all language groups together, meetings that for one group might take $1\frac{1}{2}$ hours would often take up to 4 hours to develop agreement and collective understanding. In short, while both of these processes were very democratic, they tended also to be both time consuming and cumbersome.

This lengthy decision-making process was to prove difficult for some English-speaking members of the organization who had had the ability to make fairly quick and decisive strategic decisions in the initial mobilization strategies of the measles campaign. In fact, the decision-making process led to tensions between some members of the organization whose primary language was English and those for whom English was a second language. While the organization had a commitment to a multicultural leadership structure, in the words of CTWO training director Alfredo DeAvila, "Sometimes you could just feel the impatience . . . multiculturalism is a hard row to hoe, and people are simply not used to taking the time to make sure that everyone has a common understanding of what the options are" (personal communication, September 1991).

When questioned about the structure of the organization, PUEBLO spokeswomen Gwen Hardy replied, "Actually, the structure works pretty well. It was *getting* the structure together that was a killer. Now that we've got some trust between us, the only problem we really have is getting new people to feel comfortable in the group." Hardy's analysis is echoed by PUEBLO's lead organizer, Sandra Davis, who observed:

> Building the structure was relatively easy, once we'd built trust among the members. Some of my earliest activities were organizing potlucks and small discussion groups, so people could get to know one another. Once people began to be comfortable with each other, as people, they began to make suggestions not only about how we could structure the organization or how we could beat the city council, but on how we should arrange the office and what color the stationary should be . . . that's when I knew that people were really into being a part of PUEBLO. (personal communication, January 1992)

In addition to developing the group's internal social relations, Davis also worked with the group to develop an analysis of what they would have to do to win their demand for a lead abatement ordinance. By the winter of 1990, it was clear to the group's leadership council that, for their ordinance to stand a chance, there had to be significant mobilization of support in at least three sectors: (a) additional members of the primary constituency who lived outside the target areas, (b) the press, and (c) middle-class professional and church groups. In addition, political opposition had to be neutralized. With these objectives in mind, Davis worked with the organizing committee to formulate a strategy that included plans for deeper outreach in Oakland's Latino community, outreach to potential supporters (such as legal and health professionals), and intensive lobbying of city and county elected officials to continue pressure.

Implementing these strategies between November 1990 and May 1991, PUEBLO organized a series of activities, which included the following: the hiring of a Spanish-speaking organizer to conduct house meetings and after-church meetings with members of the Latino community; the development of three outreach meetings specifically designed to gain support of health and legal professionals; formal endorsement of PUEBLO's lead abatement plan by 23 churches in Oakland; and meetings with all members of the Oakland City Council and the Alameda County Board of Supervisors to gain support for PUEBLO's lead abatement proposal.

Added to these actions, PUEBLO also pursued a legal strategy by joining with the ACLU, the Natural Resources Defense Fund, the NAACP Legal Defense and Education Fund, and several legal services programs in suing the California Department of Health and Human Services, charging that the state had failed to enforce the federal requirements for lead testing.

While all of these actions were incrementally important, probably the initiative that proved most significant in reaching PUEBLO's objectives was a full-page ad placed by the organization in the May 22, 1991, edition of the *Oakland Tribune*. Titled "How Long Will Oakland Let Children Be Poisoned?" the ad addressed "fence-sitting" city council members and urged readers to call the city council and to "tell our leaders to get the lead out!" The ordinance passed without a "nay" vote.

■ Key Factors for Successful Campaign Initiatives

While it is true that PUEBLO's organizing success could be accounted for by examining the traditional factors that contribute to winning community organizing campaigns, there were a number of both internal and external factors that affected the outcomes in both of the PUEBLO campaigns. These factors included the following: (a) how research was used in developing the campaign efforts, (b) the role the organizers played in developing the organization, (c) the organization's ability to use national connections and exploit shifts in political context, and (d) the group's strategic mobilization of key constituencies.

Research in the Organizing Campaigns

Neither of PUEBLO's campaign efforts would have been possible without a combination of background and site-specific research. In the measles campaign, it was the research hypothesis that low-income communities had inadequate access to health care that framed the community survey that launched the campaign. The stimulus for the lead campaign, in turn, was the analysis of a state report on lead contamination. Much of the local data, collected door to door, was linked to national studies conducted by environmental advocacy organizations as well as by the Centers for Disease Control. The speculation by the initial organizers of the Campaign for Accessible Healthcare that immigrant communities were underimmunized was borne out when outbreaks occurred in Fresno, Stockton, San Francisco, and San Bernardino in addition to Oakland.

PUEBLO's research work, however, was not limited to survey or background research. To motivate county officials to conduct outreach programs in low-income immigrant communities, PUEBLO's organizing committee had to develop a sophisticated understanding of the funding bases of state and county agencies.

"Target" research was conducted in both campaigns to inform the membership of the background, strengths, and weaknesses of decision makers in both appointed and elected positions. Finally, PUEBLO staff members conducted legislative research, examining lead abatement ordinances from five states, before designing a comprehensive legislative package, which included testing of children, homes, and public areas; abatement and treatment; and a funding mechanism based on an assessment per household and taxes on industries that produce leaded products.

While research is a necessary component in an organizing campaign, it is not in itself sufficient to resolve an issue or to change relations of power. For that, it takes organization. And the biggest challenge for the organizers was not coordinating the research, it was building the organization.

The Role of the Organizer

In an atomized society such as this, difference is shunned; action, when taken at all, is individual; and the notion of a democratic process is reduced to bureaucratized forms of "citizen participation." A successful community organizing campaign, which requires respect for constituent differences, interdependency, and collective planning and action, is, in terms of societal norms, a series of "unnatural acts."

To develop such a campaign, organizers must not only have a commitment to societal change, they must also have a set of unusual sensitivities and skills and the ability to develop creative methods to encourage people who have had negative experiences with "public life" to think and to act. Earlier I mentioned that both Francis Calpotura and Sandra Davis were part of a new breed of organizers possessing these skills and sensitivities. What is it about their backgrounds that assisted them, and how were these skills and sensitivities evidenced in specific situations?

First, countering the prevailing wisdom that the best organizers emerge from "the community," Davis and Calpotura were both "outsiders." Both had spent a significant portion of their formative years abroad, and they both had to struggle to legitimate their identities in a U.S. context: Calpotura as an immigrant and Davis as a biracial woman. In addition, Calpotura's background in the anti-Marcos movement and Davis's experiences in the students' and women's movements had infused both of them with a clear set of political ideals. Added to these ideals was the analytical and skills training both received through the Center for Third World Organizing. CTWO had an eclectic approach to training organizers, which included exposure to most of the major organizing approaches advocated by various networks in the United States as well as a healthy dose of analytical sessions that examined race, class, and gender dynamics in community struggles in Asia, Africa, and Latin America.

Working in a multiracial setting, PUEBLO organizers had to develop an organizing model or approach that worked in new immigrant communities, as well as established communities of color, and that could effectively challenge the established sociopolitical structure without immediately being smashed. As I discussed earlier, one of the key skills needed in internal development is the organizer's ability to create an atmosphere of trust in which a structure reflective of diverse communities could emerge. In addition, a number of other factors are important for successful internal development in a multiracial organization, including the ability to (a) put into practice outreach methods that can be effective in a variety of communities and (b) create an approach for the development of the analytical prowess of the organization's leadership and membership that is not the "laying on of ideology."

Over the course of 2 years, both PUEBLO organizers employed a variety of contact and mobilization strategies to reach and organize their primary and secondary constituencies. The initial interview with key actors is an approach most often used in institutional or church-based organizing. The building of contacts through existing agencies or organizations is mostly used by organizers wishing to build coalitions, while house meetings have traditionally been used by both the United Farmworkers to build boycott committees and the National Abortion Rights Action League (NARAL) to develop primary leadership. In addition to these techniques, PUEBLO organizers also used presentation and lobbying tactics to develop endorsements—an approach most often employed in political campaigns.

While it may seem like simple common sense to use different techniques to contact people from different social strata, such an approach is not often used. Each outreach technique is attached to a theory about the social change potential of a particular constituency. So, for example, some organizers who organize very poor people use either door knocking or house meetings, because they would argue that there are no institutions that "truly" represent the interests of the poor. Conversely, organizers who do church-based organizing would claim to be able to tap a Judeo-Christian ethic through which they can reach a social justice value base. Still others would assert that the mobilization of middle-class professionals through their associations was the "most correct" approach because middle-class people have the most political and economic legitimacy. A clear strength in the PUEBLO case was that the organizers were willing, in the words of Francis Calpotura, to "figure out and use whatever approach seemed most appropriate for the constituency." This "pragmatic flexibility" allowed them to use a variety of approaches and work with a broad spectrum of people to achieve the organization's ends.

Regarding PUEBLO's development, I've described the formal organizational structure. To understand more fully the internal dynamics of the organization, however, it is necessary to examine the membership's political development. Sandra Davis had a specific interest in the systematic development of the analytical abilities and leadership skills of PUEBLO members. To this end, Davis organized two initiatives. First, she recruited members to attend CTWO's Saturday School, a 6-week skills training seminar for leaders of Bay Area community and labor organizations. In the Saturday School, PUEBLO leaders met welfare rights activists, organizers from immigrant rights groups in San Francisco and San Jose, student activists from San Francisco State University, and gay and lesbian organizers from ACT UP.

This exposure to a variety of both people and issues was in itself valuable to PUEBLO members. Davis supplemented it with bimonthly Wednesday night issue discussions, however, which gave members an opportunity to watch films or hear speakers and to get into lively debates on important social issues. Organizing intern Josue Guillen describes the sessions:

> At first people didn't know what to expect, so only a few people came. But after the first two sessions, the war in the Persian Gulf started and almost 30 people showed up to hear a representative from one of the Arab organizations. That one got really hot, since a lot of people had relatives

in the Gulf. After that, we scheduled them about every 2 weeks and we've always had 10-15 people, good discussion and great food . . . great food helps. (personal communication, September 1991)

Thus it was a combination of formal skills training, exposure to other social movement activists, and structured internal discussions that developed a leadership core in PUEBLO able to envision and develop a multiracial organization with broad-based representation.

The organizers' pragmatic flexibility in their approach to building an organization, coupled with perseverance in their efforts to develop a structure that reflected the composition of the community and the construction of a program to develop the skills and analytical capacity of the membership, were all important variables in developing the organization. This internal development might have been for naught, however, without an additional set of abilities: the capacity to take advantage of shifts in the political terrain.

Exploiting Shifts in the Political Context

Though PUEBLO's organizing and research efforts were thorough and timely, the group's efforts might not have made a difference without the development of three additional factors: (a) increased national awareness of health care issues, (b) the definition of lead poisoning as an environmental concern for low-income communities of color by both government bodies and the national media, and (c) PUEBLO's ability to work with an emergent coalition of organizations of people of color created to address environmental issues.

Probably the most obvious indicator of an increased national awareness of health care issues is the recent development of a critical mass of organizations and individuals lobbying for national health insurance. There were other indicators that health care was rising on people's list of primary concerns, however, both nationally and in California. As early as June 1989, a statewide, California-based group called Children Now! released a report that gave California a "D" in children's health care ("California Receives," 1989). This report dovetailed with a December 1989 UNICEF report, which found that conditions for poor children were deteriorating in the United States and Great Britain. Just prior to the Campaign for Accessible Healthcare's first action, local papers had reported inadequate emergency room facilities and a general lack of personnel.

Coupled with these general problems in health care, both issues that PUEBLO zeroed in on—measles and lead poisoning—had been foreshadowed by reports in the national media. A story in *USA Today* in September 1989 ("1989 Measles") predicted that measles case totals could be higher in 1989 alone than in the previous 9 years, while an editorial in *The New York Times* in May 1989, titled "The Shame of Measles," added credibility to the campaign's claims of underimmunization and their prediction of an outbreak.

Similarly, awareness of the dangers of lead poisoning was also reaching the national press at around the same time that PUEBLO began raising the issue in Oakland. Recognition of the toxic effects of lead, in particular, was long overdue. Over the last 30 years, researchers have continually lowered the level of exposure regarded as harmful, from 60 milligrams per deciliter of blood in the early 1960s to 25 in the 1970s, down to 10 by November 1991.

In a *New York Times* story ("U.S. Opens," 1990), Dr. William Roper, director of the Centers for Disease Control, called lead poisoning "the no. 1 environmental problem facing America's children." A follow-up story in the February 25, 1991, issue of *Time* magazine refers to lead poisoning as the "most severe environmental disease in this country" ("Lead and Your Kids," 1991).

The shift in awareness of both of these health problems added legitimacy to PUEBLO's assertion that they were problems in low-income neighborhoods in Oakland and added credibility to the organization's demands that local officials take action. As Rowena Pineda, a PUEBLO organizing intern said, "It was one thing when we were the only ones who saw the problem. But after we told them that the measles outbreak was going to hit and we got state and federal reports that explained how big a problem lead was, we were at least getting heard" (personal communication, January 1992).

PUEBLO's relationship to other environmental organizations such as the Southwest Organizing Project and the National Toxics Coalition flowed from the group's relationship with the Center for Third World Organizing. Through these relationships, PUEBLO was able to gain access to important research findings, recruit student volunteers, and meet with a wide variety of activists across the country.

One of the CTWO connections had particular significance in linking PUEBLO to a broader coalition of activists of color. At the same time that a national awareness about the importance of health care issues was emerging, activists from communities of color were launching an effort geared to challenge the tendencies of white environmental organizations to ignore the environmental concerns in communities of color: tendencies called "environmental racism." Initiated by Richard Moore of the Southwest Organizing Project in Albuquerque, New Mexico, the effort, on the one hand, charged the largest environmental organizations with "an equal role in disrupting our communities" and, on the other, joined together a coalition of environmental organizations in communities of color to fight toxic dumping.

These efforts were significant not only because of the attempt to reform national environmental organizations and coalesce local communities of color but also because also of the financial resources available for environmental organizing. Francis Calpotura, who did the initial fund-raising for PUEBLO, observed, "When we were talking about immigrants and lead poisoning, only a small number of progressive funders were interested in our work. When lead poisoning suddenly was seen by funders as part of an 'environmental' agenda, we were finally able to move some money" (personal communication, January 1992).

Mobilization Strategies

A key problem for community organizers is how to use mobilization strategies to present the organization and its demands in the best possible light, before the broadest spectrum of people. Mobilization strategies must first assess the vulnerability of decision makers as well as who and what will influence them. After the assessment, the organization will strategically mobilize their primary constituency, borrow legitimacy from individuals or organizations with societal legitimacy, and present a positive case through third parties such as the electronic or print media.

Over the course of 2 years, PUEBLO organizers had a number of opportunities to implement strategic mobilizations. In an early attempt to mobilize public sympathy around underimmunization and announce the initial community survey, the Campaign for Accessible Healthcare sent out press releases to several Bay Area California newspapers. The results were mixed. In the "ethnic press," newspapers that predominantly serve the African American, Filipino, and Latino communities, all three papers reported that minority or immigrant children were at risk for childhood diseases. While most of the area's major newspapers simply ignored the campaign's release, one, *The San Francisco Chron-*

icle, filed a completely inaccurate story titled "Program to Immunize East Bay Minority Kids" ("Program," 1989) implying that the campaign's survey had the ability to provide inoculations.

As the organization matured, and staff and leaders received training in press relations from the Public Media Center, a San Francisco-based public interest media organization, the ability of the leaders and staff to influence the tone of news stories increased. Of the 34 newspaper stories reporting on the measles campaign that are archived at the PUEBLO office, only 6 could be characterized as negative. Of the 73 articles archived on the lead campaign, only 3 had a distinctly negative tone in reference to the lead abatement program. So successful was the organization's press work that a number of newspaper stories were published about the ad that the organization took out in the *Oakland Tribune*, urging the Oakland City Council to "get the lead out."

Another dimension of mobilizing public sentiment through the press was the use of public events to make the group's point. PUEBLO either spoke at, disrupted, or upstaged a range of public events including public hearings, city council meetings, town hall meetings, and installation ceremonies. The campaign was also adept at developing dramatic media events. These included sponsoring candidate forums in the mayoral campaign, press conferences at contaminated playgrounds, a group of 30 children with sand buckets demanding tests for contaminated soil, and the shutting down of two city office buildings.

PUEBLO also directly mobilized secondary constituents to act on the organization's behalf. The principles employed by PUEBLO in these strategic mobilizations were simple. Campaign staff and leaders would assess what message needed to be delivered, what the best time to deliver the message was, and who the appropriate messenger was. Following these principles, Catholic schools were mobilized to issue a measles alert before the public schools. Pastors and ministers supported the campaign by writing endorsement letters for PUEBLO's demands, letting members speak from the pulpit, and speaking on behalf of the group at city council meetings. Special committees of doctors and lawyers conducted letter writing campaigns, testified at city council meetings, and provided a local donor base for the campaign.

Language differences were also used to the group's advantage. Often the group would have a monolingual spokeswoman address the city council to make the point about language differences, and negotiations with the police during actions were also often conducted by monolingual speakers. In addition, because the victims of both measles and lead poisoning were very often young people, a separate youth brigade, Youth of Oakland (YOU), was developed to articulate young people's views. Thus, by developing a clear understanding of the skills and levels of access of the organization's primary and secondary supporters, and accessing the susceptibility of decision makers to hear and act on their messages, PUEBLO was able to project the organization's message to large numbers of people through a variety of credible channels.

■ The Shape of Things to Come

In writing about the development of PUEBLO, three things struck me as particularly significant. First, the complexity of the issues are little short of astounding. Twenty years ago, an organizer could mobilize a sizable number of people who could point out a problem and say to the state, "Fix it." Seven out of ten times, the group would get some action, not necessarily the action the group wanted, but some relief, nonetheless. In the 1980s, with fiscal cutbacks, it became harder and harder for groups to demand and get benefits. Solutions for issues also became less simple as toxic dumping proliferated, unregulated banks mired in financial crises sucked up the public surplus, and service cutbacks put hundreds of thousands of people on the streets and deprived millions of health benefits. In the case of PUEBLO, neither of the organization's efforts would have been successful without both access to national networks and a tremendous amount of research. If all local community organizations have to expend the research efforts that PUEBLO had to put forth to resolve a local issue, community organizing is in serious trouble, because the resources simply are not there.

Second, media attention was inordinately important to the organization's efforts. Had the press decided not to pay attention to PUEBLO's campaigns, the organization would not have been able to mobilize sufficient secondary support to win its demands. This was particularly true in the lead campaign. It was only extensive cultivation of local press contacts, including feeding them a series of national stories increasing the significance of PUEBLO's work, that made a difference. Without the sophisticated intervention of the Public Media Center assisting PUEBLO in press relations, the local press might have ignored the organization's efforts.

The third set of factors, while internal to PUEBLO, have implications for community, labor, and other progressive formations. PUEBLO's organizers spent a great deal of time creating an inclusive infrastructure that reflected the composition of the community. Through the organization, they also addressed the needs and interests of communities of color, particularly immigrants, a sector of society who have the least power and who are blamed for everything.

In conclusion, I would note that there are many factors that predict the success or failure of a particular organization's campaign effort. Clearly, one is the skill level and sophistication of the organizers, coupled with their ability to take advantage of shifts in the political context. Organizers, then, not only must have mastered the technical skills of constituent mobilization, they must also have decisive analytical skills, a commitment to create egalitarian relations within the organization, and the ability to teach. The availability of resources, including personnel and financial, access to media, and the specifics of resource development, affect the general development of the organization. These sets of variables are subject to a variety of external factors.

There is one internal variable that organizations have control over, however, that will be increasingly important in community struggles: the ability to build inclusive organizations. Ultimately, it will be the willingness of community and labor organizations to build multiracial alliances that address the interests of low-income people of color that will determine America's future—and the shape of things to come.

REFERENCES

Adamson, M., & Delgado, G. (1988). Deadly neglect: Childhood immunization in the Reagan era. *The Minority Trendsletter, 1*(4).

Bay Area's racial mixture is U.S. wave of future. (1992, December 4). *Oakland Tribune.*

California receives grade of "D" in study of children's condition. (1989, June 29). *The New York Times.*

Center for Third World Organizing. (1988, November). [Board memo]. Oakland: Author.

County declares measles emergency . . . free immunizations at ten clinics on Saturday morning. (1990, April 4). *San Jose Mercury News.*

Economy makes quiet comeback. (1991, August 26). *The San Francisco Chronicle.*

Epstein, B. (1990, January-March). Rethinking social movement theory. *Socialist Review, 20.*

Get the lead out of children. (1989, July 7). [Editorial]. *Oakland Tribune.*

Health officials ignoring measles outbreak danger, group says. (1989, November 30). *Oakland Tribune.*

Lead and your kids. (1991, July 15). *Newsweek.*

Lead poses health risk to 6 million children. (1990, July 19). *San Francisco Examiner.*

Measles alert . . . It's out of control says health official. (1990, March 8). *Oakland Tribune.*

1989 measles totals may be highest in 80s. (1989, September). *USA Today.*

Oakland leads in office space vacancies. (1991, March 28). *Oakland Tribune.*

Oakland: New generation of leaders believe in city's future. (1991, January 7). *Los Angeles Times.*

Program to immunize East Bay minority kids. (1989, January 27). *The San Francisco Chronicle.*

Rabin, R. (1985, July/August). Silent epidemic. *Science for the People.*

Retail jobs lost as firms leave Oakland. (1991, April 9). *Oakland Tribune.*

The shame of measles. (1990, May 22). [Editorial]. *The New York Times.*

State's kids still exposed to lead. (1990, December 9). *San Francisco Examiner.*

U.S. opens a drive on lead poisoning in nation's young. (1990, December 19). *The New York Times.*

Why young children are so vulnerable to lead. (1990, November 1). *The New York Times.*

6 Keep on Keeping On: Organizing for Welfare Rights in Massachusetts

BETTY REID MANDELL
ANN WITHORN

During the late 1960s and early 1970s, the National Welfare Rights Organization (NWRO) provided the core structure for a powerful welfare rights movement. All over the country, but especially in northern cities, poor women organized. They organized, first, simply to stop what they saw as ill treatment from welfare workers. Then they organized to change rules that made it impossible for them to survive. Next, they began making local, state, and even national-level demands for more benefits. Finally, their efforts were instrumental in leading Congress to consider a guaranteed national income and, ultimately, to reject President Nixon's Family Assistance Plan (FAP).[1]

What happened to this movement? Has the driving goal of "welfare rights" survived into the 1990s? This chapter examines the major strategic questions facing welfare rights organizing today in the United States. It focuses on the history of welfare rights efforts, in general, and efforts in Massachusetts, in particular, where a statewide welfare rights organization has been in place since the mid-1970s and where we have both been involved. And it speculates on the theoretical viability and future of welfare rights as a social movement focus for the 1990s.

We live in an era where "old" class-based social movements are said to be disappearing, where "new" social movements organized around issues of gender and race expand as well as fragment social activism. A central question here is this: What does this mean for a welfare rights social movement organized around claims against the state made by poor women who are disproportionately black and Latino?

■ The Ground on Which We Stand: The History of National Welfare Rights Organizing

The predecessors of the welfare rights movement were the organizations created by unemployed workers in major cities around the country during the 1930s. They demanded "relief" as well as pensions and jobs. They struggled to create mutual aid networks, hosted militant demonstrations, and negotiated directly with the state for assistance.[2] But it was not until the 1960s that women who were receiving state aid organized themselves in their own name and tried both to get more benefits and to increase the numbers of women applying for public relief in the name of citizen's (and later women's) rights. It took the spirit of the civil rights movement, moved into the fray of northern cities, seasoned with the reemergence of women's rights, to yield a vital and creative "welfare rights" movement.

The history of the NWRO and the first welfare rights movement has been well documented. In addition to the broad analyses offered by Guida West, Frances Fox Piven, and Richard Cloward, several useful "case studies" of local welfare rights efforts exist.[3] These historical portraits yield a picture of early organizations that were vibrant, militant, and serious in their critique of the U.S. welfare system. Women initially formed local groups out of frustration with treatment from local welfare departments and desire for mutual support. Often assisted by middle-class organizers, their anger and energy propelled them into noisy, public conflicts with local and state authorities. The structures that quickly formed to channel this intense energy were classic "movement organizations"—loosely disciplined, poorly funded, and situated on the margins of local poverty programs, church social justice committees, and other liberal groups. Women who emerged as local leaders were often strong personalities who became controversial figures in their own communities.

By the early 1970s the role of the National Welfare Rights Organization had become more pronounced, and local organizing efforts began to follow a national strategy. Nevertheless, organizing became more difficult as state and county welfare departments learned better how to routinize benefits and limit worker discretion, so that one critical focus of early organizing—its attack on the arbitrary allotment of benefits—was reduced. With the death in 1973 of NWRO founder George Wiley and the defeat of the Family Assistance Plan, the national focus of the welfare rights movement quickly collapsed. The movement splintered into remnants, with some areas losing any organizational form, while others maintained small organizations that struggled to retain at least a "watchdog" role in regard to state programs and to organize around particularly offensive policies.

Leaders moved on, some into advocacy or service jobs that could be considered "co-opting," but most simply into other stages of busy lives. In Boston, for example, a few early leaders attended college and became social service workers, while others became involved in different aspects of community organizing as their children grew up. Some national contacts were maintained, but it was not until the 1987 founding of the National Welfare Rights Union (NWRU) that the goal of a national welfare rights movement was revived.[4]

The National Welfare Rights Union was formed through the combined efforts of a national network of local welfare rights groups, advocacy and religious groups from different states, and several national left organizations. Its strategies include national networking, militant direct action, and electoral campaigns. In cooperation with the National Union of the Homeless, NWRU groups squat in abandoned buildings, particularly those owned by HUD, and then rehabilitate them for poor people. They organize "Survival Summits" where each member state can set its own agenda for the movement and develop strategy and theory. One of the main platforms these groups have adopted is a national extension of the "Up and Out of Poverty Now" campaign begun in Massachusetts. They also attempt to get more favorable media coverage of welfare as well as operating a "Fraud Watch," to counter the witch-hunt style welfare fraud investigations that have intensified throughout the country.[5] But in the face of the national antiwelfare measures and increasingly punitive policies that accompanied budget cuts in most states in the Reagan-Bush years, attempts to build a strong national welfare rights movement have been unsuccessful.

■ Welfare Organizing at the Grass Roots: The Massachusetts Example

The history of welfare rights organizing in Massachusetts embodies all the basic problems facing welfare rights activists since the demise of the NWRO. During the late 1960s and early 1970s, the earliest group, Mothers for Adequate Welfare (MAW), and the local NWRO chapter

(MWRO) organized many women on welfare to fight for their rights. The extent of their influence can be seen in decisions of most local community action agencies at the time to provide some support for welfare rights activity within Head Start and other poverty programs. Indeed, "welfare rights" became a basic principle of progressive organizers in many areas of domestic politics: legal services, health care, child care. In response to the constant organizing around special needs, in the early 1970s the governor adopted a "Flat Grant," ostensibly so that more than "squeaky wheels" could receive discretionary and seasonal benefits. In fact, the measure pulled the rug out from under organizers. Without any payoff for confrontations at local welfare offices, the logic for "militant" action faded, and the organizations that remained were neither stable nor supportive enough to maintain themselves without a target from which "victories" could be immediately won.[6]

So by 1975, despite their indisputable influence in the large advocacy and "progressive" communities in Boston, both original groups were functionally defunct. The leader of MAW, Lillie Landrum, and other MWRO activists were still around to speak out at hearings and to serve on advisory boards, but there was no functioning grass-roots welfare rights organization. This vacuum posed an immediate problem for many of the advocates who had supported the idea of welfare rights and who were then working in various poverty and advocacy agencies concerned with poor people's issues. The basic principle such activists had learned from the recent past was that poor people should speak for themselves. How could progressives, who were not receiving aid, fight for welfare rights in the legislature and within the state bureaucracy without an organization of welfare recipients to set the goals and increase pressure?

The self-conscious attempt of activists and welfare recipients to forge an answer to this question in the mid-1970s has set the pattern for welfare organizing in Massachusetts since. Briefly, the short-lived state-level federal poverty agency started to organize welfare recipients. This effort was quickly given over to a progressive community planning organization that received state and federal money to plan and advocate for poor people. A paid organizer made overtures to local poverty programs and to a small group of welfare recipients, many of whom were students at the University of Massachusetts in Boston. These eagerly started a statewide organization, the Coalition for Basic Human Needs (CBHN), with the mandate to organize, educate, and advocate for welfare rights. From the beginning, the CBHN eschewed self-help and individual advocacy in favor of a broader focus on educating, mobilizing, and affecting state welfare policy and practice.[7] Between 1976 and 1979 the new group lost all state funding and established itself as an independent organization supported through a variety of grants and fund-raising efforts. It emerged as a victorious leader within the broad coalition of labor and social service groups that defeated conservative Governor Edward King's 1979 effort to institute a harsh workfare plan. During Dukakis's second and third gubernatorial administrations (1982-1990), the group assumed statewide leadership again in a coalition to bring welfare benefits "Up and Out of Poverty" and to establish and monitor the state's Employment and Training Program.[8] Recently, as the state economy collapsed and a new governor heightened attacks on state social expenditures, the CBHN has been involved in active efforts to fight cutbacks in basic benefits.

In addition to the CBHN's various chapters, somewhat independent but affiliated groups have grown up in western Massachusetts (ARISE) and at the University of Massachusetts at Boston (ARMS). ARMS focuses on educating and training university students and community people, often providing independent study credit for welfare rights activism at the university.[9] ARMS members have joined with others to found a forum for their ideas in *Survival News*, a national newspaper for, about, and partially by low-income women. Many of the contributors are welfare claimants who not only talk about their own experiences but also develop a theoretical perspective about those experiences.

Over the years, the national network of welfare rights activists has become more cohesive. Membership has become more situated in local chapters, and the percentage of nonwhite, nonstudent members has increased dramatically. The CBHN has been a part of this network and has worked closely with other groups, such as the Massachusetts Law Reform Institute. The MLRI helped win a monumental victory in forcing Massachusetts, through the courts, to study the actual needs of claimants and to set a realistic "standard of need," even though the legislature could not be forced to provide funding up to that standard. But, while statewide welfare rights organizing has continued almost unbroken in Massachusetts since the 1960s, structural constraints and internal issues, including questions about the very salience of welfare rights organizing, pose formidable barriers. The experience of organizers and activists in Massachusetts offers a strong base from which to examine the strategic and tactical problems facing welfare rights activists today.

■ Strategic Questions for a Welfare Rights Movement

Not everyone agrees on the value of welfare rights organizing. For many radicals, organizing welfare recipients to claim their rights from the state has been a problematic strategy. They doubt whether poor women should even try to organize themselves in a claimants' movement. Many civil rights activists in the 1960s initially questioned whether it helped the cause to link blacks with welfare. More recently, some activists from African American and Latino communities have questioned whether welfare has not been more of a trap than a "benefit" for their people, arguing that "community development" strategies have more potential. Many feminists have also shied away from strong identification with welfare rights, either because of their desire to link women's concerns to those of women in the workplace and traditional families or out of more radical frustrations with the state and the "dependence" it demands even from militant recipients.[10]

For similar reasons, Marxist organizers often emphasized a "class-based strategy"—to draw women on welfare into working-class alliances for jobs, not to isolate them by association with welfare programs that are inherently stigmatized from a "workers'" perspective. The current version of this argument can be seen in social-democratic demands for political realism. Thus progressive intellectuals such as Theda Skocpol and William Julius Wilson call for "universal" programs—appealing to the middle class—over demands for "welfare rights" as a policy strategy.[11]

Within the welfare rights movement, however, demands for welfare rights are seen as arguments for the fullest extension of universal economic rights. Nonoppressive programs must be developed that will allow women to support their families as single parents, even during times when they are not employed. Welfare rights activists argue that to define anything less as a social goal is not universal, nor does it address the needs of poor women—who are also working class. Of course, special attention must still be given to how problems associated with racism and sexism are addressed.

Yet even the strongest supporters of welfare rights movements recognize profound strategic problems and theoretical tensions. What is the most effective organizing "model" for building a welfare rights movement? What about empowerment issues, coalition building, electoral strategies, the welfare state as the focus of a movement, and race and gender dynamics? Each of these, discussed below, illustrates the problems and potential in welfare rights organizing.

Organizational Form

There are two dominant approaches to welfare rights organizing. Frances Fox Piven and Richard Cloward have argued that mobilizing poor people is best done by cadre (professional organizers) when the social and political climate is ripe. They argue that, as the only power poor people possess is that of militant protest and disruption, they should mobilize massive numbers of people to disrupt and demand changes in normal bureaucratic functioning, as people did during the welfare rights movement of the 1960s and early 1970s. They also see the major focus of poor people's organizing as the state, because that is "where people meet" and where collective demands can be made.[12]

Most of the National Welfare Rights Organization did not adopt Piven and Cloward's strategy of reaching out to unenrolled people as a way to expand expectations of the state, however. Instead, they militantly organized to get larger grants for the people who were already enrolled in AFDC. Local chapters also varied in how closely they followed the mobilization by cadre approach. Perhaps the Boston MWRO followed this model most fully.

Sociologist and movement supporter Guida West calls the Cloward and Piven approach the "Boston model." In opposition to this "mobilizing" model, she sets forth what she calls the "Johnnie Tilmon model," after the founder of the early welfare rights group in California. The Tilmon model argues for creating permanent organizations, formed and maintained by poor people themselves, as the most effective way to achieve change in their lives, their communities, and the state. West argues that these self-help groups create ties of solidarity among AFDC women, develop a sense of community, and provide a vehicle for women to meet their own needs such as for child care, welfare advocacy, mutual advice, and emotional support. At the same time, such groups can be most effective in organizing for changes in the welfare system because they are internally more cohesive. The self-help model also challenges the professionalization of organizing—by insisting that even militant campaigns can best be led by poor women themselves, not by a cadre of professional organizers sent from outside the community.[13]

Many welfare rights groups combine features of both these models. The Brooklyn Welfare Action Council (BWAC), which lasted from 1969 to 1973, was the largest chapter of the National Welfare Rights Organization (constituting 40% of their membership), for example. In its early days, BWAC members engaged in militant confrontational tactics. But after setbacks in the early 1970s, the members abandoned disruptive tactics and turned more toward building the organization, advocacy, and self-help training programs.[14]

Cloward and Piven argued that BWAC reached or passed its utility when it left the streets, abandoned disruptive tactics, and became a dues paying organization.[15] Pope agrees that the group made fewer gains when it abandoned confrontational tactics, but she argues that confrontation is not enough, that disenfranchised people need more organizational support to explore the full dynamics of political process. We agree. Welfare rights must be a strategy developed and led by poor people, especially women, in their own organizations. One hopes that the times and the leadership will create as militant a strategy as possible, but, at the least, women need their own organizations if they are to experience collective and individual progress.

Empowerment

Anyone who has worked with a welfare rights group can cite numerous examples of individual women who have "found themselves" through their involvement with the organization. The validation and recognition that come to many participants, for the first time in their lives, are truly moving. Pope tells of the welfare rights organizers in BWAC who are still active in their communities 20 years later. Theresa Funiciello, a leader of the Downtown Welfare Advocate Center, said that "people who spent time with BWAC became transformed."[16] In Boston, we both know dozens of successful women who speak, like former recipient Janet Diamond, of the powerful lessons they learned "as a permanent member of the sorority" of welfare mothers.[17]

Without organizing themselves, it is easy for welfare claimants to internalize the stigma that society has placed on them, so the work of combating those "welfare myths" within its members, as well as the broader public, has always been a major goal of welfare rights groups. Organizers and advocates have learned the rules of the bureaucracy to arm claimants against arbitrary treatment by the welfare department and also to convey the power and the privilege of advocating for others.

But if the individual empowerment that comes from being an effective advocate and organizer builds leadership, it may also lead many welfare rights groups to depend too much on their founding leaders and make it difficult to spread leadership more equally among the membership. When the leader leaves, many groups fall apart. Massachusetts groups have often struggled to fight the institutionalization of entrenched leadership and then found themselves frustrated by their dependence upon paid organizers who became the key people in the organization, by default. The CBHN has therefore also struggled constantly to articulate and achieve "collective," as opposed to individual, empowerment.[18]

To be effective, welfare rights efforts must be sensitive to the conflicts that emerge between the goals of collective and individual empowerment. Women on welfare are desperately poor. Many have absolutely no other resources than their grant checks, which are never enough. So women naturally come to movement organizations with personal empowerment goals—to gain power in bureaucratic disputes, some financial assistance, a job, or a means for individual change—that may undermine efforts for collective empowerment.[19] There is a significant tension here. One woman's "empowerment" may be another woman's opportunism, and the sum of all the struggles for individual empowerment may be internal explosion, not joint progress.

Under the right conditions, schools have proven good recruiting grounds for helping women on welfare to combine personal and collective empowerment. While these projects "cream from the top" women who are prepared for college-level work, a great power can emerge when women on welfare become students, a power that can work against the individualism and internal strife that often accompany narrow individual empowerment efforts within organizations. The CBHN itself originated with, and ARMS continues to be led by, the group of welfare claimants whom CBHN cofounder Jeanne Dever has dubbed the "lumpen intelligentsia." These are women who have attended college and have experienced a flowering of their intellect that transcends individual concerns.

Most welfare rights organizations, from Johnnie Tilmon's group to ARMS, continue to combine personal and collective empowerment. They give advice about how to cope with new rules and provide mutual support in myriad ways. Yet, this "self-help" function has remained problematic for many welfare rights activists. In the CBHN, as in most groups, efforts to solve individual problems have always been seen as overwhelming the need to keep the organizational focus on "making real change." Still, as with other social movements, the underlying connection between radical, collective social goals and individual service provision is difficult to bury.[20] People's hunger for recognition and mutual support is deep and insistent, and welfare rights groups continue to provide mutual aid and individual advocacy. The hard task is figuring out how to unite these activities with continued social confrontation.

Coalition Building

Welfare rights organizing faces a dilemma of, on the one hand, needing to heighten the dialogue and build coalitions between poor women and other progressives and, on the other, understanding that such coalition building can shift the focus from the problems that loom most immediately before welfare recipients.

Coalitions begin at home. A first question facing welfare rights organizations concerns how broadly to expand their own membership. Welfare rights groups have always debated whether to allow anyone other than current recipients to join. Most welfare rights groups have restricted their membership to welfare claimants, sometimes, as with the CBHN, even excluding people who have recently stopped receiving welfare. George Wiley had opposed such an exclusionary policy for the NWRO and argued, along with Piven and Cloward, that welfare rights organizations could increase their effectiveness by including the working poor, the aged, and other groups with similar interests. In response, the NWRO developed a "Friends of NWRO" category to include advocates who did not receive welfare.

As Guida West pointed out, tensions were generated in collaborative work between the very poor and the middle class in the NWRO.[21] Such tensions continue, although perhaps less intensely. The NWRU does allow former recipients into membership and does welcome advocates whom they trust at organizational meetings. Many local groups, however, are like the CBHN in their desire to open membership only to their own constituency and to work with nonrecipients only in more structured relationships.

The strongest coalition has been between welfare rights groups and legal services. Some welfare rights groups work out cooperative relationships with particular lawyers, as the CBHN has done successfully over time with the Massachusetts Law Reform Institute. In terms of other potential coalitions, however, efforts to move unions and working-class community groups to take up welfare issues have proven frustrating, given the general hostility of the working poor toward welfare. Alliances with public sector unions have been forged, but usually around policy concerns, not around improving the day-to-day interaction between recipients and workers. Even links to other groups of welfare state recipients—such as the elderly or disabled—have been hard to maintain, except as joint members of coalitions with a broader purpose—such as progressive tax policy or expanded health coverage. Joint activities are valuable but may not forge the deep alliances necessary before mutual mistrust can be addressed. When, for example, "the plight of the homeless" became an "in" topic in the early 1980s, public and private money became available. At the same time, welfare rights groups found themselves less able to capture funding and media attention. Welfare was "out." One strategy focused on the problem of homeless families on welfare and won some policy and media victories. But, again, the effort was difficult, not insignificantly because the style of some of the homeless organizers was more "male" than that of the welfare rights activists.[22] Similar, less dramatic conflicts have occurred when welfare rights activists tried to work with health care organizers, whose focus on expanding health care coverage for low-wage workers tended to overwhelm the constantly decreasing quality of the health care available through Medicaid.

But the prerequisite for any meaningful dialogue with other interests is to have an organizational welfare rights base, whether exclusive or not, so that individual welfare activists can effectively speak for other recipients in coalitions. Because coalitions around domestic issues seem inevitable in these times, organized groups of welfare recipients become a necessity. Indeed, in Massachusetts, the need of other advocate groups for "legitimate" voices from welfare recipients helped keep the CBHN alive. If welfare rights groups understand this dynamic, they may be able to make more effective claims on other advocacy groups for support.

Electoral Strategy

Electoral strategy can be seen as the newest way for welfare rights groups to create dialogue: It gives visibility and may heighten feelings of hope. One of the more recent strategies of the NWRU is to launch electoral efforts using the slogan, "Elect the Victims of Poverty." As part of this campaign, an ARMS and CBHN activist, Dorothy Stevens, ran for governor of Massachusetts in 1990. Still, there are reasons for doubt about the value of electoral politics. Electoral campaigns require an enormous amount of energy and resources, resources that might be better used for grass-roots organizing. And even if the electoral strategy makes some sense, at what levels of government should efforts be aimed?

On the positive side, political campaigns do have an empowering psychological effect on people who have been dispossessed from the electoral arena. They present another opportunity for getting welfare issues debated in the public realm. Yet confusion can develop regarding whether the aim is actually to win an office or merely to present a symbolic campaign for the purpose of getting the issues aired in a public forum. Clearly, Stevens had no chance of winning the governorship, yet the campaign claimed to believe that it had a chance to win—if not in 1990, then in a subsequent election. She was successful in getting national media attention on the *Donahue* and *Sally Jessy Raphael* shows and in some newspapers, but the local media trivialized her campaign by putting it in the "Living Pages" section when they covered it. And both television shows slanted the presentation in such a way that prevailing stereotypes were as much reinforced as challenged. We remain skeptical, at the least, about electoral strategies for welfare rights organizing.

Welfare State Activism

Apart from the benefits they retain or gain for recipients, welfare rights organizations continue to keep advanced social welfare demands on the social agenda. The demands that have historically grown from this movement are some of the most challenging to neoconservative and neoliberal concepts of the capitalist state: a guaranteed annual income, urged in the 1960s by the NWRO; wages for caretaking, demanded in the 1970s by the Downtown Advocacy Center; substantive proposals for adequate child care, health care, housing, social services, and—for those who choose to work outside of the home—dignified jobs that pay breadwinners' wages. The current work requirements that force women on welfare to work at low-level jobs while leaving their children at home also put recipients in a position to analyze the role of poor women generally in the labor force. These constraints lead welfare activists to struggle for the right of all women to have the choice to care for their children at home or, if they choose to work outside of the home, the right to a job that lifts them out of poverty.

Yet, despite all the truly grand significance of its broadest demands, the recent Massachusetts welfare rights movement can only claim modest real world achievements. It demonstrated that, without extraordinary pressure, states will only give "more," but never enough, not even in good times. It has been extremely difficult to create the base for the simple right for state support above the poverty level, much less the broader conception of economic rights. Now that the "reality" of bad times for all is invoked to force activists to forgo new demands, benefit levels shrink quickly.

Obviously, one of the basic elements of any welfare rights movement is to organize recipients to fight for themselves, as legitimate claimants on the state. But it must also expand the vision of the economic rights that can be claimed by all citizens. If welfare rights organizations are cognizant of the inherent critical theory of the welfare state that underlies their organizing, for example, they may find themselves better able to talk with the African American, feminist, and social-democratic groups who must decide on the value of a welfare rights strategy. Such strategies can be "universal," as mentioned earlier, by seeking to establish an end to the fear of poverty for everyone—those already poor as well as those in the middle class worried about someday falling into poverty.[23]

Racial and Gender Dynamics

Piven and Cloward recall that early civil rights leaders were fearful of the NWRO. Whitney Young said that he would rather see 10 black airline stewardesses than 100 more black women on welfare.[24] These tensions have remained and help explain why there is less attention than might be expected to welfare issues from mainstream African American politicians, even those representing poor communities.

Massachusetts, like many urban states, is highly segmented racially. Its urban African American and Latino communities are large and extremely poor. In Boston the focus within minority communities for the past 15 years has been to stress community development, jobs, and housing for the community. Welfare rights demands for increases in benefit programs that are seen as inherently oppressive have received scant attention from community organizers. Mainstream leaders have not wanted to play into racial stereotypes by focusing on welfare issues. Politically radical community leaders have simply held little hope that their constituency would benefit much from welfare programs—except for those services that they could offer themselves through contracts with the state. As the CBHN's origins were not in the communities of color, the issues have been especially obscured. Here it seems as if the problem is not exactly that communities of color have not seen welfare rights as an issue but that the differing theoretical approaches of community development versus welfare rights have not been discussed in public debate. Little attention has been paid therefore to all the potential gender and racial dynamics at play.

Feminist theory has strong connections with welfare rights activities, even if welfare rights theory and leaders have not directly influenced mainstream feminism. The original welfare rights movement was not self-consciously feminist, even though most of the members were women. Guida West says it was a black women's movement led primarily by white men.[25] This created a great deal of tension in the movement, and by the time the women managed to gain organizational control, the movement was already dying.

Morrissey says that the "second wave" of welfare rights organizations that began to emerge in the mid-1970s was more influenced by the women's movement: "While the NWRO tried to ignite a poor people's movement, the second wave of welfare rights organizations stressed that welfare is not an issue for poor people, in general, but is more specifically a concern of poor women."[26] As suggested by the tensions between welfare rights and homeless organizers, many feminists now postulate that women's organizing is inherently different, in both process and product, than men's. They self-consciously try to achieve a feminist model within today's welfare rights groups. Many men, feminists say, are more attracted to the large-scale militant mobilizing model while many women are more attracted to the self-help, mutual support, neighborhood development model.[27] While this is open to debate, and certainly most recent welfare rights organizers have not necessarily been feminists, it does seem that contemporary welfare rights groups do borrow heavily from the consciousness-raising model of feminist groups, with their emphasis on relationships, emotional support, and connectedness.

Current welfare organizing in Massachusetts shows the influence of the women's movement. The Coalition for Basic Human Needs has drawn on feminist theory in its internal training. It made critical alliances with feminist groups as part of the "Up and Out of Poverty Campaign." During this effort, middle-class feminists and women on welfare engaged in real struggles with each other over style, language, and priorities. It was not easy, but much was learned, and, for a while, there were real material benefits as welfare grants actually increased.

Yet, despite the influence of feminist theory and strategy, welfare rights groups and mainstream feminist organizations have maintained an uneasy distance from one another. Welfare workshops at feminist conferences have drawn scant enrollment. In meetings we have witnessed, the class dynamics have been painfully clear, as middle class feminists either tried to present overly abstract analyses, or, usually, just retreated in the face of angry, "authentic" welfare activists. Even as feminist theorists increasingly wrote about the state, few actively engaged in welfare politics, with welfare mothers. Instead, both middle class feminist organizations and theorists have tended to focus attention on employment related issues. Sometimes militant welfare mothers have seemed almost an embarrassment, because they uncompromisinginly seek legitimacy, even payment, as mothers while seemingly rejecting employment as a personal option. The end result has been that a movement, which should have been at the forefront of welfare rights, has seldom been seen.

It is important not to caricature feminists here, however. Many welfare activists are feminists and the best of feminist theory on the state is supportive of welfare rights activism. Most important, since the summer of 1992, the National Organization of Women (NOW) has made welfare rights a priority issue, has sought alliance with the National Welfare Rights Union, and in July 1993, devoted more than half a day of its national conference to discussion of the relationship between welfare rights and feminism.

At the conclusion of her book on the NWRO, Guida West suggests that black feminists may serve as the critical link between welfare rights activists and mainstream feminists. We agree and look to see more concrete connections made in this area. We suggest that welfare rights groups must now work hard to claim links with the organized women's movement, despite any not-so-subtle discouraging messages, for the current conflict over the nature of the state has critical effects on all women's lives.

■ **Prospects for the Future: In Defense of a Welfare Rights Strategy**

The question of "what is to be done?" for welfare claimants cannot be viewed separately from that question for the entire society. We find much power in Michael Walzer's recent commentary on contemporary society: "Increasingly associational life in the 'advanced' capitalist and social-democratic countries seems at risk. Publicists and preachers warn us of a steady attenuation of everyday cooperation and civic friendship. And this time it's possible that they are not, as they usually are, foolishly alarmist."[28] Citing E. M. Forster's dictum, "Only connect," Walzer argues that

> the quality of our political and economic activity and of our national culture is intimately connected to the strength and vitality of our associations. . . . Politics in the contemporary democratic state does not offer many people a chance for Rousseauian self-determination. Citizenship, taken by itself, is today mostly a passive role: citizens are spectators who vote.

Walzer presents a vision of a "more densely organized, more egalitarian civil society" of "socially engaged men and women" and of "poor people with strong families, churches, unions, political parties and ethnic alliances [who] are not likely to be dominated or deprived for long."[29] As participants in welfare rights politics for most of our adult lives, we remain uncertain about how to meet Walzer's charge to "render the state accessible . . . [through] many organizing strategies and new forms of state action."

On the one hand, the conditions facing poor people in this country are worse than they have been since the 1930s. Twelve years of national neoconservative policy have taken away many basic social supports won, in part, by the efforts of earlier activists. The collapse of the national economy has left many more people vulnerable to poverty. And the conditions in our cities have become even more desperate. Certainly, reports coming into *Survival News* and our reading of the national press lead us to think that there may be some increase in acts of resistance. Part of us believes that such a situation should breed a new militancy, as well as new allies and a new sense of connectedness, for a renewed welfare rights movement in the United States.

But, on the other hand, our immediate fear is that the current situation is not strongly supportive of great gains for welfare recipients. As we view it, a responsible society must agree to provide a basic floor of unstigmatized economic and social benefits so that anyone can have a basic level of security, regardless of whether the wage system yields her a living wage. Single parent women often see this immediately because they can least afford to be fooled by the myth that almost any job will allow them to provide adequately for their families. So women on welfare have clear material reasons for demanding government guarantees for income, health, and social supports—even for caregivers' wages—and little hope that market mechanisms will save them. And they have more to fear from decentralization than may other workers or community activists.

Yet, as Stalinist state socialism disappears in Europe, neoconservatives continue to discredit the U.S. welfare state in general while neoliberals focus their ill will on the "dependent" poor. So, while poor men may find themselves more able, in bad times, to make strong appeals for economic democracy and for jobs, it may be even harder for women to demand the continuation, expansion, and improvement in state programs that they need to support their families.

If Walzer as well as Fisher and Kling are correct—that new social movements must reach back to old movements for a stronger ideological focus, while older movements must look to newer movements for creative strategies and nonexclusive membership—welfare rights activists may feel trapped. For them, the ideological logic of old social movements served to discount women's complex needs for a state that would protect them without controlling them, while the seemingly egalitarian, less militant style of new social movements often dismissed them for being too abrasive and too distrustful of more well off, and well meaning, "friends."

Nevertheless, the history of the welfare rights movement offers significant lessons for social movement theorists and activists. Perhaps welfare rights organizing reflects an important blending of old and new social movement forms in which class and the struggle over the state remain salient. In the struggle for the rights of the poor, class infuses gender and racial politics with militant, material demands against the state for equity and social justice. But this is not a case of simply the old social movements informing the new. It cuts both ways. Simultaneously, welfare rights organizing brings center stage the polyvocal voices and activism of women and people of color—a politics of gender and race—infusing class politics with the power and resonance of identity and cultural politics.

If an expansive and full understanding of *democracy* is to be the watchword of new movements, then women's right to support themselves and their children with dignity must be central. We must do more than fight "welfare bashing" with arguments that it is unfair to blame women for not finding jobs in bad times. Our task is not to create a constituency only for simple "economic justice" but also to legitimate differing paths to democratic participation. To raise functioning kids is of equal social value, and deserving of a fair share of society's benefits, as to produce profit or to wage a war. We find splendid models for activism in the efforts over the past two decades of those women engaged in the welfare rights struggle, who continued to fight together for their families and themselves in the face of fragmentation and disinterest from the left, selective attention from feminists, neglect from liberals, and abuse and harassment from the right. The mere fact that another national welfare rights organization has survived in the face of "underclass" rhetoric, the antiwelfare "Family Support" Welfare Reform act of 1988, and comparable antiwelfare legislation in state after state is a sign of the profound need for a class-, gender-, and race-focused claimant's movement. In Massachusetts, during the height of Reaganism, benefits were raised, punitive workfare measures put aside, and lawsuits even won to protect poor women from homelessness.

The best plan now is, using the old civil rights phrase, to "keep on keeping on" building organizations that monitor the state, reaching out to other poor women, and educating the public. In an increasingly impersonal and mechanistic nation, it is essential to help people connect with one another. For welfare claimants, this involves both organizing groups where people can find mutual support and insisting upon their legitimacy, even their leadership, within broader communities that find themselves increasingly poor.

NOTES

1. The major historical treatments of the welfare rights movement are Guida West, *The National Welfare Rights Movement* (1981), and Frances Fox Piven and Richard A. Cloward, *Poor People's Movements* (1977).

2. See Piven and Cloward (1977).

3. Illustrative case studies here are in Bailis (1975), Hertz (1981), Milwaukee Welfare Rights Organization (1974), Morrissey (1990), and Pope (1989).

4. See issues of *Survival News* for coverage of the NWRU. Or, better yet, subscribe by writing to *Survival News* (c/o Mandell, 102 Anawan St., West Roxbury, MA 02127).

5. We remain supportive of the NWRU, as the one existing national organization for welfare recipients. We are, however, worried about the movement's ability to remain an independent vehicle for welfare rights activism. It is tightly linked with the Communist Labor party, an organizational affiliation that has given the NWRU much needed support but may not lead to the most open, democratic development of grass-roots activism. For

us, in January 1992, the jury is still out regarding the future of the NWRU as a significant player in the ongoing history of welfare rights activism.

6. See Withorn (1982) for a review of this history.

7. This summary of the CBHN is based on our personal experiences and interviews conducted over the years with key participants. Also, Mary Quinn, executive director of the organization for many years, gave us an extensive interview in the summer of 1991.

8. The Massachusetts Employment and Training Program (ET) was touted as an alternative to forced work (workfare) programs. Advocates were involved in planning for it. It was, by all accounts, better than more punitive workfare programs in other states. But, from the perspective of welfare recipients, there were still serious problems with its conception and implementation. For studies of the "model" program, see Ammott (1986) and the Urban Institute (1990). ARMS also prepared an award-winning radio documentary about workfare and ET (see below).

9. ARMS serves as a useful example of a college-based welfare rights organization. Started as an organizing project by students in Ann Withorn's class on "welfare rights organizing," it developed as a recognized student organization with both an external and an internal focus. Low-income students provide information and support to each other, sponsor speakers and events, and agitate and lobby around work/education/training issues. A graduate from the first group now teaches the organizing class that continues to be the hub of recruitment of new ARMS members. For more information on ARMS, please write to them care of Diane Dujon, College of Public and Community Service, University of Massachusetts, Boston, MA, 02125-3393.

10. The early tensions between welfare rights and civil rights were documented by both Cloward and Piven and by Guida West. They are also discussed by Piven and Cloward in an interview with Ann Withorn titled, "Socialist Analysis and Organizing," in a special *Radical America* issue on organizing (1988, Spring). A special issue of *The Nation* (vol. 253, no. 19, December 1991), edited by Adolph Reed and Julian Bond, on racism and contemporary politics addresses the connections between racism and the welfare state, if not welfare rights organizing. For the best of feminist criticism regarding welfare, see Fiona Williams (1989) and a bibliographical essay by Linda Gordon in her edited collection, *Women, the State and Welfare* (1990).

11. Perhaps the clearest elaboration of Theda Skocpol's ideas is in "Universal Appeal: Politically Viable Policies to Combat Poverty" (1991). See also William Julius Wilson (1987).

12. See Piven and Cloward (1977, 1988, Spring).

13. See West (1981).

14. See Pope (1989).

15. Cited in Pope (1989, p. 32).

16. Cited in Morrissey (1990, p. 203).

17. Janet Diamond (1986, p. 189).

18. An example of this problem occurred when local groups had to determine which members should receive the very small amounts of money available through now-defunct Commonwealth Service Corps grants. These small state-sponsored internship appointments generated terrific struggles, so much so that many organizers wanted to forgo them, even when recipient members saw the small stipends as a significant benefit. We find Kathy Ferguson, *The Feminist Case Against Bureaucracy* (1984), helpful in understanding some of this dynamic.

19. We are especially indebted to the CBHN's Mary Quinn for her conceptualization of the difference between individual and collective empowerment within welfare rights organizing.

20. For a full discussion of this, see Withorn (1984).

21. See West (1981).

22. This generalization comes from our experience in Boston. The review of early NWRO organizing strategy in Boston as examined in both Bailis (1975) and West (1981) also give typical examples of the problems of "male" organizing style.

23. Here again, the December 1991 issue of *The Nation* is extremely helpful.

24. Piven and Cloward (1988, Spring, p. 23).

25. See West (1981).

26. Morrissey (1990, p. 204).

27. The Women's Organizing Project at Hunter College has created a helpful bibliography and material for exploring this dynamic: Center for Community Organizing, Hunter College, New York, NY.

28. Michael Walzer (1991, pp. 293-304).

29. Walzer (1991, pp. 298-300).

REFERENCES

Ammott, T. (1986). *ET: A model for the nation? An evaluation of the Massachusetts Employment and Training Choices program.* Cambridge, MA: New England Regional Office, American Friends' Service Committee.

Bailis, L. (1975). *Bread or justice: Grassroots organizing in the welfare rights movement.* Lexington, MA: Lexington.

Diamond, J. (1986). The skies are not cloudy all day. In *For crying out loud: Women and poverty in the US.* New York: Pilgrim.

Fergusen, K. (1984). *The feminist case against bureaucracy.* Philadelphia: Temple University Press.

Gordon, L. (Ed.). (1990). *Women, the state and welfare.* Madison: University of Wisconsin Press.

Hertz, S. H. (1981). *The welfare mothers movement: A decade of change for poor women.* Nadham, MD: University Press.

Milwaukee Welfare Rights Organization. (1974). *Welfare mothers speak out.* Milwaukee: Author.

Morrissey, M. (1990). The Downtown Welfare Advocate Center: A case study of a welfare rights organization. *Social Service Review, 64*(2), 189-207.

Piven, F. F., & Cloward, R. A. (1977). *Poor people's movements.* New York: Pantheon.

Piven, F. F., & Cloward, R. A. (1988, Spring). Socialist analysis and organizing. *Radical America, 21*(1), 21-31.

Pope, J. (1989). *Biting the hand that feeds them: Organizing women on welfare at the grass roots level.* New York: Praeger.

Skocpol, T. (1991, Summer). Universal appeal: Politically viable policies to combat poverty. *Brookings Review*, pp. 29-33.

Urban Institute. (1990). *Evaluation of the Massachusetts Employment and Training (ET) Choices program.* Washington, DC: Author.

Walzer, M. (1991, Spring). The idea of a civil society. *Dissent*, pp. 293-300.

West, G. (1981). *The national welfare rights movement: The social protest of poor women.* New York: Praeger.

Williams, F. (1989). *Social policy: A critical introduction.* New York: Basil Blackwell.

Wilson, W. J. (1987). *The truly disadvantaged.* Chicago: University of Chicago Press.

Withorn, A. (1982). *The circle game: Services for the poor in Massachusetts 1966-1978.* Amherst: University of Massachusetts Press.

Withorn, A. (1984). *Serving the people, social services and social change.* New York: Columbia University Press.

7   The Career of Urban Social Movements in West Germany

MARGIT MAYER

Over the last decade, urban protest has drastically changed its appearance. In the 1970s and early 1980s, massive protests of rehab squatters, citizens' initiatives, tenant groups, and housing activists brought prevailing forms of urban development in many German cities to a halt. Today such movements are reported only occasionally. Headlines are filled instead with reports of increasing numbers of youth street gangs and, more recently, racist and violent attacks on immigrants and refugees. No longer a site for struggle over alternative and popular ways of appropriating the city, the urban terrain instead appears fractured: Community organizations are now on the "inside" and unemployed youth, foreigners, and other marginalized social groups are on the "outside." These and other new cleavages find expression in unfamiliar forms of protest activity, in right-wing and neo-Nazi militancy, in attacks by "autonomous" radicals on Greens in city councils, or in puzzling rituals of street fighting over New Year's Eve or May 1. While similar changes have been observed in most Western nations, this chapter traces one particular country's experience of urban social movements in terms of the specific West German (and later unified) political opportunity structure as well as in the context of a broader crisis and transformation of a mode of accumulation and regulation, the latter having created new patterns for urban politics and a different space for social movements.

We can identify distinct phases of urban opposition movements in Germany, beginning with a first wave of mobilization by citizens' initiatives during the early 1970s against large-scale renewal projects and in defense of residents' living conditions. These struggles soon expanded into struggles over the cost and the use value of the public infrastructure, into which cities invested heavily during the short era of social reform (1969-1973) and created a fertile milieu for various types of grass-roots and community groups, into which leftist projects of the now dissolving extraparliamentarian opposition of the student left inserted themselves. Squattings, rent strikes, and massive demonstrations against renewal and displacement policies marked the high point of this first phase of urban movements and left behind a new political actor in most West German cities: a self-confident and politically active urban counterculture.

The transition from the reformist modernization politics of the Brandt government to the crisis-induced "Model Germany" of the Schmidt government in 1974 also marked a new phase for urban-based protest movements. While governments increasingly sought to delegitimize protest, their modernization policies exacerbated the negative effects of urban restructuring and led the various urban movements into tighter cooperation and highly politicized antistate orientations. Moderate citizens' initiatives, radical leftists, and local projects of the newer women's and ecology movements became united not only in their opposition to urban renewal but also in contesting the established parties' monopoly to articulate political interests. During this phase, electoral alliances (green, colored, and alternative lists) were formed and gained seats on local city councils.

The early 1980s squatters' movements in various German (and other West European) cities is a result of the politicization and homogenization of urban protest during the late 1970s and also shows the effects of a changed economic and political opportunity structure. The period's economic crisis fell especially on local governments as they are responsible for dealing with growing unemployment and higher welfare dependency rates, while the federal government's austerity policies severely restricted their scope for action. Looking for ways to deal with these dilemmas, many municipalities "discovered" the problem-solving potential and innovative capacities of local movement milieus: Their labor gradually was acknowledged and upgraded in a manner that would have been inconceivable in the highly polarized German political culture of the 1970s. Many movement projects received funding and some were even incorporated as "model projects" into municipal social or employment programs of the "entrepreneurial city." Community and movement groups' participation in different policy sectors was routinized, and, last but not least, movement issues and demands were now firmly represented in many local governments by the Green party.

These various incorporation processes have had effects that have become visible since the late 1980s in an increasing heterogenization of the social composition and political orientation of the urban movement milieus. While a social movement sector has now clearly become a stable, permanent element within German urban politics, with its own public sphere, alternative life-styles, and infrastructure, it also manifests more and more polarizations, cleavages, and forms of implosion. "Incorporated" segments frequently find themselves attacked by groups, whose economic and social problems have been ignored by the incorporation discourse of the 1980s and thus marginalized. The problems caused by mass unemployment, by the lack of opportunities for unskilled young people, as well as those engendered by the rapid multiculturalization of many city neighborhoods are intensifying under unification pressures and creating a new agenda for urban movements, which has yet to be seized.

This career of urban social movements does not correspond to typical patterns described by social movement theory. None of the concepts of a gradual diffusion of movement sectors, patterns of cyclical rise and decline of mobilization, or the "natural death" of a social movement through institutionalization processes is helpful in accounting for these transformations. Clearly, a movement sector has consolidated that is still able to mobilize for different occasions. But its relations to intermediary sectors and the state are less clear and its constituent elements are fragmented and even polarized in new ways.

Therefore to understand the developmental patterns of urban social movements in Germany, we will examine the actors, goals, internal organization, and transformations in their roles for social change as they relate to various phases of urban development and their respective conflict patterns.

■ Phases of Urban Conflict and Urban Social Movements

Opposition to Fordist Urban Renewal

While the immediate postwar development was dominated by the cold war and the German economic miracle, with the expansion of the (social-democratic) Keynesian-welfare state model of development from the mid-1960s on, new lines of conflict emerged. The instruments and agencies of central state planning and global steering were expanded so as to distribute the blessings of the Fordist modernization process all over the country. Local governments implemented this scheme by expanding the urban social and technical infrastructure (streets, schools, kindergartens, hospitals, social housing, and so on), by servicing land provision, and by managing large-scale urban renewal. All over Germany, and not merely in localities that were governed by Social Democrats, large-scale urban renewal and modern housing construction were at the core of local politics. The demolition of whole turn-of-the-century neighborhoods and their replacement by modern housing construction marked a high point, and simultaneously a crisis, of social-democratic local politics.[1]

This type of urban infrastructure and of collective consumption expansion accelerated the segmentation of urban space into monofunctional zones of residence, shopping, working, and entertainment and thereby destroyed vital fabrics and milieus of neighborhoods. While serving to raise consumption levels, it also standardized ways of living and monotonized urban life. It was against these effects of the growth strategies that the first phase of urban oppositional movements during the 1960s and beginning of the 1970s mobilized.

In 1965 Alexander Mitscherlich's book *The Inhospitability of Our Cities* already offered a harsh critique of the dominant patterns of urban development, their fixation on the automobile, the consequent decay of the inner city, and suburbanization's destructive effects on the countryside. Other precursors of the first wave of mobilizations include the early 1960s youth revolts and the situationists' revolt against urban emptiness and hegemonic norms. Both revolts challenged the still hegemonic norms of self-discipline, self-sacrifice, and the belief in progress, and they contributed to a gradual cultural pluralization of postwar Germany. In 1968 this cultural opposition merged with the extraparliamentary opposition to nuclear armament and the emergency laws passed by the grand coalition. From then on, the fundamental critique of society of the new left became most influential for the movements of the period.

Citizens immediately threatened by urban renewal plans or large-scale projects formed the initial opposition to the growth strategies. These citizens' initiatives often developed out of traditional citizen associations made up of middle-class notables. They used conventional, pragmatic methods to defend their neighborhoods and chose cooperative tactics and professional strategies such as "planning alternatives from below." Confronting unresponsive technocratic city administrations, however, they frequently resorted to unconventional forms of politics, including direct action and street protest. Contested issues included not only infrastructure expansion but also cost, quality, and participation in its design. In many cities, broad mobilizations occurred that were directed toward lowering costs and influencing cultural norms expressed in the institutions of collective consumption (especially schools, kindergartens, and public transportation). These protests were joined by initiatives from the youth protest movements, whose roots were in the 1960s antiauthoritarian movement. In the course of the 1970s, this local scene was gradually "infiltrated" by a wave of leftist community organizing groups that had grown out of the political projects of the extraparliamentarian opposition. The new left saw the "reproductive sector" as an area of politicization where disadvantaged groups could be mobilized (see Roth, 1990a).

The first squatting in Germany took place in 1970 in Cologne, but the Hamburg and Frankfurt housing struggles were even more militant. During the first half of the 1970s, squatting took place in many West German cities (see Brandes & Schön, 1981, pp. 174 ff.). The most favorable conditions for a concentrated and relatively long period of squatting activities were present in Frankfurt, where from 1972 to 1974 squatting actually dominated the local movement sector. The issue here was restructuring of neighborhoods near the central business district for expanding tertiary functions. In other cities, the triggering events were large-scale renewal projects. In each case, renewal plans and large-scale demolition of turn-of-the-century housing did not include open and democratic planning processes but instead nonpublic and generous deals between city agencies and investors. This political process stimulated speculative behavior whereby whole blocks were bought up, temporarily rented out to "transitory residents" like students and immigrant workers, or left vacant. The real estate owners could expect huge profits from the demolition and eventual construction of high-rise office buildings. Both the undemocratic nature and the detrimental social effects of such urban development politics sparked (in Frankfurt as early as 1968) protest organized by conventional citizens' associations, which usually saw themselves as nonideological and quite distinct from the radical, student-led groups, which were also forming at the time.

In this climate, the first squat in Frankfurt was carried out by students and social workers who had already been active in SDS and community groups. The squatters had formed a "collective living experiment" and occupied a large, turn-of-the-century building together with Italian immigrant families. Two similar squats followed a month later and their success bred imitators in other circles (Dackweiler, Poppenhausen, Grottian, & Roth, 1990, p. 210). In Hamburg the first squat took place in 1973 in a similar atmosphere of widespread protest against demolition plans (Schubert, 1990, p. 35). Explicitly political projects, the goal of these first squats was to radicalize political work in the "reproductive sphere." The squatted houses both symbolized the criticism of urban renewal that consisted in demolition for luxury housing or offices and served as organizational bases for further squats; their residents also played important roles in initiating other movement activities (in Frankfurt, for example, the rent strike movement).[2]

Because the issue of urban destruction was easily presented as a political scandal, public reactions were initially quite positive.[3] The occupation and subsequent violent eviction of a building in September 1971 encouraged more squats, because widespread indignation over the brutal police actions and bloody street battles forced the Frankfurt mayor to rescind his earlier eviction order. Similar sympathies arose in Hamburg over the city government's repressive and criminalizing response to their first squattings. Citizens' initiatives, tenant groups, and professionals came to the support of the squatters and formed a broad housing movement. In Frankfurt, from October 1971 to July 1972, 10 more mostly successful squattings took place, broadening the infrastructure for political work and the movement's alternative living arrangements. During this expansive phase of the squatting movement, a curious coexistence and even productive relationship prevailed between the radical, antireformist protest and social-democratic reform policies, which attempted innovative and socially responsible solutions to the problem. The lines of conflict were drawn between the squatters, their supporters, and the ruling SPD against what appeared to all as the common enemy: the speculators and irresponsible real estate owners.

Reasons for the decline of this first wave in the squatting movement differed according to the local situation. While in Hamburg or Berlin, community and tenant initiatives worked pragmatically to prevent demolitions and to create and maintain alternative housing forms (see Bodenschatz, Heiser, & Korfmacher, 1983), thus building an organizational basis for another massive mobilization during the early 1980s, in Frankfurt the movement's strong infusion with political and existential radicalism eventually turned into a limitation. Left radicalism and militancy became quite synonymous, both because of the strong presence of new left groups within the movement, who understood their activities in the reproductive sector as part of broader revolutionary activities, such as party building or internationalism, and also because of the SPD city government's changing political strategy. In 1973-1974 the city began urging evictions while simultaneously presenting itself as the savior of the existing housing stock and the fabric of the threatened neighborhood (Dackweiler et al., 1990, p. 214). The stiff repression and criminalization of the squatters during two protracted eviction conflicts in particular intensified the movement's critique of SPD reformism and its own self-radicalization (Stracke, 1976, p. 123) while the distance to the more moderate citizens' initiatives increased and the supportive environment began to crumble.

In spite of such setbacks, this phase produced, by the mid-1970s in most German cities, a new political actor—a self-confident urban counterculture with its own infrastructure of newspapers, self-managed collectives and housing cooperatives, feminist groups, and so on, which was prepared to intervene in local and broader politics. In Frankfurt the movement scene reacted to the setback with a drastic shift in orientation. Trying to learn from the failure of the "mass militancy" of the housing struggle, its leaders turned toward the new women's movement and its motto, "The personal is political." This shift brought to the foreground the social experiments that had actually been implemented in the squatted houses, covered up by the revolutionary power politics dominant during the period.

Institutional effects of this phase of mobilization included modest participatory concessions by city administrations: More groups and interests were to be heard and allowed participation in the urban planning process. But the slogan of the short social-liberal reform era, "Let's risk more democracy!" was not applied to the local opposition. *Legitimate* political action was still restricted to party-based action and limited to those parties that were seen as safeguarding the "free, democratic basic order." The radical opposition was threatened with the Berufsverbote 1972 (i.e., the decrees against radicals; see Narr, 1976). Thus the social-democratic governments during this reform phase (1971-1974) provided a peculiar opportunity structure for urban protest: They were quite supportive of reformist citizens' initiatives as these supplied necessary social pressure "from below" for envisioned reform initiatives "from above." The left-radical opposition also benefited from some participatory concessions[4] and from the general climate of reform, but whenever it took the promise of "more democracy" too seriously, it confronted severe repression.

Project Phase and Greening
of the Opposition (1974-1982)

From 1974 to 1977 social-democratic governments remained in place on all levels but now engaged in crisis management instead of reform politics.[5] The social-liberal government under Chancellor Schmidt (since 1974) returned institutional politics to its (prereform) era state of being closed off and protected from pressures and interests from below. Urban opposition and protest were publicly delegitimized and attacked, while, as a consequence of crisis management and modernization, pressures on the conditions of urban life intensified. Through a series of centralizing measures, even the space for political action by local authorities was severely restricted.[6]

The worldwide economic recession of 1973-1974 indicates the break in the postwar growth model and when the crisis of Fordism became felt in many different sectors. Markets for consumer durables and mass products were saturated; the labor process could not be further Taylorized; economists noted a structural crisis of capital reproduction; and the consensus around Keynesian policies dissolved (Leaman, 1988, pp. 205 ff., 212). In other words, the social and technical limits of the Fordist growth model had become apparent: The rigidities of the production structure, the rising costs of mass production and mass consumption, and the politicization of those costs and effects slowed down growth rates and triggered social conflicts and social movements that put these costs on the agenda.

Citizens' initiatives protesting the threats to and infringements on their quality of life contributed to making the social limits of the Fordist regime visible, particularly the way its resource and waste intensity creates barriers to expansion. The ecology and other movements also challenged technological fixes as solutions to the Fordist relationship to nature, fearing their negative effects on democracy and social responsibility.

The economic restructuring efforts undertaken to overcome this crisis of Fordism—including the world market-centered modernization strategies of the "Model Germany"[7]—augmented the proportion of social groups that remain excluded from the "blessings of Fordism" as unemployment rates (affecting especially the younger age groups) skyrocketed.[8] Economic restructuring oriented toward the world market also intensified such spatial restructuring as urban renewal and tertiarization (see Häußermann & Siebel, 1989). These negative effects on urban living conditions and the growth cartel's exclusivity, attacking even moderate citizens' initiatives as "internal enemies of the state" (for blocking investments), encouraged not only more protest activity but also a coming together of heterogenous movements and their creation of independent organizational structures quite opposed to the state and its parties.[9] As repressive and marginalizing measures by the authorities provided repeated cause for cooperation among the movement groups and for confrontation with the authorities, alternative projects, frustrated citizens initiatives, and local new social movement campaigns (peace, women, ecology) developed tighter solidarities and a shared radical-oppositional self-image.

The most significant innovation within the local movement scene was that alternative projects and communal experiments came to the fore more strongly. During the late 1970s, projects in all types of production and service activities and collective living arrangements were initiated (see Bertels & Nottenbohm, 1983; for economic projects, Kück, 1985; for social projects, Huber, 1980). At the same time, the continued experience of political exclusion and marginalization during this phase[10] led the movement groups, in some localities more than in others, to shift their political interventionism in the direction of electoral alternatives. During the second half of the 1970s, the first *local electoral coalitions* emerged: green, rainbow, and alternative lists, which ran candidates for city halls and municipal elections (see Roth, 1991). In 1978 they joined on a statewide basis in Hessia (and out of these developments in 1980 the national Green party was to be formed). This electoral alternative helped to create a common denominator for the various and particular local movements—ecology. "Ecology" came to signify the search for fundamental and generalizable alternatives and a radical opposition to the dominant policy of crisis management (Roth, 1990b).

Shifts in the Relationship Between the Movements and the State

As 1982 marked another year of recession in Germany, stagnation reached the formerly expansive service sector (Leaman, 1988, p. 234), introducing a period of intensifying distributive struggles and reductions of social benefits by the state. The simultaneous change in national government brought the conservative Christian Democrats into power and led to a revival of local and urban issues in the public sphere. While an intense second wave of squatting and housing struggles swept the country in the early 1980s, this time the solution was sought in the selective adoption of movement initiatives at the local level. Local governments, forced to find new and alternative ways of dealing with the fiscal restrictions imposed by the consequences of economic restructuring, unemployment, and rising welfare costs, began to look to community groups and alternative organizations for their innovative potential. Thus, in the course of the decade, a transition occurred from urban social movements challenging the state to a less oppositional relationship between "interest groups" and a local welfare bureaucracy increasingly confronted with its own limitations.

The squatting movement of the early 1980s was soon known as the "rehab squatting movement." This time, the movement was strongest in Berlin, where it started in 1978 as the last desperate step of a 10-year-long defensive community- and tenant-organizing endeavor to stop the deterioration, forced vacancies, and speculation carried out by private landlords. When a powerful youth and alternative movement emerged and coalesced with local community groups, squatting became a form of self-help in which the squatters not only occupied vacant buildings but also attempted to restore the properties into livable condition after years of physical deterioration (see Katz & Mayer, 1985). Again, these forms of occupation managed to attract the support of broad sectors of the population alienated by the rotten building policies of the Berlin government and by the disruptive effects of—and huge profits made by—massive housing development, real estate, and tax shelter syndicating firms. During the movement's peak in 1981, about 160 buildings were "rehab-squatted" in West Berlin, directly involving about 5,000 people.[11]

The joint actions of the squatter movements brought together citizens' and tenants' initiatives, marginalized youth, and alternative political groups. While the former were interested in careful urban renewal and self-help in housing rehabilitation, the latter sought niches for themselves in a relatively protected milieu, used the actions as a stage for their struggle against the state, or were simply interested in suitable space for political projects. What they had in common, at least initially, was a radical critique of the state housing policy and a desire for unfettered self-realization, for private spheres without state control.

As the fruits of their self-help labor were repeatedly destroyed by evictions and demolitions, more squatters sought agents to mediate their interests with the local state. While evictions, arrests, trials, police investigations, and street fighting were still going on (one demonstrator was killed in the protest against the eviction of eight squatted buildings in September 1981), some squatters and support groups worked up a variety of proposals for the transfer of squatted houses into public ownership, "legalized" self-management and long-term leaseholds, as well as an institutionalized third party mediator and manager between the houses and the state. After years of struggle and many setbacks, which gradually fragmented the movement, the first alternative renewal agent, Stattbau, began to administer the buildings on behalf of the Berlin Senat, which would in turn purchase the buildings from their current owners and give squatters long-term leases with extensive self-management rights (see Clark & Mayer, 1986, p. 412). Following this example, similar alternative renewal agents were established in Hamburg in 1984 (Schubert, 1990, pp. 37 ff.) and over the next few years in other West German cities.

A similar process of "approximation" took place with the alternative collectives and citizens initiatives and the state. In Berlin these groups had formed an umbrella organization, Arbeitskreis Staatsknete, to secure public funding for their projects. And while the founding activists among them framed this demand as a political offensive on the "new voluntarism" propagated by the Christian Democratic government, more and more projects joined the Arbeitskreis, which were new, had little political experience, but had high hopes for *individual* funding. This changing composition among the activists reflects the fact that deteriorating economic conditions and increasing marginalization (especially youth unemployment) were beginning to undermine the position of alternative projects all over Germany (see Beywl, 1983, p. 97, 1989). A consequence was that the projects sought to professionalize and were increasingly willing to participate in the political bargaining process wherever it would open up to them.

And open up it did. Because the effects of the Fordist crisis and of restructuring efforts made themselves felt most of all on the local level, many cities began to develop unconventional, cost-effective policies to deal with the challenges they faced. Local budgets were under intense pressure through increasing unemployment and poverty rates; welfare programs (for which local authorities are responsible) had to be expanded, but fiscal austerity at the federal level severely restricted the ability of local governments to act. Additionally, municipal budgets began to feel the strain from years of environmental neglect, as polluted soils, traffic congestion, waste disposal, and water provision are largely municipal responsibilities. To devise solutions to these crises, cities began to look to the alternative scene as an *innovative reserve*.

The West Berlin administration spearheaded these "opening-up" processes[12] and were soon followed by other (at first especially Christian Democratic-run) local governments. In 1983 a social services program was established in response to demands for state funding of alternative social, cultural, and political projects but also as a solution to the problems of the local welfare state (see Fink, 1984, who was then the Berlin senator for social affairs). While the umbrella organization Arbeitskreis Staatsknete had demanded funding for a self-administered fund from various departments, the CDU offer was limited to social services and health-related activities but geared toward projects based on client self-help and voluntary coproduction of health services. Over the first few years of the program, a number of groups found the state's control over their work and the redefinition of their goals too intrusive and dropped out, but the program endures and has funded hundreds of self-help groups in social projects working with women, immigrants, youth, drug addicts, and so on (see SEKIS, 1987). Similarly, in response to the housing problems that the rehab squatters publicized, the Berlin Housing Senat institutionalized a self-help rehabilitation program featuring the inclusion of various intermediary organizations and both technical assistance and socially oriented renewal agents in the planning, formulation, and implementation of housing and social policies (see Mayer, 1987, pp. 354 ff.).

These examples of involving community-based and alternative groups in municipal policies are part of a larger change in local service provision in which the responsibility for the implementation of a variety of formerly municipal tasks is delegated to other (nonmunicipal) private and voluntary sector agents (see Mayer, 1991, 1992). While traditional welfare state benefits are reduced, new mediating structures are installed and new forms of (often state-initiated) self-steering are explored, into which former social movement organizations are tied. This occurs in the classical areas of urban renewal, housing, and social policies where self-help groups, women's centers, youth centers, and special programs for foreigners are affected but also in the area of employment and job training policies where community and alternative groups have already experimented with innovative schemes addressing social marginalization and long-term unemployment. Administrative activity now seeks to connect the neighborhood and alternative groups and their social service work to state employment policies, thereby saving local welfare expenditure and activating marginal social groups for whom traditional means of welfare state integration have failed.

Whether they create projects in urban repair, in environmental protection, or in social and cultural infrastructure, the intermediary organizations or renewal agents turn into employment agencies of a new type. While tackling social and ecological problems, they mediate cheap labor through municipal rehabilitation and training programs and, in the course of managing the new organization, professionalize themselves. The municipality's increasing readiness to accommodate solutions developed by the alternative scene has had ambiguous consequences for the movement groups. The public acknowledgment, funding, and upgrading of their labor led to an erosion of their original orientation to social change but led as well to a stabilization of local movement sectors, the strengthening of their infrastructure, and to making them, finally, a normal and permanent feature of German politics. While facilitating local improvements that are in many respects superior to anything the state or corporations have been able to achieve, the new organizations also find themselves "used" to establish urban-cultural "ambiance" or to assist the micro-management of intensifying social problems. In their less radical segments, metropolitan movement milieus are displayed by the city as (cultural) locational factors in the competition to attract investors.

These particular incorporation processes on the local level were paralleled by institutionalization processes in other social movements such as the peace or ecology movements. During the early 1980s, the peace movement expanded, reached new levels of mobilization in 1983-1984, and, throughout the 1980s, protests against a planned nuclear reprocessing plant continued, which, together with the protests caused by the Chernobyl catastrophe in 1986, led to the consolidation of movement networks and infrastructures. From informal grass-roots collectives to very professional movement organizations, all types of organizational patterns now coexist side by side and together constitute a new political sector adjacent to the other institutions of political interest intermediation, such as parties, unions, and associations. The influence of the New Left within these movement sectors has diminished, however, and in many ways it seems that, to the extent that the protest issues and motives have become more widespread, the movement lost its former radical edge.

One of the most important social movement institutionalization processes was of course their incorporation via the Green party's parliamentary representation. Since its foundation in 1980, approximately 6,000 people have been elected to local councils on Green or Green-alternative lists. Today, the Greens participate in governmental coalitions in four states (Hessen, Lower-Saxony, Brandenburg, Bremen), and there are numerous Red-Green local governments. As an electoral alternative to the established parties, the Greens have forced them to acknowledge and deal with the movements and their issues, and they have managed to negotiate many concessions and benefits for the movements (see Roth, 1991). The ambivalent consequences of "parliamentarization" on the social movements are the topic of many studies (see Mayer & Ely, 1993; Zeuner, 1985) and also have particular local manifestations. The constraints of parliamentary compromise, the concentration on elections and budgets, and the pressure to jettison symbolic counterpolitics have led local Greens to adopt a rather limited strategy, focusing on few issues, such as funding for women's centers and shelters, establishing affirmative action agencies, reducing traffic, and so on, and giving up more comprehensive political challenges. Thus the presence of the Green party in local governments, while aiding the public recognition of movement issues and movement practice, has also served to shift the political weight from protest politics toward cooptation and lobbying (see Dackweiler et al., 1990, p. 147; Roth, 1991, p. 85).

In sum, this phase features repeated waves of opportunities for urban movement groups to enter their demands and plans into city development. First, in the context of the housing struggles, so-called gentle urban renewal programs were created,[13] for which new agents were established and residents' input was routinized. Then, in the context of social policies, issues that the traditional bureaucratic welfare state was not able to handle well—youth, drugs, battered women, and foreigners—were addressed with new self-help and funding programs. Next, labor market problems were addressed with training programs, often coupled with environmental and social policies and also relying on community organizations' know-how and connections. As cities experience the need for urban regeneration, they tap into their own "endogenous potential" of an organizational landscape of local movement milieus, offering local movements an opportunity to influence urban politics while simultaneously instrumentalizing them.

■ New Polarizations: Urban Social Movements in the 1990s

The restructuring processes triggered by the crisis of Fordism resulted in a more pronounced, uneven regional development than postwar Germany had ever known; for the first time, urban development was no longer shaped by growth. Instead, two different patterns emerged: expanding cities (primarily in the new-growth South) and declining cities (primarily in the deindustrializing North; see Friedrichs, Häußermann, & Siebel, 1987). Even within metropolitan areas, disparities intensified (Häußermann & Siebel, 1989). Simultaneous with this intensification of social-spatial polarization processes, interurban and interregional competition (for growth industries, state funding, skilled workers, or consumer spending) has intensified, conferring new challenges on the local level. Many urban governments try to stimulate growth through active management, through public-private partnerships, and by developing their particular local assets as a tool in the competition over positional advantages (see Mayer, 1992). So far, such policies have not counteracted the tendencies of "flexible specialization" characteristic of the emerging regime, which intensifies the hierarchical differentiation between cities and regions.[14] Furthermore, the deregulated, flexible forms of growth tend to create new forms of exclusion such as homelessness, precarious and casualized forms of employment, and long-term structural unemployment for certain population groups.

Winners in the new growth, however, are not only the expanding numbers of well-paid, highly skilled professionals in the advanced services and high-tech sectors. They are also to be found among the staff and founders of many of the newly subsidized projects and intermediary organizations whose work now enjoys social recognition and whose position is now relatively secure. The process of inclusion of formerly excluded social groups has produced both winners and losers and thereby created new contradictions and cleavages between insiders and outsiders.

The "new insiders" are to be found among Green city council members as well as in the new institutions local authorities created in response to movement politics. To Green members of a city government, movement politics is no longer as relevant as party politics. As a consequence, they appear to young activists as established, co-opted, and even corrupted.[15] To an extent, the institutionalization of alternative local politics, as it turns movement participation into lobbying and interest group politics, contributes to the marginalization of the new movement actors and new protests. A similar mechanism is at work in the organizations and intermediaries that are now partially incorporated into the provision of services and into the emerging, decentral negotiation structures. While community development organizations are busy developing low-income housing, those who do not qualify for the waiting lists or who still prefer to squat see themselves confronting "established" development organizations. These tensions were expressed in violent actions by autonomous groups against Stattbau, the alternative renewal agent in Berlin noted above. Furthermore, the rehabilitation of old buildings usually prepares the way for gentrifiers to move into the area. As this occurred, protests were directed toward the symbols of advancing gentrification such as chic yuppie restaurants.[16] These actions are often led by the so-called autonomous scene, the most radical segment of the social movements.[17] They indicate that the movement scene has split into antagonistic fragments, where one group attacks as "yuppification" what to another is an achievement of gentle, participatory urban renewal.

But there are more—and growing—social groups who cannot be reached even by the instruments of the last innovative phase of urban politics. In fact, some of the new political alienation is precisely an outcome of the recent incorporation processes.

Marginal groups are far worse off today than even during the early 1980s: The competition on the labor market has become most intense; the unemployment rate has now reached 11.8% (2.7 million);[18] and the number of people depending on welfare has reached 4.2 million.[19] The number of homeless people is now estimated at 150,000 and increasingly includes young people and women. The economic, social, and ecological problems have all been exacerbated through the addition of former East Germany, which even served to encourage a political backlash.[20] Social groups with limited skills and training, who feel powerless and politically alienated, now tend to exert pressure on those groups who had barely been integrated, as, for example, some immigrant groups. German working-class kids, who never participated in the alternative scene and never had a chance to be clients of the progressive community work (which preferred immigrants as clients), now join gangs and act out their anger against "foreigners" (see Farin & Seidel-Pielen, 1991, p. 49). The Christian Democratic party's campaign against foreigners and refugees has given public recognition to a racist discourse, which is supposed to deflect attention from and offer an illusionary solution to some very real problems. Currently, racist mobilization in Germany threatens to seriously damage the still fragile democratic political culture developed during the last 40 years.

The field of urban social movements is structured rather differently in the 1990s than during the 1980s. It is more fragmented and displays far more heterogeneous orientations, some of which are quite antagonistic with each other. Also, the movements have generated new forms of institutionalization and even provide impulses for innovative municipal policies. Yet, one cannot say that urban movements have disappeared: Massive mobilizations around urban issues continue (recently especially against highway construction plans, for traffic reduction, and against the housing shortage) carried out by citizens' initiatives; autonomous groups carry on the struggle against gentrification and urban renewal, which is about to destroy the urban milieu they thrive in; all currents of the so-called new social movements, such as the women's, ecology, and peace movement as well as self-managed enterprises, are active locally and use the local political channels; there are violent riots, often in a ritualized form (e.g., every May 1 and New Year's Eve) but also as political protest (e.g., the campaign against the IMF meetings in Berlin in 1988; see Gerhards, 1991). In early 1991 the Gulf War triggered massive mobilizations involving existing infrastructure, networks, and, especially, local organizations. Houses are still squatted and defended (though the stage for these struggles has moved mostly to the East)[21] and eventually "processed" by the alternative renewal agents, who follow the state funding programs. Recently, such different components of the urban movement scene as members of the autonomous scene and punks prone to militancy, as well as peace and religious groups, defended asylum seekers from racist attacks and organized shelter for refugees who were fleeing a second time, this time from East Germany.

While in this case, groups with differing political conceptions and repertoires came together, there are also developments in very opposing directions. For example, movements have emerged pursuing goals contrary to those of the ecologically and socially oriented movements discussed so far but who make use of the same action repertoire and unconventional forms, which, due to the particular statist history of postwar Germany, have always been associated with the left. For months an active movement mobilized organizing demonstrations and an intense public debate *against* "Tempo 100," that is, against speed reduction on urban highways and *for* unlimited freedom for the automobile. Increasingly, the right seems to be using more and more elements of a social movement repertoire than the traditional forms of (hierarchical and formal) organization. Gangs of skinheads and neo-Nazis have developed a particular counterculture, squatting houses (in the East) and militantly attacking their enemies (leftists, foreigners, gays; see Farin & Seidel-Pielen, 1991, p. 52; Holthusen & Jänecke, 1991). Over the last 20 years, urban movements have been transformed from fundamental opposition via societal marginalization to modernizing and innovating forms of urban renewal, social policy, and forms of governance and have left behind a different terrain.

While the boundaries of the social movement sector have become less clear, and while the movement field has lost energy to other intermediary sectors, cities remain sites of social movements. But the issues are more and more defined by harsher social realities, new marginalization processes, and cleavages reflecting an increasing polarization into "dual cities." The actors are more heterogeneous, and some of them turn against the former movement actors who are now "insiders." Unifying visions and shared forms of praxis have given way to the coexistence of diverse forms of movement politics, organized in all types of forms from spontaneous initiatives to professional movement entrepreneurs. Our analysis of urban movements found that these changes have to do with the changing political opportunity structures, particularly the established parties' selective appropriations of movement issues and the Green party's 1980s electoral successes. These openings were especially manifest on the local level because the crisis and transformation of Fordist modes were first and most sharply expressed here and led to an upgrading of local politics. Though radical utopias confront harsher social conditions in the 1990s than before, the impacts of the last decades' urban movements (returning politics to civic self-activity in a traditionally state-fixated society) and the openings that have been created in local politics provide opportune conditions for movement politics. One task will be to link the resources of the privileged movement sectors with the concerns and demands of the new marginalized sectors.

NOTES

1. From 1969 to 1973 the majority of governments on the city, state, and federal levels were led by the Social Democrats, who, during this phase, were strongly reform oriented. From 1966 to 1969 a so-called grand coalition ruled on the national level, that is, a coalition of two large parties: the SPD and the CDU/CSU. With its "Act for the Promotion of Stability and Economic Growth," it tied local budgets, which represent the lion's share of public investment, to the central government's Keynesian strategy of countercyclical measures. From 1969 to 1972 a social-liberal coalition made up the government on the federal level.

2. The population group most discriminated against, immigrant families, went on rent strike (by the end of 1972, about 1,000 people participated) to reject the role that the renewal process had forced them into, that is, to profitably fill out the last time span before the deteriorated housing stock would be demolished (Stracke, 1976, p. 134). Despite the large number of rent-striking buildings and despite the support they received from the citizens' initiative, leftist activists, squatters, and community groups, as well as the positive resonance they received from the media, the rent strike movement lost in court.

3. In Frankfurt the SPD mayor even welcomed the first squats as "symbolic actions," which served to legitimate and strengthen the local SPD's reformist efforts. After the third squat in November 1970, however, the mayor decided there were enough symbols and declared that further occupations would not be tolerated.

4. The only significant participatory measures passed during the period were the information and hearing rights established with the Urban Renewal Act of 1971.

5. On the local level, many Social Democrats lost to Christian Democrats years before the shift occurred nationally (1982). In Frankfurt, for example, the conservative era started in 1977.

6. Centralizing measures carried out during the second half of the 1970s (*Gebietsreform*) reduced the number of local governments by about one third, reduced their power and authority, and created yet greater distance between citizens and the administration at the lowest level of government.

7. See Markovits (1982).

8. Unemployment remained abnormally high right up until the next recession in 1981 (see Leaman, 1988, pp. 216, 233).

9. These movements were, in fact, not altogether independent of the state given that to a large extent their resources stemmed, if indirectly, from the benefits of the German welfare state: to university students as stipends and to other political activists as welfare or unemployment compensation, rent subsidies, and so on.

10. These were highlighted by the "German Fall" of 1977 (see Mayer, 1978).

11. There were also widespread squatting movements in Zurich, Amsterdam, Frieburg, and other German cities related to the *new housing needs,* a term coined for what appeared to be a new problem at the beginning of the 1980s. A more limited squatting movement in Frankfurt at the time was mostly carried out by younger radicals at the margin of the "established" movement scene, many of whom were primarily interested in cheap housing. The local opportunity structures were no longer conducive to their efforts as the CDU city government would not tolerate illegal occupations. Intense gentrification processes in the districts had displaced those groups who might have been willing to

support and use radical forms of self-help. The dominant movement issues of the period, the struggle against the airport expansion and the new peace movement, did not leave much space for other mobilizations, and the activists of the earlier housing struggles had meanwhile gone into Green electoral politics (see Dackweiler et al., 1990, pp. 206 ff., 219 ff.). The unresolved housing problems eventually contributed to the fact that in 1989 a Red-Green city government became possible.

12. Berlin has often been used as a testing ground for innovative social policies. This is due to its unique political and economic situation during the cold war period and to the fact that it attracted such large numbers of marginalized groups.

13. This obviously did not apply to central city areas, where housing policies encouraged high-income groups to move back into the city. Once they appropriated the social space, it was no longer available for alternative life-styles and disadvantaged social groups.

14. Instead, they often go hand in hand with the new ways of urban development: revitalization and gentrification of the inner city, expansion of polycentric agglomerations, and new forms of small-scale segregation that dissolve the homogeneous Fordist zones. Current government programs subsidizing new housing construction and renovating existing housing privilege private developers over publicly controlled production companies. While small-scale procedures have been introduced to renew deteriorated housing stock, rent laws have been liberalized, and the ensuing market-led restructuring has led to unplanned but massive displacements of low-income residents (for Frankfurt, see Bartelheimer, 1991; for Berlin; Krätke & Schmoll, 1991, p. 546).

15. In Frankfurt, conflicts between movement veterans and a younger movement generation erupted during the 1980s. At a teach-in in October 1985, after the death of an activist who was killed at an anti-Nazi demonstration by a police water tank, Fischer and Cohn-Bendit (radical activists during the housing struggle who became Green-Realo politicians) were attacked with eggs because they refused to withdraw from negotiations with the SPD to form a Red-Green coalition in the Hessen state government.

16. As, for example, in the so-called *Kübel-Aktion* when buckets of excrement were emptied in the up-scale Maxwell restaurant in Kreuzberg (see Kramer, 1988).

17. In response to the harsher state repression, which constructed squatters as a criminal conspiracy (to repress them with antiterrorist measures), a so-called autonomous scene formed in most large cities, with a radical, antistate orientation and with militant praxis forms.

18. See *tageszeitung* (January 10, 1992): "Mehr Arbeitslose."

19. See *tageszeitung* (January 3, 1992): "In Deutschland wächst die Armut."

20. Because of the authoritarian structures the GDR society brought with it, social movements have lost some of the status and clout gained during the last couple of decades. This is perceived by many in Germany as a political backlash to the 1950s.

21. In the fall of 1990, more than 100 large tenement buildings were occupied by (about 1,500) squatters in East Berlin. The use of massive police force to evict some of them in November 1990, for which the SPD was responsible, led to the Greens' leaving the governing coalition. After the following elections, a "grand coalition" of Christian Democrats and Social Democrats was formed ("to deal with the massive problems of unification"), which replaced the Red-Green government of the previous $1\frac{1}{2}$ years.

REFERENCES

Bartelheimer, P. (1991). "Neue Urbanität": Vom sozialen Anspruch zur Wachstumspolitik. Armut in der Dienstleistungsmetropole Frankfurt. *Alternative Kommunalpolitik, 13*(1), 30-34.

Brandes, V., & Schön, B. (Eds.). (1981). *Wer sind die Instandbesetzer?* Bensheim: päd extra.

Bertels, L., & Nottenbohm, H. (Eds.). (1983). *Außer man tut es: Beiträge zu wirtschaftlichen und sozialen Alternativen.* Bochum: Germinal.

Beywl, W. (1983). Alternative Ökonomie: Modell zur Finanzierung von Selbsthilfeprojekten. In L. Bertels & H. Nottenbohm (Eds.), *Außer man tut es: Beiträge zu wirtschaftlichen und sozialen Alternativen.* Bochum: Germinal.

Beywl, W. (1989). Stand und Perspektiven der Forschung zur Alternativokönomie. *Forschungsjournal Neue Soziale Bewegungen, 2*(2), 7-12.

Bodenschatz, H., Heiser, V., & Korfmacher, J. (1983). *Schluß mit der Zerstörung? Stadterneuerung und städtische Opposition in West-Berlin, Amsterdam und London.* Gießen: Anabas.

Clark, S. E., & Mayer, M. (1986). Responding to grassroots discontent: Germany and the United States. *International Journal of Urban and Regional Research, 10*(3), 401-417.

Dackweiler, R., Poppenhausen, M., Grottian, P., & Roth, R. (1990). *Struktur und Entwicklungsdynamik lokaler Bewegungsnetzwerke in der Bundesrepublik: Eine empirische Untersuchung an drei Orten.* Unpublished DFG Research Project Report, Freie Universität Berlin.

Farin, K., & Seidel-Pielen, E. (1991). *Krieg in den Städten: Jugendgangs in Deutschland.* Berlin: Rotbuch Verlag.

Fink, U. (1984). Hilfe zur Selbsthilfe: Ein Berliner Modell. *Aus Politik und Zeitgeschichte, B 11,* 31-45.

Friedrichs, J., Häußermann, H., & Siebel, W. (Eds.). (1987). *Süd-Nord-Gefälle in der Bundesrepublik?* Köln: Westdeutscher Verlag.

Gerhards, J. (1991). Die Mobilisierung gegen die IMF-und Weltbanktagung 1988 in Berlin: Gruppen, Veranstaltungen, Diskurse. In R. Roth & D. Rucht (Eds.), *Neue soziale Bewegungen in der Bundesrepublik Deutschland* (pp. 213-234). Bonn: Bundeszentrale fur politische Bildung.

Häußermann, H., & Siebel, W. (1989). *Neue Urbanität.* Frankfurt: Suhrkamp.

Holthusen, B., & Jänecke, M. (1991). *Thesen zur neueren Entwicklung des Rechtsextremismus in beiden Teilen Berlins und in den fünf neuen Ländern.* Unpublished discussion paper, Berlin.

Huber, J. (1980). *Wer soll das alles ändern: Alternativen der Alternativbewegung.* Berlin: Rotbuch.

Katz, S., & Mayer, M. (1985). Gimme shelter: Self-help housing struggles within and against the state in New York City and West Berlin. *International Journal of Urban and Regional Research, 9*(1), 15-45.

Kramer, J. (1988, November 28). Letter from Europe. *New Yorker, 64*(41), 67-100.

Krätke, S., & Schmoll, F. (1991). The local state and social restructuring. *International Journal of Urban and Regional Research, 15*(4), 542-552.

Kück, M. (1985). Alternative Ökonomie in der Bundesrepublik. *Aus Politik und Zeitgeschichte, B 32,* 26-40.

Leaman, J. (1988). *The political economy of West Germany, 1945-1985.* London: Macmillan.

Markovits, A. (Ed.). (1982). *The political economy of West Germany: "Modell Deutschland."* New York: Praeger.

Mayer, M. (1978). The German October of 1977. *New German Critique, 13,* 155-163.

Mayer, M. (1987). Restructuring and popular opposition in West German cities. In M. P. Smith & J. R. Feagin (Eds.), *The capitalist city: Global restructuring and community politics* (pp. 343-363). Oxford, UK: Basil Blackwell.

Mayer, M. (1991). Politics in the post-Fordist city. *Socialist Review, 21*(1), 105-124.

Mayer, M. (1992). Shifts in the local political system in European cities since the 1980s. In M. Dunford & G. Kafkalas (Eds.), *Competition, regulation, and the new Europe.* London: Belhaven.

Mayer, M., & Ely, J. (Eds.). (1993). *The German Greens: Paradox between movement and party.* Philadelphia: Temple University Press.

Mitscherlich, A. (1965). *Die Unwirtlichkeit unserer Städte: Anstiftung zum Uńfrieden.* Frankfurt: Suhrkamp.

Narr, W. (1976). Threats to constitutional freedoms in West Germany. *New German Critique, 8,* 20-41.

Roth, R. (1990a). Stadtentwicklung und soziale Bewegungen in der Bundesrepublik. In R. Borst et al. (Eds.), *Das Neue Gesicht der Stadt* (pp. 209-234). Basel: Birkhäuser.

Roth, R. (1990b). Städtische soziale Bewegungen und grün-alternative Kommunalpolitik. In H. Wollmann & H. Heinelt (Eds.), *Lokale Politikforschung in den 80er und 90er Jahren* (pp. 167-186). Basel: Birkhäuser.

Roth, R. (1991). Local Green politics in West German cities. *International Journal of Urban and Regional Research, 15*(1), 75-89.

Schubert, D. (1990). Gretchenfrage Hafenstraße: Wohngruppenprojekte in Hamburg. *Forschungsjournal Neue Soziale Bewegungen, 3*(4), 35-43.

SEKIS (Selbsthilfe Kontakt und Informationsstelle). (1987, April). *Selbsthilfe Rundbrief, 7.*

Stracke, E. (1976). *Innerstädtische Umstrukturierungsprozesse und soziale Bewegungen in Frankfurt am Main.* Unpublished doctoral dissertation, University of Frankfurt.

Zeuner, B. (1985). Parlamentarisierung der Grünen. *Prokla, 61,* 5-22.

8 The Silent Valley (Kerala, India) Dam Abandonment: A Case of Successful Community Mobilization

MATHEW ZACHARIAH

The poor and the powerless constitute the vast majority in the nations of Asia, Africa, Latin America, and the Caribbean. Although the governments of most of these nations pursue development, they do so mainly through policies and actions that seek to stimulate general economic growth. Growth, however, does not equal development: It does not necessarily improve the living standards of poor people and, indeed, can create large groups of development victims. In this context, it is instructive to analyze the experience of the Kerala Sastra Sahitya Parishad (KSSP) in successfully mobilizing public opinion against the construction of a large dam in the state of Kerala, India. A study of the KSSP's campaign against the Silent Valley dam can help illuminate the processes of conscientization and explore the limits and possibilities of antihegemonic popular education.

The KSSP emerged out of the unique history and political configuration of the state of Kerala; still, it needs to be understood within a much larger context. For, while Indian state planners and administrators, especially in the past decade, have emphasized economic growth,

AUTHOR'S NOTE: The author's research on the KSSP in 1986-1987 was supported by a University of Calgary Sabbatical Fellowship, a Social Sciences and Humanities Research Council of Canada (SSHRCC) Leave Fellowship, and a Shastri Indo-Canadian Institute Research grant. The research affiliate status that the Centre for Development Studies in Trivandrum extended to the author, the labor of research assistants (particularly R. Sooryamoorthy), and the cooperation of several officeholders of the KSSP made this work possible. Two SSHRCC International Conference Travel Grants are also gratefully acknowledged. *Science for Social Revolution,* by the author and Sooryamoorthy, will soon be published by Sage (India).

many people's movements in India have come to emphasize, instead, participation, redistribution, and ecological sensitivity. If, as some have said, India—a political democracy struggling to recast its largely feudal social structures—epitomizes all the problems of the cultures and countries in the southern hemisphere, then the study of locally based movements and groups in that country, as they have struggled with the problems created by growth and misarticulated visions of development, may hold some lessons for other areas of the world as well.

The KSSP dates it origins back to 1962, when a small group of intellectuals began an effort to make scientific knowledge available to Malayalis—as the people of Kerala are called—through books and periodicals written in Malayalam, the language of Kerala. Its name, in fact, can be translated as "Kerala Science Literature Society." Today the Parishad—as it is informally called—continues to publish magazines and books that have a popular focus and that attempt to educate ordinary people on significant issues in the field of science. In the 1970s, however, the KSSP began to expand both its base and its range of activities. It now organizes and conducts popular education classes on a variety of subjects, engages in campaigns to protect the environment, protests the pollution of rivers by large industries, and promotes healthful living habits in the population. It also actively opposes the militarization of science and organizes to resist the manipulative practices of multinational corporations.

While the focus of this chapter will be on the KSSP's involvement in the Silent Valley dam controversy, I shall begin by describing some of the major features of Kerala as a part of the federal state of India and then provide a brief history of the KSSP. The middle section of the chapter will discuss the major issues involved in the dam controversy and trace the steps by which the government of Kerala eventually decided to abandon the project. The leading role played by the KSSP in this episode won for it a new name in the Indian academic and political vocabulary: ecological Marxists (Guha, 1988, p. 2579).

The final sections of the chapter will attempt to suggest which features of the KSSP, and which specific conditions prevailing in Kerala, might have contributed to the successful outcome of the campaign against the dam. At the same time, we will try to understand some of the limitations of the movement. For, while the KSSP has borrowed heavily from Marxist images of a new society, it remains without a strongly formulated and indigenous vision of its own.

At their best, the main contributions of new social movements like the KSSP are to resist oppression, to demand reformulation of social priorities, and to pressure existing structures to take greater account of poor and powerless people. Such movements, however, have been singularly unable to articulate a viable, constructive, and credible alternative to "command systems"—whether they are of the capitalist or the state socialist varieties.

■ Kerala in India

The subcontinent of India ends in the south in Kanyakumari, where three seas clash: the Bay of Bengal, the Arabian Sea, and the Indian Ocean. Kerala begins barely 100 kilometers to the northwest of this land's-end apex of the inverted triangle that is South India. Shaped somewhat like Chile, it is a relatively narrow strip of land, some 590 kilometers in length and ranging in breadth from 120 kilometers at one point to 30 kilometers at another. It is only the 18th largest of the 25 states in the Indian Union, which is the legal name of India's federal state.

Kerala falls into three natural regions. The highlands are to the extreme east. They contain 24% of the state's dwindling forest area. Here one can find the highest peak (2,694 m.) south of the Himalayas, Anaimudi. Tea, coffee, rubber, cardamom, and other spices are grown on mountain plantations. These plantations, once largely owned by British corporations, are now controlled by Malayali and other Indian private companies.

The second geographic region is the midlands. These are dotted with rice (paddy) fields. Coconut and mango trees offer shade, and there is an abundance of tapioca, banana, ginger, black pepper, sugarcane, and other tropical fruits and vegetables. The coastal lowlands constitute the third region, one broken up by green rivers, river deltas, lakes, lagoons, and winding canals. Fisherfolk, known by their wide conical hats, live along the beaches; navigating canoes, they bring in their bounty from the Arabian Sea, whose blue waters wash the state's sparkling white coastline.

If the mountains and hills in the east prevented invaders from conquering Kerala, the sea in the west brought many different groups to its shores. One might say that the well-known self-confidence of Malayalis stems from the state's unconquered history; the Malayali openness to new ideas is influenced by the open sea.

Two prominent cultural features of Kerala society deserve brief mention here: its religious traditions and the practice of matriliny among its dominant castes, particularly the Nairs. There is a subtle cultural difference between the way the dominant, northern Indian, orthodox Brahminical tradition understands the god Bali, for example, and the way Bali is understood in the Kerala tradition. In the North, Bali is demon king of the Asura family, in contrast to the good gods of the Pandava family. But in Kerala Bali becomes Mahabali (great Bali), who was tricked by Vishnu into surrendering his entire kingdom to keep his word. Mahabali—or Maveli in common parlance—thus deprived of his reign, asked for and received permission to return from the nether world once a year to visit his people. The day of his return, the festival of Thiruvonam, is celebrated with great enthusiasm every year in the month of Chingham (August-September), the first month of the Malayalam calendar after the main harvest.

The notion that kings and others in power should be concerned about justice and the welfare of their people is a strong element in Kerala's cultural ethos. Although, up until the beginning of the twentieth century, Kerala had an extremely strong and iniquitous caste system, almost every Malayali—irrespective of religion—participates in the annual Onam festival and sings the following verse:

When Maveli ruled the land
All the people were equal . . .
There were no lies, no deceit.
Not even a little hypocrisy.

Thus there were latent tendencies toward equality in Kerala, expressed in yearnings for a golden age, which later social movements were able to harness.

Matriliny (marumakkathayam) and patriliny existed side by side in Kerala. Among the Nairs, matriliny centered on the *tarwad*, the family unit. This consisted "of all the descendants of a common ancestress in the female line; a man's children had no rights within the tarwad, since they belonged to his wife's family" (Woodcock, 1967, p. 104). It is wrong to romanticize this system as a matriarchy, that is, as a familial system where the women held institutional power over the men. The eldest male member of the family, called *Karanavar*, had almost absolute power to decide how the land and the affairs of the tarwad should be managed. Nevertheless, the matrilineal system gave women far greater status than would have been available to them under either a patrilinear or a patriarchal system. Women participated in discussions of tarwad matters; as girls, they were educated in literature, music, dancing, and sometimes in physical activities associated with warfare. It is arguable that the widespread practice of matriliny had the latent effect of predisposing people to accept alternate forms of social organization and to develop a frame of mind that was open to pluralism. The spatial pattern of the villages in Kerala may be another contributing factor to the region's progressive political orientation. Villages in other parts of India tend to be concentrated in one area, surrounded by very large, open, cultivated or uncultivated spaces. In Kerala, however, villages appear to be everywhere. As Woodcock writes:

> [Kerala] villages are the most open in the world, with the possible exception of Malayan Kampongs; the dwellings are scattered wherever there are trees to give them shade, and with . . . little sense of the need to concentrate around a focal point. (Woodcock, 1967, pp. 44-45)

One of the outcomes of this panorama of scattered rural habitats has been good communication links between all parts of Kerala. These links have facilitated the work of social movements such as the KSSP.

Kerala's experience challenges conventional definitions of urbanization. Measured in conventional terms, in fact, such as industrialization or commercial trade, Kerala is clearly rural. Yet, it is also very advanced in the provision of modern services and exhibits many of the features associated with developed urban economies. To fully understand the context in which its social movements have taken root, it is important to grasp these contradictory aspects of Kerala society.

Basically, Kerala is agricultural; 81% of the state's population is classified as rural, while only 5% of its area is classified as urban, well below 10 other states and two Union Territories, namely, Delhi and Chandigarh. According to the 1981 Census of India, only 27% of Kerala's population could be considered as participating in the wage sector of the economy. Kerala—with some 3,000 registered companies—ranked well behind Maharashtra, West Bengal, Delhi, Tamil Nadu, Gujarat, Karnataka, Andhra Pradesh, and Punjab in the total number of government and nongovernment companies. There were only 26,500 small-scale industrial units in Kerala in 1984. As opposed to being concentrated in a few urban centers, these units can be found scattered all over the midlands and the lowlands.

Nevertheless, other demographic features of Kerala are more consistent with a developed, urban-based political economy. For example, although Kerala occupies only a little more than 1% of India's land area, its over 28.5 million population is the 12th largest of all the states and Union Territories. Given its small size, this makes its average population density per square kilometer the highest in the country. For India overall, this density is 261; for Kerala, it is 655.

Reproduction rates are lower in Kerala than in India generally: The 1988-1989 rate was 1.3 for Kerala compared with 1.67 for the country as a whole (*Economic Review*, 1989, p. 97). Furthermore, Kerala is the only state in India where there are more women than men: 1,032 females per 1,000 males. The age at marriage is higher in Kerala than in any other region, especially for women. And life expectancy for women is higher than it is for men: in 1987, 70 for females and 67 for males. The respective figures for India in 1987 were 54 (females) and 55 (males). In addition, Kerala's 1985 infant mortality rate of 26 per 1,000 live births is the lowest in India and compares very favorably with some of the "developed" countries. The maternal mortality rate for Kerala is below 2 per 1,000 deliveries in contrast to the Indian average of 5.8. These statistics are to some extent accounted for by the fact that, for every 1,000 Malayalis, there is almost one medical institution.

Generally speaking, these are demographic features more commonly associated with "developed" countries than with "developing" ones. But they do not exhaust the picture. For example, Kerala has the highest literacy rate of all the Indian states and Union Territories. According to the 1981 census, in India as a whole close to 47% of the males and almost 25% of the females (or 36% of the entire population) were literate. But in Kerala over 75% of the males and 65% of the females were literate (or more than 70% of Kerala's population). Ernakulam, the only major urban, industrial city in Kerala, claims the distinction of having achieved almost 100% literacy, a situation for which the KSSP can take much credit. And, at every level, Kerala has the highest percentage of females enrolled in the educational system.

Moving beyond demographic factors, one finds in Kerala a more advanced infrastructure than might be expected in most agricultural societies. Thus every village in the state is connected with an all-weather road and, according to the Indian Postal Service, even has a post office; Kerala leads all the other states in this respect. Since 1985 a protected water supply has been available to over 66% of the urban and 41% of the rural population. In 1986 Kerala had 4.5 telephones per square kilometer compared with 1.05 for the country as a whole; the average number of telephones per 1,000 persons in Kerala is 7.1 against an all-India average of 5.06 (*Economic Review*, 1986, p. 46; See also, Franke and Chasin, 1980). Finally, as of 1984-1985 rural electrification had reached 100% of Kerala's 1,268 villages. This particular aspect of infrastructure development, of course, created those very pressures that led, eventually, to the proposal to build the Silent Valley dam.

There is a less happy side to the ledger, however. For the beauty of Kerala's landscape, its encouraging population statistics, and its progressive infrastructure hide many grim socioeconomic realities. While the use of financial institutions such as banks is extensive, for example, indicating a high degree of monetization of the economy, in 1987-1988 per capita income was estimated to be Rupees 2,754, below the per capita national income of Rupees 3,286. This placed Kerala in the bottom half of all the states in India (*Economic Review*, 1989, p. 8).

Unemployment is high. "At the end of July 1989, there were [3.67 million] job seekers on the live registers of the Employment Exchanges." Of these, 1.86 million had completed high school, and some had gone beyond (*Economic Review*, 1989, p. 3). A June 1989 report pointed out that the rising suicide rate among young people could be attributed primarily to frustration over unemployment among educated youth, mainly from the lower and lower middle classes (Jayachandran, 1989, p. 76). In recent years the authoritative annual *Economic Review* has published data on heavy losses incurred by public sector undertakings, a steady decline in foreign currency remittances from nonresident Indians primarily in West Asia (the Middle East), dwindling prices in the international market for cash crops such as coffee, and declining production of food grains such as rice and other cereals and vegetables (in contrast to increases in milk production and tons of fish caught inland and in the sea), leading to a growth rate in 1985-1986 of 2.9%. India's overall growth rate for the same period was 5.1%.

This unusual combination of a somewhat progressive cultural tradition, rural economy, good lines of communication, widespread literacy, and relatively sophisticated infrastructure with bleak economic conditions may help explain the uniqueness of Kerala's political situation: Soon after its formation as a state in 1957, it stunned the world by becoming the first state or province within a federated country anywhere to *elect* a communist government. Communist and socialist parties continue to be very strong in Kerala. The KSSP, though conceived as an organization for the popular dissemination of science, rather than as an explicitly partisan political movement, is rooted in Marxist traditions.

■ The KSSP: A Brief Account

Historical Background

The KSSP remained a rather small organization until about 1973 when, at its 11th Annual Conference, it adopted the slogan "Science for Social Revolution." That slogan signified three important changes in the KSSP's approach to science. (a) Science, instead of being equated with certain branches of knowledge, such as physics and biology, was now to be conceived as a process through which human beings attempted to explore relationships between cause and effect in the social as well as the natural world. (b) The processes of science, and the uses to which its conclusions and applications (i.e., technology) were put, were now to be understood as depending on human decisions. (c) Those human decisions were currently resulting in grave social problems such as imiseration. For such decisions to be changed, science had to be compelled to serve the people and not just the elites. This stance both increased the organization's popularity among a great many ordinary people and made it a target of sustained controversy.

There was a noticeable increase in membership in 1977. The "official" histories of the KSSP do not discuss this important matter. Let us recall that in 1975-1977 Emergency Rule had been imposed on the nation. This was a dark period for Indian democracy, with severe restrictions placed on the activities of political parties. Many left-wing political activists, specifically members of the Communist Party of India (Marxist)—CPI(M)—, found themselves without their usual forums.[1] The left-wing activists then turned to the KSSP, because the organization was not overtly political and was allowed to continue to function during the emergency.

The entrance of a large number of CPI(M) activists around 1976-1977 into the ranks of the KSSP had two long-lasting effects. First, the KSSP almost overnight became an organization with a large membership. Second, Marxist modes of thought began to dominate its perspectives. Another significant increase in membership occurred in 1983, mainly as a result of the success of the KSSP's street theater program, which covered the entire state.

By 1988-1989 there were almost 1,200 local units, with a combined membership of approximately 37,650 persons. My investigations in 1986-1987 indicated that approximately 60% of the KSSP's active workers were teachers in the region's schools and colleges. Physical scientists, workers, peasants, and technicians can also be found in the membership rolls.

The KSSP's Activities

The KSSP has a three-tier organizational structure. At the base are the units in the villages, towns, and cities; in the middle, the regional and district councils and committees; and, at the apex, a State General Council and a Central Executive Committee. The Parishad publishes three magazines: *Eureka*, for elementary school children; *Sastrakeralam*, for high school students; and *Sastragathy*, for adults. It has also published over 500 books for people of all ages, most of them inexpensive paperbacks on scientific topics. Some are from a "Marxist Science" perspective; a few are expensive reference works. The units sell the books and use the commission they obtain for their activities.

The Parishad also organizes popular education classes with such titles as "Nature, Science and Society," "Resources of Kerala," and "The Cheated Consumer" (Parameswaran, 1987, 1988). Over a 5-year period, support from sympathetic groups enabled the KSSP to organize up to 15,000 "Nature, Science and Society" classes. It has conducted thousands of classes on the other topics as well. But the KSSP does not restrict itself to formal educational programs. It extends its concern for the social implications of science to political action. It once organized a protest outside a posh hotel where a multinational drug company had invited all the doctors of the area to an all-expenses-paid seminar to promote their newest drugs. It distributed pamphlets urging people to demand that government-owned pharmaceutical companies produce and distribute drugs without using brand names—which would cost a fraction of the prevailing price. With assistance from the state and federal governments, the KSSP has also developed a smoke-minimized oven (chulha) for poor people's dwellings.

The KSSP has extensive activities in schools and colleges (Zachariah, 1989, 1990). Two of these are particularly worth mentioning: widely popular Eureka Science Quizzes for elementary school children and the Sastrakeralam Quizzes for high school students, conducted with the cooperation of the Kerala government's Department of Education. The KSSP is also active in the area of teacher retraining in science subjects.

Since 1980 the KSSP has been experimenting with the use of folk art in its mass contact programs. It organizes an annual 37-day march, called Sastra Samskarika Jatha (Science Culture March), across the state. Three separate teams of artists visit several hundred villages, towns, and cities using the medium of Kerala's folk arts to perform street plays, songs, and other forms of spectacle. Progressive screenplay writers, musicians, and lyricists donate the first draft of their works to the KSSP for the march. Amateur artists are selected from mostly working-class, unemployed, and peasant backgrounds to perform; they attend weeklong workshops with experienced KSSP people and, if necessary, revise the scripts as they practice. The plays are performed in open air theaters, in school or college auditoriums, and on street corners, where hundreds of thousands of people see them and interact with the cast and crew.

The songs are based on folk tunes familiar in Kerala, while the dramatic formulas draw, in large part, on the great Hindu myths that most Malayalis know. One play that I saw in 1986 was named *To the 21st Century* and another, *Blood*. The twenty-first century was depicted as a place to which a chariot full of technological gadgets, rich people, and experts were going; it had no seats for ordinary people. *Blood* depicted the needless death of an industrial worker whose fellow workers, out of superstition and ignorance, would not donate blood to save him.

With the help of friendly groups, the KSSP has taken its Jatha program to other states and regions. Programs have been carried out in the states of Gujarat, Madhya Pradesh, Tamil Nadu, Pondicherry, Delhi, Karnataka, Andhra Pradesh, Rajasthan, and Maharashtra. These programs were all presented in their respective regional languages. Overall, the march offers an intense period of KSSP contact with the people, enabling the organization to sell its publications, identify socioeconomic problems, and spread its reach to newer areas.

The KSSP's Ideology and Objectives

The KSSP's official slogan, "Science for Social Revolution," captures the essence of its ideology in one pithy phrase. In the KSSP's vision, *science* stands for all critically evaluated and accepted knowledge that has the potential to empower people; science in this sense is the exploration of the relationship of cause and effect to eliminate the superstition and fatalism that help keep the vast majority of Indians poor and oppressed.[2]

Almost all the intellectuals who founded the KSSP were socialists in a very general sense. The dominant national political party in India at the time, the Indian National Congress, was committed to building "a socialistic pattern of society." Almost all Indian political parties and leaders of the early 1960s paid lip service to socialism. In the early years of the KSSP's growth, social democrats, Gandhian socialists, and scientific socialists (i.e., Marxists) kept their political differences in check and united to promote scientific thinking, in an abstract sort of way. But in the late 1960s and early 1970s, their differences broke out into the open. Marxists asserted that Marxism is *the* science of society and that an organization dedicated to promoting science must do so through the perspectives and tools of Marxism. The adoption of the official slogan in 1973 represented a victory for this view. The entrance of a large number of CPI(M) members in 1975-1977, referred to above, reinforced this tendency. Many of the early founders left the KSSP during this period and began to publicly attack it as a "CPI(M) front." Some of them established associations to counter the KSSP's ideology and popularity. Yet, as I shall argue in the pages to follow, the KSSP has not been a mere CPI(M) front and its ideology has been undergoing significant challenge and evolution.

■ The Silent Valley Dam Controversy

A Brief Chronology of Events

While, as early as 1928 or 1929, a British engineer had identified Silent Valley as an ideal site for hydropower generation, the first technical investigations for a hydroelectric dam did not take place until 1958. In 1973 the government of India's Planning Commission sanctioned the project in the hope that 120 megawatts of electricity would be produced immediately and 240 megawatts within a few years.

In April 1976 the government of India appointed Zafar Futehally— then vice-president of the World Wildlife Fund in India—as chair of a 19-person Task Force for the Ecological Planning of the Western Ghats (D'Monte, 1985). The committee's report, presented a year later, concluded that, if a dam were constructed in the Silent Valley, then "the last Vestige of natural climax vegetation of the region, and one of the last remaining in the country, will be lost to posterity." The task force strongly recommended that the project be abandoned and the area declared a biosphere reserve (D'Monte, 1985, p. 33). The committee nevertheless seemed to leave the door open to dam construction by listing 17 safeguards that, it felt, had to be implemented should the authorities insist on proceeding with the proposal.

The Kerala State Electricity Board (KSEB) and the government of Kerala chose to interpret the task force report as permitting construction—given the safeguards. In response, Futehally, in a letter dated October 19, 1979, stated his opposition to the dam under any circumstances and accepted personal responsibility for the report's earlier ambivalence (Prasad, 1984, pp. 131-132).

In 1976, around the time the task force issued its report, the KSSP became involved in the question of the Silent Valley dam. In 1978 at the KSSP Annual Conference, M. K. Prasad, a professor of botany and a leader in the campaign against the dam, moved to request a halt to the hydropower scheme. The motion was approved, and the KSSP then organized the first of several mass signature and poster campaigns in opposition. Despite these actions, however, the Kerala Legislative Assembly—with many sitting CPI(M) members—passed a unanimous resolution for the speedy implementation of the project. This episode was significant, in part, because it showed clearly that the KSSP was not necessarily a "front" for the Communist Party of India (Marxist), as was so often alleged. Indeed, after the passage of the Legislative Assembly resolution, the KSSP stepped up its campaign to stop the Silent Valley dam. Its local units and district and state-level committees continued to organize discussions in rural and urban public forums. In addition, the KSSP sponsored a pamphlet published by a five-person group in 1979 titled *The Silent Valley Hydroelectric Project: A Techno-Economic and Sociopolitical Assessment*. This pamphlet played a key role in mobilizing opposition to the dam, and we shall look at some of its arguments more closely in the next section.

In April 1979, quite independently of the KSSP, environmental activist Joseph John filed a writ petition before the Kerala High Court, resulting in the grant of a 2-week stay in the construction of the dam. Although the High Court, on January 2, 1980, finally dismissed the claim regarding the adverse effects of the dam, the temporary stay galvanized both supporters and opponents. A month after John submitted his petition, Prime Minister of India Morarji Desai wrote the chief minister of Kerala, approving resumption of work on the Silent Valley project. On the other side, the International Union of Conservation of Nature and Natural Resources (IUCN) intensified its campaign in support of the environmentalists, helping to widen opposition. The primary motive of the IUCN was to protect the lion-tailed macaque, an arboreal primate, and other threatened species.

In January 1980 Mrs. Indira Gandhi returned to the prime minister's chair. In contrast to her predecessor, Desai, Mrs. Gandhi was opposed to the dam. In the same month, a new CPI(M)-led government came to power in Kerala. Alarmed, it pressed the central government for a decision in favor of dam construction, but the Kerala regime was nevertheless sharply divided over the issue. One Marxist leader, Govinda Pillai, declared in a public forum, "Even if Karl Marx tells me to support the project, I won't do so" (D'Monte, 1985, p. 51).

In August 1980 the CPI(M) chief minister, E. K. Nayanar, took a delegation to New Delhi to press the Kerala government's case. Prime Minister Gandhi appointed another committee to examine all the evidence and arguments developed by scientific groups. This committee, under the chairmanship of Professor M. G. K. Menon, presented its report in April 1983. Although the report was cautiously worded, the chairman, in his letter of transmittal, supported conservation. In November 1983 the Kerala Congress-dominated government gave in and scrapped the Silent Valley dam project.

It is to the role of the KSSP in this outcome to which we now turn.[3]

The Role of the KSSP

A constellation of factors seems to have been responsible for the campaign's success. One point of view, for instance, gives Mrs. Indira Gandhi most of the credit for delaying, and finally killing, the project. Another suggests that expressions of public concern from outside Kerala, particularly in the West, played crucial role in turning the tide. It is especially important to note that a large number of organizations in Kerala participated in the "Save the Silent Valley" movement and that some of their spokespersons have expressed irritation about what they perceive as the KSSP's attempt to take all the credit. It is necessary therefore to clearly identify the KSSP's contribution.

There can be no question that KSSP publications on the Silent Valley controversy were a significant element both in bringing the question before public consciousness and in educating people on the issues involved. Its report, *The Silent Valley Hydroelectric Project* (Prasad et al., 1979), was a key element in this process. While the publication ultimately concluded that the dam should not be built, its account was carefully drafted and presented all the major arguments for and against construction as carefully, and as objectively, as possible.

Both sides agreed that Kerala was facing a critical shortage in electricity and that, for at least two reasons, there was a legitimate need to find new sources of electric power. First, electricity was essential for the industrial development that would, among other things, help reduce the state's high levels of unemployment, and, second, the household demand for electric power was increasing at a rapid rate. In support of the project, the *Silent Valley* report pointed out that the proposed site was one of the most ideal in the state for hydropower generation; that the people of Northern Kerals (Malabar), irrespective of their political affiliations, had been agitating for the project for 20 years or more; and that work on the dam, along with allied activities, would provide employment opportunities for between 2,500 and 3,000 persons for a period of 5 to 6 years. Further, the dam could impound and store the monsoon waters of North Kerala so as to avoid floods in the rainy seasons and drought in the summer seasons. Also, hydroelectric power was preferable as an energy source to coal, which was costlier and more polluting. Finally, the document made as strong a case as it could that construction of the dam need not adversely affect the ecosystem (Prasad et al., 1979, p. 3).

The report then arrayed the arguments against the dam. The case for the opposition started with the fact that tropical rain forests are the richest expressions of life on the planet, having a history of several million years of evolution. The Silent Valley was estimated to have been in existence for no less than 50 million years, and its continued integrity was important for the survival of certain endangered species, such as the lion-tailed macaque. Many of the valley's flora and fauna were unique to the area and its flora so diverse and complex that plant breeders found it an invaluable gene pool. The benefits from the dam by way of additional irrigation facilities and energy generation would be marginal in relation to the adverse effects on the ecological system and the destruction of unique species. Finally, the report concluded that the hydrological impacts of the dam had not been studied carefully enough and that the Silent Valley area should be declared a biosphere reserve (Prasad et al., 1979, p. 4).

Along with its printed material, the classes conducted by the KSSP on the Silent Valley dam issue—along the lines of their earlier "Nature, Science and Society" and "Resources of Kerala" classes from 1980 on-ward—resulted in the debates "percolating to the people," as Fernandes puts it (1987, p. 30). KSSP leaders were careful to ensure that the debate did not focus only on the dam but that the issue of dam construction was seen as part of the larger issue of energy production and consumption in the state generally. Thanks mainly to the KSSP's superb organizational ability, many Malayalis became interested in the environmental consequences of large-scale dam construction and other development projects. What are often considered esoteric topics (such as protection of endangered flora and fauna) were discussed in myriad public platforms and in "Letters to the Editor" columns of newspapers.

Since Marxists were often arrayed against each other on this issue, the KSSP's leaders were particularly careful to ensure that the debate was conducted fairly. *The Silent Valley Hydroelectric Project*, for example, presented its arguments in a reasoned and dispassionate tone. In marked contrast to some other KSSP publications, the document was consistent with the movement's declared mission to promote scientific attitudes and information among the people.

The Silent Valley episode was a salutary lesson for the KSSP and the people of Kerala. It reminded them that there are really few black and white issues in development and that policy questions must address options shaded in many gray hues. It made clear, once and for all, that Communist party membership was no guarantee of unity on development issues. No objective student of the controversy could reduce the arguments to simpleminded slogans such as "Humans Versus Nature," "Man Versus Monkeys," "Pro-development Versus Anti-development," "Development Versus Environmental Protection," and so forth. Given the KSSP's public acknowledgment that Kerala needed more electricity and that the northern region was relatively underdeveloped, the intellectuals associated with the KSSP were compelled to offer suggestions for alternative power generation. These alternative suggestions, arguments, and counterarguments helped maintain the debate at a relatively high level (see Vijayachandran, 1980).

Implications for Community Mobilization

The abandonment of the Silent Valley dam proposal illustrates the KSSP's ability to oppose the state by using the power of mass persuasion. It has helped create among ordinary people a sense of their power as citizens. But the KSSP developed into its current form in Kerala, which has been the home of many movements for social equality. We need to understand, therefore, the ways in which such contextual factors as Kerala's history, culture, and social structure might have contributed to the KSSP's success.

First, there have been many social uplift movements in Kerala, of which the KSSP is only one recent example. Then, too, there is the high literacy rate, which makes it possible for the KSSP to get its message across through the production and distribution of written materials. The movement also uses Kerala's well-developed infrastructure: telephone lines linking most of the state, very good connections to the interior by roads, and a very efficient and widespread postal system. All these assist the organization to work well. These contextual factors, however, do not explain why the KSSP was able to succeed in helping defeat the Silent Valley dam. They only set out some of the social and cultural conditions under which that victory took place. We need to look more closely at three elements central to the organizational life of the KSSP itself: its ideology, the credibility of its leadership, and its notions of effective political strategy.

1. The KSSP's specific ideological stance grew from the fact that many of the intellectuals who became active in the organization accepted Marxism as the science of society. Marxism propagated a vision of a classless society and a program to capture state power as a method to realize that vision. These features made it far more appealing to most members of the KSSP than the indigenous vision, Sarvodaya, which Mahatma Gandhi had promoted to change people's consciousness and, eventually, Indian social institutions (see Zachariah, 1986). Marxism did not appear to suffer from two fatal weaknesses of Sarvodaya: (a) political irrelevance and (b) association, however indirect, with the Indian National Congress party, which, in most Indian states, had been in power since the 1951 elections for two decades.

The KSSP's ideological stance in relation to both science generally and the impact of development on people's lives in particular has been crucial to the support it has won. The KSSP, in its attempts to promote the scientific temperament, teaches that ordinary people can benefit if science is used by society in new and creative ways. There is another factor as well: In their life experiences, people notice that, although economic development is taking place, ordinary people are not fully benefiting from it. This is especially true in Kerala, which is one of the poorer states in India. The KSSP's emphasis on development for the people thus holds a strong appeal for the working and middle classes.

2. It is not only ideology that is a factor in the KSSP's success at mobilizing people, I believe, but also the credibility of its leadership.

In most organizations, for example, we find that the top and intermediate leadership are very distant from the rank and file. In the KSSP, however, leadership is functional. Leaders and followers sleep in the same hall when there are overnight meetings. They go to the same wells to drink, the same bathrooms to wash and use latrines. Leaders are not assigned to 5-star hotels while followers find themselves relegated to meager accommodations—as often happens with many organizations in India.

Another element contributing to the effectiveness of the KSSP is that many people in top leadership positions already have secure jobs. The KSSP is their avocation. As soon as their regular job is over, they arrive at KSSP offices to do the hundreds of mundane but essential activities that keep it going. They do this work for many reasons, not the least of which is their commitment to the cause and the camaraderie that develops between them and the other volunteer workers. It is an organization where people are involved, but not for narrow self-interest. Whether in day-to-day administration or the performance of street plays, expenses are voluntarily kept to a minimum.

To ensure maximum impact, the active volunteer workers must be willing to devote a considerable portion of their nonremunerated work time to the progress of the movement. The absence of significant financial rewards may mean, on the one hand, that the movement will not immediately "catch fire," that it will take time to achieve a sufficiently large following to achieve "critical mass" status. But it will also mean, as a prominent KSSP leader said to me, that selfish, egotistical people will not be attracted to the movement as would "flies to a honeypot." It follows, of course, that the offices of the KSSP, and its organizational work, must be as spartan as possible to save costs and to make poor people feel at home in its day-to-day work spaces.

3. Finally, there are some key strategic principles that the KSSP has learned to follow. Because it is not difficult for the powerful forces of the status quo to isolate and demoralize an antihegemonic movement, the movement must align itself (openly or secretly, as circumstances warrant) with similar organizations or with political parties sympathetic to its stance on particular issues. To resist successfully unwelcome blandishments, lobbying, blackmail, or other threats that will be brought to bear on its independence, such a movement must also ensure that it has a sufficient, self-reliant financial base. It is important, as well, for the movement to cultivate influential persons in government, the arts, the sciences, technological units, and entertainment fields who are

supportive of its cause. And, finally, the arts—music, drama (including street theater), poetry, effective posters—all must be pressed into service to spread the message of the organization.

Theoretical Explorations

The KSSP has not been able to create an energizing vision that will appeal to those ordinary people—for instance, most of the poor Christians and Muslims and many poor Hindus—to whom Marxism is anathema. Such a vision will have to be necessarily indigenous and cannot, especially in this decade, take comfort in communist shibboleths. Three implications follow.

The main reason the KSSP's stance vis-à-vis the dam received accolades is because of its extraordinary efforts to keep the intellectual debate honest. The specific impetus, of course, was the presence of Marxists on both the pro-dam and the anti-dam sides. But there is a general lesson to be learned here. On many matters that affect the people—such as the poor quality of education in government-run schools—the KSSP can present credible, defensible arguments based on carefully conducted investigations instead of resorting to worn-out slogans that make it seem like a mere CPI(M) front.

In view of the clearly demonstrated inability of communist practice to create a just society in the former Soviet Union and Eastern Europe, the KSSP should rethink its approach to the social revolution it wants to promote. In this connection, we should applaud its decision of the past 3 years to focus on a campaign for the eradication of illiteracy in Kerala. Pursuit of positive middle-range objectives of this nature can probably broaden its appeal. Such objectives, of course, need to come to terms with the view that, while development including the participation of people is a slower process, it is also a better one.

Third, the Sri Lankan version of the Sarvodaya movement has been struggling to articulate a vision of a "no affluence as well as no poverty" society (see Ariyaratne, 1989, p. 229). The KSSP might also attempt similar searches based on Kerala's history and its unique place in India and the world.

The abandonment of the Silent Valley dam was a significant victory for community mobilization, and the role played by the KSSP in defeating the project was central. Yet the unique features of the struggle to keep Silent Valley as a biosphere—such as the late Mrs. Gandhi's support, the high literacy rate among Kerala's people, and Kerala's activist traditions—means that there are no general principles that can automatically be learned from this effort and applied elsewhere. Other huge dams in India are currently being built despite popular opposition. Nevertheless, it is surely as important to celebrate and learn from small victories as it is to learn from great defeats. The KSSP has succeeded very well in being an oppositional force. It has been effective in creating among ordinary people a sense of participation and enthusiasm in development issues. Perhaps there are some aspects of its character and practice that can be taken beyond Kerala and the struggle over the Silent Valley dam. This chapter, in fact, suggests at least three.

The KSSP has shown its ability to remain committed to a clear and focused but at the same time fairly flexible ideological stance in regard to development issues. It retained this openness in the Silent Valley dam controversy. It has, second, insisted upon a leadership that, in its day-to-day practice, struggles to live the values of equality and social concern that the movement claims as its foundation. And, certainly in the case of the Silent Valley movement, the KSSP carefully followed a set of strategies that sought coalition, even as they maintained and protected the organization's independence.

These are all features of KSSP organizational life that can, perhaps, be generally related to community mobilization and extended to other settings.

NOTES

1. There are three major Communist parties in India. The Communist Party of India—CPI—is the oldest continuing party in the country; it is often seen as closely allied with the former Soviet Union. The Communist Party of India (Marxist)—CPI(M)—broke ranks with the CPI for theoretical and practical reasons. It takes a more militant stance than the CPI by insisting that participation in electoral politics should not blind communists to the need to use violence to bring about change when the circumstances are right. The Communist Party of India (Marxist-Leninist)—CPI(ML)—is the smallest group and advocates the violent overthrow of the Indian state as a precondition for profound societal change. There are also many splinter groups.

2. In its 1986-1987 Workers' Diary, the KSSP listed seven major objectives. The first, and most important, objective reads as follows:

"To develop in all sections of the people scientific consciousness and the scientific perspective. In this way, to build the foundation for a meaningful social revolution."

Some of the others were:

"To conscientize and help organize the people and people's associations to oppose the anti-people actions of scientific and technical knowledge purveyors."

"To line up the people against old understandings, ignorance and traditions that are obstacles to social progress."

"To propagate ways through which scientific and technical knowledge can be appropriately utilized to promote genuine development in our country."

3. D'Monte (1985) and Fernandes (1987) provide excellent detailed accounts of the individuals and events associated with the abandonment of the dam project. They discuss such actors as Dr. Salim Ali, the famous author on birds in various regions of India, and Steve Green, an American who had studied the lion-tailed monkey. Therefore, in the brief account that follows, we only mention a few highlights.

REFERENCES

Ariyaratne, A. T. (1989). *Collected works: Vol. 4. Moratnuva.* Sri Lanka: Sarvodaya Shramadana Movement.

D'Monte, D. (1985). Storm over Silent Valley. In *Temples or tombs? Industry versus environment: Three controversies* (pp. 28-59). New Delhi: Centre for Science and Environment.

Economic Review. (1985). [annual]. Trivandrum: Government of Kerala, State Planning Board.

Economic Review. (1986). (1989). [annual]. Trivandrum: Government of Kerala, State Planning Board.

Economic Review. (1989). [annual]. Trivandrum: Government of Kerala, State Planning Board.

Fernandes, J. (Ed.). (1987). *Silent Valley: A look back* (The DEEM—Documentation of the Experience in Environmental Management—series). New Delhi: World Wildlife Fund—India.

Franke, R. W., & Chasin, B. H. (1989). *Kerala: Radical reform as development in an Indian state* (Food First Development Report 6). San Francisco: Institute for Food Development Policy.

Guha, R. (1988). Ideological trends in Indian environmentalism. *Economic and Political Weekly, 23*(49), 2578-2581.

Jayachandran, F. (1989, July). Dynamics of attempted suicide and strategies for prevention: A study from Calicut. *Loyola Journal of Social Sciences, 3*(2), 73-81.

Parameswaran, M. P. (1987). *KSSP: Movement for a mass education.* Trivandrum: KSSP. (mimeo)

Parameswaran, M. P. (1988). Art as medium of communication of science. *Science for Social Revolution, 1*(1), 15-16.

Prasad, M. K. (1984). Silent Valley: An ecological assessment. *Cochin University Law Review,* pp. 128-138. (reprint)

Prasad, M. K., et al. (1979). *The Silent Valley Hydroelectric Project: A Techno-economic and socio-political assessment.* Calicut: KSSP.

Vijayachandran, K. (1980). *Silent Valley: Myth and reality.* Trivandrum: Parisara Asoothrana Samrakshana Samithy.

Woodcock, G. (1967). *Kerala: A portrait of the Malabar Coast.* London: Faber and Faber.

Zachariah, M. (1986). *Revolution through reform: A comparison of Sarvodaya and conscientization.* New York: Praeger. (also New Delhi: Vistaar/Sage, 1988)

Zachariah, M. (1989). People's movements and reform of formal education. *Canadian and International Education, 18*(1), 319.

Zachariah, M. (1990). Dilemmas of a successful people's education movement in India. *Perspectives in Education, 6*(3), 157-175.

9   "Deepening" Democracy: Popular Movement Networks, Constitutional Reform, and Radical Urban Regimes in Contemporary Brazil

SONIA E. ALVAREZ

South America's recent democratic transitions provided fertile terrain for the growth of a wide variety of social movements and other forms of collective resistance to regressive economic policies, cultural authoritarianism, and repressive military regimes. In Brazil new movements of the urban and rural poor, along with other grass-roots movements linked to the progressive Catholic church, newly militant sectors of the labor movement, the human rights movement, and the feminist, black, gay, and environmental movements articulated democratic demands for expanded citizenship, social justice, and political

AUTHOR'S NOTE: Elements of the arguments presented in this chapter were elaborated in presentations delivered at the Center for Latin American Studies, University of California, San Diego; the conference on "Social Movements and Cultural Politics," at the University of California, Santa Cruz; the Center for Latin American Studies, University of Washington; and the A. E. Havens Center for the Study of Social Structure and Social Change, University of Wisconsin, Madison. I am grateful to my colleagues at these institutions for comments that helped me clarify and refine the analysis presented here. As always, I am greatly indebted to numerous Brazilian scholars for their help in conceptualizing this project and their insights into the dynamics of popular movement politics, most especially Ruth Corrêa Leite Cardoso, Simone Coelho de Castro Alves, Julio Assis Simes, and Aldaiza Sposati. Anne Blair ably assisted in collecting data in the field; Gabrielle Watson generously shared her data on movements for water and sanitation in São Paulo; and Vince Chhabria, Brian Wampler, and William Veiga provided valuable research assistance at UCSC. This research was supported by faculty research grants from the University of California, Santa Cruz.

191

and cultural transformation, adding new dimensions to the struggle against military authoritarian rule. As negotiations between civilian and military elites increasingly narrowed the scope of democratization, some observers vested great hopes in the transformative potential embodied by Brazil's new social movements, heralding them as portenders of a deeper, more thoroughgoing, more genuine democracy—the "last, best hope" for "real" democratization.

Since the first civilian administration in 21 years was installed in 1985, Brazilian movements arguably *have* contributed to the democratization of social and cultural life by challenging hegemonic discourses and chipping away at societal patterns of domination and subordination. But Brazil's democratic institutions remain elite dominated. The "political class" enthroned in the new democracy shows remarkable continuity with its authoritarian predecessor.[1] The party and electoral legislation "favor weak parties, limit accountability, and encourage personalistic, clientelistic, and individualistic styles of representation" (Mainwaring, 1991, p. 39). Access to and influence in policymaking arenas remain restricted to powerful national and transnationalized economic interests and traditional clientele networks. And most Brazilians continue to be excluded from meaningful participation in the formal political process. At the institutional level, at least, the hopes once vested in the democratizing potential of grass-roots and liberation movements would appear to have been dashed.

Most movement demands for expanded citizenship and social justice, moreover, have been indefinitely deferred. Though some basic civil liberties were restored and suffrage was extended to illiterate adult citizens in 1985, the institutional and ideological continuities between authoritarian and postauthoritarian politics have severely restricted the scope of social, political, and economic reform undertaken by Brazil's civilian rulers. The structural adjustment and neoliberal economic policies implemented in Brazil's "New Republic," moreover, differ little from those pursued under authoritarian rule, further dampening movement hopes that democratization would bring about a new politics of redistribution and thus expand social citizenship.

But, as I will suggest, the struggle over the nature and future course of Brazilian democratization is hardly over and social movements are still actively contesting the would-be entrenchment of restricted, elite democracy. Radical democratic alternatives, inspired by grass-roots social movement practices, grounded in the poor and working classes, and articulated by social movement networks and progressive political parties, are very much alive in Brazil today, as in several other South American nations. In countries as diverse as Brazil, Colombia, Venezuela, and Uruguay, coalitions of social movements and "new" or "reconstituted" parties of the left are articulating competing conceptions of social *and* political citizenship and democracy, though these democratic experiments currently are largely restricted to the local level (see Escobar & Alvarez, 1992).

Such efforts to "deepen" South American democracy stand out as islands of resistance to the tide of neoliberalism and elite-dominated democratization that has swept the region since the mid-1980s. Deepening political democracy—especially in dependent capitalist societies characterized by egregious social and economic inequalities—entails devising political-institutional arrangements that *redistribute* information about, access to, and influence in the governmental arenas in which collectively binding policy decisions are made. In Latin America, even under formally democratic political regimes, such information, access, and influence have been enjoyed by a very small, privileged fraction of the population but effectively have been denied to subaltern groups and classes.

Since the return of civilian rule in Brazil in the mid-1980s, social movement activists and their political allies in the church and on the left have struggled to develop concrete, if not yet fully coherent, strategies for promoting alternatives to the restricted democratic regime envisioned by the military and civilian elites who seek to control the democratization process; their strategies are the focus of this chapter. My principal empirical examples are drawn from metropolitan São Paulo, a "megacity" of some 15 million inhabitants that accounts for close to a third of Brazil's industrial production.[2]

I first trace the evolution of urban popular movements in São Paulo over the course of Brazil's transition, underscoring the strategic role of "political articulators" in weaving together disparate urban struggles, other social movements, and progressive opposition political currents to advance an alternative radical democratic vision. I then turn to an analysis of how such movements worked to expand the institutional parameters of Brazil's postauthoritarian regime through their participation in the process of drafting new federal, state, and municipal constitutions.

Focusing on local politics, the final section discusses the efforts of the Workers Party's (Partido dos Trabalhadores, or PT) "popular democratic" municipal administrations to implement an alternative democratic project at the local level, a project whose professed goal is to transform and democratize the relationship between poor and working-class citizens and the state. Founded in 1980 by militant trade unionists, social movement activists, practitioners of liberation theology, members of Marxist political organizations, and leftist intellectuals, the PT today defines itself as a "democratic and socialist mass party." As a party "born of popular movements," its professed goal is to give "institutional expression" to such movements and thus dispute the hegemony of Brazil's political and economic elites through both institutional and social struggle.[3] Since it assumed the reins of municipal power in São Paulo and over two dozen other Brazilian cities after impressive (and largely unexpected) victories in the municipal elections of 1988, the PT has been struggling to put its long avowed goal of "popular democracy" into practice.

■ **Urban Social Movements and Democratization in Brazil: Articulatory Practices and the Evolution of a Radical Democratic Vision**

The urban "popular movements"[4] that today form the PT's principal base of support in São Paulo are products of the social struggles of the 1970s and 1980s, struggles guided by new political methodologies (or, in movement parlance, "new ways of doing politics"). Though the actual political practices of these "new" movements vary considerably and do not always conform fully to their stated egalitarian ideals, most reject hierarchical organizational forms, encourage participants to develop a critical consciousness of how structures of domination and exploitation shape their daily lives, and value the direct participation of community members in seeking community improvements. Such participation, movement discourse proclaims, is a means to social empowerment, an end in itself, and not just a means to secure rights or social services from the state. The practice of "direct democracy" at the community level and the mobilization of neighborhood residents to make collective demands on the state are at the core of the political methodologies of these new movements.

Since their emergence, however, the popular movements of the last two decades—which include, among others, the progressive Catholic church's Christian Base Communities, organizations of the urban landless, the shantytown dwellers, or *favelados*, grass-roots women's organizations, cost-of-living, day care, and health care movements—have had to dispute the associational terrain of São Paulo's urban periphery with "older" neighborhood civic organizations, which are crucial links in the urban chain of traditional clientelistic politics.

In São Paulo these "older" neighborhood civic associations, the most common of which are called *Sociedades de Amigos do Bairro* (SABs, or Societies of Friends of the Neighborhood), expanded steadily from the 1940s through the 1960s. Though originally organized by residents of the urban periphery who sought the expansion of social services to their neighborhoods, the SABs began to flourish when local politicians found them to be fertile ground for the extension of urban clientele networks. The politics of *troca de favores*, or exchange of favors, thus provided the primary impetus for the expansion of the SABs throughout the populist period.[5] By 1970 there were over 1,100 SABs in the state of São Paulo, of which 800 could be found in metropolitan São Paulo alone (Singer, 1980, p. 87).

Today, the vast majority of SABs are formal, hierarchical membership organizations whose leaders are elected in assemblies of association members. These formal mechanisms of leadership selection, though usually involving only a small fraction of neighborhood residents, are what permit the SABs to claim the legitimate, delegated authority to "represent" all local residents vis-à-vis city officials. Community mobilization in pursuit of urban services typically is shunned by the SABs whose leaders frequently become neighborhood political brokers, or *cabos eleitorais*, for urban party organizations.

After 1964 Brazil's military authoritarian rulers availed themselves of these "representative" neighborhood associations to control and co-opt poor residents of the urban periphery. Many of the SABs came to be dominated by politicians from ARENA, the military regime's official party. The associations' prime activities increasingly centered on extracting personal favors for their members from the military-appointed mayor and ARENA municipal councilmen. The SABs thus gradually lost their "representativeness" and much of their legitimacy vis-à-vis local residents, and whatever influence they might have once had on the social fabric of their neighborhoods increasingly eroded.[6]

The erosion of the SABs' legitimacy coincided with the emergence of new organizational initiatives among the urban poor, largely commandeered by progressive sectors of the Catholic church.[7] Clergy and religious and church lay workers, inspired by the teachings of liberation theology, organized tens of thousands of Christian Base Communities

(Comunidades Ecclesiais de Base, or CEBs) throughout Brazil. And by the late 1970s, these and their "popular movement" offspring far outnumbered the SABs and other "older" associational forms in São Paulo's urban periphery. Seeking to combat the socially perverse consequences of the military's model of development and promote critical consciousness and fraternity among the faithful, the church stimulated CEB participants to organize community self-help projects and encouraged them to demand urban services from the authoritarian state, not as political "favors" but as integral components of their "rights" as "citizens."

This pro-participatory language on rights and citizenship, coupled with the condemnation of both military authoritarianism and its populist-corporatist predecessors, became the discursive thread that, over the course of the 1970s and early 1980s, wove dispersed, localized urban struggles together into loose-knit and increasingly militant popular movement networks. These movement networks provided the political party opposition with a crucial social base and quickly became a thorn in the side of the military's controlled project of *abertura*, or "political opening," launched in 1974 as the authoritarian regime's foundational project began to falter.

Though abertura by no means signaled the end of the military's repressive measures, it did permit more explicit opposition to be voiced in civil society, at least among elite sectors. In the mid-1970s the Brazilian Bar Association, the Brazilian Press Association, and other professional groups joined the Catholic church in denouncing authoritarian policies and demanding the restoration of democracy. Many of these middle-class dissidents—including intellectuals, architects, doctors, and other professionals—along with former student activists and guerrilla combatants, radical Catholics, opposition party activists, and members of incipient feminist and black movements, became the advisers or "political articulators"[8] of the new popular movements taking shape in the urban periphery. Many began working in peripheral neighborhoods, attending and often organizing the activities of local mothers' clubs, youth organizations, health care groups, and so on.

The more radical of these political articulators, especially those inspired by socialist and/or feminist ideologies, emphasized the structural and political roots of the particularistic demands typically advanced by local movements (e.g., for running water, paved streets, local health clinics). In working with movements of the urban landless, for example, they stressed that, to obtain adequate housing, it was necessary to struggle against the larger "pact of domination" and not just for more government-funded housing units to be built in the neighborhood. Feminists, drawn to popular movements by the fact that the overwhelming majority of participants in the new movements were (and still are) women, worked to instill a critical gender consciousness among neighborhood activists.[9] Advisers also helped establish connections among local movement leaders and sometimes articulated protests and other joint movement strategies—establishing fluid nets of horizontal linkages among movement organizations. They facilitated movement contacts with government bureaucracies; indeed, many articulators were or would become public servants. It should be stressed that many local leaders of popular movement groups—whose organizing experience provided them with "mobilizational capital" that rivaled the "cultural capital" of university-educated advisers—also become the articulators of citywide or regional movement networks.

Though linkages among movement groups were typically informal and joint actions or conjunctural articulations were most often organized around specific urban problems (e.g., public housing, health services, day care, and so on), many leaders and advisers of the various issue-specific movement networks often interacted in opposition party arenas and exchanged logistical support and crucial political information. Through this sort of political and ideological mediation, the new urban struggles became ever more articulated with the struggle against the military's authoritarian regime and its economic model.

But the opposition to military rule itself was riddled by internal divisions and these surfaced unmistakably when the military decreed the forcible splintering of the sole post-1965 legal opposition party, the MDB (*Movimento Democrático Brasileiro*, or Brazilian Democratic Movement), in late 1979. As Margaret Keck argues, by the late 1970s, there was a "growing consensus in Brazilian society on the need for democratization. The powerful contradictions within this consensus were bound to be released once the discussion moved from opposition to the regime to constructing political organizations that would shape the democratization process" (Keck, 1986, pp. 67-68). While some members of the political opposition insisted on the strategic necessity of maintaining opposition unity, most in the loose-knit urban popular movement networks articulated by the church, the Marxist left, intellectuals, professionals, feminists, and gay and black movement activists joined with some progressive sectors of the MDB and the "new trade union movement"[10] to found the PT, insisting that the goal of unity "hid substantial disagreement about the kind of democracy to be instituted" (Keck, 1986, p. 68).

Many Societies of Friends of the Neighborhood and other "older" civic associations—some of which had adopted some of the organizational innovations of "newer" popular movement groups and had built ties to the left or *autentico* wings of the MDB during 1970s—opted for the PMDB, the party founded by those who championed the unity of opposition forces. Still other SABs and neighborhood associations of the "older" variety established new clientelistic ties to the most conservative wing of the party, currently its dominant wing, under the leadership of former São Paulo governor, Orestes Quercia. The antagonisms that had characterized the relationship between newer popular movements and older neighborhood associations, stemming from different organizational goals and divergent "ways of doing politics," thus took on explicitly partisan, ideological overtones during the 1980s.

Whereas democracy had been the universal rallying cry for the opposition as a whole under the artificially imposed two-party system, the party reform of 1979 brought fully to the fore the competing conceptions of and projects for democracy and, underlying the visions, the practices of various MDB party factions and their respective social movement constituencies. Three distinctive democratic projects began to take shape in the early 1980s. Dissident elements of the authoritarian regime coalition and conservative sectors of the opposition advocated the restoration of liberal democracy, with multiple qualifiers—that is, though basic civil and political freedoms and political competition would be restored, Brazil's dependent capitalist economic model would suffer few alterations, radical political and social forces would remain marginal to politics and policymaking, and the military would retain significant political prerogatives. A second project, which centered on institutional reforms and parliamentary action and championed socioeconomic reforms and the expansion of social, as well as formal political, citizenship, was advanced by the progressive and center-left wings of the PMDB (which, in 1988, left the party to form the PSDB, the Party of Brazilian Social Democracy).

The Workers Party shared the social-democratic opposition's concern for the expansion of social rights but its "popular democratic" project was distinctive in its insistence that meaningful democratic citizenship also required the promotion of popular participation—both within and beyond the parliamentary and electoral arenas—in the pursuit of social and economic justice and empowerment. The kind of democracy envisioned by the PT found its principal inspiration in the "political methodologies" developed by popular movements. Its discourse on "popular participation," for example, is quite close to that of the liberation theology church (Keck, 1986, p. 86). Thus, while the PT proposed to give institutional voice to the demands of subaltern groups and classes in the parliamentary arena, it viewed the democratic struggles of popular and liberation movements in civil society as integral components of its "popular democratic" project for postauthoritarian Brazil. Its radical democratic vision thus led the party to insist on the centrality of social empowerment through grass-roots participation and to promote the growth of "autonomous" popular movements without imposing its political agenda on those movements.

■ Expanding Representation and Extending Citizenship

The first and most restricted of the three democratic projects described above can be said to have triumphed in 1985, as civilian leaders from the "ancien regime" and conservative sectors of the political opposition assumed the reins of power in Brazil's first civilian federal administration in 21 years. Even in an increasingly conservative national political climate and amid an economy careening ever more rapidly into crisis, however, movement networks and their progressive allies in political society persisted in their efforts to deepen Brazilian democracy.

These efforts reflect a partial reorientation of the political methodologies adopted by popular movements under military rule. That is, after 1985 many in the loose-knit network of movement organizations and advisers came to view participation in formal processes of representative democracy as a complementary means for furthering the goals of social empowerment and meaningful citizenship, to be pursued alongside continuing efforts to promote economic justice and redistribution, *concientizao* (critical consciousness), and community participation and mobilization.

Some movement leaders and their allies in civil and political society turned their efforts toward influencing the drafting of the constitution that was to shape Brazil's postauthoritarian regime, thus working to break the hegemony of economic and political elites over the democratization process. Some active in the loose-knit network of movements and articulators, now formalized into coalitions such as the Constituent Assembly Popular Education Project,[11] played a crucial role in mapping out national strategies, bringing movement leaders together to work toward the expansion of citizenship and representative democracy. Many groups worked to elect "popular representatives," candidates with "organic links" to movement organizations, to the 1986 Congress that was to draft the federal constitution. After the congressional Constituent Assembly was installed, efforts turned to pressuring the assembly to create mechanisms that would ensure citizen input and participation in the drafting of the constitution.

To this end, coalitions or articulations of movement organizations, progressive sectors of the Catholic church, and labor unions established "popular lobbies" in Brasília in 1986 and 1987.[12] These lobbies represented both an innovative adaptation of "historic" popular movement tactics developed under military rule and the maturation of new pressure group tactics essential to movement effectiveness in representative democracies. The historic tactics employed by the popular lobbies included, for example, numerous citizen caravans to Brasília—massive mobilizations of busloads of citizens from throughout Brazil who would descend on Congress to press for the inclusion of their demands or issues in the Draft Charter; this was a tactic previously most often deployed at the municipal level. Some popular lobbies also engaged in fairly aggressive, confrontational tactics. DIAP, the trade union lobby, for example, distributed lists and photos to the media of members of Congress deemed "popular enemies" for opposing the inclusion of social and labor rights in the Constitution.[13] Other movement coalitions and popular lobbies staged sit-ins and hunger strikes in Congress. And hundreds of mass rallies, petition drives, and letter-writing campaigns were mounted.

The "new" pressure group tactics developed by the popular lobbies clearly reflected the radical democratic political methodologies or practices typical of Brazil's popular movements. For example, while a national coalition of grass-roots groups, the National Pro-popular Participation Plenary, established offices in the nation's capital and regularly engaged in lobbying legislators, it was more than a conventional lobby. During the Constituent Assembly's deliberations, the plenary held regional and national meetings of popular movement activists and published newsletters to evaluate the constitution-drafting process in its various stages. The plenary defined itself as a loosely structured network or "articulation" of groups, not a formal peak organization. In keeping with the political practices typical of Christian Base Communities and other popular movement organizations, the plenary rotated leadership at the local, state, and national levels and also engaged in continuous efforts at political education aimed at promoting a deeper and broader conception of democratic citizenship.

Movement lobbies and articulators succeeded in persuading the dominant party (then the PMDB) to include three key mechanisms that facilitated citizen input to the Draft Charter. First, individual citizens or organizations of civil society were invited to submit initial suggestions for the preliminary constitutional draft. Second, the internal rules of the Constituent Assembly provided for citizen testimony at public hearings held by the 24 subcommissions responsible for elaborating different sections of the preliminary draft. And, third, movement lobbies and progressive legislators secured a "popular amendment" process to that preliminary draft, which provided that amendments could be submitted for congressional consideration if signed by at least 30,000 registered voters and sponsored by at least three organizations of civil society.[14]

Over 11,000 initial suggestions were received by the assembly and were routed to the appropriate subcommissions for consideration.[15] Dozens of popular movement representatives testified at subcommission hearings; groups either were invited to testify or could request a hearing. For example, members of urban landless movements and *favela* associations testified in five subcommissions, including one that dealt with urban reform, a matter never before addressed by Brazilian constitutional law.

After the preliminary constitutional draft, based on the reports of the 24 subcommissions, was published on July 15, 1987, congressional constituents and civil society had until August 15 to propose amendments. In that brief period of time, 122 popular amendments were presented, signed by 12,277,423 registered voters—between 6% and 18% of the Brazilian electorate.[16] This impressive feat could never have been accomplished without the organizational infrastructure provided by popular movement groups, especially those tied to the Catholic church. Again, movement leaders and articulators and the informal intramovement networks established over the course of the 1970s and 1980s played a crucial role in this campaign.

What was the net result of these grass-roots efforts to expand representation and participation in postauthoritarian Brazil? At the institutional level, the federal constitution allows for elements of direct democracy to be built into Brazil's political system at various levels. For example,

Title One reads, "All power emanates from the people, who exercise it through their elected representatives or directly, pursuant to this Constitution." The word *directly* was included at the insistence of popular lobbies and their progressive congressional allies and was fiercely opposed by the political right. The 1988 Constitution provides for "popular legislative initiatives," which require the endorsement of 1% of the electorate from at least five states. It also recognizes the legitimacy and representativeness of civic associations and movement organizations. For example, it mandates that urban movement organizations be consulted in urban planning. It grants trade unions, professional associations, and other organizations of civil society the right to represent their members in any judicial or administrative instance. The Constitution also inscribes new social rights for women, racial/ethnic groups, and labor and expands the formal political and civil rights of all Brazilian citizens.

According to most movement leaders, lobbyists, and political analysts, the process of citizen participation in the Constituent Assembly also contributed to expanding and deepening democratization insofar as it exposed broad sectors of the population to formal democratic procedures and, through political education, helped to further a more democratic political culture. It unquestionably fueled political learning among popular movement organizations that were pushed to develop more effective pressure group tactics. A growing number of parliamentarians, in turn, came to accept and even encourage citizen participation in the policy process.

The increased legitimacy and growing acceptance of citizen participation in the business of government was also reflected in the new state and municipal constitutions promulgated in 1989 and 1990, respectively. The movement-party networks that mobilized around the federal Constituent Assembly, now aided by the inclusion of various rights to participation in the 1988 Constitution, were also relatively successful in securing, and sometimes expanding, those rights at the state and local levels. In São Paulo, for example, the state constitution of 1989 established several citizen councils in the areas of education, health, women's rights, culture, and the environment.

The "Organic Law" (Lei Orgânica), or municipal constitution of São Paulo, drafted by a local legislature with a significant progressive presence,[17] guaranteed an unprecedented series of rights, including popular legislative initiatives, plebiscites and referendums, public audiences on budgetary and other matters of great significance to the municipality, and citizen access to information on the workings of government. It further recognized the rights of "users" of social services to participate in the formulation of social policy and in monitoring its implementation. This participation was structured by the Organic Law to take place within either "sectoral councils" (i.e., dealing with policy sectors such as health, education, housing) or any other such participatory channels that the executive or legislative branches decided to create (Assambleia Municipal Constituinte, 1990, pp. 22, 29).

Many of the rights guaranteed in the federal, state, and municipal constitutions await regulation through ordinary legislation before they can be made effective by governments and enjoyed by citizens. Moreover, the federal government's neoliberal policies and the concomitant rolling back of the national state from the arena of social welfare and service provision are unlikely to generate the conditions that would enable citizens to reap the benefits of substantive entitlements now inscribed in constitutional law. Nevertheless, these constitutions lay "the groundwork for future improvements in the distribution of income and property" (Cammack, 1989, p. 32), legitimate the participatory claims of popular movements and other social sectors historically excluded from Brazil's representative institutions, and create a "constitutional space" in which movements might continue the struggle to deepen Brazilian democracy. Furthermore, it would be a mistake to undervalue the "symbolic effectiveness" of movement participation in these constitution-drafting processes and the expanded citizenship rights the new constitutions confer.[18] The mobilization of ordinary citizens to prevent "mere redemocratization" (that is, a restoration of Brazil's elitist pre-1964 democratic system) confirms the existence of a sizable and heterogeneous political constituency that supports more thoroughgoing democratization and is invested in participating in the formal democratic process.

■ Building Participatory Democracy at the Base: Citizens and the State in the PT's "Popular Democratic" Municipal Administrations

That constituency, largely composed of popular movements and movement networks, had been gaining increased legitimacy vis-à-vis public authorities over the course of the Brazilian transition process.

Since at least the late 1970s, in an effort to shore up their waning base of political support, local administrations controlled by the military regime's official party began to engage in dialogue with neighborhood organizations that claimed to "represent" local residents, sometimes responding to the demands of "new" popular movements as well as SABs and other neighborhood civic associations.[19]

Though many SABs continued to engage in the politics of *troca de favores*, based on a logic where "he or she who gives, receives," a different logic of "he or she who organizes and mobilizes, receives" came to rival the traditional clientelistic logic over the course of the 1980s. Since at least the beginning of that decade, Brazilian neighborhood-based movements guided by this mobilizational logic have been increasingly effective in advancing their goals. In asserting a collective political identity as urban citizens with specified rights to urban services, popular movements also indirectly undermine clientelistic, neopopulist hegemonic politics and thus further democratic consolidation.[20]

After opposition parties came to control several state and municipal governments in the early 1980s, movement activists and their advisers/articulators pressured public authorities to expand opportunities for citizen participation in the design of social and urban policy. In the state of São Paulo, governed by the centrist and progressive wings of the PMDB from 1983 to 1986, local associations of urban residents were granted the status of "legitimate interlocutors" by many state and municipal officials.

In response to the pressures of movement activists working within the PMDB, Governor Franco Montoro created citizen "councils" where different social movement constituencies (such as women's movements, the black movement, and the ecology movement) were to be represented.[21] The councils were made up of public servants from relevant state agencies and "representatives" of these various movement constituencies, who were appointed by the governor. The councils were charged with advising the administration on policies of particular interest to their constituencies and monitoring the implementation of such policies.[22]

The São Paulo PMDB municipal administration of Mario Covas also tried to establish some formal channels for citizen participation in each of the city's regional administrations. These local councils were to be made up of members of neighborhood associations that claimed to represent the interests of local residents. But as Ruth Cardoso and others analysts have noted, the "representativeness" of particular local associations became the source of acute political conflict among and within popular movements and SABs and between both types of organizations and the local government bureaucracy, especially when more than one neighborhood group claimed to be the sole "legitimate interlocutor" of residents' demands.[23]

Popular movement groups, many of whose participants had become avid supporters of the PT, now the most vocal opposition party in São Paulo, were among the most vehement critics of the PMDB's institutionalized channels for citizen participation. These groups, along with some sectors of the PT, denounced the PMDB-created participatory mechanisms as pseudodemocratic shams, created from the "top down" and intended to "harness" (*atrelar*) movements to the government, depriving them of the autonomy so central to their vision of social struggle. Moreover, the fact that the popular movements' archrivals, the SABs, were sometimes viewed by the PMDB as legitimate representatives of the population, further discredited these citizen councils in the eyes of newer, more radical groups.

Many of the most militant movements and some PT activists defended the idea of autonomous popular councils, created from the "bottom up." Such councils would be constituted democratically by "truly representative, more combative" popular movement organizations who had been demanding their rights to social services and urban improvements from conservative administrations and who would now exercise their hard-won rights to influence the design of urban policy and monitor its implementation.

Since the late 1970s, the grass-roots health movement, one of São Paulo's most radical popular movements, deeply influenced by the PT and its sympathizers in the progressive wing of the Catholic church, had organized into "Popular Health Councils." These involved movement members in monitoring the services provided by the neighborhood clinics—clinics that the movement had won from the state and municipal governments after years of struggle. These councils secured official recognition from the state and local health departments but established their own internal rules and selected their own representatives in elections designed and supervised by the movement.[24] Critics of the PMDB councils held the movement-created Popular Health Councils to be exemplary channels for popular participation.

The condemnation of the PMDB's citizen councils and the insistence on autonomous formulas for "representing" popular demands would come back to haunt popular movements and the PT when the party came to power in the city of São Paulo in 1989. For, since its 1988 municipal electoral victories and a nearly successful bid for the presidency in 1989,[25] the PT has been forced to translate its "oppositional" political vision into a distinctive, proactive "popular democratic" project for postauthoritarian Brazil. And translating this vision into a viable local political project has proven a tortuous and vexing task for the PT in the municipalities it controls, including São Paulo.

"Popular participation" together with the "inversion of local government priorities" were the twin pillars of the PT's municipal campaigns throughout urban Brazil in 1988. Both were seen as crucial to the party's goals of democratizing the relationship between poor and working-class citizens and the state. The PT's platform, developed for that campaign, declared: "Participation is a political activity . . . and . . . should involve, therefore, the power to *decide* on policy and *control* its execution." The platform then committed itself to five conditions necessary for the realization of meaningful participation: (a) political-administrative decentralization, (b) the democratization of information, (c) planning, (d) the creation of institutional channels for participation and control, and (e) stimulus to the autonomous organization of the population (popular councils, for example) and the recognition of diverse forms of political representation of the population.[26]

When the PT came to power in São Paulo and elsewhere, there was little concrete sense, much less consensus, within the party as to how this radical democratic vision would be put into practice. With regard to popular participation, there was considerable dissent. All *petistas* agreed that, whereas dominant economic interests had determined the priorities of local government in the past, ordinary citizens must now be given greater say in local government planning, policy formulation, and implementation. Most also insisted that participation should build on, rather than replace, the autonomous community struggles spearheaded by urban popular movements.

Even before the party's mayoral candidate was selected, however, supporters of the two principal contenders disagreed on several crucial dimensions of popular participation. Plinio Sampaio's supporters, mostly drawn from moderate sectors of the party, advocated the creation of "consultative" popular councils. These, created and formally institutionalized by the municipal administration, would advise the administration on matters of concern to local residents.

Luiza Erundina's supporters, drawn from the party's more radical social base, including radical Catholics and Trotskyite political groups organized within the PT, favored the formation of "deliberative" popular councils. These, created by popular movements themselves and recognized as "legitimate representatives" by the administration, would have the power to decide on matters of policy and budgetary priorities of interest to their neighborhoods. Council representatives would be designated in whatever way the movements chose to do so.[27]

It was the more radical perspective of Luiza Erundina that won the mayoralty. Erundina repeatedly emphasized that there would now be three "coequal" powers at the municipal level: executive, legislative, and "popular." According to her early pronouncements as mayor, the precise shape and political scope of the Popular Councils would emerge "from the people themselves." Municipal "popular power," in her mind, would be modeled after the now legendary Popular Health Councils. There were more than 80 of these by now, the members of which had been elected by over 100,000 local residents.

The party undertook to stimulate the creation of the Popular Councils and explicitly charged the 20 regional administrations of the municipality with the task. But during the first year of the PT administration, "the people themselves" did not organize spontaneously to form Popular Councils. In a few neighborhoods, primarily where there was a preexisting history of territorially articulated urban struggles, embryonic Popular Councils were formed but soon ceased to function. Two principal difficulties came to the fore as "popular power" began to take on a more institutionalized form in São Paulo.

First, the "newer" urban popular movements in São Paulo that formed the PT's political base typically had organized around "sectoral" issues—that is, in a particular neighborhood, the local health movement group would articulate its demands vis-à-vis the municipal or state health departments, the local day-care group would make demands on the social welfare department, and so on. Thus, in most neighborhoods, issue-specific local groups lacked a history of articulation or of territorially based organization that would seek to establish local priorities for urban services—that is, should the neighborhood first seek a clinic or a day-care center?

Second, the PT administration's desire to "govern with the people" brought long-standing animosities between popular movements and "older" neighborhood associations such as SABs to the fore. And in embryonic Popular Councils and in the dozens of "Popular Plenaries" and public audiences held by local officials to "hear" the demands of the popular sectors, "the people" proved to be quite divided in their interpretation of the interests of "the population." In many neighborhoods, SABs and similar civic associations, many with ties to the PMDB or other opposition parties, appeared at PT plenaries and forums to challenge the representativeness of popular movement organizations who sympathized with the government party.

Some of the more radical popular movements also rejected the PT's councils, claiming that "the State was the State" and that, though many of their former allies were now in power, participation in the councils would still taint movement autonomy.

These difficulties continued to plague the Erundina administration's efforts to promote greater citizen participation in the business of local government. In mid-1991 "sectoral" councils were functioning only in the municipal health department, where, significantly, there was a previous history of participation and, perhaps more important, where the popular health movement, whose PT ties are unmistakable, had established effective local hegemony in the articulation and representation of demands for better health services for the poor and working classes.

Where there was no history of ongoing local participation, and where movement hegemony was disputed by different types of neighborhood organizations, the councils had yet to materialize. The process of establishing Popular Housing Councils, which I followed closely between August and October 1991, is illustrative of the difficulties in procedurally determining who are the "legitimate interlocutors" of popular sector interests.[28] HABI (Superintendência de Habitao Popular), the municipal bureau in charge of public housing for the poorest sectors of São Paulo's urban landless (families with incomes of less than five minimum monthly salaries or approximately U.S.$200), set out to create Municipal Popular Housing Councils in early 1991. HABI invited a broad cross section of neighborhood-based groups and associations to partake in several structured "Popular Plenaries" on how these councils should be constituted.

At the plenaries, popular movement activists, particularly from the radical *Movimento Sem Terra,* or Urban Landless Movement,[29] far outnumbered members of the SABs or other neighborhood associations with PMDB or other opposition party links. Their majoritarian presence can be explained by the fact that the Sem Terra movement had, from the mid-1980s, been one of the most active and vocal popular movements in São Paulo. Since its inception, it had been deeply influenced by the PT and its sympathizers in the progressive wing of the Catholic church;

its numerous land invasions and other radical actions had extracted significant concessions from state and municipal housing authorities.[30] At the plenaries, the popular movement groups advocated their "popular democratic" conception of the Housing Councils. These would be organized in each of HABI's administrative subdivisions in the city; their members, like those of the autonomous Popular Health Councils, would be directly selected by local residents in communitywide elections supervised by HABI officials and monitored by movement groups.

On the other hand, members of SABs and other PMDB-influenced neighborhood associations insisted that council members should be "indirectly elected," that is, selected by "legally recognized associations" formally registered with the city.[31] Each association would be entitled to a specified number of representatives to each regional council. Such a representational formula virtually assured the SABs and other "older" neighborhood associations the majority of seats on the would-be councils because many popular movement groups, given their historic mistrust of the state, were not officially registered with the city. Popular movement groups and their advisers, many of whom were now HABI public servants, vehemently opposed this electoral procedure, claiming that many of the "older" neighborhood associations had not genuinely been involved in struggles for public housing and lacked a real social base (i.e., were "phantom" organizations that, for all intents and purposes, existed only on paper).

As of late October 1991, after 3 months of often volatile negotiating sessions, no agreement had been reached and the PT and the Sem Terra movement, on the one hand, and the PMDB and the SABs and neighborhood associations, on the other, were each planning to introduce separate bills on the housing councils to the municipal legislature. This fierce conflict over democratic procedures reveals that devising representational formulas that allow for the constitution of "legitimate interlocutors" for "popular interests" remains a major stumbling block in the PT's efforts to advance its popular democratic project at the municipal level.

Some of the more radical left sectors of the party and of popular movements have long dismissed formal procedural issues and representational formulas as elements of "bourgeois democracy." "Popular democracy" has often been held up by the left in Brazil, as elsewhere in Latin America, as the polar opposite of its putatively bourgeois variants. Yet the institutional and constitutional contours of popular democracy have seldom been specified. Creating Leninist "mass organizations" tied to the party, as a complement to standard representative institutions, as was done in Sandinista Nicaragua's version of popular democracy—though still supported by some left sectarian groupings within the party—would be inimical to the PT's historically antivanguardist stance and its professed respect for the autonomy of social movements.

If we define *popular democracy* as a set of redistributive political-institutional arrangements that facilitate information about, access to, and influence in governmental policymaking by those subaltern groups and classes who historically have been denied the effective exercise of democratic citizenship, and if we assume—in a postmodern sense—that the interests of the "popular classes" are neither given, nor fixed, nor "scientifically knowable," then it is imperative that representational schemes be devised that would enable democratic governments on the left to determine who are the "legitimate interlocutors" of the popular sectors. Importantly, significant sectors of the Workers Party and many social movement activists in São Paulo are today grappling with the complex question of how participatory channels can be made both accessible to and genuinely representative of all poor and working-class citizens.

Creating institutions that would involve poor and working-class citizens in the workings of government is but one of several ways in which the PT has proposed to transform the relationship between poor and working-class citizens and the local state apparatus. In the realm of urban services provision, as Gabrielle Watson's incisive study of community struggles for water and sanitation services suggests, the PT administration in São Paulo has also introduced innovative programs that simultaneously seek to address urgent community needs and involve local residents in the planning and execution of urban policy and community improvements (Watson, 1992). Whereas some previous municipal administrations encouraged neighborhood residents to volunteer their labor in reurbanization projects in the city's shantytowns and other marginal settlements in the urban periphery (primarily to reduce costs), the PT has also involved community groups in the design and planning of urban infrastructural projects. Similarly, HABI in São Paulo has developed a number of public housing projects that are community designed and administered; municipal housing authorities transfer funds for construction directly to neighborhood organizations, which, in turn, hire their own technical staff and specialized construction crews and devise their own schemes for allocating volunteer community labor.

Many PT administrations have undertaken efforts to democratize information about local government through more fluid, "direct" democratic mechanisms such as forums, "Popular Plenaries," and public hearings on budgetary and planning matters, for example. In some PT municipalities in the state of São Paulo, such as that of Santo André, the party and the administrations have encouraged the creation of autonomous, territorially based popular movement councils that could more effectively challenge the SABs' exclusive claim to neighborhood representation.[32] Arguing that the local population "organizes episodically or permanently to *demand* and guarantee its goals" but "still is not in the habit of organizing to *get informed, get educated* or learn to *administer*" (Prefeitura Municipal de Santo André, 1990) so as to more effectively advance its goals, the PT in Santo André, as in the coastal port city of Santos, has also promoted increased collaboration between city employees and community residents in pursuit of urban improvements and encouraged more fluid forms of citizen involvement in the business of local government. Out of this process of popular education and citizen-state collaboration, the Santo André administration contends, "more solid and permanent channels of relating to the community" will gradually evolve (Prefeitura Municipal de Santo André, 1990).

As Robert Gay persuasively argues, "The establishment of very different ties between civil society and political society is critical for the Left if the power of traditional elites is to be undermined" because historical forms of corporatist, populist popular incorporation into the political process have created a pragmatic "allegiance of the popular classes to traditional political elites" (Gay, 1990, pp. 447, 449).[33] Clientelism is one concrete expression of that pragmatic popular class posture vis-à-vis the state. Majoritarian sectors of the PT therefore view the party's municipal administrations as part of a larger strategy of disputing the societal hegemony of Brazil's owning classes, a strategy that hinges on democratizing citizen-state relations through popular participation and the inversion of government priorities at the local level.

■ **Conclusions**

Discussions of democratization in Latin America today typically center on the requisites of institutional consolidation and democratic stability.[34] And though we must certainly be concerned with how more viable and effective democratic institutions might be crafted, I believe it is also imperative for political analysts and activists to explore how more inclusive and meaningful democratic institutions might be designed, to consider how the *quality as well as the stability* of Latin America's new democracies might be enhanced.[35] In particular, we need to pay closer attention to channels and strategies that increase nonelite access to policymaking and implementation. And in the context of highly stratified Latin American societies, we must also explore how democratic institutions might be structured so that the basic interests of the bourgeoisie are not "virtually guaranteed" (Pzeworski, 1986, p. 60) and those of the popular classes are not "virtually excluded."

Examining the role of social movements in democratic consolidation processes allows us to begin to address these pressing political questions, to explore the nexus between institutional and extrainstitutional democratic struggles. I have argued that social movements, specifically urban popular movements, have contributed to deepening Brazilian democracy in at least three ways. First, movement articulatory practices helped inspire and advance an alternative democratic vision that emphasized citizen participation as a crucial component of meaningful democracy. Second, movement networks and coalitions were instrumental in promoting constitutional reforms that extend new social rights and potentially expand the opportunities for political participation to subaltern groups and classes. And, third, urban popular movements have formed the core constituency of an innovative democratic party of the left, the Workers Party, which, since 1989, has worked to democratize the relationship between poor and working-class citizens and the state at local levels.

Social movement practices were central to the development of the PT's popular democratic project, one that has emerged as a clear and imaginable alternative to the restricted conceptions of democracy advanced by parties of the center and the right. To be sure, locally based democratic experiments cannot illuminate larger questions concerning how to promote more equitable national economic development strategies or how to control and democratize the coercive apparatuses of the state. And despite the increased autonomy granted to municipalities by the 1988 federal constitution, such experiments are, of course, significantly constrained by their subordination to state and federal policy directives. They may, however, help undermine clientelistic, state corporatist, and authoritarian state-society relations in local politics, historically one of the principal sources of antidemocratic political practices in Brazil.

At the national level, moreover, the neoliberal imperative of rolling back the state from the realms of redistribution and social provision has been accompanied by a devolution of those governmental responsibilities to regional and local instances of the state. And whether or not one views this as a positive development, it nevertheless enhances the importance of local politics in Brazil, as elsewhere in the Americas, both theoretically and politically.[36] Despite the constraints imposed by an increasingly global economy and the Brazilian federal government's unrelenting fiscal crisis, the local political arena, I have tried to show, is one in which Brazilian urban movements have nevertheless secured social and political rights, however limited and inadequate to the ever more daunting task of redressing flagrant social and economic inequalities on a national or global level.

In a global era, local political arenas could become increasingly central to the pursuit of more meaningful political participation and more expansive social rights. Local instances of the state are "closer to home," potentially more permeable and more vulnerable to citizen scrutiny and intervention. As the PT's efforts to "invert" local government priorities suggest, local governments can potentially mitigate the perverse effects of national structural adjustment policies such that the burden does not fall disproportionately on poor and working-class citizens. In Brazil, as elsewhere in Latin America, the devolution of responsibility has not, however, been accompanied by a devolution of state resources from the national to the state and local levels. But incipient political struggles for more effective decentralization of state authority and resources are currently under way, adding yet another dimension to ongoing movement efforts to deepen Latin American democracy.

NOTES

1. For an analysis of the intraelite negotiations that narrowed the scope of Brazilian democratization, see especially Hagopian (1990), Moreira Alves (1988), and Smith (1987).

2. This research forms part of a larger comparative project on social movements, urban politics, and democratic alternatives in contemporary South America. This chapter is based on field research conducted in BrasAlia and São Paulo in June and July 1998 and in metropolitan São Paulo and four other Workers Party-led municipalities in the state of São Paulo from August through October 1991. The analysis draws on 62 interviews with participants of urban popular movement groups, neighborhood civic associations, political party activists, members of municipal councils, municipal public servants, and administration officials; primary documents from the movements, the Workers Party (PT) and

other parties, and official municipal government publications; media coverage of movements and the PT municipal administrations; and observation at numerous movement assemblies and movement-party and movement-state negotiating sessions.

3. For the most compelling and comprehensive account of the emergence and development of the PT, see Margaret Keck (1986; see also Keck, 1986-1987; Meneguello, 1989; Sader & Silverstein, 1991). Many of the PT's principal organizational and programmatic documents are collected and analyzed in Gadotti and Pereira (1989).

4. Urban popular movements, as movement analysts have stressed, are a "subset of social movements." As Scott Mainwaring explains, the term *social movements* encompasses "a wide amalgam of movements, including the feminist movement, the labor movement, the peasant movement, the ecology movement, the human rights movement and others. . . . Urban popular movements attempt to improve urban living conditions, usually through demands on the state for public services including sewers, paved roads, better transportation facilities, better medical facilities, running water, and electricity" (1987, p. 133).

5. On the influence of populist clientele networks on the political worldview of residents of São Paulo's urban periphery, see Teresa Caldeira's excellent study, *A Política dos Outros* (1984). See also Gay (1990). On the early history of the SABs, see Singer (1980) and Gohn (1991).

6. Many SABs today are little more than empty organizational shells with little actual social base in their neighborhoods. The typical SAB in São Paulo has a handful of regular participants, among whom are the formally elected president, vice-president, secretary, and so on. There are, of course, exceptions to this rule; in some neighborhoods, the leadership of SABs has been successfully disputed by social or political forces less inclined to engage in the politics of *troca de favores*.

7. On the political transformation of the Brazilian Catholic church, see especially Mainwaring (1986). For a recent and comprehensive analysis of the Christian Base Communities, see Hewitt (1991).

8. I borrow this concept from Simone de Castro Tavares Coelho (1991b). Ruth Corrêa Leite Cardoso refers to movement advisers as "external actors" to highlight their "exteriority" to the communities in which they organize. See her "Movimentos Sociais Urbanos: Um Balanço Crítico" (1983). Carlos Nelson Ferreira dos Santos uses the term *catalizadores*, or "catalyzers," to describe the impact of advisers on the movements. See *Movimentos Urbanos no Rio de Janeiro* (1981). In *Engendering Democracy in Brazil: Women's Movements in Transition Politics* (Alvarez, 1990b), I labeled these actors "extra-community agents." The term *political articulator*, however, more accurately describes the role of (often middle-class) advisers in popular movement organizations. For, while they are in a position of exteriority to the local community when they begin working with local groups, they play an increasing role in the *internal* dynamics of the community and its local groupings when their organizing efforts persist over time.

9. These activities often brought feminist activists into open conflict with the local church. On these tensions and on women's participation in CEBs and other church-related movements, see Alvarez (1990c).

10. On the role of the new trade unionism in Brazilian transition politics, see especially Keck (1989).

11. This coalition brought together a number of organizations who had a long trajectory of collaboration with Brazil's popular movements, including ISER (Instituto de Estudos da Religio), IBASE (Instituto Brasileiro de Analises Sociais e Economicas),

CEDAC (Centro de Aço Comunitaria), SEP (Serviço de Educaço Popular), CEDI (Centro Ecumênico de Documentaço e Informaço), CPO (Comisso Pastoral Operária), CPT (Comisso Pastoral da Terra), and FASE (Federaço de Orgos para a Assistência Social e Educacional). Together they launched the National Movement for Popular Participation in the Constituent Assembly. For a comprehensive account of their activities, see Whitaker et al. (1989).

12. The ensuing discussion draws on interviews with Joo Gilberto Lucas Coelho, director of the Center for the Study of the Constituent Assembly (CEAC) at the University of Brasília (Brasília, June 30, 1988); Ulysses Riedel de Resende, director of the Inter-Union Parliamentary Assistance Department (Departamento Intersindical de Assessoria Parlamentar, or DIAP; Brasília, July 1, 1988); two members of the National Conference of Brazilian Bishops' (CNBB) Executive Coordination of the Constituent Assembly (Brasília, June 29, 1988); and Francisco "Chico" Whitaker Ferreira, member of the executive commission of the National Pro-popular Participation Plenary (São Paulo, July 13, 1988).

13. See DIAP (1988) for the "scores" ultimately awarded to each parliamentarian based on his or her voting record on "popular rights."

14. Indeed, the constitution-drafting process in Brazil was more open to genuine citizen input than were similar processes in other recent democratic transitions, including those of Spain, Portugal, and Greece.

15. This figure and others given below are taken from Assembleia Nacional Constituinte, Comisso de Sistematizaço, *Emendas Populares* (1987).

16. The range stems from the fact that any registered voter could sign up to three amendments. As Whitaker et al. point out, if each citizen signed one amendment, then approximately 18% of the electorate can be said to have participated in the process. Alternatively, if each participating citizen signed three amendments, then that figure becomes 6%. They suggest that the most likely figure would be around 10% to 12% participation. See *Cidado Constituinte* (Whitaker, 1989, p. 104). That this number of signatures was collected in so brief a time span is all the more remarkable when one considers that each signatory had to show proof of voter registration at the time she or he signed an amendment and each citizen could sign no more than three amendments.

17. In October 1991, of the 53 members of the municipal legislature, 15 belonged to the PT, 6 to the social-democratic PSDB, 2 to the PCB or Brazilian Communist party, 1 to the PCdoB, or Communist Party of Brazil, 1 to the PSB or Brazilian Socialist party, and 2 to the PV or Green party. Due to a number of conjunctural factors, the elaboration of which is beyond the scope of this chapter, citizen input into the drafting of the municipal constitution appears to have been fairly limited.

18. On the significance of the symbolic politics of social movements, see García (1992) and Alvarez and Escobar (1992).

19. On the impact of urban movements on social policy in São Paulo during the 1970s and 1980s, see especially Jacobi (1989). On the relationship between the day-care movement, which mobilized thousands of women in São Paulo's urban periphery during the 1970s and early 1980s, and the PDS (regime party) administration of Reynaldo de Barros, see Alvarez, *Engendering Democracy in Brazil* (1990b, especially chap. 9).

20. See Cardoso (1992). See also Gay (1990), Abbaszadeh (1991), and Mainwaring (1987).

21. The idea of creating government councils for citizen participation was not entirely new to São Paulo city politics. In 1956 Mayor Wladimir Pizza had tried to install District

Councils in an effort to "institutionalize" the SABs. In 1979 Mayor Reynaldo de Barros resurrected the idea, creating Community Councils that would be composed of "representatives of the 'community forces' of each of the [city's 35] Regional Administrations— class associations, social organizations, religious social movements, SABs—and whose objective would be to participate in discussions of the municipal budget, to discuss, in public audiences, demands relative to the concrete problems with the competence of the prefecture, etc." Neither of these councils ever became effectively institutionalized, and as Singer notes, "It was clear that the Community Councils would have no decision making power, but would be mere channels for demand-making, through which role they would substitute the associations created by the population at its own initiative" (1980, p. 106).

22. On the dynamics of the São Paulo State Council on the Status of Women, created by Montoro in 1983 at the urging of feminists active in the PMDB, see Alvarez (1990a, p. 35).

23. See especially Cardoso (1992). See also de Castro Tavares Coelho (1991b) and Cardoso and Simes (1990).

24. On the health movement and its evolving relationship to institutional politics, see Jacobi (1989) and Cardoso and Simes (1990).

25. The PT's presidential candidate, Luis Inácio "Lula" da Silva, won 46% of the vote in the second round (runoff) of the 1989 presidential election, losing to Fernando Collor de Melo by only 4%.

26. "Documentos Políticos dos Pre-candidatos do PT," cited in Dias Paz, Accorsi Pereira, and Rodrigues da Silva (1990).

27. Interview with Felix Sanchez, Projeto Integrado de Educaço Popular, Gabinete da Prefeita (August 26, 1991, São Paulo).

28. The ensuing discussion draws on observation at seven negotiating sessions about the would-be housing councils held between August 30 and October 3, 1991; on observation at strategy sessions of the PT and the Sem Terra movement and the PMDB and neighborhood associations concerning the creation of the housing councils; and on formal interviews with Beatriz Abramides, Assessora de Participaço Popular, Superintendência de Habitaço Popular (HABI), Secretaria Municipal de Habitao e Desenvolvimento Urbano (October 11, 1991, São Paulo); Alana Madureira, Assessora de Comunicaço, HABI (August 21, 1991, São Paulo); Maria de Lourdes Lima, staff person for PMDB municipal councilman and leader of the PMDB in the municipal legislature, Antonio Carlos Caruso, president of a Sociedade de Amigos de Bairro (September 24, 1991); Vereador Antonio Carlos Caruso (September 24, 1991); and Vereador Jose Indio Nascimento, member of the small conservative party, the PST (September 12, 1991); and informal interviews with popular movement participants, neighborhood association members, and HABI staff.

29. On the Sem Terra movement, see Gohn (1991), Ammann (1991), and de Castro Tavares Coelho (1991a).

30. Formal interviews with "Padre Tico," parish priest and key articulator in the Unio de Movimentos de Moradia de São Paulo and the national campaign for the Fondo Nacional de Moradia Popular (September 2, 1991, São Paulo) and Paulo Comforto, coordinator of the Unio de Movimentos de Moradia de São Paulo and staff person for PT municipal councilman, Henrique Pacheco (September 6, 1991).

31. The urban landless/housing movement is ideologically heterogeneous, and distinct factions within the movement have established ties to different political parties and

sectors of the state bureaucracy. For an analysis of the various tendencies in the movement in São Paulo, see Gohn (1991).
32. Formal interview with Teresa Santos, Secretaria de Governo (municipal cabinet member), Prefeitura Municipal de Santo André (October 1, 1991, Santo André).
33. On the corporatist political-institutional arrangements that secured that allegiance from the organized working class, see especially Cohen (1989).
34. See, for example, Pastor (1989), Diamond and Linz (1988-1989), and Linz (1990).
35. Scott Mainwaring (1987, p. 132) draws this important distinction.
36. The urban political arena has not figured prominently in the comparative literature on democratic consolidation. Recent Latin American scholarship has begun to correct the "national" bias of the debate, however. See especially, Borja, Calderon, Grossi, and Penalva (1989), Borja, Valdes, Pozo, and Morales (1987), and Laurelli and Rofman (1989).

REFERENCES

Abbaszadeh, B. (1991). Urban popular movements, the state and the political system: The case of São Paulo within the Brazilian political structure. In H. P. Diaz, J. W. A. Rummens, & P. D. M. Taylor (Eds.), *Forging identities and patterns of development in Latin America and the Caribbean*. Toronto: Canadian Scholars' Press.
Alvarez, S. E. (1990a). Contradictions of a women's space in a male-dominant state: The political role of the commissions on the status of women in post-authoritarian Brazil. In K. Staudt (Ed.), *Women, international development, and politics: The bureaucratic mire*. Philadelphia: Temple University Press.
Alvarez, S. E. (1990b). *Engendering democracy in Brazil: Women's movements in transition politics*. Princeton, NJ: Princeton University Press.
Alvarez, S. E. (1990c). Women's participation in the Brazilian "People's Church": A critical appraisal. *Feminist Studies, 16*(2).
Alvarez, S. E., & Escobar, A. (1992). Social movements in contemporary Latin America: Theoretical and political horizons of change. In A. Escobar & S. E. Alvarez (Eds.), *The making of social movements in Latin America: Identity, strategy, and democracy*. Boulder, CO: Westview.
Ammann, S. B. (1991). *Movimento Popular de Bairro: de Frente para o Estado em Busca do Parlamento*. São Paulo: Cortez.
Assembleia Municipal Constituinte. (1990). *Lei Orgânica do Municipio de São Paulo*. São Paulo: Câmara Municipal.
Assembleia Nacional Constituinte, Comisso de Sistematizaço. (1987). *Emendas Populares* (Vols. 1, 2). Brasília: Senado Federal.
Borja, J., Calderon, F., Grossi, M., & Penalva, S. (Eds.). (1989). *Decentralizacion y Democracia: Gobiernos Locales en America Latina. Santiago:* CLACSO/SUR/CEUMT-Barcelona.
Borja, J., Valdes, T., Pozo, H., & Morales, E. (1987). *Decentralizacion del Estado: Movimiento Social y Gestion Local*. Santiago: ICI/FLACSO/CLACSO.
Caldeira, T. (1984). *A Política dos Outros: Os Moradores da Periferia e o Que Pensam do Poder e dos Poderosos*. São Paulo: Brasiliense.

Cammack, P. (1989). The politics of democratization. In *Democratization and the state in the Southern Cone* (B. Galjart & P. Silva, Eds.). Amsterdam: Center for Latin American Research and Documentation.

Cardoso, R. C. L. (1983). Movimentos Sociais Urbanos: Um Balanço Crítico. In B. Sorj & M. H. Tavares de Almeida (Eds.), *Sociedade e Política no Brasil Pós-64*. São Paulo: Brasiliense.

Cardoso, R. C. L. (1992). Popular movements in the context of the consolidation of democracy in Brazil. In *The making of social movements in Latin America: Identity, strategy, and democracy*. Boulder, CO: Westview.

Cardoso, R. C. L., & Simes, J. A. (1990). *Políticas Sociais: A Relaço entre as Agências Públicas e seus Usuarios* (Relatório final, mimeograph).

Cohen, Y. (1989). *The manipulation of consent: The state and working-class consciousness in Brazil*. Pittsburgh: University of Pittsburgh Press.

de Castro Tavares Coelho, S. (1991a). *A Emergência da Aço e a Construço de Identidades Coletivas* (mimeograph).

de Castro Tavares Coelho, S. (1991b). *Os Movimentos Sociais e a Institucionalizaço da Participaço Política—Alguns Conceitos Basicos* (mimeograph).

Diamond, L., & Linz, J. (1988-1989). Introduction: Politics, society, and democracy in Latin America. In L. Diamond, J. Linz, & S. M. Lipset (Eds.), *Democracy in developing countries: Latin America*. Boulder, CO: Lynne Reinner.

DIAP. (1988). *Quem Foi Quem na Constituinte nas Questes de Interesse dos Trabalhadores*. São Paulo: Cortez; Obore.

Dias Paz, R., Accorsi Pereira, M., & Rodrigues da Silva, F. J. (1990). São Paulo: Privilegiar "a Reproduço da Vida." *Proposta, 45*, 17-18.

Escobar, A., & Alvarez, S. E. (Eds.). (1992). *The making of social movements in Latin America: Identity, strategy, and democracy*. Boulder, CO: Westview.

Ferreira, C. N. (1981). *Movimentos Urbanos no Rio de Janeiro*. Rio de Janeiro: Zahar.

Gadotti, M., & Pereira, O. (1989) *Pra Que PT: Origem, Projeto e Consolidaço do Partido dos Trabalhadores*. São Paulo: Cortez.

García, M. P. (1992). The Venezuelan environmental movement: Symbolic effectiveness, social practices, and strategies. In A. Escobar & S. E. Alvarez (Eds.), *The making of social movements in Latin America: Identity, strategy, and democracy*. Boulder, CO: Westview.

Gay, R. (1990). Popular incorporation and prospects for democracy: Some implications of the Brazilian case. *Theory and Society, 19*, 447-463.

Gohn, M. (1991). *Movimentos Sociais e Luta pela Moradia*. São Paulo: Edicoes Loyola.

Hagopian, F. (1990). "Democracy by undemocratic means"? Elites, political pacts, and regime transition in Brazil. *Comparative Political Studies, 23*(2), 147-170.

Hewitt, W. E. (1991). *Base Christian Communities and social change in Brazil*. Lincoln: University of Nebraska Press.

Jacobi, P. (1989). *Movimentos Sociais e Políticas Publicas: Demandas por Saneamento Básico e Saúde, So Paulo 1974-1984*. São Paulo: Cortez.

Keck, M. (1986). *From movement to politics: The formation of the Workers' party in Brazil*. Unpublished doctoral dissertation, Columbia University.

Keck, M. (1986-1987). Democratization and dissension: The formation of the Workers' party. *Politics and Society, 15*(1), 67-95.

Keck, M. (1989). The new unionism in the Brazilian transition. In A. Stepan (Ed.), *Democratizing Brazil: Problems of transition and consolidation.* New York: Oxford University Press.

Laurelli, E., & Rofman, A. (Eds.). (1989). *Decentralizacion del Estado: Requerimientos y Politicas en la Crisis.* Buenos Aires: Fundacion Friedrich Ebert/Ediciones CEUR.

Linz, J. (1990). The perils of presidentialism. *Journal of Democracy, 1*(1), 51-70.

Mainwaring, S. (1986). *The Catholic church and politics in Brazil, 1916-1985.* Stanford, CA: Stanford University Press.

Mainwaring, S. (1987). Urban popular movements, identity and democratization in Brazil. *Comparative Political Studies, 20*(2).

Mainwaring, S. (1991). Politicians, parties, and electoral systems: Brazil in comparative perspective. *Comparative Politics, 24*(1).

Meneguello, R. (1989). *PT: A Formaço de um Partido, 1979-1982.* São Paulo: Paz e Terra.

Moreira Alves, M. H. (1988). Dilemmas of the consolidation of democracy from the top: A political analysis. *Latin American Perspectives, 15*(3), 47-63.

Pastor, R. A. (Ed.). (1989). *Democracy in the Americas: Stopping the pendulum.* New York: Holmes & Meier.

Prefeitura Municipal de Santo André, Secretaria de Governo. (1990, November 6). [Contribuio para a Discusso sobre Participao Popular na Administrao Petista] (mimeograph).

Pzeworski, A. (1986). Some problems in the study of the transition to democracy. In G. O'Donnell, P. Schmitter, & L. Whitehead (Eds.), *Transitions from authoritarian rule: Comparative perspectives.* Baltimore: Johns Hopkins University Press.

Sader, E., & Silverstein, K. (1991). *Without fear of being happy: Lula, the Workers Party, and Brazil.* London: Verso.

Singer, P. (1980). Movimentos de Bairro. In P. Singer & V. C. Brant (Eds.), *São Paulo: O Povo em Movimento.* São Paulo: CEBRAP.

Smith, W. C. (1987). The political transition in Brazil: From authoritarian liberalization to elite conciliation to democratization. In *Comparing new democracies: Transition and consolidation in Mediterranean Europe and the Southern Cone.* Boulder, CO: Westview.

Watson, G. (1992). *Water and sanitation in São Paulo, Brazil: Successful strategies for service provision in low-income communities.* Unpublished master's thesis, Massachusetts Institute of Technology.

Whitaker, F., et al. (1989). *Cidado Constituinte: A Saga das Emendas Populares.* São Paulo: Paz e Terra.

Part III

Identity Politics and Social Mobilization

10 Friends and Neighbors: Knowledge and Campaigning in London

JUDITH ALLEN

Everyday, in myriad ways, the modern European state invites its citizens to subject themselves to its administrative power—through the provision of routine information (name, age, gender, nationality, address) for routine purposes (applying for driving licenses, library tickets, bus passes, social security; registering births, deaths, marriages); fulfilling obligations (paying taxes, voting, responding to the census); consuming local services (rubbish collection, education, water and sewerage, sports facilities); participating in local or national politics (as voters, as members of pressure groups, as members of political parties, in response to consultation); and so on. There is virtually no activity in daily life that is not touched by the state.

In subjecting themselves to the routines of state administrative power, modern citizens soon grow accustomed to defining themselves within the categories that the state uses to regulate them and their relationships with one another. Each citizen's sense of her- or himself as a unique individual comes, imperceptibly, to be shaped by the methods and techniques the state uses to shape its administration of the social body as a whole and the social bodies within that whole (Foucault, 1965, 1973, 1975a).

The state's power over its citizens, and its citizens' power over it, come to rest on the knowledge each provides to the other, rather than on superior force or moral hierarchy. Most of the time, in most places, this reciprocal power/knowledge relationship is taken for granted, routinized, accepted without question. But now and then, here and there, these relationships are questioned. Citizens reserve the right to define themselves as they see themselves, to contest the definitions of themselves inherent in state administration, to challenge the practices and discourses of that administration, and to create new visions of what it means to be a citizen, an individual, an active subject. Sometimes these challenges are small, localized, specialized. Sometimes they mobilize large groups in new and changing perceptions of themselves (Foucault, 1982).

If participation is the everyday activity of knowledge exchange between the state and its citizens, then organizing and campaigning activities are essentially about challenging the nature of the discourses and practices that underlie participation. Effective participation is founded on the self-defined identities of acting subjects rather than on the subjectivities arising from subjection to administrative methods of exercising power. Campaigning and organizing seek to alter the relationship between state and citizen or to change the effects of existing relationships (Foucault, 1982, 1988b, 1988c).

I use these ideas, drawn from the work of Michel Foucault, to tell the story of the Paddington Federation of Tenants and Residents Associations and of how it came to define itself in the context of organizing and campaigning against the administrative power of central and local government. I want to show how a disparate group of people created a set of relationships among themselves, thus giving an identity to the federation while simultaneously forming a subjectivity for themselves. It was from within this subjectivity that they could contest subjection to, or subjectification by, the modern state.

What is remarkable in the story is the failure of the Thatcherite ideological and administrative project to infect the federation's own definition of itself and its work as well as its members' sense of the necessity for speaking out collectively against oppression. Thus the federation stands as an example of the strengths of people making their own lives together, reflecting the radical root image of democracy wherever it occurs (Forester, 1989).

■ Michel Foucault: The Modern Subject

What does an abstruse, modern French philosopher have to offer in telling the story of the Paddington Federation?

Michel Foucault took up a challenge laid down by Immanuel Kant. Commenting on the French Revolution, Kant remarked that the democratic ideal carried within it a new conceptualization of what it meant to be an individual. Most subsequent political philosophy has focused on the changing nature of the sovereign state's relationship to its citizens, ignoring an evolving conceptualization of individuals and the relationships among them, except insofar as these have been necessary to understand the expansion of civil administration in policing relationships between its citizens (Foucault, 1979, 1978b). Over a lifetime's work, Foucault inverted and subverted this conceptualization of political philosophy. He delineated a new concept of the individual, one that focused on a dual concept of subjectivity. In Foucault's thought, subjectivity both gives the individual a sense of uniqueness as a subject and, simultaneously, provides the basis of the individual's subjection (Foucault, 1978c; Wood, 1985).

To develop this concept of the individual, Foucault radically reformulated concepts of power. For Foucault, the individual is not only acted upon/subjected by the exercise of administrative, economic, political, and social power but, in turn, articulates, as an acting subject, a multidirectional flow of power outward. Thus power, for Foucault, is not something that flows from the "center" to the "peripheries" of society, as in traditional juridical concepts of the nature of the state. Rather, power "circulates" through individuals, linking them together in networks or webs of relationships. Power is what happens when each of the parties within a relationship has choices open to it, including, critically, the choice to leave the relationship altogether (Foucault, 1976, 1982).

Relationships between individuals are formed within practices that define, mark, measure, and identify them in relationship to each other. Yet, these practices are both institutionalized and built into the forms of knowledge—discourses—that underpin, accompany, and legitimize the institutions within which the practices are carried out (Foucault, 1973, 1975b, 1978a). Tracing the ways in which knowledge and power are connected through the practices and discourses of specific institutions is crucial to understanding the nature of modern societies. It is also crucial to understanding how refusing to have one's subjectivity defined by these forms of knowledge, that is, refusing to act as if one were the subject embodied in these knowledges, creates the space and means for contesting the power of the modern state. Thus resistance is born in the interplay between subjectivity and subjection. To refuse to be subjected is to insist on one's own subjectivity. To define one's own subjectivity is to refuse subjection (Foucault, 1982; Weeks, 1989; Wood, 1985).

Nevertheless, Foucault rejects any kind of individualistic essentialism as the basis for defining subjectivity. Rather, he sees complex modern societies as offering a diversity of discourses and practices, organized within broad blocks or disciplines, which can be drawn upon by individuals. How we know "others" and "ourselves," our own marking characteristics, is defined relative to these diverse discourses and practices (Foucault, 1978a).

To develop the significance of this method of exercising power by defining, measuring, and marking out individuals, Foucault needed to develop a new concept of the state and state power. In his view, modernity is characterized by a state that has dual concerns, one for the social body as a whole and one for the individualized bodies of the persons whom it governs. It "polices" the social body through administrative means rather than through the exercise of force as in the medieval state or through the use of "confession" as in Christian ecclesiastical institutions (Foucault, 1975a, 1978a, 1988a). The administrative means the state uses to govern in modernity are based on distinguishing individuals from each other, categorizing them, and intervening in their lives in ways based on these categorizations. To do this, the state must acquire a detailed knowledge of individuals, which it does through their abilities to verbalize, to talk about, to tell of, to confess their own characteristics, behaviors, desires, and aspirations—elements of their lives that would otherwise be hidden from the state. Thus the state has taken over the techniques of "confession" developed by the late Christian church and uses them to constitute its citizens, the individuals it seeks to "govern" and whose relations it seeks to survey, regulate, and control (Foucault, 1978a, 1988a).

Democracy, within this framework, can best be seen as an incitement to individuals and groups of individuals, however defined, to talk about and assess the practices through which the state's administrative mechanisms, techniques, methods affect them. The processes of verbalization, of self-knowledge in relation to political and cultural practices, allow people to define themselves differently than the ways in which the state defines them. Once the concept of "difference" is embedded in the whole range of discourses and practices that characterize contemporary Western society, individuals and groups are empowered to define themselves, their own subjectivity, in terms that do not necessarily or fully refer to the administrative categorizations of the state, terms therefore that can form the conceptual bases for resisting the administrative intrusions of the state into the conduct of their lives. They discover and invent new categories through which to describe and understand themselves, categories that have the potential to challenge, disrupt, and redirect administrative power (Foucault, 1978a, 1982; Weeks, 1989).

Again, in Foucault's image of social structure, there is no center from which power emanates; rather, there are only complex webs or networks within which a multiplicity of actors seek to exercise power over each other, interacting, intersecting, altering their purposes, adapting and adopting each others' ideas and activities, and changing themselves and society as a consequence (Cousins & Hussain, 1984; Foucault, 1976). Nevertheless, these social webs are loosely structured into "disciplines," within which power and knowledge are linked through specific methods and techniques of exercising power. Most crucially for Foucault's epistemologically based concept of social structure, each of these disciplines constitutes within itself an "ensemble of rules" as to what constitutes "truth." What is considered "true knowledge" within one discipline may well be regarded as irrelevant or false within another (Foucault, 1988a).

Part of what the Paddington Federation attempted to do was to change the notion of what was accepted as "knowledge" in the context of struggles with local authorities over housing and local land use control policies. The federation became a site for articulating disciplines and practices defined by the subjectivities of its membership, not by the rules, assumptions, interpretations—"knowledges"—of those controlling the local state apparatus. This chapter will recount at least some of the practices by which the federation provided a way for its constituencies to find and name their own subjectivities, construct their own discourses, and insert them into the day-to-day politics of community struggle. Indeed, the main purpose of the chapter is to explore how "knowledge-based campaigning" works within a modern democracy: how knowledge can be used within different kinds of power relationships to resist subjection to the practices and discourses of the state and landlords and how knowledge itself is produced by specific practices and discourses.

■ Knowledge and Campaigning: The Paddington Federation of Tenants and Residents Associations

In the remainder of this chapter, I use Foucault's ideas to explore the experience of a group of tenants' associations in Central London between 1974 and 1990. The Paddington Federation was formed in 1974 as an umbrella group for tenants and residents associations throughout the northwest quadrant of the London Borough of the city of Westminster. Its boundaries were those of the Metropolitan Borough of Paddington, which became part of the city of Westminster after local government reorganization in 1964. (The city of Westminster is 1 of 32 boroughs that make up the administrative area bounded by the Greater London Council. The cities of Westminster and London constitute the central core of London.)

Initially, the federation's membership spanned both public and private tenants as well as owner-occupiers. From 1980 onward, local authority tenants formed a separate organization, to take advantage of requirements within the 1980 Housing Act for local authorities to formally consult their own tenants on a number of policy matters. Thus the federation came to represent private tenants and owner-occupiers. During its life, the federation sustained a membership of approximately 40 groups throughout the area.

The main aim of the federation was to represent tenants and residents groups on issues of common concern. In practice, this ranged from helping to form tenants associations, supporting individual tenants in negotiations with their landlords, and campaigning around local housing issues to give voice both to its member associations and to the interests of private tenants more generally.

The individuals who were involved in the federation can be divided into roughly four groups. First, there were the representatives, "activist" tenants from member associations, largely self-selected with the tacit or explicit endorsement of their associations. Second, there were tenants from properties where there were no formal tenants associations, "individuals" who had been helped by the federation and who wished to return their appreciation. Third, there were community workers from other organizations in Paddington, who saw participation in the federation as part of their jobs. And, fourth, there were the federation's own workers. Not surprising, in a highly socially mixed area, the people involved in the federation spanned an immense range of class, age, political experience, and affiliation.

The ethos that united these disparate individuals was based on four shared understandings: first, that the power relationship between landlord and tenant is unequal; second, that acting together is more effective than acting individually; third, deep concern for the misfortunes any individual might face; and, fourth, that all issues should be discussed together until a common basis for action is found within which each participant can see her- or himself (Allen, 1986). Most of the discussion that led to this shared understanding took place in the federation's monthly general meetings, a forum in which everyone who was involved in the federation could contribute, sharing their experiences, discussing how to proceed together, and supporting each other. For many, these encounters were equally important as social event and working meeting. Some members would speak more at meetings than others, yet the "listeners" came to have a unique significance for the federation: as the quiet observers that every political speaker needs at his or her elbow, as repositories of moral strength, as keen judges of character, and as symbols of those whom the federation was aiming to help. Their careful listening practices taught the speakers both how to speak and how to listen, contributing to the development of a unique form of discourse within the federation. Thus the federation developed a distinctive set of internal relationships and style of working, which gave it stability and cohesion within a highly turbulent external political environment.

The federation's history can be divided into four periods. Between 1974 and 1977 the federation depended on community workers "on loan" from other voluntary groups in Paddington. From 1977 to 1979 it relied on the energies of its activist members. Between 1979 and 1986 the federation received funding from the Greater London Council to employ its own workers. Between 1986 and 1990, when the federation wound itself up, it had almost no funding or workers. Throughout the whole of its life, the organization's ethos and continuity were carried by the activist tenants, with an increasing number of individual tenants from 1980 onward. While these periods roughly parallel major national and London-wide political upheavals, the federation's history is by no means a simple reflection of these wider changes. Nevertheless, before discussing the federation's campaigns, it will be useful to outline the broader political environment within which the federation worked.

■ Modernizing the Local State

Both issues that brought down the Thatcher government in 1990—Europe and the poll tax—reflect a set of broader dynamics that strongly affected the ability of community-based organizations within a "modern" democracy to give voice to contesting their subjectification and forming new subjectivities.

The oil crisis in 1973 accelerated more general changes in the world economy. These changes supported the development of an international money market in which London's place was central. At the same time, rising interest rates and the globalization of production undermined the United Kingdom's already shaky industrial base, leading to important shifts in domestic power from industrial to financial capital. Altogether, these structural changes generated a severe fiscal crisis for the British state and laid the basis for the Thatcherite program to modernize British government.

Conditions on the IMF loans to the British government in 1967 and 1976 required a reduction in public expenditure and the development of a monetarist economic policy. The politically strategic elements in controlling public expenditure were local authority spending and housing, which would bear the main brunt of reduced spending (Cooper, 1985; Holmans, 1991; Malpass, 1990). The shift to monetarist economic policy has been reinforced by the progress of economic and monetary "harmonization" and the Single Market Programme within the European Community (Drake, 1991; Ghekiere, 1991).

It has taken nearly 15 years for governments of both parties to implement the changes demanded by the IMF. The financial strategy had two main components. The first was to force local authorities to restructure the administration of their housing stock by effectively setting up housing as an independent, nonprofit business within local government, while progressively removing housing subsidies (Ball, Harloe, & Martens, 1988). The second component was to bring the general level of local government expenditure under direct control by the central government, which involved a major restructuring of the political and administrative relationship between central and local government.

The Thatcher government sought to transfer the local authority housing stock out of the state sector. Since 1979 about one sixth of the stock has been transferred through sales to individual tenants. The restructuring of local authority housing administration is designed to facilitate a second spate of "wholesale" transfers into the not-for-profit sector. Such transfers are being "encouraged" by withdrawing personal housing subsidies from local authority tenants to force rents up while continuing the level of personal subsidies to not-for-profit tenants. (Local authorities currently own 25% of the national housing stock, while not-for-profits own 5%.) Local authorities have been stopped from building any more houses, and all subsidies for new development have been shifted to the not-for-profit sector (Back & Hamnett, 1985; Cope, 1990). At 50,000 units a year, the level of public sector house building is below the level required to keep pace with the deterioration of the stock. Other capital spending by local authorities is restricted to the modernization of a few of the worst estates, as often as not in conjunction with transfer of ownership.

The second component of the government's strategy of controlling public expenditure was to restructure the relationship between local and central government. Thus the election of the Thatcher government in 1979 ushered in one of the most turbulent periods ever for British local government. The reorganization of local government in 1974 (1965 in London) had more or less simply redistributed local authority functions into new geographic units and, by and large, had bipartisan support. The Thatcherite reforms left the geographic structure more or less intact, except for the abolition of the metropolitan counties, but strongly centralized control over how local authorities carried out their functions. Thus the 1980s "reorganization" struck directly at the heart of local democracy within a modern state.

Ironically, the 1974 reorganization set the stage for the conflicts of the 1980s by creating larger, more efficient, more internally centralized, more professional, more party politicized, and more powerful local authorities (Cockburn, 1977; Lansley, Goss, & Wolmar, 1989; London Edinburgh Weekend Return Group, 1979). More than 1,600 small authorities were replaced by just over 500 larger ones, organized in a "two-tier" structure. Administrative functions were divided between counties and districts (in London between the Greater London Council and the London boroughs). With the exception of planning, all local government functions were allocated either to counties or to districts.

Massive Labour electoral defeats in the 1978 local government elections paved the way for a generational shift in both parties. On both left and right, the "generation of 1968" came of political age in the local government elections between 1978 and 1981. The New Urban Left brought with them a vision of democracy as participation in debates over the decisions affecting particular groups (Gyford, 1975). Their vision was forged in a wide variety of disparate settings: feminist, antiracist, and gay struggles; left splinter politics; community action; single issue campaigns such as CND, the Anti-Nazi League, and Chile Solidarity; and the white- and blue-collar local authority trades unions. What united the New Urban Left was their vision. What distinguished different New Urban Left-controlled local authorities was their ability to overcome the conflicts inherent in these origins. In those local authorities where the New Urban Left took control, they sought to include previously excluded groups by setting up new types of democratic consultative and participatory forums within local government and funding community-based voluntary groups to provide services directly. Both initiatives supported a plurality of local voices in wider public debates.

The New Urban Right shared the Thatcherite vision, which saw the role of a democratically elected, but highly centralized, government as creating the conditions under which individuals could compete for rewards within a broader society (Offe, 1984; Thornley, 1991). They saw little place for voluntary groups, preferring a strategy of "contracting out" service provision to professionally based business organizations. Initially, the New Urban Right acquiesced to centrally imposed expenditure cuts, rapidly withdrawing funding from voluntary groups. The New Urban Left authorities had no choice but to withdraw funding after 1985, when expenditure controls became inescapable. Thus the economic logic of spending cuts was also from the beginning a political logic of suppressing local democratic debate.

In London the Thatcherite program played itself out in a specific way. In 1981 control of the Greater London Council (GLC) passed from the Conservatives to a New Urban Left-controlled Labour administration. With County Hall symbolically located directly across the river from the Houses of Parliament and with a budget that made it the "fourteenth largest nation-state in the world," the GLC led the political opposition to the Thatcher government's reform of local government finance. (In a spatial irony, control of Westminster City Council, the borough within which the Houses of Parliament are located, passed to the New Urban Right in 1982.) In 1983 a proposal to abolish the Greater London Council (together with the six other metropolitan county councils) was inserted into the Conservative Manifesto, and in 1986 the GLC ceased to exist (Carvel, 1984; Lansley et al., 1989; Young & Kramer, 1978a).

Thus the political environment within which the federation worked from 1979 onward was politically divided and highly charged. The immediate focus of much of its work, Westminster City Council, was in the hands of the New Urban Right, yet the federation was funded by the Greater London Council. Moreover, as the Thatcherite financial strategy worked its way through, there was less and less point in arguing for more capital spending on housing and more and more point on focusing on the ways relationships between landlords and tenants were regulated (or not) in practice.

In the remainder of this chapter, I explore how the federation created its own identity through a series of pamphlets and events that it produced. The central principle behind these pamphlets was presenting "factual" information in a way that exposed the effects of the state's administrative activities on the lives of tenants and residents in Paddington. I treat the federation's publications and public events as *confessions* in Foucault's sense of the term (1978a); as ways of verbalizing the federation's identity as an organization and the shared subjectivity of its members. I discuss how the "writing" and "speaking" practices and discourses of participants within the federation allowed them to construct and articulate this newly subjective identity.

In what follows, I will look at three specific issues that Foucault poses about understanding knowledge-based campaigning in a specific context. The first issue deals with the extent to which the federation's self-definition was shaped by both (a) the practices and discourses of local government—which viewed and treated it as political subject—and (b) the ways that the relationships among individuals within the federation, its own practices and discourses, contested its subjection to local government. The second issue concerns the ways in which the effects of the federation's activities were sometimes unpredictable, reflecting the complex webs of relationships that characterize modern democracies. The third issue turns on the question of how different practices and discourses implicitly define what constitutes "truth" in relation to both knowledge and power.

■ Speaking Out: Finding a Voice

The following discussion is structured around three campaigns by the Paddington Federation: "Home Truths" in 1977, the District Plan Inquiry in 1980, and "Taken for Granted" between 1980 and 1984. All three of these campaigns focused on the local authority, the city of Westminster. They have been selected because the federation's response to this immediate and conflictual relationship was central in forging its identity. Other campaigns, with other groups in Paddington and throughout London, only built on and extended this identity.

"Home Truths"

In 1964 a central government Committee of Inquiry on Housing in London identified north Paddington as one of the twelve worst areas of housing in London, characterized by intense overcrowding in the private rented sector (Milner Holland, 1965). In 1967 the newly formed Westminster City Council proposed to redevelop half of this housing and rehabilitate the remainder. The city's commitment to private sector improvement reflected its very weak commitment to direct housing provision, although the city and the GLC together owned 30% of the housing stock within the borough. The proposed redevelopment was to be carried out by the GLC. Similarly, the city tended to take a laissez-faire approach to poor physical housing conditions, both within its own stock and toward enforcing the Health and Housing Acts, which lay down minimum standards of repair and management in the private rented sector.

By 1974 Paddington was fertile ground for organizing tenants. In this context, the Paddington Federation was set up by a group of professional community workers. They were employed by a number of local organizations, most of which were funded by Westminster City Council. The council shared the common belief at the time that community development was a way of helping poor people to help themselves (Cockburn, 1977). The community workers, however, were all strongly inspired by neo-Marxist theory and saw organizing local groups as a form of struggle against the capitalist local state.

The federation's first major campaigning publication was *Home Truths: An Investigation into Westminster City Council's Housing Policies,* published in 1977. The main effect of *Home Truths* was to establish the federation as a political subject within Westminster City Council housing politics. Nevertheless, the process behind writing the pamphlet and its style did little to challenge the ways in which local government deploys knowledge in support of power.

Home Truths was largely written by the group of community workers then supporting the federation, although it was initiated and researched by an officer at Westminster City Council acting covertly. The liaison with the council officer was kept secret, not only from his employer but also from the other members of the federation, reflecting the professional distance between the community workers and the tenants they were organizing as well as some of the ideological and ethical conflicts of local authority professional officers (Kaufman, 1987; Thomas & Healey, 1989). The core issue behind the pamphlet was the level of housing capital investment by the city council. It "played back" to the council information from its own technical reports, showing how this information could support quite different conclusions. It did not use any information arising out of the personal experience of tenant members of the federation. Thus both the content and the writing process mirrored the professional control over technical information, over what constitutes relevant "facts," that characterizes the political decision-making process within British local government. The sheer technical quality of *Home Truths* made it difficult for the council to refute. It was what the federation did with the report, however, that established its position as a political subject in Westminster. In 1977 the central government introduced a national system for controlling public expenditure on housing. Local authorities were asked to submit detailed capital spending plans to the central government, which then allocated national capital spending targets among the authorities (Holmans, 1991). In a brilliant tactical move, the federation submitted an "alternative" capital spending plan for Westminster based on *Home Truths*. This led to a meeting between the federation (the community workers and two token tenants) and the Labour housing minister. As a consequence, the government gave the Conservative city council permission to spend an extra £4 million. In effect, the conspiratorial aspirations of the community workers were fully diverted into normal party political networks. The alternative capital spending plan contested neither the right of central government to determine spending limits for local authorities nor the right of local authorities to decide how to spend that money. All it did was argue that more should be spent.

Nevertheless, *Home Truths* did insert the federation into the housing politics of the city council at quite a high level of visibility. It built the reputation of the federation as not just another local pressure group but as a group with some considerable, unusual, and unexpected technical and political skills. *Home Truths*, however, challenged the local authority's monopoly of technical expertise without challenging the general practices and discourses associated with the use of this expertise in local politics. It did nothing to change the relationship of tenant members of the federation to the power/knowledge processes characterizing local government administration. It simply inserted the community workers, another group of professionals, into the existing practices and discourses of local authority administration. It did little to build a subjective identity among tenant members. Instead, and despite its tangible results, it simply confirmed their subjection to existing techniques of power by demonstrating their "lack of knowledge."

The District Plan Inquiry

The District Plan Inquiry in 1980 was the key event that shaped the federation's own identity. The Foucauldian problem is clear. Local authority land use planning documents in Britain are highly formalized. The central government gives clear and strong guidelines about their form and function. Because their main function is to provide a consistent and coherent set of policies to govern applications for the development or change in use of properties, plans are structured as a series of separate chapters that lay out the conditions under which changes to different land uses will be permitted.

Plans articulate three different types of power relationships and the planning process contains very clear images of the administrative subjects within it. The heart of any plan is the power relationship between planners, granting or refusing planning permission, and developers, applying for planning permission. The second power relationship is between the local authority and the population it "governs." In administrative terms, the local authority is responsible for the well-being of the people who live within its area. In a strongly party-politicized system, however, this administrative responsibility becomes biased toward those groups that support the ruling party in the local council. The third power relationship in planning arises from the roles that it assigns to individual citizens. They can only act as "objectors" to policies that are determined through a combined political and quasi-judicial process, or, if they happen to be adjacent property owners or members of a "recognized" amenity group, to specific planning applications.

The legislation governing planning makes a number of formal "participation" requirements on local authorities. The last stage is a formal "public inquiry," held under the auspices of the Planning Inspectorate, officials within the central government ministry whose function is to adjudicate conflicts between the local authority and objectors over the content of the plan before it is formally approved by the secretary of state for the environment. The problem for the federation was how to break out of these administratively defined roles and to find an idea that would give form and voice to all their various experiences within a single framework.

In 1977 the community workers who had set up the federation were withdrawn by their employing organizations. Between 1977 and 1979 three distinct local groupings emerged within the federation. The first was in north Paddington, where tenants associations had formed a consultative grouping around a number of local authority small area initiatives in housing and planning. The second was in Bayswater, where local groups were concerned about the environmental effects of rapidly expanding tourist accommodations. The third was in Maida Vale, where virtually all the housing was owned by a single large landlord, the Church Commissioners (the property holding agency for the Church of England). Each of these groupings had a strong identity, but there were no themes that knitted them together across Paddington as a whole. The Draft Plan prioritized housing uses within the city. The main policy was to draw a line around the central area of the city (the "central activity zone") and give housing first priority outside this area and significant priority within it. When the Draft Plan was circulated for comment, the federation divided the work of reading it chapter by chapter among its various members. Its organization into separate land use chapters, however, inhibited members from seeing how it related to immediate local housing problems. Then, two things happened simultaneously. The federation employed its own worker, who had a radical planning education. And one member observed that the expansion of the hotel trade in Bayswater seemed to be taking over houses that had been privately rented, mostly as single room tenancies in "houses in multiple occupation." This observation was the necessary catalyst.

District Plan Inquiries can be thought of as a highly ritualized form of drama. The proceedings are very formal, quasi-judicial in nature, and involve both written objections and oral evidence. Giving oral evidence may involve the examination and cross-examination of witnesses. The roles in an inquiry are set by the legislative framework: an inspector, planners from the local authority and its barrister, the objectors and their barristers (if any), and any expert witnesses that either side may wish to call. Thus the problem for the federation was how to act effectively within this framework to assert a view of housing and planning problems that was fundamentally different than that contained in the Draft Plan.

The federation concluded that one answer to the question: "How to act?" was to write a play. The federation had the roles: itself the objector, and its members the expert witnesses on living in Paddington, and, in the framework of examination and cross-examination, it had the plot, familiar from countless television programs and films. The formality and social distance of the procedures were subverted by their familiarity. All that was required was the dialogue. In writing the script, an important problem was to clarify precisely what the federation was doing by "objecting," because its main aim was to support the housing policies in the Draft Plan but the inquiry procedures only allow for "objectors," not "supporters." The other available option was to object to the tourism policies, but this would confine the evidence to what planners regarded as "tourism." Neither option was satisfactory, as the federation's main focus was on the interaction between tourism and housing. So the federation created a new kind of planning knowledge and language. It developed the concept of "hotelization" to describe the interaction between tourism and housing, resulting in "quasi hotels" and "creeping conversions." In other words, it challenged the existing discourse and definitions of the problem by introducing a discourse and set of definitions of its own.

The method the federation used to write the script was to hold a series of meetings that drew in both existing members and others who had not yet been actively involved in the federation. At the first meeting, each person described his or her experiences. Five general issues emerged. First, there were the usual effects of tourist provision: transport congestion, traffic safety, loss of local-serving shops, overprovision of *bureaux de change*, late night noise nuisance, and inadequate rubbish collection. Second, quasi hotels were identified as properties used partly as hotels and partly as houses in multiple occupation. The issues in these properties included pressure on rents to match what could be gained form tourists, sharing premises with temporary residents who had no interest in the general conditions of the property, and harassment as landlords sought to evict tenants to let their rooms to tourists. A third set of issues arose from the use of "holiday lets" to genuine tenants as a way of evading the Rent Acts governing residential landlord-tenant relationships. Fourth, the federation identified the scale of "creeping conversions," that is, changing the use of residential property to hotels without the benefit of planning permission. Fifth, there was the impact on tenants of the use of residential premises for prostitution.

The first meeting clarified the issues, followed by two more meetings that led to a collective script-writing exercise. At the second meeting, each person who was to be an expert witness was questioned by the rest of the group. This both elicited further information and gave every member of the group a way of relating their individual experience to that of the other members. At the third meeting, the person who was speaking for the federation as the objector went through the list of questions from the previous meeting with the expert witnesses answering, closely observed by all to ensure that none of the questions undermined the general line of argument. This sharpened the questions, provided the basis for deciding the order in which the evidence should be presented, and made it relatively easy to write a very brief "proof of evidence" outlining the main points.

The public inquiry went very smoothly, involving well over 20 people in what one of the local authority planners remarked was the "best floor show he had ever seen." In addition to the five substantive points about the interaction between housing and tourism, the play conveyed three important messages, both to the local authority and to the federation's own members. First, the federation seeks to make a positive contribution to the governance of Westminster; we do not wish simply to be carping critics. Second, each one of us is a person whose life makes sense as a whole and cannot be understood within the administrative categories of planning. And, third, no matter how individually disparate you may think we are, we see ourselves as "friends and neighbours who care about each other."

Seeing the inquiry procedures as a part of popular culture subverted the subjectifying experience of participating in the inquiry. By formulating and acting within a discourse of its own, the federation created a new form of "knowledge" about planning and housing. By presenting tenants as experts with their own practices and discourses, the federation rejected its previous subjectification as a technically sophisticated pressure group within the framework of the prevailing authority structures and assumptions. It was this latter achievement, seeing tenant members as experts, which shaped much of its later work. Conversely, the federation's professional members and workers were seen simply as people whose particular skill was articulating what the "actual," participant experts were saying.

"Taken for Granted"

After the District Plan Inquiry, the federation became interested in how improvement grants to renovate older properties were associated with the harassment of tenants. This campaign had three stages. The first was the publication of a pamphlet, *Taken for Granted . . . Improvement Grants in Westminster* (1981). The second involved written and oral evidence to a committee of the House of Commons. The third included two formal complaints to the District Auditor, the central government agency responsible for overseeing local authority accounting practices.

The 1969 Housing Act introduced local authority improvement grants for older properties in need of renovation. The grants paid a substantial proportion of the costs of improvement and were often concentrated in small action areas. They were intended to make the full renovation of rented property profitable, particularly in areas where rents were insufficient to give an adequate return to landlords. (Grants were also available to owner-occupiers.) The combination of grants and a major house price boom in the early 1970s fueled gentrification and displacement in inner-city areas.

The 1974 Housing Act contained provisions to limit these negative effects of improvement grants. Virtually all private tenants were given security of tenure. In addition, landlords of tenanted properties within the action areas were required to rent the improved property at less than market rents for at least 7 years after the works were completed. Local authorities were not obliged to impose these conditions outside the action areas, although in practice virtually all did.

In 1976, however, in response to lobbying by the Church Commissioners, who were seeking to gentrify their slum holdings in Paddington, Westminster City Council stopped imposing conditions on grants outside the action areas. In addition, another type of landlord entered the market in Paddington in the late 1970s. These landlords specialized in buying fully tenanted properties and harassing the tenants out. They then applied to the city council for a grant on the empty property, thereby evading the conditions on grants.

In 1981 the federation wrote to the leader of Westminster City Council expressing its unease at the scale of harassment in the area, harassment accompanied by national increases in grant levels, which were making the improvement grants even more attractive to private developers. The letter was not answered. The federation then wrote to the chair of the Housing Committee. This letter also went unanswered. So the federation published the second letter in the local newspaper. Now the council responded—in the newspaper. It made three points. First, the conditions on grants were unnecessary statutory and administrative restrictions (implicitly on "free enterprise"). Second, the council regretted that "those seeking to raise less important issues are bound to experience delays in having their correspondence answered." Third, the council admonished the federation for seeking "to debate . . . political decisions of the Council" through the local newspaper.

When the issue came before the Housing Committee, which had long since passed into the hands of the New Urban Right, council officers confirmed that 8 of the 22 cases of harassment documented by the federation had been associated with grants. They recommended that conditions on grants be reimposed. The Housing Committee made a great show of "compromising," by lowering the amount of money to be paid in grants for landlords who did not wish to accept the conditions. The federation responded by publishing a pamphlet *Taken for Granted* (1981). It simply recounted the story to date, included the various relevant documents, and asked the next full council meeting to change the decision of the Housing Committee. The pamphlet was limited in numbers and circulated only to members of the council, the press, and the federation itself.

What happened next was totally unexpected. During the Conservative party conference, *The Times*, not yet under the control of Rupert Murdoch, published a front-page story based on the pamphlet. The housing minister, finding himself under pressure at the conference, in turn, pressured Conservative councillors in Westminster. The Housing Committee's decision was substantially altered.

In the autumn of 1981, the federation submitted written evidence to the House of Commons Environment Committee's Inquiry into the Private Rented Housing Sector. In January 1982 it was asked to give oral evidence before the committee. The federation concentrated on the range of ways in which landlords were evading the Rent Acts regulating landlord-tenant relationships. Its evidence was designed to draw the attention of members of Parliament to the ways that their legislative intentions were being subverted. The committee was interested, but their report had very little effect on a Thatcher government committed to freeing private enterprise from the fetters of government regulation (House of Commons, 1982, 1983).

Following the House of Commons inquiry, the federation tried a different tactic. Each November, local authorities are obliged to open their accounts to scrutiny by any elector within their area. From this source, the federation obtained a list of all improvement grants given in Westminster between 1969 and 1981. Together with the *Sunday Times* Insight Team, the federation was able to show that, in Westminster, property renovation was so profitable that there was no need for improvement grants. The federation then decided to submit a complaint to the District Auditor. The legal grounds for the complaint were that the decision to remove conditions on improvement grants was "unreasonable"—that, given the knowledge of harassment caused by unconditional improvement grants, no "reasonable" local authority would remove the conditions. The District Auditor dismissed the complaint. Undeterred, the federation complained again the next year, arguing that the city council did not monitor whether or not conditions were met. Without monitoring, it could not reclaim grant money when the conditions were broken. Therefore the city council was willfully "losing" money. This complaint was upheld. The subsequent internal audit identified a number of cases of fraud among council officers responsible for administer-

242 IDENTITY POLITICS AND SOCIAL MOBILIZATION

ing grants. The council eventually stopped giving grants altogether outside the small action areas, justifying the decision by referring to central government limits on their level of capital spending, against which the grants counted.

After the Greater London Council was abolished in 1986, the federation received no further funding. Although many groups collapsed at this time (London Voluntary Service Council, 1987), the federation persisted for another 4 years. It wound itself up in 1990, because nothing is more painful to activists than enforced passivity. The federation's activists are now all involved in other local organizations. The individual members who sustained the activists are still cared for through the networks of friendship and support that the federation established during its life.

Each of the federation's campaigns had unintended consequences or, rather, consequences that emerged from the social networks of power and knowledge in unexpected ways. The 1988 Housing Act introduced draconian penalties for harassment and illegal eviction as well as a more highly accountable improvement grant system. At the same time, it introduced new forms of tenancy, regularizing the evasions of the Rent Acts. The concepts of "creeping conversions" and "quasi hotels" have entered into general local authority planning discourse. In addition, the federation strongly influenced both the planning and the housing strategies of the Greater London Council. These still underpin cooperation across the political spectrum of local authorities in London. Beyond this, many of the federation's ideas have been taken up and used by both campaigning groups and local authorities outside London as well.

There is no single answer to the question of what made all this work. But among the most crucial factors was the relationship between the techniques that the federation used to speak within itself and the shared subjectivity that grew from those discussions—the practices and discourses based on its own subjectivity and refusal of subjection. A significant part of the federation's subjectivity was never to define itself or its members as victims but to celebrate the courage and persistence of those of its members who were willing to speak out against the consequences of state power or the economic power of landlords. This led to a process of discussion and "publication" based on telling the stories of its members, displaying the federation's subjective view of itself as "friends and neighbours caring about each other."

■ Conclusions

Foucault's work provides a means of analyzing the nature of "knowledge-based campaigns." These campaigns use knowledge in two ways: first, to form relationships within the campaigning group based on distinctive subjectivities and, second, to subvert the techniques of administrative power by refusing to act as the subjects these techniques envisage. Such campaigns use the practices and discourses associated with democracy to "speak out," to exploit the divisions within the state's own networks of power, and to alter what happens there by creating new "knowledge" of subjects within the body politic.

Within this framework, specific actors pursue their own programs. But the articulation of social networks throughout society means that, most often, what is achieved is something different than the ends that motivated their programs. Indeterminacy and unforeseen consequences are the result of all action, as ideas circulate through society in unpredictable ways.

Distinctively modern struggles are about forming subjectivities that refuse subjection to administrative techniques of exercising power, whether by the state or by economic institutions. Insofar as modern techniques of administrative power are based on the individual's ability to verbalize her- or himself, then "confession" forms the ground both for subjection to administrative power and for forming a subjectivity that refuses the categories established by that power. The institutional forms of democracy incite confession and, in so doing, leave open the bases for individuals to speak to each other and to define themselves as distinctively different than the knowledge of them imposed by administrative technique. The networks of modernity, that is, hold us "in place," subjecting us to the power of others, while, simultaneously, existing as means through which subjects, acting in relationship and connection to other subjects, articulate power and come to assert ever-shifting levels of control over their world.

REFERENCES

Allen, J. (1986, September). *Smoke over the Winter Palace: The politics of resistance and London's community areas.* Paper presented at the Conference on Planning Theory in Practice, Politecnico di Torino, Italy.

Allen, J., & McDowell, L. (1989). *Landlords and property: Social relations in the private rented sector.* Cambridge, UK: Cambridge University Press.

Back, G., & Hamnett, C. (1985). State housing policy formation and the changing role of housing associations. *Policy and Politics, 13*(4), 393-411.

Ball, M., Harloe, M., & Martens, M. (1988). *Housing and social change in Europe and the USA.* London: Routledge.

Carvel, J. (1984). *Citizen Ken.* London: Chatto and Windus.

Cockburn, C. (1977). *The local state.* London: Pluto.

Cooper, S. (1985). *Public housing and private property: 1970-1984.* Aldershot, UK: Gower.

Cope, H. (1990). *Housing associations: Policy and practice.* London: Macmillan.

Cousins, M., & Hussain, A. (1984). *Michel Foucault.* Basingstoke, UK: Macmillan.

Drake, M. (1991). *Housing associations and 1991: The impact of the single European market.* London: National Federation of Housing Associations.

Forester, J. (1989). *Planning in the face of power.* Berkeley: University of California Press.

Foucault, M. (1965). *Madness and civilisation: A history of insanity in the age of reason.* New York: Random House.

Foucault, M. (1973). *Birth of the clinic: An archaeology of medical perception.* London: Tavistock.

Foucault, M. (1975a). Body/power. In C. Gordon (Ed.), *Michel Foucault: Power/knowledge: Selected interviews and other writings: 1972-1977.* Hemel Hempstead, UK: Harvester Wheatsheaf.

Foucault, M. (1975b). *Discipline and punish: Birth of the prison.* London: Allen Lane.

Foucault, M. (1976). Two lectures. In C. Gordon (Ed.), *Michel Foucault: Power/knowledge: Selected interviews and other writings: 1972-1977.* Hemel Hempstead, UK: Harvester Wheatsheaf.

Foucault, M. (1978a). *The history of sexuality: The will to knowledge* (Vol. 1). London: Allen Lane.

Foucault, M. (1978b). On power. In L. Kritzman (Ed.), *Michel Foucault: Politics, philosophy, culture: Interviews and other writings 1977-1984.* London: Routledge.

Foucault, M. (1978c). The West and the truth of sex. In V. Beechey & J. Donald (Eds.), *Subjectivity and social relations.* London: Open University Press.

Foucault, M. (1979). Politics and reason. In L. Kritzman (Ed.), *Michel Foucault: Politics, philosophy, culture: Interviews and other writings 1977-1984.* London: Routledge.

Foucault, M. (1982). The subject and power. *Critical Inquiry, 8,* 777-795.

Foucault, M. (1988a). Technologies of the self. In L. Martin (Ed.), *Technologies of the self: A seminar with Michel Foucault.* London: Tavistock.

Foucault, M. (1988b). Truth, power, self. In L. Martin (Ed.), *Technologies of the self: A seminar with Michel Foucault.* London: Tavistock.

Foucault, M. (1988c). The political technology of individuals. In L. Martin (Ed.), *Technologies of the self: A seminar with Michel Foucault.* London: Tavistock.

Ghekiere, L. (1991). *Marches et Politiques du Logement dans la CEE.* Paris: La Documentation Francaise.

Gordon, C. (Ed.). (1980). *Michel Foucault: Power/knowledge: Selected interviews and other writings: 1972-1977.* Hemel Hempstead: Harvester Wheatsheaf.

Gyford, J. (1975). *The politics of local socialism.* London: Allen & Unwin.

Holmans, A. (1991). The 1977 National Housing Policy Review in retrospect. *Housing Policy, 6*(3), 206-219.

House of Commons, Environment Committee. (1982). *The private rented housing sector: Vol. 1. Report, Vol. 2. Minutes of Evidence, Vol. 3: Appendices.* London: Her Majesty's Stationery Office.

House of Commons, Environment Committee. (1983). *The private rented housing sector: A report on the memorandum from the Department of the Environment in response to the committee's first report* (Session 1981-82). London: Her Majesty's Stationery Office.

Kaufman, J. L. (1987). Teaching planning students about strategizing, boundary spanning and ethics: Part of the new planning theory. *Journal of Planning Education and Research, 6,* 108-115.

Kritzman, L. (Ed.). (1988). *Michel Foucault: Politics, philosophy, culture: Interviews and other writings 1977-1984.* London: Routledge.

Lansley, S., Goss, S., & Wolmar, C. (1989). *Councils in conflict: The rise and fall of the municipal left.* London: Macmillan.

London Edinburgh Weekend Return Group. (1979). *In and against the state.* London: Pluto.

London Voluntary Service Council. (1987). *After abolition: A report on the impact of abolition of the Metropolitan County Councils and the Greater London Council on the voluntary sector—and the outlook for the future.* London: Author.

Malpass, P. (1990). *Reshaping housing policy: Subsidies, rents and residualisation.* London: Routledge.

Martin, L. (Ed.). (1988). *Technologies of the self: A seminar with Michel Foucault.* London: Tavistock.

Milner Holland. (1965). *Report of the Committee on Housing in Greater London* (Cmnd. 2605). London: Her Majesty's Stationery Office.

Offe, C. (1984). *Contradictions in the welfare state.* London: Hutchinson.

Paddington Federation of Tenants and Residents Associations. (1977). *Home truths: An investigation into Westminster City Council's housing policies.* London: Author.

Paddington Federation of Tenants and Residents Associations. (1981). *Taken for granted . . . Improvement grants in Westminster.* London: Author.

Saunders, P. (1979). *Urban politics: A sociological approach.* London: Hutchinson.

Thomas, H., & Healey, P. (1989). Ethics, skills and legitimacy in planning practice in Britain. *Planning Theory Newsletter, 3,* 63-65.

Thornley, A. (1991). *Urban planning under Thatcherism: The challenge of the market.* London: Routledge.

Weeks, J. (1989). Uses and abuses of Michel Foucault. In L. Appignanesi (Ed.), *Ideas from France: The legacy of French theory.* London: Free Association Books.

Wood, N. (1985). Foucault on the history of sexuality: An introduction. In V. Beechey & J. Donald (Eds.), *Subjectivity and social relations.* London: Open University Press.

Young, K., & Kramer, J. (1978a). *Strategy and conflict in metropolitan housing: Suburbia versus the Greater London Council 1965-75.* London: Heinemann.

Young, K., & Kramer, J. (1978b). Local exclusionary policies in Britain: The case of suburban defence in a metropolitan system. In K. Cox (Ed.), *Urbanisation and conflict in market societies.* London: Methuen.

11 The Difficulty of Leaving "Home": Gay and Lesbian Organizing to Confront AIDS

VALERIE LEHR

AIDS (acquired immunodeficiency syndrome) organizing within gay and lesbian communities became a central focus of political work in the 1980s and remains a focus in the 1990s. This organizing has been difficult because it must simultaneously confront two challenges: the necessity of combatting the association of AIDS with risk groups and the reality that both AIDS politics and gay and lesbian organizing are rooted in identity politics, a form of political organizing in which the necessity of affirming difference has often been denied. Although reacting to the construction of AIDS as an epidemic concentrated in risk groups (because of what some see as the "unnatural actions" of members of these groups) has been aided by the orientation of gay activism to identity politics, this same orientation creates difficulties when white, middle-class-dominated gay male communities need to work with people who are not male, gay, white, and/or middle class.

From the time that AIDS was first recognized by epidemiologists, it has tended to be associated with "risk groups." The earliest name given to AIDS was GRID—gay-related immune deficiency. Political organizing around AIDS must constantly fight the identification of groups of people as at risk while using the cultural understandings and norms of these groups to fight the spread of the disease. In the introduction to their special issue on AIDS, the *Radical America* editorial board recognized the difficulties that the gay community and communities of color have faced in their confrontation with the AIDS epidemic: "We want to challenge the notion that AIDS is acquired by a particular kind of person, while simultaneously challenging the current mythology that 'everyone is equally at risk' because it denies the special vulnerability and experience of gay men, blacks and Hispanics, I.V. drug users, and other groups where cases have been concentrated" (1986, p. 3). It is necessary to recognize "risk groups" as stigmatizing and inaccurate, yet preventing AIDS and confronting the problems of people with AIDS (PWAs) proves to be most effective when community standards of sexuality/drug use can be transformed and when community-based services can be provided. Activists must base AIDS organizing on identity, while avoiding turning AIDS politics into narrowly defined identity politics.

Josh Gamson's (1989) analysis of the AIDS Coalition to Unleash Power (ACT UP), a predominantly white, gay male organization, begins with the understanding that, for gay men, AIDS activism requires that gay identity be affirmed. ACT UP's actions, he suggests, are difficult to assess because they are designed to challenge an "invisible enemy"— the construction of boundaries between "normal" and "abnormal." That is, the ability to talk about "risk groups" has come from the dominant culture's desire to separate acceptable behavior from unacceptable, or deviant, behavior, not by using the coercive power of the state but by labeling and stigmatizing those who challenge the norms. In this sense, AIDS is an "epidemic of signification" (Treichler, 1988). Activists have had to fight against views of PWAs and people whose practices put them at risk for acquiring HIV, the virus believed to cause AIDS, as inherently perverted and unnatural and therefore deserving of AIDS. The groups that ACT UP most targets, the medical establishment and the media, are primarily responsible for constructing the view that AIDS results from who people are rather than from practices in which they engage—practices that can be changed.

Because AIDS politics is about fighting stigmatization, it is a politics that requires attention to identity. Gamson writes, "Identity-forming strategies are particularly crucial and problematic when the struggle is in part against a society rather than against a visible oppressor" (1989, p. 363). It becomes problematic, he continues, because, in challenging the identity imposed by outside, organizing takes place around that identity. This creates the possibility that, by reinforcing the identity that is intended to be challenged, politics based on identity, and on the challenge to normality, may be ineffective as a long-term strategy because it makes working with those who do not share the identity difficult.

In this chapter we will explore this question by examining works that argue that identity politics is ineffective as a long-term strategy as well as theoretical work in feminism that suggests that organizing can move from narrow identity politics to broader alliance building. By exploring AIDS politics, an exploration that also requires a discussion of gay and lesbian organizing, we will be able to see whether identity politics is leading to an activist movement based on alliance building. The example of ACT UP, particularly ACT UP/New York, demonstrates that alliances can be formed but only if political groups are structured in such a manner that different "identities" are explicitly recognized and valued within the group.

■ Identity Politics and Alliance Building: History and Theory

The social movements of the 1960s and 1970s differed from previous social movements in their emphasis on the connection between political work and identity. These movements politicized areas of life that had previously been seen as outside the realm of public, political discussion, such as sexuality and culture (Kauffman, 1990, p. 67). One reason identity politics arose was that the process of fighting against the cultural construction of one's identity as inferior required that people come to see themselves as different than those cultural images and to see themselves and the group of which they are a part as valuable, based on a different definition of what is desirable. "It's important to note," Adams writes of feminism, "that identity politics encompasses a celebration of a group's uniqueness as well as an analysis of its particular oppression" (1989, p. 23). Politics based on identity locates resistance not primarily in traditional political channels but in the transformation of self-understanding and group understanding. Bernice Johnson Reagon recognizes both the necessity of this process and its dangers:

> You come together to see what you can do about shouldering up all of your energies so that you and your kind can survive. There is no chance that you can survive by staying *inside* the barred room. That will not be tolerated. . . . But that space, while it lasts, should be a nurturing space where you sift out what people are saying about you and decide who you really are. (1983, p. 358)

The tendency of movements, however, has been to try to remain in the "barred rooms," thus creating difficulties in moving beyond analysis and the building of culture to political action. In fact, as Adams notes, what is likely to happen, and what has happened in the women's movement, is that the values of the dominant subgroup define the understanding of oppression and the process and content of discussion (1989, p. 27). The result is a fragmented movement composed of different identity groups with little communication between groups. A movement structured in this way does not have the ability to confront difficulties between women; it is most successful when all anger can be directed externally. Lorde (1984) understands the need to confront the anger that exists between women within groups as a result of differences in race, class, and sexuality, if feminism is to bring about change.

Barbara Epstein agrees that identity politics will not lead to the development of a successful movement for social and political change, arguing that identity politics emphasizes the formation of culture, which leads away from a focus on the strategies necessary to bring about change (1990, p. 53). Kauffman makes a similar point, suggesting that identity politics has tended to result in the creation of "life-styles." This is a problem because "lifestyle politics suggests that external structures don't really have to be confronted" (Kauffman, 1990, p. 76). Rather, isolated communities with their own cultural norms are created; political correctness within communities replaces political action. Furthermore, because identity formation attempts to value that which is devalued, it tends to be reactive. The demand for identity politics is strongest when there is a felt need for "barred rooms." If this need decreases, even if few structural changes have been made in society, the energy necessary to continue organizing can also decrease. Thus the lack of focus on structural change is a serious problem.

Identity politics can be an important component of political action, but it will progress only if the exploration of identity can be balanced with structural analysis and the creation of ties to other identity groups (Kauffman, 1990, p. 79). In discussing this possibility, some feminist authors have rejected the idea of coalition politics, preferring to discuss the need to build alliances between groups. In differentiating between alliances and coalitions, Albrecht and Brewer suggest that a coalition has "traditionally referred to groups or individuals that have come together around a particular issue to achieve a particular goal. These groups operate autonomously and are usually not connected to each other; most groups have different agendas as well" (1990, p. 3). Alliance is intended to refer to something deeper: "Out of our vision of alliance we see allies as people who struggle together on a number of progressive fronts, not just a single issue that might emerge in a short-term coalition. We see coalitions as short-term solutions and alliance formation as ongoing, long-term arrangements for more far-reaching structural change" (Albrecht & Brewer, 1990, p. 4).

To form alliances, consciousness-raising and the presence of separate spaces used in identity politics are necessary. But in such a model of politics, consciousness-raising must go further than it does in identity politics. "In addition to reclaiming positive aspects of one's own heritage and learning about other groups' histories and current status," Alperin argues, "activists are asked to evaluate how different types of oppression interact in specific historical situations" (1990, p. 28). We can further develop this by observing that there is also a need to move from politics based simply on anger directed outside of the identity group to analytic politics that recognizes the complexity of identity and the anger within the group that may result from this complexity. These additional steps lead to an understanding of the connections between different forms of oppression, thus paving the way to a greater understanding of the structural problems underlying different forms of oppression. With such an understanding, withdrawing into one's life-style is no longer a feasible option.

In discussing the need for alliance formation, Albrecht and Brewer specifically discuss AIDS as a social problem that will only be confronted if alliances are built (1990, pp. 18-19). At the most basic level, it is obvious that this is true because AIDS has most severely affected gay male communities and communities of color. Without responses to AIDS that consider the differing forms of oppression affecting these communities, the social forces that have produced a crisis of the magnitude of AIDS cannot be understood. At the same time, as the alliance model suggests should be the case, it is clear that identity politics has played an important role in allowing gay men, in particular middle-class white gay men, to begin to control the spread of AIDS within their community and to build a social movement in response to the AIDS crisis. What remains unclear is whether the alliances necessary to build a lasting movement able to confront the multiple social problems apparent to AIDS activists will be forged. This challenge is particularly difficult because the contemporary gay and lesbian movement has a history not of alliance building but of identity politics. Thus, in exploring how identity politics and alliance building are taking place within AIDS politics and gay and lesbian politics in the 1990s, it is helpful to have an understanding of the difficulties confronted within gay and lesbian politics prior to the onset of the AIDS crisis.

■ History of Gay and Lesbian Politics

Gay men, the group that in 1981 AIDS was first recognized as striking, had organized politically over the preceding 40 years. The conditions that gave rise to this organizing include the development of capitalism and the impact of World War II on society. The development of capitalism, John D'Emilio (1983a, 1983b) has argued, was a necessary condition for the development of gay identity in the United States because it created a wage labor system that, by severing the economic connection between private life and public life, freed individuals from family-based labor. In large cities there were gay and lesbian meeting places by the early 1900s. World War II furthered this development by increasing the mobility of people, while furthering sex segregation at a time when homosexuality was already being defined as a "disease" that threatened the nuclear family, traditional gender roles, and reproduction among the middle class (see D'Emilio, 1983b, pp. 96-101). The definition of homosexuality, although intended as a means of control, also provided an understanding around which organizing could occur. The resurgence of support for heterosexual families after World War II, accompanied by the condemnation of gay men and lesbians by the military and through the McCarthy hearings, further encouraged the formation of a sense of identity.

Cities were a primary place for gay and lesbian communities to form initially because of the location of manufacturing and professional jobs there. This dual class structure was prominent, and led to conflict, in early gay/lesbian communities. The majority of identity-based organizing, however, has been dominated by middle-class gay men and lesbians, while bars have been a more traditional gathering place for working-class gays and lesbians. For middle-class gay men and lesbians, employment as professionals and in the service sector has allowed for the continued growth of gay/lesbian communities, even as industry left cities. The gay movement should be seen as an excellent example of what Manuel Castells describes as an urban movement based predominantly on the goal of creating/maintaining an autonomous cultural identity. Such an identity allows residents to defend themselves against the standardization of culture while defining an independent social meaning (1983, p. 319).[1]

The first attempt to create this identity-based movement occurred in the 1950s as the homophile movement developed in many American cities.[2] Pressures gays faced combined with the conservative political environment of the 1950s quickly led the homophile movement to become not identity based but, instead, a liberal movement that tried to gain the support and acceptance of experts. It was not until the 1969 Stonewall riot that identity politics became central to gay and lesbian organizing. Ironically, the riot was started by a lesbian refusing to be quietly arrested during a bar raid and was continued primarily by poor, black or Hispanic, gay men and/or transsexuals, all groups later excluded from the identity-based political movement. Even in the political environment of the 1970s, an environment supportive of recognizing the "personal as political" and dominated by identity-based movements, it was difficult for gay men and lesbians to sustain an activist political movement. Although there were always gay men and lesbians who understood their gay and lesbian identities as a challenge to the institution of the patriarchal family, for many more gay men and lesbians, organizing to openly challenge these systems was less important than building safe spaces and responding to homophobic attacks.

In 1982 Dennis Altman evaluated gay and lesbian organizing: "The problem with depending on our opponents to rally support is that it also allows them to determine our agenda. One of the most critical steps that must be taken is to build on the anger aroused by specific anti-gay campaigns to construct a more permanent and inclusive movement" (p. 138). He observed that for gays in the United States there were three challenges: the lack of political analysis generally in the United States, the ability of gays to pass, and "the hedonistic lifestyle available to many gays (men at least)" (p. 138). These challenges, as well as those posed by unanalyzed racism, classism, and sexism, need to be discussed because they still exist within gay politics and within AIDS politics. A final obstacle should also be added: the inability or unwillingness of the left to incorporate identity-based gay and lesbian analysis into its understanding.

Most gay men and lesbians, as Altman noted, can pass as heterosexual, a possibility that is generally not faced by other identity-based movements. For many gay men in the 1970s, publicly coming out and asserting their gay identity was less important than ending bar raids and arrests so that they could continue to pass as heterosexual and enjoy the privileges that this brought while also having access to gay sex and social life. For these men, the goals of gay politics were at most to fight for privacy rights within the existing social and political systems, not to analyze and challenge those systems. Further, the differences in what being gay means to those who want success within current economic, social, and political systems and those who want to challenge those systems made it impossible to develop a common understanding of gay identity. This created difficulties for developing either a gay agenda or a gay leadership; because there was no unified community but there was an ideology of a gay community, gay leaders were always being attacked for not defining "gayness" as particular subgroups desired. It is this that Jernigan believes made the development of an activist movement impossible: "Efforts to build anything but the least common denominator [a movement focused on civil rights] were largely unsuccessful" (1988, p. 48).

Similarly, a number of authors have argued that the gay movement, given both its own divorce from other radical issues[3] and the decline of new left politics on the whole, became more focused on gaining power and privilege within the economic and social systems that existed. This was particularly true for white, middle-class gay men who, despite being gay, were privileged in other important respects. Adam writes, "The paradox of the 1970s was that gay and lesbian liberation did not produce the gender-free communitarian world it envisioned, but faced an unprecedented growth in gay capitalism and a new masculinity" (1987, p. 97). The lack of direction was great enough so that some, such as Tommi Avicolli, editor of a Philadelphia gay newspaper, suggested in 1979 that the gay movement had been co-opted by consumerism (1979, p. 2). Adam argues that even sexuality became commodified as the number of bars and baths expanded and profited.

With a decrease in police harassment, particularly in bars, many cities became sites for flourishing gay, particularly gay male, subcultures, with these subcultures often being defined in terms of particular gay identities and behaviors. In San Francisco the dominant gay culture of the Castro differed from the working-class gay culture of the Tenderloin. The identity-based gay movement was most successful in creating places where gay life-styles could flourish. As gays have built cultural areas where gay life can openly be lived, the areas that Levine (1979) identified as "gay ghettoes," tensions have arisen between white, middle-class gays, particularly gay men, and the residents of the neighborhoods in which these "ghettoes" have developed. The development of gay urban areas occurred at a time when the economic function of cities was changing and many urban dwellers were losing their jobs. In a changing urban environment where many were becoming displaced, gays were an easy target for that anger of those being displaced. In San Francisco, according to Manuel Castells, gays were able to move into the Castro because of nontraditional living arrangements and because they renovated houses themselves. Despite these realities,

> As often happens in the process of social change, groups inconvenienced by the progress of another are not properly recompensed. . . . These hardships have been at the root of the hostility of ethnic minorities against gay people, a hostility often translated into violence. Class hate, ethnic rage, and fear of displacement by the invaders have clearly held greater sway than prejudices from family traditions or machismo ideology. (1983, p. 167)

A series of articles in Boston's *Gay Community News* (GCN) makes it clear that this was not only a problem in San Francisco. Such stereotyping, whether of gay men as rich speculators or ethnic communities as homophobic, remains a challenge for AIDS activists. This has been made more difficult by the reality that middle-class gay men have been particularly adept at receiving grants to develop AIDS service organizations, often winning competitions with less wealthy, less politically astute, or less bureaucratically organized groups (Sadowick, 1991, p. 38).

In examining the pages of *GCN*,[4] it is clear that civil rights issues and the negative portrayal of gay men and lesbians in the media were the focus of much energy in the early 1980s, when AIDS was first being identified. Aside from reacting to problems such as the loss of child custody by lesbians, the need to defeat California's Briggs initiative, which would have allowed gay male and lesbian teachers to be fired, the need to respond to Anita Bryant's crusade to repeal gay rights in Florida, and the need to contest negative portrayals of gay men and lesbians in the films *Cruising* and *Windows*, it was not entirely clear where gay men and lesbians wanted the movement to go. Thus the movement was, as Altman recognized, only dynamic when it could respond to actions of others that threatened the developing gay lifestyle. This is identity politics at its most restrictive, leading to action when the "barred rooms" are directly threatened and when anger can be directed to those who pose this threat, but lacking the structural analysis necessary to challenge the dominant system or to work with others oppressed by similar social constructions. The divisions that arose between gay men and lesbians are illustrative. Many lesbian feminists identified the gay male movement as oppressive because it failed to analyze and criticize patriarchy (see Frye, 1983). These women left the gay male movement to focus on building a lesbian feminist community. At the same time, both the gay male movement and the lesbian feminist movement failed to adequately address the impact of racism within their communities. Thus gay men and lesbians of color confronted the racism of these communities and the homophobia and sexism in communities of color and the dominant culture. Often these men and women participated in political work in the white-dominated gay and lesbian communities while also being active politically in communities of color; finding a true "home" was difficult.

By the 1980s many lesbians, and some gay men who had explicitly analyzed and rejected the values and institutions of the dominant culture, had left exclusive lesbian or gay organizing, focusing on social agendas such as the peace movement, the environmental movement, and the reproductive freedom movement in organizations such as the Reproductive Rights National Network, the Women's Health Movement, Battered Women's Shelters, and the People's Anti-War Mobilization. "Through the 1980s," Epstein notes, "lesbian affinity groups were a major part of actions and of the ongoing life of the direct action movement: they have stayed with the movement when others have disappeared" (1991, p. 181). Despite the leadership roles that lesbians have come to play in these groups, lesbian identity was not always explicitly recognized as central to the political goals for which lesbians fought, even if this identity was central to their political involvement. Torie Osborn observes, "We have a rich—and totally unacknowledged—tradition of community activism and leadership in every social change movement in this country's history, from abolitionism, to civil rights, the '60s antiwar movement, and women's liberation" (1991, p. 90).

Perhaps the failure of gay men and lesbians to build an identity-based, transformative movement during the 1970s was most clearly apparent at the 1979 March on Washington. Some had hoped that the march would refocus gay men and lesbians on gay and lesbian liberation, rather than gay pride, yet the march produced little long-term organizing. In addition to the difficulties within gay politics that we have examined, the inability to build a more transformative political movement must be seen as connected to both the decline of an organized left in the United States and the hesitancy of progressive movements to take gay and lesbian identity seriously. In a recent interview, Urvashi Vaid, executive director of the National Gay and Lesbian Task Force, observed:

> When gay people work in the labor movement, or the peace movement, or the women's movement, we have experiences such as this: "Well, we support equal rights for gay people, but that's not what we're here to talk about—we're here to talk about housing, we're here to talk about peace." But there are gay and lesbian perspectives on each of these issues. We have experiences of discrimination that are particular, and should be aired in these forums. The left has a long history of problems in dealing with the lavender question, and dealing with sexuality in general. (1991, p. 7)

Sarah Schulman has explicitly discussed this failure in relation to AIDS: "The progressive community's response to the AIDS crisis has revealed how incapable they are of addressing any issue in which homosexuality is central. After 20 years of occasional lip-service and no honest investigation, the theoretical foundations of the contemporary left are apparently irrelevant to AIDS activism" (1988, p. 3). Thus gay and lesbian politics prior to the onset of AIDS reveals the challenges to creating an alliance-based response to the AIDS crisis in gay and lesbian communities.

■ Gay Politics After AIDS

The October 11, 1987, March on Washington for Lesbian and Gay Rights was a critical event for gay and lesbian organizing as well as for AIDS activism. The march was organized as a response to the Supreme Court's 1986 *Bowers v. Hardwick* decision, in which the court upheld Georgia's sodomy law by declaring that homosexuality is not protected by the right to privacy. *Hardwick,* combined with *Mosely,* a later decision in which the Georgia Supreme Court ruled that the sodomy law did not apply to heterosexuals, made clear "not that sodomy—an act—is illegal, but something else is illegal—*homosexual* sodomy, a set of acts tied to an identity" (see Cerullo, 1987, pp. 68-69).

The *Hardwick* decision came at a time when AIDS had already become a major concern within gay communities. If the *Hardwick* decision suggested that gays and lesbians were vulnerable to state regulation, the responses to AIDS by federal, state, and local governments, as well as the scientific establishment and the media, made it clear that the gay population and the IV drug-using population were considered expendable. Thus, although it may have been possible for significant segments of the gay population to believe that political power in local communities and access to economic resources guaranteed a degree of safety for gays unmatched in previous times, by 1987 the realities of AIDS made it clear that gay men, regardless of race or class, were in need of political activism if they were to survive physically. Similarly, the regular occurrence of violence in the lives of gay men and lesbians, perhaps increased by the overt homophobia of the Supreme Court and the acceptability within the dominant culture of blaming gays for AIDS, combined with the lack of response to this violence from police, further confirmed the need for activism.

Between 500,000 and 700,000 people came to the March on Washington, which provided a meeting place for many activists, including those from ACT UP/New York, a group formed in March 1987 and important in planning for the Supreme Court Civil Disobedience on the day following the march.[5] The combination of the march, meetings, and civil disobedience led to the formation of many new activist groups in cities throughout the country, many named and patterned after ACT UP/NY. Chris Bull reports that "ACT UP/NY has served as a model for more than three hundred groups which have sprung up around the country since the March on Washington" (1988, p. 1). Autonomous branches of ACT UP have formed in such American cities as Chicago, Los Angeles, San Francisco, Buffalo, Portland, Kansas City, Atlanta, Seattle, New Orleans, Denver, Boston, Washington, DC, and Philadelphia. Additionally, chapters have formed in Minnesota, Paris, Berlin, and London.

In forming an AIDS activist movement, there have been difficulties due to the race, class, and gender divisions in the gay and lesbian community and the lack of alliance building between white middle-class gay men and lesbians and other identity groups. It is clear that these divisions continue to have an influence (see Gomez, 1989; Johnson, 1987). Additionally, difficulties continue to result from the stereotype of white gay men as wealthy real estate speculators as well as the reality that some white gay men have exercised their class and male privileges to build a comfortable life-style, one that, if they are PWAs, affects their ability to receive treatments for AIDS, to have health insurance, and to have adequate housing. At the same time, it must be recognized that lesbians and gay men are working together in a way that was impossible in the past. The role that lesbians played in establishing an alternative women's health care network, for example, has been critical for the AIDS movement.

A new complication has arisen, however: A schism has increasingly developed between those who identify their primary identity in terms of their PWA status and those whose primary identity is gay or lesbian. These conflicting identities are connected to a problem in AIDS activism not common with other social movements. In "Coalition Politics," Reagon wrote about the need to understand that change is a long-term process, one in which we "must not think that the issue we have at this moment has to be faced or we will die" (1983, p. 366). For PWAs, however, maintaining this perspective is more difficult than for others; the reality is that, unless issues, particularly medical issues, connected to AIDS are addressed, PWAs *will* die. Currently, life expectancy for PWAs is increasing, but it is still only approximately 15 years from the time of infection. Thus alliance building and social movement building can appear less critical than pressuring the government to "get drugs into bodies." Peter Staley writes:

> A rift has occurred between those of us who joined as a matter of survival and those who joined seeking a power base from which their social activism could be advanced. The common denominator that was missing was the crisis mentality—the view that time was our ultimate enemy. Defeating racism, sexism, and homophobia will take decades at best and become a never ending fight at worst. Successfully countering the anti-abortionists or America's imperialist tendencies will take more time than people with AIDS have. (1991, p. 98)

An examination of writings about the internal dynamics of many gay- and lesbian-dominated AIDS activist groups can leave one very pessimistic about the future of this movement, particularly given the split between those who believe that improving the treatment options of PWAs must be the most important concern of AIDS activists and those who believe that AIDS must be seen and fought within the context of fighting racism, sexism, and homophobia. This dynamic has led to the splitting up of ACT UP groups in San Francisco, Portland, and Chicago. It has also led to tensions within ACT UP/NY.

The difficulties that have arisen concern both the process of decision making to be used in ACT UP chapters and the goals of the organization.

In San Francisco the question of process concerned whether the use of consensus decision making was practical or whether it was too time consuming.[6] Yet here, as in the other ACT UP chapters, the question of process is tied to other difficulties. In San Francisco,

> Those in the original chapter argue that the best way to combat AIDS is within the context of other social ills, while most of those who left to form the new chapter of ACT UP [ACT UP/Golden Gate] believe that ACT UP had gotten too concerned with wider social issues like sexism, racism, and homophobia, thus diluting the group's impact on AIDS. (O'Loughlin, 1990, p. 48)

Sadowick suggests similar difficulties in other ACT UP chapters, specifically connecting them to gender divisions: "ACT UP chapters in Portland, Oregon, and Minnesota are also polarized between the women who are more geared to long-term change and the men who are too impatient for them" (1990, p. 54). Similarly, there have been debates within ACT UP/NY about whether the democratic rules of procedure are too time consuming to be useful. Those who make this argument also discuss their perception of ACT UP/NY as a group increasingly abandoning gay men PWAs as it examines the impact not only of homophobia but also of sexism and racism. Harding reports, "Michael Petrelis, an ACT UP member in Washington, D.C., said he worries that 'gay men are being pushed not to the back burner, but totally out of the picture.' And Chicago AIDS activist Daniel Sotomayor said he worries that as gay men with AIDS become 'yesterday's news,' they will be neglected by activist groups" (1991, p. 21).

An additional difficulty is that many gay men and lesbians have been politicized by AIDS but have come to focus their energy on the more specific identity issue that drew them to AIDS: being gay or lesbian. As a result, they have left ACT UP to form newer activist organizations, such as Queer Nation and the Pink Panthers. (This group has been renamed the Panthers Patrol as the result of a lawsuit.) Queer Nation formed in New York in April 1990. Chee describes QN members as "people who had been in ACT UP but were HIV negative or interested and wanting something other than the emphasis on treatment issues" (1991, p. 15). Queer Nation groups have formed in response to such events as queer bashing in New York and arrests for cruising in Philadelphia (Podolsky, 1990, p. 52). The Pink Panthers is a group that formed in New York, also as a result of gay bashing, in July 1990. This group's organizers "had already seen street action with the New York chapter of ACT UP and with Queer Nation" (Merrett, 1990, p. 55). Their goal is to make the streets safe for openly gay and lesbian people.

The combination of tensions and splits within AIDS activist organizations and the tendency of more focused gay and lesbian activist organizations to split off from AIDS activist groups could be interpreted as an indication that identity politics cannot lead to alliance building. This interpretation, however, is unable to account for the fact that AIDS activist groups, particularly ACT UP chapters, have created what remains a dynamic movement with the ability to confront issues beyond the medical concerns of PWAs and the identity concerns of gay men and lesbians. For example:

■ 1991: The Second AIDS Treatment Activists Conference was attended by 300 activists from 30 ACT UP chapters. The primary focus of the conference was access to treatment. The People of Color Caucus began planning a conference for treatment activists of color. The ACT UP Network's call for universal health care was discussed (Wofford & Yang, 1991, p. 1).

■ 1991: ACT UP/NY planned a 24-hour "Day of Inspiration" with actions all over the city, including a rush-hour blockade of Grand Central Station. Harlem ACT UP focused on homeless issues, working with Emmaus House, an advocacy center for homeless people. The Latino Committee "stormed the offices of Bronx Borough President Fernando Ferrer" (Nealon, 1991, p. 1).

■ 1991: Antiwar actions were planned by ACT UP and Queer Nation chapters in many cities during the Gulf War. ACT UP/SF cosponsored a demonstration with Pledge of Resistance (Woffard & Zeh, 1991, p. 6).

■ 1990: ACT UP/Atlanta organized two actions on consecutive days. The first, which included reproductive rights activists, was to combat sodomy laws, the second to confront the Center for Disease Control. The CDC action demanded that the CDC recognize that AIDS is increasingly affecting IV drug users, people of color, women, and children (Gerber, 1990, pp. 1, 3).

■ 1990: ACT UP/DC planned a demonstration demanding that the Social Security Administration "alter its criteria [for benefit eligibility] to accommodate the changing nature of AIDS and HIV." Such a change is particularly critical for women with AIDS (Nealon, 1990, p. 1).

■ 1990: ACT UP/Chicago and ACT NOW, "an umbrella organization of AIDS activist groups," jointly planned a demonstration focusing on the AIDS-related concerns of people of color, women, and children. As a result of actions focusing on women, children, and people of color with AIDS, the first woman PWA was admitted to Cook County hospital (Gould, 1990, p. 1).

That these actions continue to occur suggests that, although identity politics continues to play a central role in both AIDS politics and gay and lesbian politics, this focus has not precluded the development of a thriving alliance-based political movement. In fact, the reality that within AIDS politics and gay and lesbian politics, identity is now understood by many individuals to encompass class, race, and HIV status, as well as sexual identity, and this identity has been both a primary source of strength and a primary challenge to this movement. We can see this more clearly by discussing ACT UP/NY, a group that has greatly influenced AIDS politics.

■ Alliance Building, Identity Politics, and Aids Activism

ACT UP/NY was formed in March 1987 in response to a speech by Larry Kramer delivered at New York's Lesbian and Gay Community Service Center. Kramer, critical of both the government and AIDS service organizations such as Gay Men's Health Crisis, which he helped to found, asked, "Do we want to start a new organization devoted solely to political action?" Two days later 300 people answered Kramer's question by attending a meeting and founding ACT UP. The group's organizational structure and tactics clearly reflect both a leftist and gay orientation. "ACT UP started out fairly small and has always been entirely open, leaderless, grass-roots, anarcho-democratic" (Crimp & Rolston, 1990, p. 34). The initial goals of the group were to "get drugs into bodies" (Crimp & Rolston, 1990, p. 37), though they have expanded since that time. Strategies employed by ACT UP range from public civil disobedience and protests, often employing traditionally gay camp humor, to meeting with scientific "experts" to discuss drug trials, to publishing documents for PWAs detailing drug effectiveness. Peter Staley, an ACT UP member since the group's inception, writes, "If saving our lives meant going to jail, we'd do it. If it meant damaging property at a pharmaceutical company, we'd do it. If it meant sitting down to a candlelight dinner with Tony Fauci through four bottles of wine and a quiet debate, we'd do it. If it meant kissing ass or kicking ass, we'd do it" (1991, p. 98).

Since the early period when the organization was focused on the needs of white gay male PWAs, the goals of the organization have become more complex. The presence of committees has helped to broaden the agenda. Crimp and Rolston write about the developing emphasis on women's issues, issues that were first publicly confronted in a protest over a *Cosmo* article, which suggested that heterosexual women were not at risk of acquiring HIV:

> By the time of the publication of the *Cosmo* article, a group of ACT UP women had been getting together at informal "dyke dinners" for several months to discuss the role of women, *lesbian* women in particular, in AIDS activism. That role often took the form in Monday night meetings of broadening the debate, keeping inequities determined by class, race, and sex on the agenda. But with the *Cosmo* article, the women had a galvanizing issue specific to the lives of women, and they quickly took action to form a Women's Committee and organize a demonstration. (1990, p. 162)

The Majority Actions Committee, "so named because the majority of people with AIDS in New York are people of color and because the word *minority* is rejected by those very people as marginalizing" (Crimp & Rolston, 1990, p. 58), provides support and serves as a base of action for people of color.[7] In addition to the existence of focused committees and caucuses within ACT UP, ACT UP has worked with other activist organizations to plan actions. For example, in response to the Supreme Court's *Webster* decision, ACT UP teamed with WHAM! (Women's Health Action Mobilization) to plan an action at St. Patrick's.[8] ACT UP/NY has also worked with ADAPT (Association for Drug Abuse Treatment and Prevention) to demand the distribution of needles to IVDUs.[9] ACT UP's ability to work with WHAM and ADAPT is important not only because it illustrates the influence that focus groups within an organization may have but also because it suggests a strategy for analyzing the links between issues and the means by which focus groups can have an impact on the larger group of which they are a part. In March 1989 "the Women's Caucus of ACT UP (21 women at the time) organized two 6-hour long evenings of in-reach: prepared talks packed with statistics and analysis, conversation, and food. At the same time, the women collectively produced a handbook to accompany the presentation because so much information was being gathered and so few outlets existed for its circulation" (Saalfield & Navarro, 1991, p. 359). Crimp and Rolston connect this teach-in with ACT UP and WHAM's St. Patrick's action as well as ACT UP members' involvement in other prochoice demonstrations. The strategy of doing teach-ins for the group's at-large membership during regular weekly meetings has been used to expand the concerns of ACT UP's membership: "These think-tanks were not politburos or steering committees. Rather, the function of the 'teachers' was to expand ACT UP's focus by including the different agendas of people who aren't gay identified, white, male, or middle class, but are, in vast numbers, living with AIDS in NYC" (Saalfield & Navarro, 1991, p. 360). Teach-ins have focused on issues such as homelessness and IV drug use. The teach-in on IV drug use was conducted by ADAPT (Saalfield & Navarro, 1991, p. 360).

These efforts have not allowed ACT UP/NY to directly deal with all of the difficulties faced by an organization attempting to confront a social problem like AIDS, that is, a social problem that clearly demonstrates the racism, sexism, homophobia, and classism of American society. Examining AIDS demonstrates how these broad social forces influence health care, housing, education, and scientific research and development. Despite the enormity of the task and the pattern of racism and sexism in gay life, ACT UP/NY, as well as other ACT UP chapters, has been critically important both in influencing change and in helping to organize opposition to governmental policies that are not obviously and directly connected to AIDS. The ability of ACT UP/NY to continue functioning must be seen as connected to the presence of the committees and caucuses. Although it is problematic that, without these focus groups, the agenda that would be supported by ACT UP probably would not consider the needs of women and people of color, the fact that they do exist provides a "home" for constituencies whose needs have been heard and have contributed to the larger group's analysis. This is recognized by New York member Tom Cunningham: "Had not the gay white male power structure been counterbalanced by the growing influence of the Latino/a Caucus, the Women's Caucus, and the Needle-Exchange Program, we would have split apart" (Sadowick, 1990, p. 53). The tensions currently present in the group must be seen as arising from the fact that people of color and women have influenced the agenda of ACT UP/NY to such an extent that some gay white men fear that their needs are no longer being met by the organization. Yet the presence of the focus groups provides these men with the opportunity to continue to focus on the "drugs into bodies" approach.

The Treatment and Data committee of ACT UP/NY has been instrumental in making changes within the clinical trial system for drugs, publicizing drugs that are effective for treating opportunistic infections, and, in general, challenging the idea that PWAs should not have an influence on their own treatment. This has been done by protesting and becoming active participants in the scientific process. The extent to which some members of the subcommittee have become co-opted by federal agencies has been another source of debate and conflict within ACT UP. Sadowick reports:

> ACT UP members, including Bill Dobbs and Jon Nalley of New York and Michael Petrelis of the Washington, D.C. chapter made public their irritation with perceived elitism within ACT UP. . . . They criticized T&D for hoarding information, said it was dominated by a small group of media stars, wrote that "women have been forced to do their own AIDS treatment activism," and added that T&D "dumps on alternative treatments." They questioned T&D's relationship to federal officials such as NIAID's Fauci. (1990, p. 54)[10]

Despite these difficulties, ACT UP/NY has not split apart. In fact, it may be that the most effective organizing against AIDS requires an organization that is in itself an alliance of different groups, with different identities. Although in meetings of the whole this may be frustrating, leading members to feel that nothing is being accomplished, it creates the possibility of mobilizing large numbers of people when necessary and, despite the intentions of some members, building a social movement. Simultaneously, it allows smaller numbers to focus on specific issues or policies in a more detailed, analytical manner. ACT UP/NY member Maxine Wolfe observes, "One of the advantages for ACT UP now that it's so large is that you can have people working on multiple things at once. But you can't lose sight of the larger goal. National health care with no treatments available is not going to be helpful for people" (Bull, 1990, p. 49). Wolfe is recognizing that AIDS activism will only be successful if it is built as an alliance between people who, largely as a result of identity, perceive their needs differently but understand, through analysis, how their needs are connected to those of other identity groups.

The size of ACT UP/NY may be a critical factor in allowing the organization to build alliances within. Splits may have been avoided not because there is not conflict but because the large number of activists has provided for effective committees. Additionally, within ACT UP chapters that are smaller, the anger that arises due to competing identities and needs can easily be more personally focused and therefore more divisive. In discussing ACT UP/Portland's split, Gallagher writes, "The philosophical aspects of the split in Portland parallel those that led to a split in San Francisco's ACT UP chapter last fall. But members of both factions in Portland said the small numbers of people involved in the dispute there made Portland's schism more emotional" (1991, p. 24). It is important to note that, even though ACT UP/San Francisco split into two groups, the less emotional nature of the split allowed them to continue working together. Thus here it has been more effective to build an alliance between two groups rather than creating a single organization that is an alliance of identity-based committees.

■ Conclusion

The AIDS activist movement has been the most dynamic ongoing political movement in the United States in the past 10 years. In addition to directly affecting AIDS and issues connected to AIDS, this movement has helped lead to a resurgence in gay and lesbian organizing, provided a model for people with other diseases who wish to challenge the medical establishment, and, as a result of the demographic characteristics of the AIDS epidemic, begun the process of building connections between white, middle-class gays and lesbians and people of color. Gay men and lesbians of color, who have been analyzing racism, sexism, and heterosexism, are critical leaders in AIDS activism. Their work in communities of color, gay and lesbian organizing, and feminist organizing throughout the 1980s means that AIDS activism has had participants with connections to the two hardest hit communities and with analyses of how racism, sexism, and heterosexism have come together in the construction of AIDS. The increasing ability of gay men and lesbians to work together, an ability that is particularly positive given the already existing connections between lesbians and other social movements, has also been important. Thus, although racism, sexism, and classism continue to be problems in AIDS politics and in gay and lesbian politics, there has also been increasing interaction between races and sexes and increasing analysis of the differing impact that AIDS has on people as a result of differences in race, class, sexuality, and gender.

One issue that has the potential to further the building of alliances is national health care. The future of the movement may depend upon the extent to which AIDS activists can work with others, including progressive movements that, if able to unify, could form the basis of a renewed and redefined left, to demand the creation of a national health care system that is able to meet the needs not only of white middle-class men but also of women, people of color, and poor people. There are obvious difficulties in creating the broad-based support necessary for success. These include the continued homophobia of the left, the lack of activist organizations fighting AIDS outside of gay and lesbian dominated organizations, and the reality that, for many communities, AIDS is not the only health care problem that is significant, yet it is the problem that has been the focus of activism. Brownsworth writes, "Gay men and lesbians have become pivotal forces in health-care activism. But for all the intensity of this health care movement, the focus has remained almost exclusively on gay men and AIDS" (1990, p. 44). The focus on AIDS has been seen by some lesbians as a continued sign that the gay male community is concerned only with its own needs (Brownsworth, 1990). The challenge for AIDS activists will be to work with other communities and people concerned with other health care issues to mobilize people to act on their anger. In October 1991 ACT UP organized a civil disobedience action in Washington, DC, to demand national health care. ACT UP members were disappointed by the lack of involvement in the march by other organizations, though they also saw their own lack of organization as a factor. In 1991 ACT UP discussed organizing a March on Washington for universal health care in spring or summer 1992. Their goal was to cosponsor the march with the AFL-CIO. If it had happened, this march might have proven as critical for continuing the task of alliance building between gay and lesbian activists and other identity-based groups as the 1987 march was for encouraging activism within the gay and lesbian community. Urvashi Vaid recognized the potential that such a march could have had:

> My vision is that it would be a truly broad coalition—the kind of coalition effort that I have yet to see—where gay and lesbian people, people with AIDS and HIV, unions, feminist groups, health care people, all would be sitting around the table and producing this national demonstration that would speak to all of the constituencies. No one would be put to the back of the bus. (1991, p. 8)

Although it would be desirable for such a march to occur, even though this does not happen, the AIDS movement has been important for moving the gay community beyond the narrow identity-based politics of the past that led to a "least common denominator" movement. The devastation of AIDS has occurred not only because of a new virus; it has occurred because of homophobia, racism, poverty, and failures in the health care system as well as other social problems. Making these connections has meant beginning to move beyond the "barred rooms" of narrowly defined identity politics to alliances that respect, and often thrive on, difference, creating new "homes" within the gay and lesbian movement while expanding activists' understandings of the need to look beyond "home" to build long-term change.

NOTES

1. In San Francisco, as Castells argues, there has also been an attempt to organize a gay community that will fight for broader citizen control through political power. The desire to create and support the institutional structures necessary for gay life-styles to exist has been the more primary goal, however, both in San Francisco and in other cities.

2. For discussions of the homophile movement, see D'Emilio (1983b), Berube (1991), and Timmons (1991).

3. There were disagreements from its inception within the Gay Liberation Front, formed immediately after Stonewall, over whether to integrate with other militant groups or to remain separate. The conflicts came to a head over the issue of support for the Black Panthers, with many leaving GLF to form Gay Activists Alliance, a group that fought solely for gay liberation. GLF ceased to exist soon after this split (see Adam, 1987; Teal, 1971).

4. *GCN* provides national coverage of gay and lesbian politics and culture.

5. It is also important to note that lesbians played a central role in organizing the civil disobedience for the march. For a discussion of lesbian participation in the civil disobedience, see Pratt (1991).

6. Whether the process of consensus decision making can work when issues of class, race, and gender are divisive issues within an organization can also be seen in the demise of Queer Nation/SF. Former QN member Mitchell Halberstadt's recent letter to *GCN* states that he blocked the passage of a proposal designed to combat racism, sexism, and classism in QN, which he saw as creating a "Thought Police" (1992, p. 5). The ability of a single individual to block action thus has the potential to make it impossible to confront a difficult issue.

7. The Majority Actions Committee is now ACT BLACK. In addition to ACT BLACK, ACT UP/NY has the Latino/Latina Caucus, the Asian-Pacific Islander Caucus, and the Foreign Nationals Caucus, thus allowing for more culturally specific discussion, support, and actions.

8. WHAM! is a direct action group whose members, about half of whom are lesbian, "negotiated a broad health care agenda, including not only reproductive rights but AIDS, cancer, lesbian health, and social-security benefits" (Gessen, 1990, p. 12). Thus it is a group that recognizes the need to move beyond seeing all women's needs as common.

9. In addition to working with ADAPT, ACT UP/NY has set up its own needle exchange program, a program that serves drug injectors in communities throughout New York City (see Elovich & Sorge, 1991).

10. For a further discussion of the Treatment and Data Committee's involvement and successes working with federal agencies, see Nussbaum (1990).

REFERENCES

Adam, B. D. (1987). *The rise of a gay and lesbian movement.* Boston: G. K. Hall.
Adams, M. (1989). There is no place like home: On the place of identity in feminist politics. *Feminist Review, 31,* 22-33.
Albrecht, L., & Brewer, R. M. (1990). Bridges of power: Women's multicultural alliances for social change. In L. Albrecht & R. M. Brewer (Eds.), *Bridges of power.* Philadelphia: New Society.
Alperin, D. J. (1990). Social diversity and the necessity of alliance: A developing feminist perspective. In L. Albrecht & R. M. Brewer (Eds.), *Bridges of power.* Philadelphia: New Society.
Altman, D. (1982). *The homosexualization of America.* New York: St. Martin's.
Avicolli, T. (1979). Liberation for sale. *Gay Community News, 7*(2), 2.
Berube, A. (1991). *Coming out under fire.* New York: Plume.
Brownsworth, V. (1990). Lesbians press for more attention to their health concerns. *The Advocate, 562,* 11-12.
Bull, C. (1988). AIDS actions coast to coast. *GCN, 15*(40), 1.
Bull, C. (1990). Which way ACT UP? *The Advocate, 558,* 48.
Castells, M. (1983). *The city and the grassroots.* Berkeley: University of California Press.
Cerullo, M. (1987). Night visions. *Radical America, 21*(2-3), 68-71.
Chee, A. S. (1991). A queer nationalism. *Out/Look, 11,* 15-19.
Crimp, D., with Rolston, A. (1990). *AIDS DEMO GRAPHICS.* Seattle: Bay Press.
D'Emilio, J. (1983a). Capitalism and gay identity. In A. Snitow, C. Stansell, & S. Thompson (Eds.), *Powers of desire: The politics of sexuality.* New York: Monthly Review Press.
D'Emilio, J. (1983b). *Sexual politics, sexual communities.* Chicago: University of Chicago Press.
Elovich, R., & Sorge, R. (1991). *Toward a community-based HIV prevention outreach strategy which incorporates needle exchange for New York City.* New York: ACT UP.
Epstein, B. (1990). Rethinking social movement theory. *Radical America, 20*(1), 36-63.
Epstein, B. (1991). *Political protest and cultural revolution.* Berkeley: University of California Press.
Frye, M. (1983). *The politics of reality.* Trumansburg, NY: Crossing Press.
Gallagher, J. (1991). Oregon activists split over sexism charges. *The Advocate, 573,* 24.
Gamson, J. (1989). Silence, death, and the invisible enemy: AIDS activism and social movement "newness." *Social Problems, 36*(4), 351-367.
Gerber, J. (1990). Southern discomfort. *Gay Community News, 17*(26), 1, 3.
Gessen, M. (1990). WHAM! Takes action on women's health. *The Advocate, 562,* 12.
Gomez, J. (1989). We haven't come such a long way, baby. *OUT/LOOK, 5,* 55-56.
Gould, D. (1990). Chicago actions slam US health care. *GCN, 17*(41), 1, 6.
Halberstadt, M. (1992). Queer proposals? *GCN, 19*(22), 5.

Harding, R. (1991). Activist women debate tactics at AIDS meeting. *The Advocate, 568,* 21.

Jernigan, D. (1988). Why gay leadership is hard to find. *OUT/LOOK, 2,* 33-49.

Johnson, D. J. (1987). Double struggle. *GCN, 15*(4), 7.

Kauffman, L. A. (1990). The anti-politics of identity. *Radical America, 20*(1), 67-80.

Levine, M. (1979). Gay ghetto. In M. Levine (Ed.), *Gay men: The sociology of homosexuality.* New York: Harper & Row.

Lorde, A. (1984). *Sister outsider.* Trumansburg, NY: Crossing Press.

Merrett, J. (1990). Gay and lesbian anticrime patrol prowls the streets of New York. *The Advocate, 561,* 55-56.

Nealon, C. (1990). Actions focus on HIV and women. *GCN, 18*(13), 1, 7.

Nealon, C. (1991). Day of inspiration. *GCN, 18*(27), 1, 7.

Nussbaum, B. (1990). *Good intentions: How business and the medical establishment are corrupting the fight against AIDS, Alzheimer's, and cancer.* New York: Penguin.

O'Loughlin, R. (1990). San Francisco ACT UP splits into two chapters. *The Advocate, 563,* 48-50.

Osborn, T. (1991). Is a unified queer nation possible? *The Advocate, 569,* 90.

Podolsky, R. (1990). Birth of a queer nation. *The Advocate, 561,* 52-53.

Pratt, M. B. (1991). *Rebellion.* Ithaca, NY: Firebrand.

Radical America Editorial Board. (1986). Introduction. *Radical America, 20*(6), 2-7.

Reagon, B. J. (1983). Coalition politics: Turning the century. In B. Smith (Ed.), *Home girls: A black feminist anthology.* New York: Kitchen Table, Women of Color Press.

Saalfield, C., & Navarro, R. (1991). Shocking pink praxis: Race and gender on the ACT UP frontlines. In D. Fuss (Ed.), *Inside/out: Lesbian theories, gay theories.* New York: Routledge.

Sadowick, D. (1990). ACT UP: Split-up or growing pains? *The Advocate, 556,* 52-54.

Sadowick, D. (1991). Cities in crisis. *The Advocate, 568,* 34-40.

Schulman, S. (1988). The left and passionate politics. *GCN, 15*(41), 3.

Staley, P. (1991). Has the direct-action group ACT UP gone astray? *The Advocate, 592,* 98.

Teal, D. (1971). *The gay militants.* New York: Stein and Day.

Timmons, S. (1991). *The trouble with Harry.* Boston: Alyson.

Treichler, P. A. (1988). AIDS, homophobia, and biomedical discourse: An epidemic of signification. In D. Crimp (Ed.), *AIDS: Cultural analysis, cultural criticism.* Cambridge: MIT Press.

Vaid, U. (1991). An interview with Urvashi Vaid. *Democratic Left, 19*(3), 7-8.

Wofford, C., & Yang, J. S. (1991). AIDS treatment strategies debated. *GCN, 19*(12), 1.

Wofford, C., & Zeh, J. (1991). Gays, lesbians to Bush: "Justify your war." *Guardian, 43*(16), 6.

12 Pioneering Moslem Women in France

SOPHIE BODY-GENDROT

In democratic countries governed by majority rule, it is crucial to understand how newcomers or people who are distinct from majorities because of their origins, their modes of integration, or their values manage to have their demands taken into account and to become actors per se. The central question in political science—"Who gets what, why, how?"—leads to two subsequent ones: How, granted the constraints that weigh on them, do disadvantaged people mobilize? Within which structural parameters do they operate?

This chapter will approach the question of how people become actors through the example of minorities within minorities in France, that is, immigrant women of Moslem origin. They are among the least likely to be moving forces.[1] Their culture, their status as immigrants or recent French citizens, their poverty, and the legacy of colonialism weigh against them.[2] Yet I will show that at the beginning of the 1990s theirs are voices that count.[3] Their actions are even more impressive when the importance of the historical context (they are the daughters of "colonial workers") and of economic changes (they operate in cities in crisis) are emphasized.

In France, there are no structured "ethnic" or minority neighborhoods in the American sense. Rather, deprived populations from 20 or 30 different countries (with a majority of French) tend to live in the same deindustrialized areas simply because of networks leading them there and cheap rent. In such areas, with a high social homogeneity, yet with differentiated ethnic populations, people, including foreign populations

AUTHOR'S NOTE: I wish to thank M. P. Smith for his comments in the editing of this chapter.

themselves, attempt to create symbolic distances within the spaces of daily life. In those close spaces, hierarchies of social relations appear, founded on social origins, allowing people to compensate for the representation they have of their own marginalization.

In these communities, organizations provide the tools that residents need to mobilize before moving into more secure structures. People resort to what R. Dahrendorf (1963) calls "political secondary rights," that is, mediating structures such as associations and formal or informal networks. In these organizations, the role of culture as a dimension is inseparable from material demands; it is the key to "self-created resistance."

Physical proximity or propinquity in residential communities generates some common interests, in this case reinforced by common gender, ethnic background, and historical experiences. Likewise, geographic concentration facilitates efforts to organize diverse populations of various generations at the community level. Associations such as the ones that will be described here give a sense of empowerment and resources to "forgotten" inhabitants once state services have abandoned the field. Such residents do not use their voting rights (either because they are not French or, if they are, because, since the decay of the Communist party in the 1980s, there is no collective structure capable of answering their specific problems and needs); they turn, rather, to home-based organizations.

Neither their social adjustment nor their forms of resistance to the existing articulations between capital, class, and ethnicity can be dissociated, therefore, from the spaces out of which these responses emerge. For spaces also give rise to everyday struggles and to innovative strategies. Certainly people experience their determinative productive situations and relations as needs, interests, and antagonisms; but, as E. P. Thompson remarks, they "handle" their experiences of constraint within their consciousness and their culture and they act on their determinate situation in their turn (Thompson, 1978, p. 164). Or, as Pierre Bourdieu would say, their "habitus," their inherited dispositions, help them strike the dice and play the game in the semiautonomous subspaces that they occupy in a way favorable to them. However dominated they might be, they perceive that there are stakes that can be called into question and they know that they may possess trump cards that may change the game in their favor. "The social world, is, to a large extent, what agents make of it, at each moment; but they have no chance of un-making and re-making it except on the basis of realistic knowledge of what it is and what they can do with it from the position that they occupy within it" (Bourdieu, 1985, p. 734).

Immigrant Moslem women offer a perfect example of these very sorts of discreet challenges to the existing order that generate social change. Their strategy to create diverse collective forms of resistance and advancement, which lead from the formation of community organizations to community businesses, is especially significant. In their struggle to find voice through independent entrepreneurship, these women cut new and unexplored paths for themselves. Their experiences form the focus of this chapter.

The analysis that follows begins by introducing the context of the Moslem experience in France. It then explores the impact of community organization strategies on the day-to-day life of this population as well as the role played by the central state. Finally, female Moslem community leaders appear as fully committed actors who begin to exercise independence and control over their lives through community-based entrepreneurship.

■ The Historical Context of Ethnic Segregation and Tensions

A Fictitious Ethnicity

For a long time, France was perceived to be an ethnically homogeneous country, deeply anchored in her history of nation building. In contrast with the experience of the American nation ritually celebrating her immigrants, in most works in search of France, the contribution of foreigners to the building of the nation is forgotten. It is the centrality, the continuity, and the unitary identity of France that is emphasized. Research on workplaces, working-class history, family, housing, and remedial education do not take into account foreign-born populations, and until recently no one knew how these aliens' children had made the French nation and imprinted their marks on the cities in which they settled.

One explanation of this omission stems from the fact that immigration significantly occurred in France in the mid-nineteenth century, when the institutional and territorial building of the nation-state was completed. Immigration remained, therefore, an external phenomenon for the French, despite its massive volume. In the nineteenth century, demographic concerns (low birthrate starting earlier than in other European countries) and military interests (marked losses due to wars and new soldiers being needed) inspired a policy of expanding immigration to compensate for labor shortages—first in agriculture, then, in the 1930s when the 8-hour work day was legalized, in industry. Yet immigration was not perceived as a problem for nineteenth-century policymakers. What appeared then as a more central issue of majorities and minorities was the incorporation of culturally distinct regions, counties, villages into one central cultural matrix. Their integration was accomplished by the powerful institutions of the Third Republic (1870-1940)—the school system, the army, the church, and the political parties. Foreigners were not perceived as such in spaces that were themselves fragmented into tiny social enclosures (Weber, 1976). The migration of the peasantry to cities after 1800 incorporated both French and foreigners, who together became part of a massive working-class proletariat that lived on the margins of the nation. At that time, the cleavage line was established on the basis of class, and externality was not linked to nationality. Cultural specificities were kept within the private sphere and, unlike the United States, were denied political recognition. Yet, in 1931, according to the census, France had the highest percentage of immigrants in the world, with foreigners constituting 6.6% of the population, that is, 515 immigrants for every 100,000 inhabitants (compared with 492 immigrants for every 100,000 inhabitants in the United States). Foreigners came from neighboring countries: Belgium, Italy, Switzerland, Spain, and Eastern Europe. But it is important to note, as well, that in those years the first Algerian immigration was already underway, the "colonial workers," as they were called at the time, prefigured the Third World immigration that France experiences today.

The Legacy of Colonization

In a way, France was the first country to "invent" the use of proletarian labor from underdeveloped countries for industrial goals (and not for settlement, as in the United States). Colonized Algeria, in return, was the first of all underdeveloped countries to have started and organized rationally, in the beginning, the emigration of those of her men who were available for wage labor abroad and whose departure would not be too disruptive to the daily processes of their communities. What is exceptional, sociologist A. Sayad says, is the precocity of the trend and the mode of political treatment that those emigrants experienced. Algerians were indeed immigrant workers in France while being French. They were not part of a political space that was homogeneous, yet they were not outside of it either. They were therefore in a deeply ambivalent situation, forming a sort of "experimental population." While both colonizers and colonized belonged to the same French nationality, no one could deny the hegemony of the first category over the other or the persistence of paternalist attitudes in the treatment of the colonized French in the workplace and the neighborhood in France. At the same time, the haunting question for the foreign workers, one that still persists today, was this: "How to be French in France without being completely French while nevertheless being French?"

Departing from the national norm of individual integration, the French policymakers of the time set forth special welfare institutions that at the same time were under police control. Thus hostels and soup kitchens created specially for isolated Algerian males also provided medical facilities, organized pilgrimages, and took care of the burying of the dead while, at the same time, providing control "to remove them from the temptation of the bars and of the streets" (Sayad, 1991). There was a consensus shared by the state, the private sector, and charitable organizations to mix welfare and police functions in the "help" provided to these workers.

This historical account exemplifies a logic of social segregation meant for a special category operating in and through space. A logic that still holds today, it once seemed exceptional, born of necessity. But it was reinforced as the spatial exceptionalism of this category was allowed to deteriorate. The stigmatization of the locale where the workers, and later their children, lived, would have two opposite effects: either to prevent them from mentioning their address or, on the contrary, to push them to defend symbolically their "community turf."

The Algerian War and Cultural Differentiation

The legacy of colonialism continues to activate wounds left by decolonization. Indeed, one of the greatest influences upon racial attitudes in metropolitan France remains that of the Algerian war. This issue is so traumatic that the French are still unable to deal with it, a fact reflected in the bitter and violent revolts in 1991 of young Harkis, the sons of those Algerians that chose to remain with the French when the war ended.[4] The war heightened racial tensions and brought the collapse of the Fourth Republic against a background of civil war and military takeover. Immigrant Moslem workers were the obvious scapegoats for all the negative feelings that a divided French society then experienced.

These memories linger only subconsciously and they explain the "special relationship" of hostility existing in metropolitan society between those who identify with the main ethnic majority and those of Islamic Algerian descent (Silverman, 1991). Furthermore, a cultural gap explains the difficult integration of Moslem populations in France. Racism in France, as E. Balibar remarks, is not based on theories of biological superiority, on the "cult of blood" or a mystical *Volksgeist,* but on cultural distinctions (Balibar & Wallerstein, 1988). As J. Kristeva remarks, however well treated you are in France, there is hardly a country in the world where you feel more a foreigner (Kristeva, 1988). Cultural distinctions (based on class) are part of the social fabric. The idea therefore that French traditions and culture would have to step down so as to take Islam as a component of French culture is unbearable to the more conservative elements of society, who are still eager to preserve "the universal cultural mission" of France. Such ideology hierarchizes people according to their resistances to cultural assimilation. In that view, Moslems, who require prayer rooms and mosques, *hallal* meats, *coranic* scarves for women, and so on, are set on the last rungs of the ladder, after francophone Africans (brought up in French Catholic schools).[5] The paradox is that, the more immigrés become legally part of the French nation, the more racist stereotypes stigmatize their difference.

The New Urban Context

The xenophobia expressed toward "Arabs" intensified when family reunification was authorized after the immigration gates closed in 1974. One of the unintended consequences of that political decision was to turn nomadic, single birds of passage of North African origin into sedentary families with numerous children. These families were to remain for good in the low-income periphery or decayed neighborhoods of large French cities like Paris, Lyons, and Marseille. Their visible needs for welfare services triggered the anger of French taxpayers and of those who claimed to have established the best health system in the world—a system for the culturally appropriate, not for (sometimes French) foreigners.

A "Quiet" Islam

The hostility the foreigners could feel in the circumscribed territories where they were assigned explains in part why those first migrants remained usually silent, except for strikes that developed in semipublic workers' hostels (*Sonacotra*) between 1976 and 1980. Revolts occurred due to poor management, ostentatious racism, and the policing of the workers' daily lives in those places. For the first time, these strikes revealed that immigrants could launch an urban social movement and sustain it with success for several months (Body-Gendrot, 1982; de Rudder, 1991). Culturally (and this demand was unnoticed by both the media and the researchers), Moslem workers demanded prayer rooms, just as, in another context, the Moslem fathers living with their families in high-rise projects did.

In a rapidly changing urban environment, these uprooted individuals and families were trying to reconstitute a familiar ground and to find an anchor in religion, all the more as prayer rooms not only provided moral and religious support but established social links in sponsoring multicentered activities and in offering material support, if necessary. In other words, they re-created micro societies populated with familiar figures. Such sites provided support for quiet resistance, building on the reproduction of cultural symbols and on the perception those migrants had of the appropriation of a space of their own.

Islam is the second and fastest growing religion in France. There are 1,000 mosques (few of them have minarets and most of them are not visibly religious from the outside). At the beginning, French local authorities saw in Islam a way to regulate dispersed populations, and building permits were granted to religious leaders.[6] After the Iranian revolution and with the demagoguery of extreme-right French leaders seeking scapegoats for electoral returns, however, Islam, immigration, and insecurity became linked in the public discourses, and the controversies over the building of mosques in large cities like Lyons and Marseille revealed a NIMBY (not-in-my-backyard) syndrome.

Ethnic tensions are also the product of French privatization policies enacted after the oil crisis (Bourdieu & Rosis, 1990). This was the time when it was decided by the central government that subsidies for the building of social housing (aide à la pierre) were too costly and should be transformed into financial (and private) support for individual projects (aide à la personne), a policy encouraging the building of detached or semidetached houses in the very areas where decayed high-rise projects were stigmatized. Consequently, new tensions arose between, on the one hand, the mobile segments of the French working-class that had access to those houses and that aspired to change the image of their neighborhood and, on the other, the multiracial poorer and newer families who were "trapped" in the social housing because they had no other option. The malaise generated by these rapid changes is reflected by the social workers working in these tough neighborhoods.

Exclusion: French Style

In the 1960s social work aimed at integrating newcomers from rural or Third World areas into the working class. The meaning of this work was the collective promotion of marginal segments at the local level. After 1968 such action changed and became openly critical of bureaucratic procedures, of social reproduction, of law and order. Today a deconstruction process has taken place among those social workers strongly identified with the marginalized poor immigrants who are their clients. They feel unable or refuse to question contradictions, such as troublesome immigrant families who should be expelled at the demand of other residents, or the swelling numbers of African families who provoke an image of "ghettoization" in the neighborhood. They feel powerless and burnt out. As Martucelli and Wieworka note, these practitioners

> could act as a superb lever for potential changes, with their numbers and the consciousness they have of their responsibilities in society. But this lever is not used. Without really reacting, they experience the loss that the end of the labor movement represents and the fading away of older models in which universalist values supported their action. Closer contacts with local authorities (due to decentralization) do not bring a new legitimacy to them. . . . They are now without great plans, without utopia, the hospital attendants or stretcher-carriers of a social world collapsing in front of them . . . and nothing shows that this situation will change rapidly. (1990, p. 11)

Alain Touraine bluntly makes the same point: Now is no longer the time for social movements. Today the problem is exclusion, not exploitation. French society based on classes carried with it conflicts and inequality. The laissez-faire society that France is becoming carries the ghetto within it (Touraine, 1991).

Despite the image of a homogeneous ghetto frequently projected by the French media and by French politicians for obvious symbolic benefits, these low-income areas are, nevertheless, not the South Bronx. First of all, 20 to 30 nationalities live together in those spaces, which is not the case in black U.S. ghettos. Second, the French are still frequently a majority there. Third, for years and years, state financial subsidies have been poured into these areas at the request of local authorities. It may be true that bureaucratic procedures have had their costs and that these grants have frequently been poorly used. Yet a control exists from above about the evolution of such sites and *laissez-faire* is not an appropriate term to describe what is going on. This intervention of the state in social matters also explains why French residents mobilize less and are not eager to pull up their sleeves to take care of their own neighborhoods. Centuries of centralization and rigid regulations have sterilized initiatives. Residents' organizations exist—there are about 700,000 associations in France—but they are rarely in competition with the state domain. They are more frequently an extension of the state.

■ The Mobilization of Moslems

Each generation of residents produces its own meanings, constructs its own history and identity, then reacts back upon other spheres. As the networks cross geographic boundaries and endure for generations, those migrant populations have been sustained by collective strategies for survival and accommodation that have proved to be more and more efficient.

Compared with other waves of immigration, Moslems in France and Moslems of France have generated fewer organizations than others and those they have produced emerged at a much later time. The expression of demands through legalized channels was made possible by a law of 1981, enacted by the socialist government. Public Law 81-909, passed October 9, 1981, allows foreigners, for the first time, to create their own associations. This was the only legitimate space recognized as such by the central and local governments, because foreigners do not have voting rights. Several factors explain why only recently have Moslems, and Moslem women in particular, been able to take an active part in grass-roots organizations. These factors include the slow decline in the 1980s of moral and financial dependence upon the home countries, the influence of religious and union leaders from abroad, and the cultural dependence of "colonial workers."

Demography and Destiny

Recent demographic transformations help explain why Moslem women in the French population have become conscious of their potential strength. While between 1975 and 1982 the increase of male immigrants was only 2.1% (the gates were supposed to be closed), the increase in female immigrants was 14% (entries due to family reunification and marriages). From 1982 until 1986, the proportion of foreign women continued to grow (5.6% compared with 3.1% for men) and they represent 44% of the immigrant population, that is, 1,541,600 persons out of 3,462,200 (Bentaïeb, 1991, p. 5). To this figure one must add the women of foreign origin who are French because (a) they have been born in France of a French parent, (b) they have lived in the country until they were 18, (c) they have chosen to become French through naturalization, or (d) they were French through the colonization process. A more inclusive figure of foreign women in France therefore totals about 3,170,000. Half of them are under 30 and 65% of them were born in France. North African women form about half of this population.[7]

An important number of those women have attended school in France and feel closer to their French peers than to those in the home country. A growing proportion benefited from a higher education. "Studying is sometimes a form of shelter," an interviewee remarks. "In immigrant communities, the relationship to knowledge is extremely valorized. Parents hope that their children will get what they could not get. Girls especially carry those hopes. In the high-rise projects, I know a girl who is a sophomore in medical school while her two brothers are drug addicts. The father pays for her education." Girls understand that higher education is a way to be recognized in the receiving country (and a way to be recognized by the interviewer, which may explain the emphasis put on the issue).

The older the wave of immigration, the more women are part of the labor force. In 1990, 50% of those between 25 and 49 years old worked. Work reflects both a search for autonomy from their traditional family and a desire for social mobility. Despite jobs specifically designated for foreign workers, a complex means of access to the labor market is now in progress: The jobs held by foreigners in the secondary sector have declined from 45% to 36% in the 1980s and in the service sector have increased from 20% to 37.5% and become the major source of employment. Half the workers are now qualified, while only one third were 15 years ago. The young and female forces are well represented in that sector. "Contraction, feminization, tertiarization": The foreign profile is close to the French one. Strikingly, the number of small companies owned by Portuguese or Maghrebi has doubled within 3 years (Maurin, 1991, no. 4). The leading women that we will now look at are representative of this economic emancipation. They are not a majority.[8] Yet they are all the more striking as they represent the embryo of an elite whose numbers will grow in the years to come.

Pioneering Moslem Women

It is into space at the neighborhood level that disadvantaged people, as they challenge the existing order, project the discreet practices and tenuous strategies that they develop individually and collectively. The constraints of French political and social life are indeed present and, every day, people continually experience them: racism, bureaucracy, collapsing economic order, disintegration of social units (Bourdieu, 1985; Thompson, 1978). What is impressive, however, is the way the Moslem women of these neighborhoods have relied on practices of their own to engage and interact with these constraints. To mark their identity and mobilize followers, these women, through associations and strategies that vary according to particular social environments, have creatively reappropriated the physical and symbolic spaces in which they live.

Difficult Mornings

While the associations Moslem women organize differ, the organizing process itself follows a distinct pattern. From the start, they experience numerous difficulties in creating their organizations, first because they are women, second because they are Moslem women, third because they are young. Banks refuse to grant them credit, landlords to rent them space. "You are Arab women, there will be fights, your brothers and your fathers will come to get you with knives. . . . Such was the image . . .," a French Moroccan woman recalls. After months of struggle, however, these women begin to acquire a knowledge of potential resources and manage, in general, to obtain recognition from the state. (According to a law passed in 1901, France requires each new association to formally declare its existence. This is a necessary step to receive grants from the state.) Because there is hardly any tradition of philanthropy and very few foundations in France, most immigrants' community-based organizations are funded by the Social Action Fund (SAF). This fund is located within the Ministry of Social Affairs and provides 90% of the community organizations' resources.

More than 2,500 immigrant associations are funded by the SAF throughout France, but mostly in the three big areas of urban concentration: the Paris region, Lyon, and Marseille.[9] Grants also come from the French secretary of women's affairs, the ministry for youth, and the ministry in charge of neighborhoods in trouble. In the private sphere, churches frequently provide space and material support. This support came randomly after these women, to support the creation of their organizations, knocked persistently on all kinds of doors to obtain funds, material support, and legitimacy. Getting one door to the bureaucracy to open then opened other, previously closed ones. A single victory led to subsequent victories by other female leaders.

In France, in contrast to the United States, it is only *after* constituencies know that the state will not intervene that civil society, namely, grass-roots organizations, comes into action. Yet, if you want to eat with the devil, you need a big spoon: Organizations have to mark their boundaries from the state. In the words of a leader of Turkish origin:

> In the Xth and XIth districts of Paris, social workers are constantly asking for our help . . . because they have difficulties with Turks, because they do not understand certain situations, they need us. . . . Sometimes, they feel unable to meet Turks if they are alone, sometimes they require material help (shelter, money) or information, or they want to send us their clients because they cannot meet the demands.

But immigrant organizations do not want to become institutional actors and they refuse to adjust their innovative work to routine state regulations. For instance, when a center for runaway (mostly Moslem) girls was opened, the state sought efficiency and profitability, that is, 100% occupancy. But this would have negatively affected the atmosphere that the leader wanted to create in her center. Moreover, the state is never monocentered. French departments (labor, health, social affairs, and so on) are jealous of each other's interventions. This means the associations have to carefully diversify their sources of support, securing funding while maintaining independence and distance from state oversight.

Funding remains a persistent problem. Leaders are aware that the use of public monies makes them dependent upon government approval but, nevertheless, see this as a more effective alternative than requiring a fee from community members, who are often young and poor. One leader remembers: "I had been careful to keep my job while starting the association. I have often had to provide part of my salary and, later, unemployment benefits, to keep the association going. . . . It was not easy to work all week long and spend evenings and weekends with the girls over here." The leaders often have to make key decisions to maximize the benefits of the collective. Such efforts generate the fear that if somehow the leader fails to provide resources and sustain the organization there will be no younger potential leader to replace her. Organizational membership fluctuates: 10 members in one case, 100 in another; all kinds of nationalities and religions here, exclusively Algerian or Turkish there. Moreover, the diversity of these organizations complicates efforts at linkage. "There is always a fear that an organization will take over and exercise its hegemony. As long as such problems are not solved, there is no future to an umbrella organization," a leader remarks. Organizations are indeed living cells, subject to emotional crises, loyalty and infidelity, harmony and dysfunction, rebellious members and supportive ones, in poor or good connections with other networks. Such upheavals and changes endanger the fragile life of the organization, all the more as it begins to organize in a fluid and frequently conflicted neighborhood where the image of "Moslem" generates suspicion and hostility.

Action More Than Mobilization

Due to these constraints, action is a feat. Rather than conventional social action, multicentered, innovative decisions more aptly describe the activities of the organizations of Moslem women, mixing cultural, sociopolitical, and educational approaches as well as economic ones. At the start, a potential leader becomes conscious that a demand is not filled, that welfare is not adequately provided, or that a public service does not exist in her neighborhood. She then decides to fill the gap and to answer the demand that institutions either cannot meet or do not want to meet.

Activities range from rehabilitation work performed in jails via dance workshops and plays in the locale reflecting the daily problems of Maghrebi families in France (which initiate subsequent debates) to art, music, and storytelling education for young children in cooperation with neighborhood schools. Ideas lead to other ideas, to other creations, and to the strengthening of identities; this is often how these leaders perceive their linkage roles. *Mediation* is a key word. Social activities are organized so that neighborhood people of various generations and nationalities meet, enjoy, and exchange views. It is sometimes out of such meetings that political decisions to mobilize against a racist crime or against an unpopular public decision or even toward international events, for example, those relating to the Israeli-Arab conflict, occur. Such mobilizations may remain at the community level or, when the circumstances are favorable, take on a national dimension. The marches against racism in 1983-1985, the march to rehabilitate the suburbs' image in 1991, and the Harkis' riots were all launched by French youth of foreign origin—including an important number of young women—who believed that they had the right to express their malaise nationally.

"They are no longer isolated workers who can be ignored. They exert an influence on society and today they even vote. They are somewhere part of the city. They live in buildings, they shop in commercial malls, they steal radios, they become students, they belong to the social landscape . . . they are actors," an Algerian hairdresser remarks. They have been socialized in France and are attached to the locale. This younger generation finds opportunities to take action, because they know how to use the media to accomplish their ends. Not only do they want to fight against the poverty-stricken image conveyed by the term *immigré,* but they want to be actors, subjects who participate in defining and shaping the realities that they confront and the images through which they are perceived (Body-Gendrot, 1993).

The dominant central strategy of national associations such as SOS-Racism was to engage in highly public national campaigns. But after 1985, these national organizations discovered that the more visible they became, the more they became the targets of extreme-right supporters. Moreover, the strategy proved politically inexpedient, because the French state does not recognize ethnicity. Particularist campaigns, localist political strategies, and community organization proved more beneficial. For, as the major political parties began to show interest in the votes and candidates of these constituencies, the Moslem activist groups discovered they were able to exercise some influence through local elections. The female leaders of Moslem organizations have also been courted politically by the major parties. But these women have cautiously kept their distance. Significantly, when they have sought to go forward, it is to the economic sphere, and not the political one, to which they have been drawn.

From Grass Roots to Entrepreneurship

The new trend on the part of many Moslem women is to become entrepreneurs.[10] We can observe the emergence of an important dynamic in the creation of trades and innovative firms started by young North African women, who are eager to use both their know-how and the social capital that they have accumulated as leaders of community organizations. Such organizations serve as the foundation for the creation of restaurants, jewelry stores, dance centers, beauty parlors, *hammams* (Turkish baths), and so on, mixing economic and social goals. Examples abound.

D. A. is an exotic restaurant, created in 1986 by a community organization in an immigrant neighborhood in response to the demands of unskilled immigrant women who wanted to become active. The catering of ethnic meals in this diversified neighborhood in Paris was developed after many months of struggle. The board of the company is composed of Maghrebi, African, and Portuguese women. Another company promoted by French, Algerian, Moroccan, and Spanish women produces fine-quality dresses inspired by the traditional costumes of their home countries and adjusted to French taste. Financial difficulties plague the firm, but important grants help it to survive.

The creation of a beautiful hammam in a difficult neighborhood challenged the poverty-stricken image of a suburb of Lyon, Les Minguettes, where riots had started in 1981. The enterprise required a heavy investment. The decision to develop this hammam was in response to an official demand aimed at maintaining the residents in the neighborhood. It was a deliberate choice to create something aesthetically beautiful at the foot of a high-rise project belonging to the state. Despite the healthy benefits of the hammam, after 2 years the investments' interest created a financial crisis. The Public Office for Social Housing offered to provide its help in exchange for 51% of the shares. The young Moslem woman and her unemployed husband who had conceived the idea of the hammam, and who had invested all their resources in it, refused to yield control over their patrimony. They demanded from the state a "generous attitude." The state (SAF) resisted. It is prepared to provide funding for social causes and projects; but an "economic" approach embarrasses officials who are unaccustomed to this type of enterprise. On the other hand, it is not in the tradition of the private sector in France to take risks and bet on an innovative project of this sort. Obviously a public/private partnership could be a solution but, at this point, it is unlikely that the creator of the hammam will open up her family enterprise to other shareholders. The new actors learn how to change their strategies and tactics, but if their goals and politics do not jibe, the transition can sometimes be painful. In other cases, know-how and responsibilities have accumulated as organization leaders have given individual entrepreneurs the social qualifications and perspectives necessary to develop their projects. These projects reflect the experience of cultural crisis, changing values, distance toward the immigration experience, and integration within a specific turf. For instance, a hairdresser and former sociologist has opened a beauty parlor that is also a music room. "Violin and hair-blown-dry: it is the same struggle," she remarks. "You can't play the violin on an empty stomach and with an empty head. . . . I look to the future, I want to act before the problems occur, before the kids drop out of school. Without music, without culture, a community dies, it has no history, no memory to insert into its daily life and that's dangerous." Economic enterprises are carried on in an environment in constant flux. Leaders therefore have to foresee what the leisure society will be like in 20 years in order to create new adaptive structures now. Another example—opening a hammam/fitness club—shows the same type of vision. "Beyond generations, it implies a construction, a duration, roots, making a space, saying at the same time we want to stay but we want to stay with our culture."

Social Concerns Over Profit

It would be tempting at this stage to put to the test the theory developed by various authors that, in the 1970s, American community-based organizations (CBOs) and grass-roots organizations were somewhat the victims of their success. Having been selected by either public or private partners, they had become bureaucratized and cut off from their base in the local community (Fainstein & Fainstein, 1991; Katz & Mayer, 1985). Our interviews suggest that a different perspective emerges in France. The jump into entrepreneurship by Moslem women in leadership provides them with a new energy. After the fatigue of organizational life, it provides an increased legitimacy in French society and a clearer recognition of their work, power, and potential. "How to be French without being completely French" is still the haunting question. Due to their origins, due to their fathers' experiences in France, due to prevailing racism, the need to prove that they are effective actors is extremely important. A Moroccan woman explains it this way: "For a long time, I was a street social worker. I became conscious of the huge potentialities that were in the neighborhood. . . . At the same time, I was aware that no one thought deeply about the meaning of one's work, that there was a blindness oblivious of people's assets . . . I became enraged."

Enraged is a recurrent term used to describe the feeling of waste produced by huge bureaucratic procedures, by fatigue, by stereotypes. It is a feeling that leads to a strategy of self-empowerment. It is understandable that immigrant female leaders, former social workers, or grass-roots leaders should have felt "enraged," powerless, and ready to try new forms of communication. They sought to substitute relations of autonomy for ones of former dependence on either organizational structures or French society at large. The owner of a Moroccan restaurant explains:

> In commercial transactions such as a restaurant, there is a way to work without submission—equal to equal. . . . There are no longer barriers and misunderstandings between cultures. You can transmit a lot of messages. . . . The making of meals is a cultural message, an image of myself and of the traditional women working with me that I would like my patrons to keep in their mind in order to discard stereotypes.

She now prefers to use her living experience rather than words to accomplish her goal.

Speeding Mutants

It may seem strange to defend the virtues of consumerism over and against those of community organizing. But one needs to understand the spirit that pushes these women to undertake such adventures. They have an almost philosophical perception of their creations; they are aware of the complexity of their generation, a generation that they define as neither first nor second but as "the generation of their age." In other words, their specific experiences and social trajectories define their identity. It is not a specifically French identity, nor a specifically ethnic one, but universal. They are defined by their will to act and by their urgency to accelerate the evolution of conservative French and immigrant societies. "We have the feeling that so many things are to be done. Our community [of entrepreneurial women] is like a crossroads. We are all the communities at the same time and all the generations as well."

Their specific attitudes, in contrast with those of first-generation immigrant women, can partly be explained by the hardships they have gone through. It was difficult to break new ground, to oppose their fathers, their relatives, their friends. As veterans and survivors, they have turned such struggles into assets and have become overmotivated. Their personal itinerary comes as a secondary explanation. H., for instance, has a Moroccan father who has lived in France for 50 years and a French Judeo-Christian mother. She was born in France but, as a Moroccan, has a double nationality. She has a Ph.D. in economics. She remained with her parents and her six brothers and sisters until she finished high school with a "baccalaureate." Both her parents wanted her to achieve a higher social status via education. Her mother had dropped out of school at 8, and she wanted her daughter "to be more intelligent" than she. Her father wanted her to get out of the "ghetto," off the assembly line. They were very strict regarding her education. They all lived in a bleak neighborhood north of Paris, near her father's best friend who lived in a surrounding Algerian community and had also married a French woman. Chinese, Italian, Portuguese factory workers also lived nearby. Gypsies did as well. Her mother came from a farmers' family and was even more puritanical than H's Moroccan father. H. struggled with her parents over the need for formal education. But that H. fought with her parents, that she was beaten with a rod on her back until she was 21, meant her younger sister had an easier time when she struggled for her own emancipation. H. was making a living with odd jobs when she met, by accident, a former philosophy teacher who encouraged her to go to college. She studied for 9 years, working at such jobs such as secretary, adviser in a summer camp, tutor, lunch program supervisor, and so on. She finished college when she was 30 and then began to demonstrate in the streets with a few other women of foreign origin. It was something new at the time. But she became conscious that things could change if women of her culture somehow took an active role. "I know that I am often too brutal," she admits. "The process of emancipation of Moslem women is very different from that of French women. I am Maghrebi, I emphasize my identity, I demonstrate for my claims, my rights, my citizenship. But I am not anti-racist. This is not my problem, but the problem of French society."

As can be seen from this example, education makes such women self-confident. Knowledge allows them to reflect upon their environment and their experience and to find ideas, support, and financial resources to carry on their reforms. They reappropriate what has been transmitted to them, what they have experienced among their French peers, and "invent" a third way. Being neither from there nor totally from here, they enjoy an artistic freedom, escaping from the rigid codes that each culture historically produces, creating their own markers that they want to share with the younger ones.

Self-interest is not their primary motivation. As they did when they were community organization leaders, they continue to see themselves as linkages. "What is the interest of escaping alone?" one remarks. In that respect, the embryo of a movement can be perceived. These women feel responsible for the younger generation and act as role models, trying to protect Moslem girls from oppressive families, boys from crisis and from drug temptations. They incorporate the young people into their actions, through initiation to art, ethnic cooking, craftsmanship, and so on. But they also want to rehabilitate their mothers, "the passive first generation," which is a way for them to enhance their cultural heritage. "The assertion in terms of continuity of the historical and affective memory with their mothers, beyond individual confrontations taking place inside families, expresses a will to rehabilitate the negative image glued on their mothers, and at the same time, a violent rejection of the protective behaviors they have experienced" (Golub, 1988, p. 3). Even if they have much reason to rebel against both their mothers and the women from the home countries who transmit the values of the households, they acknowledge that they are the products of that culture. They recognize that, frequently, from those "oppressed" mothers they have had instilled into them the motivation not to reproduce the traditional models of their community.

In sum, this new generation of Moslem women, who start with the handicap of being minorities in a society technically and culturally ruled by a historical majority, nevertheless prove that they are creating the elements of a new elite. The future, of course, is most uncertain, as this dialogue reveals: "We are women, we are immigrés, we are poor, we do not vote . . . and you would like us to represent something? Are you dreaming? Maybe in 50 or in 60 years, we will represent something." To which another interviewee replies: "In half a century, no one will talk any longer about our integration."

It indeed remains to be seen whether these women will be able to maintain their empowerment and, through their personal charisma, generate the sorts of mobilizations among younger followers that will eventually improve the status and well-being of the Moslem communities in the cities where they live.

NOTES

1. The term *Moslem* is the common denominator of a heavily heterogeneous population. *Maghrebi* or *North African*, which are also used, do not refer to increasingly numerous African and Turkish populations. Although *Moslem* conveys a religious connotation, its use here does not necessarily imply that the Moslems of France practice their religion. Less than 10% of them attend the Friday prayer.

2. The French use the derogatory term *immigré*, a word with a passive connotation, in opposition to the actively connoted term *immigrant*.

3. The fieldwork for this study is based on 2-hour taped qualitative interviews that I have been conducting among Moslem women who are heads of organizations in large French cities. These interviews are part of a large survey on the political attitudes of Moslems in France carried out under the auspices of the National Foundation of Political Science for the French Ministry of Social Affairs in 1989. It led to a report under the authorship of R. Leveau and C. de Wenden, "Modes d'insertion des populations de culture islamique dans le système politique francais."

4. In the summer 1991, young Harkis mobilized nationally to protest against the "oblivion" their families had been the victims of since their forced settlement in former military camps in 1962. The subsequent logic of spatial segregation, a specific welfare allocation to Harkis, and a general lack of recognition from the French led, for the second and third generations, to the combined phenomena of poverty (80% of young Harkis are unemployed; 85% of them are school dropouts), petty delinquency, racism, and exclusion in the areas where about 6,000 of them are concentrated (*Le Monde*, July 8, 1991).

5. In a recent opinion poll, 31% of the French say they fear a Maghrebi immigrant; only 18% fear a Black immigrant (*CSA/Evénement du Jeudi*, July 4-10, 1991).

6. Legislation on the separation of church and state was passed by the National Assembly in 1905. At that time, the three major religions (Catholic, Protestant, Jewish) had a status. This is not the case for Islam. When the question of a national representation occurs, the lack of consensus among competing Moslem populations accentuates the sources of controversies between established authorities in France and in the home countries.

7. Older foreign women from Spain, Portugal, and Italy saw their percentage decline to 39.6% in 1986.

8. Officially, less than 24% of North African women work. Yet, this figure must be seen as real progress, given their traditions. It is explained by the fact that a large percentage of Moslem women are born in France, where they attended school.

9. The SAF was created in 1958 to improve the living conditions of Algerian workers. It is linked in people's minds to the colonial history of France despite the fact that it became autonomous after 1983 and is no longer dependent on the French ministry in charge of law and order. Unlike the British CRE, which funds its own programs, its function is to fund immigrant organizations' actions.

10. Between 1975 and 1982, the creation of immigrant businesses increased by 26.2%, compared with 7.3% for the French (Jourd'hui & Padrun, 1991).

REFERENCES

Balibar, E., & Wallerstein, I. (1988). *Race, nation, classe: Les identités ambiguës.* Paris: La Découverte.

Bentaïeb, M. (1991, March). Les femmes étrangéres en France. *Hommes et Migrations, 1141,* 4-12.

Body-Gendrot, S. (1982). Urban social movements in France and the U.S. In N. Fainstein & S. Fainstein (Eds.), *Urban policy under capitalism.* Beverly Hills, CA: Sage.

Body-Gendrot, S. (1993). Ville et violence. *L'irruption de nouveaux acteurs.* Paris: Presses Universitaires de France.

Bourdieu, P. (1985). The social space and the genesis of groups. *Theory and Society, 14*(6), 723-744.

Bourdieu, P., & Rosin, C. (1990, March). La construction du marché: Le champ administratif et la production de la "politique du logement." *Les Actes de la recherche en sciences sociales,* pp. 81-82.

Dahrendorf, R. (1963). Recent changes in the class structure of Western European countries. In S. Craubard (Ed.), *A new Europe?* Boston: Beacon.

de Rudder, V. (1991). Housing and immigrant integration in French cities. In D. Horowitz (Ed.), *Immigration and ethnicity in France.* New York: New York University Press.

Fainstein, S., & Fainstein, N. (1991). The effectiveness of community politics: New York City. *CUCR, 3,* 108-132.

Golub, A. (1988). *Femmes issues de l'immigration maghrébine dans le processus d'intégration de la société francaise.* Unpublished manuscript.

Jourd'hui, Y., & Padrun, R. (1991, March). Les femmes immigrées créent et entreprennent. *Migrants-formation, 84,* 160-170.

Katz, S., & Mayer, M. (1985). Gimme shelter: Self-help housing struggles within and against the state in New York City and West Berlin. *International Journal of Urban and Regional Research, 9*(1), 15-45.

Kristeva, J. (1988). *Etrangers à nous-mêmes.* Paris: Fayard.

Martucelli, D., & Wievorka, M. (1990, December). Le travail social, l'immigration et la ville. *Les annales de la recherche urbaine, 49,* 5-12.

Maurin, E. (1991, April). Les étrangers: Une main d'oeuves a part? *Economie et Statistique, 242,* 39-50.

Sayad, A. (1991). Immigration in France: An "exotic" form of poverty. In K. McFate, R. Lawson, & W. Wilson (Eds.), *Urban marginality and public policy in Europe and in America.* Washington, DC: Joint Center for Political Studies.

Silverman, M. (Ed.). (1991). *Race, discourse, and power in France.* Hants, United Kingdom: Avebury.

Thompson, E. P. (1978). *The poverty of theory and other essays.* New York: Longman.

Touraine, A. (1991, February). Face à l'exclusion. *Esprit,* pp. 7-13.

Weber, E. (1976). *La fin des terroirs.* Paris: Le Seuil.

13　The Bay Area Movement Against the Gulf War

BARBARA EPSTEIN

The national movement against the Gulf War failed to prevent that war or to bring it to an end before tens of thousands of Iraqis were killed and the United States proclaimed victory. The movement also failed to generate broad popular opposition to the war. In the months before the war began, while policy toward Iraq was still being debated in Congress, there was widespread opposition to, or at least misgivings about, military intervention. These misgivings evaporated as soon as war was declared, and the antiwar movement rapidly found itself isolated and powerless. It is probably fair to describe the Gulf War as the worst defeat that the U.S. peace movement has suffered since the late 1940s, when public support for cold war policies was created and the peace movement of the time was successfully labeled as un- or anti-American.

Although the nation as a whole was plastered with yellow ribbons throughout the war (and beyond), there were cities where the peace movement was able to mobilize tens of thousands of people as soon as war was declared. The San Francisco Bay Area (including Berkeley and Oakland in the East Bay) and Santa Cruz, some 80 miles to the south, were two such cities. San Francisco and Washington, DC, were the sites of the major national antiwar demonstrations. Unlike the Washington demonstrations, which drew protesters from the East Coast and the Midwest, the San Francisco demonstrations were primarily an expression of greater Bay Area opposition to the war (southern Californians could attend the simultaneous demonstrations held in Los Angeles). As soon as Bush announced that war was imminent, tens of thousands of Bay Area residents took to the streets. The Bay Area peace movement was able to turn public life upside down for about 10 days, with countless demonstrations, teach-ins, forums, and other public events.

Santa Cruz, a city of about 50,000, was the other major focus of antiwar activity in the larger Bay Area. As soon as war was declared, 8,000 people gathered to march through the streets in protest, the largest demonstration in the history of the city. The University of California, Santa Cruz, campus was shut down for 2 days, and for the next 2 weeks life in Santa Cruz, as in the Bay Area, was dominated by antiwar demonstrations, educational events, and discussions.

Without an empirical study of antiwar activity elsewhere in the country, it is not possible to answer the question of why such activity was particularly visible in the Bay Area. But it is possible, on the basis of a study of one geographic area, to ask what facilitated the organization that took place there and why that movement nevertheless fell apart.

With the collapse of socialism and what appears to be the collapse of any basis for any unified movement of the left, the question emerges of whether identity politics is likely to become the salient form of progressive politics, and, if so, what that will mean for the possibility of coalitions. The movement against the Gulf War was the first major effort of what have been called the "new social movements" to join forces around one issue. It tested the ability of movements that represent discrete constituencies and that celebrate difference to coalesce. Looking back at the war and the formation of an antiwar movement, in an area where antiwar activity was particularly strong, allows us to look at both the strengths and the weaknesses of the new social movements at a moment when unity is called for.

This "test," of course, did not take place in a vacuum but under circumstances that were particularly difficult. First, the war came and went in a flash. Unlike the Vietnam War, in which U.S. ground troops were introduced only after nearly a decade of gradually increasing levels of U.S. involvement, the prospect of massive U.S. military intervention in the Gulf seemed to appear out of the blue. The Vietnam War lasted long enough for large sections of the public to rethink not just that war but the political and cultural assumptions that legitimated U.S. intervention. The Gulf War was over before any such process was possible. Second, the Gulf War came at a moment when what might be called the left, or progressive forces, were extremely weak in the United States. The fact that it is no longer clear what this sector should be called is an indication of the depth of its crisis. It was also a symptom of the crisis of the left as a whole that it was possible for sectarian organizations, discredited in the eyes of the great majority of left activists, to dominate the structures that gave direction to the movement on a national level.

Many local peace organizations participated in the national mobilizations organized by the national antiwar organizations, but the influence of the sects within these national organizations created widespread skepticism and distrust. As a result, the national antiwar organizations were not able to give leadership to the antiwar movement beyond holding national mobilizations. The antiwar movement needed a coherent strategy that would go beyond holding large demonstrations. Such a strategy could only have been formulated by activists from around the country coming together in an atmosphere of trust; this could not happen in national antiwar organizations dominated by sectarians.

The reason that it was possible for sectarian groups to provide organizational leadership for the antiwar movement was that that role was abdicated by those left and peace organizations that enjoy widespread respect and that might have been expected to provide more substantial leadership for the antiwar movement. This abdication speaks to the crisis of the progressive sector of U.S. politics. The largest organizations on the left, at the time of the Gulf War, were the Democratic Socialists of America (DSA), which for a number of years had been in decline, and the Communist party, which lacked any legitimacy whatsoever outside of very narrow circles and was on the verge of collapse. The largest peace organization was Sane/Freeze, which had represented a mass movement in the mid-1980s, through the Freeze campaign, but had since lost its mass constituency and, with (presumably) the end of the cold war, much of its sense of purpose. At least DSA and Sane/Freeze were prone to a certain timidity because they were trying to hold on to a prestige and influence that seemed to be slipping away from them. Both organizations were also particularly reluctant to address issues having to do with the Middle East. Both organizations have been anxious to maintain good relations with the liberal wing of the Democratic party and also with liberal groups, including mainstream Jewish organizations. Addressing issues of the Middle East raises the possibility of criticizing Israel, which could jeopardize these ties. The fact that the major organizations of the left and the peace movement were weak, disoriented, and prone to timidity, especially around questions of the Middle East, undercut their ability to provide leadership for a movement against the Gulf War. This situation created an opening for the sectarian left; it also created a vacuum of national political leadership and largely left the task of building an antiwar movement to local groups, some of them entirely new, some of them coming out of movements ordinarily concerned with issues of domestic rather than foreign policy.

The perspective that I bring to this chapter is shaped by my own involvement in the movement against the Gulf War both in the Bay Area and in Santa Cruz. I live in Berkeley; I teach at UC Santa Cruz. I was involved in the antiwar movements in both communities before and during the war. In the East Bay, I was a member of Middle East Peace Action, a group of Middle East and antiwar activists, most of us with experience in the nonviolent direct action movement, who came together in the late summer to begin sponsoring educational events and holding demonstrations against U.S. intervention. A left Jewish group that I belong to organized a candlelight vigil in San Francisco's Union Square for New Year's Eve; the vigil drew between 1,500 and 2,000 participants. At UCSC shortly before war was declared, along with several other faculty members, I organized a group that called itself Faculty Against the War, which promoted discussion among faculty, compiled a reader on the war and its background that was widely disseminated, sponsored antiwar educational events, and supported student antiwar efforts. The following chapter is based not only on my observation of the antiwar movement from these vantage points but also on interviews with about 20 antiwar activists.

In the first week of August 1990, Iraqi troops entered Kuwait. Saudi Arabia (with U.S. encouragement) requested that the United States send troops. President Bush made statements to the press posing the possibility of a U.S. military response and set the machinery in motion toward sending U.S. troops to the Middle East. By October there were more than 200,000 U.S. troops in Saudi Arabia; in early November Bush announced that he would send 200,000 more. The first steps toward war, through the late summer and fall, were met by what appeared to be a troubled and questioning public. A poll conducted on November 19 by *The New York Times*/CBS indicated 21% favoring a military response in the near future; 51% indicated that they had not heard a convincing reason for U.S. involvement in the Gulf. Until mid-January, when Bush gave Saddam Hussein a January 15 deadline to withdraw from Kuwait, and the next day began bombing Iraq, public opinion polls continued to indicate high levels of public uneasiness about the possibility of a war in the Middle East.

Through the late summer and fall, Bush's steps toward war were met with opposition, or at least questioning, from a diverse set of arenas.

There was substantial dissent from Bush's policies in Congress, especially in the House of Representatives, based on the argument that economic sanctions would be more effective and less dangerous than a military response. Two former chairs of the Joint Chiefs of Staff and seven former secretaries of defense warned, in testimony before Congress, against the dangers posed by a war in the Middle East. After the war was over, it became clear that these hesitations had been shared by current Pentagon officials. Rumor, among peace movement Washington-watchers, had it that the State Department, or at least the Middle East desk, was not enthusiastic about the possibility of a war (Michael Klare, personal communication, April 1991). There had not been so much high-level dissent from U.S. policy since the foreign policy establishment split over the war in Vietnam in the months leading up to President Johnson's announcement that he would not run for office in 1968.

Though Bush appeared to be bent on a confrontation, and probably a military confrontation, with Saddam, the extent of elite dissent from Bush's policies exerted what in retrospect appears to have had an unduly soothing effect on what might be called the peace movement establishment. Many leading figures associated with the peace movement made public statements not only deploring the Iraqi invasion of Kuwait but giving guarded support to Bush's decision to send troops to Saudi Arabia—while arguing that economic sanctions would be more effective than military action and expressing the hope that the U.S. troops would remain, as an unused threat, in Saudi Arabia. Jesse Jackson made such a statement; so did Samir Amin; so did Daniel Ellsberg (who later apologized for his naïveté in believing that Bush would send troops to the Middle East but refrain from using them in military actions that would increase the power of the United States in the region).

What was most remarkable about the growing opposition movement, in the summer and fall of 1990, was that the major organizations of the peace movement, and of the progressive wing of U.S. politics, were largely absent from it. Sane/Freeze was not in evidence; neither was DSA (the Democratic Socialists of America, representing the democratic socialist tendency). Both of these organizations had national offices, and resources, that would have permitted them to give cohesion to the emerging, but diffuse, protest movement. Through this period, many people in progressive/peace movement circles found it difficult to believe that the United States would actually go to war, partly because it appeared to be such a dangerous move and partly because there was so much high-level opposition to it. Representative Ron Dellums, of Berkeley and Oakland, was later to argue that, if only the peace movement had opposed the war more vigorously, earlier than it did, the vote in Congress could have gone against rather than for the war. (In the House of Representatives, the vote for the war was 250 to 183; in the Senate, 52 to 47.)

Perhaps one of the reasons that the organizations that might have given the antiwar movement leadership earlier in the trajectory toward war failed to do so is that they were lulled into the belief that there was not going to be a war. Another reason was that what might be called the peace movement and left/liberal establishment in the United States has for many years avoided issues having to do with the Middle East out of the fear of taking stands that might offend and alienate the liberal Jewish establishment (and also out of internal dissent over the same issues). Peace movement and left/liberal organizations depend on the liberal Jewish community for financial support. They also highly value influence and respectability (with liberal members of Congress, with the liberal wing of the Democratic party generally), and they fear that open criticisms of Israel could destroy this influence and support. Because the peace movement establishment has avoided taking stands on the Middle East, it has also for the most part failed to educate itself about the Middle East. Caught off guard by the Gulf crisis, the peace movement not only was reluctant to respond but also was unprepared to do so.

As a result, the opposition movement that sprang up, in the Bay Area and elsewhere around the country, included a vast number of local groups, many of them with little or no previous political experience; a significant level of support from the churches, including both leading Catholics and Protestants; and statements of opposition to the war from many trade unions. Ultimately, it was the local peace centers that held the movement together. Some of these centers were slower to become involved than the noninstitutional activist groups that responded immediately, but each of the peace centers eventually devoted its full attention to the Gulf crisis, enabling local peace movements to attain some degree of cohesion.

What national leadership existed was provided by two umbrella organizations of antiwar groups, the Coalition Against a Vietnam War in the Middle East (generally referred to as the "Coalition") and the National Campaign Against the War in the Middle East (referred to as the "Campaign"). Both had national offices in New York; on the local level, each brought together antiwar activists and organizations. The

Coalition sponsored the major demonstrations in Washington, DC, and San Francisco on January 19; the Campaign, the demonstrations in those two cities on January 26.

Unfortunately, organizations of the sectarian left had considerable influence in both of these organizations. The Coalition was initiated by people associated with the Trotskyist Workers' World party; the Campaign, though initiated by independent activists determined to build a broad, inclusive antiwar movement, was dominated in the Bay Area by Socialist Action, another Trotskyist group. Of the two, the Coalition (with its Workers' World leadership) was the more overtly sectarian: in Coalition meetings in San Francisco, any criticisms of Iraq's invasion of Kuwait were likely to be shouted down. But Socialist Action, while more appreciative of the need for a broad antiwar movement, was nevertheless as insensitive as the Workers' World to the need for open, democratic discussion. Socialist Action wanted a broad antiwar movement that it would dominate. In San Francisco, where Socialist Action dominated the Campaign, steering committee meetings were struggles for power. The Campaign held a national meeting in New York in November; Socialist Action packed, and controlled, this meeting. The demonstrations of January 19 and January 26 were major contributions to the antiwar movement, and the availability of dedicated, if sectarian, activists helped make those demonstrations possible.

The sectarian influence in the coalitions had relatively little impact on the national demonstrations: People attended to protest the war, not to support particular organizations. Probably the vast majority of demonstrators were at most dimly aware of what organizations were sponsoring the demonstrations. What was unfortunate about the sectarian influence was that it undermined the possibility that a national antiwar movement might coalesce. The sectarian groups took up the space in which there otherwise might have been discussion of an overall strategy for the peace movement.

Because the antiwar movement had no national leadership that was able to go beyond planning demonstrations, it was essentially a local or regional movement. The Bay Area and Santa Cruz both had the progressive political culture and the institutional resources to back up large and vibrant protest movements. In both areas there were teach-ins and demonstrations before the war began; these began to draw large numbers of people in late November, December, and early January, as it seemed increasingly likely that there would be a war. On January 6, an antiwar interfaith service at St. Mary's Cathedral drew 6,000 participants. On January 13, an antiwar rally in Santa Cruz drew a crowd of 6,500, to that date the largest demonstration ever held in that city. But in both Santa Cruz and the Bay Area, the focus was on planning for a response after war was declared.

In the Bay Area the Pledge of Resistance, in coordination with other local peace organizations, announced that there would be a demonstration and civil disobedience at the Federal Building in San Francisco the morning after war was declared. When Bush announced January 15 as the deadline for an Iraqi withdrawal, the Pledge circulated word that there would be a demonstration on the morning of the 15th; about 10,000 people arrived early in the morning to protest, a decision was made on the spot to take over the Bay Bridge, which was shut down for several hours; about 1,000 arrests were made. Bombing began the afternoon of the next day. The Pledge of Resistance has its roots in the religious peace and social justice community; in the Bay Area it represents the radical wing of that community and forms a bridge between the church-based protest movement and the left more generally.

The demonstration on January 15, like all demonstrations organized by the Pledge, was nonviolent, and it featured the participation of the various communities making up the peace movement. On one side of the Federal Building, the gay and lesbian community led the protest; straight people were welcome but were requested to join in gay and lesbian chants. On another side of the building, religious activists, some of them in robes, led a protest that included prayer in various traditions. On another side, women led the protest; women linked arms, forming a wall and holding an antiwar banner that spanned the lengths of the building. On the fourth side of the building, protest was led by the Central America solidarity community. The next day the bombing began; in the evening protesters again took to the streets, this time under the aegis of the more anarchist-oriented wing of the movement and this time with a more confrontational approach. The next morning the Pledge again held a major demonstration at the Federal Building, drawing an even larger number of protesters. Again the protests on the various sides of the building were led by various sections of the antiwar movement; this time the environmental movement took the place of the Central America activists; they brought oil barrels and held banners protesting the impact of war on the environment. The same morning, the Pledge held a demonstration at the Stock Exchange, closing it down. These demonstrations resulted in about 1,300 arrests.

In Santa Cruz the student antiwar coalition had announced that if bombing began during the day protesters would gather at the quarry, the large meeting site at the center of the campus, and march downtown together and join with townspeople for an antiwar demonstration; the university would then be closed for 2 days. When the bombing began, student activists went from classroom to classroom announcing that war had begun.

Most classes ended; several thousand students and faculty met at the quarry and marched downtown together to join a demonstration of about 8,000, the largest demonstration that Santa Cruz had ever seen. In the days preceding, a hastily organized faculty antiwar group had promised to support the undergraduate call for strike by calling off classes for 2 days; a parallel organization of graduate students had also given its support to the strike. For 2 days the campus was effectively closed down; for those 2 days, and for about 10 days following, there were so many demonstrations and antiwar events of all kinds that even with the smallest available type it was difficult for the staff of the Nuclear Weapons Freeze, a downtown peace organization, to crowd them all onto the one-page Persian Gulf Events Calendar, which was published every day and circulated on the campus and in town.

In both the Bay Area and Santa Cruz, the antiwar movement was held together by the combined efforts of the various institutions of the peace movement, which served as information centers and gave the local antiwar movement whatever degree of cohesion it had, and ad hoc groups, mostly but not entirely made up of young people, who dropped everything else to organize against the war. In the Bay Area the main institutions that coordinated activities and served as focal points of information were the American Friends Service Committee office in San Francisco and the Pledge of Resistance office in Oakland; the Middle East Peace Action/Middle East Children's Alliance office in Berkeley, a considerably smaller operation than the AFSC and the Pledge, played a similar role on a smaller scale. In Santa Cruz it was the Resource Center for Nonviolence and, to a lesser degree, the office of the Nuclear Weapons Freeze that performed the same function.

The Pledge of Resistance and the Resource Center for Nonviolence are alternative institutions, foci of progressive political activism in the Bay Area and Santa Cruz. They are staffed by people who have long histories as activists. These institutions, and the people who run them, are respected and trusted by large numbers of activists; they are able to mobilize these networks rapidly. Darla Rucker, who works at the Pledge of Resistance, told me that, if the Pledge got a phone call about a political emergency in the afternoon, they could have a demonstration on the streets the evening of the same day, complete with monitors, legal observers, speakers, and sound equipment (Darla Rucker, personal communication, June 12, 1991, Oakland).

Seven or eight years ago Darla and most of the other staff at the Pledge were activists in the Livermore Action Group; they were building a mass movement against the arms race. Now they are the leading movement institution of the East Bay; they are a bureaucracy that keeps a progressive response to U.S. foreign policy alive by holding demonstrations—but they are no longer trying to build a mass organization. The Livermore Action Group brought people into a large organization that collectively decided what actions it would hold. The Pledge calls demonstrations and decides what will happen at these demonstrations; most participants are not part of this decision-making process. The Resource Center, in Santa Cruz, plays the same role. During the Gulf War the Resource Center played a crucial role in bringing activists together, initiating and sponsoring demonstrations and educational events. But it did not attempt to build a movement based on mass participation.

The strength of the antiwar movement in the Bay Area and Santa Cruz was a result not only of the fact that there are large numbers of politically progressive people in these two areas, people ready to attend antiwar demonstrations and events, but also of the fact that the Bay Area and Santa Cruz have institutions like the Pledge of Resistance and the Resource Center for Nonviolence that are devoted to sustaining a politically progressive culture in the area and had the political experience and resources to coordinate antiwar groups, call demonstrations, and hold antiwar events. The Bay Area and Santa Cruz are unusual not only for the broad progressive sentiment in both communities but for the fact that progressive institutions such as the Pledge, the AFSC, the Resource Center, and to a lesser degree many smaller institutions have survived the 1980s and maintain an uncompromising oppositional stance. But given the fact that both the Bay Area and Santa Cruz have in the past been the sites of progressive and antiwar organizations, movements based on mass participation, it is also striking that the most experienced activists in both communities were holding events rather than developing mass organizations.

One reason that activists concentrated on organizing events rather than mass organizations was that the Gulf crisis came on fast and was over quickly. The war in Vietnam and the arms race both developed more slowly and lasted much longer. Building mass organizations takes time. Furthermore, the activists of the early 1990s who have experience in struggles based on mass organizations are now mostly in their forties and want some stability, as well as political activity, in their lives. The alternative bureaucracies of the peace movement provide at least a minimal degree of stability; building a mass organization would not. Finally, experienced activists sense that this is not the moment to build a mass organization. In a crisis, large numbers of people will come to demonstrations and educational events. They may come together with others in settings in which they already feel some connection (in neighborhood, workplace, or occupational groups or in groups based on racial or sexual identity). They are much less likely to join organizations that are defined simply by an issue.

The movement against the Gulf War was in fact based on countless groups defined by preexisting affiliations, formal or informal. The impulse to form such groups came partly from a desire for a sense of community in the face of a frightening war and partly from a sense that one had to find a particular vantage point from which to speak out. One of the earliest constituencies to come together against the war was relatives of people in the military. In the East Bay, Parents Against the War, a group that included many people of color, held press conferences, demonstrations, and a weekly vigil against the war. Just Peace, a group of East Bay therapists, began meeting in October to talk about the danger of war and about what they as therapists could do. As war became more imminent, more therapists and related mental health professionals attended the meetings. The meetings included announcements of general antiwar events and discussions of ways in which therapists could speak out against the war. As a result of these discussions, some members of the group went on radio and television shows to discuss such issues as the psychological impact of the war. At the meetings of Just Peace, time was set aside for people to talk about their fear, anger, and depression about the war; in an evaluation meeting held after the war, many people said that the group had given them a sense of community that they greatly needed during the war (Andrea Aidells, personal communication, June 26, 1991, Berkeley). Other antiwar groups came together around particular skills useful to the antiwar movement: Artists and Writers for Peace, Artists and Videomakers Against War, Poets for Peace.

The most vibrant sections of the antiwar movement, especially in San Francisco, were organized not around categories of skill or occupation but around the more emotionally charged categories of sexual and racial identity. San Francisco's network of politically progressive gay and lesbian organizations provided the strongest and most vital community base for antiwar activism in the city. ACT UP, the largest of San Francisco's radical or at least militant homosexual organizations, had split in two prior to the war. In the summer of 1990 ACT UP had played a leading role in protesting the exclusion of gays and lesbians from a national conference on AIDS that was held in San Francisco; ACT UP had also used this opportunity to publicly insist that the issue of AIDS be treated with greater urgency by the federal government and also by the medical profession. In the months after the conference, some members of ACT UP argued that it was not enough to go from one action concerned with AIDS to the next, that the issue of AIDS must be integrated into a broader radical analysis and strategy. Many of the more experienced ACT UP members were included in this group, and virtually all of ACT UP's lesbian members took this position. The other side argued that ACT UP should continue to address AIDS alone, that taking on other issues would mean diluting the organization's focus and militancy.

When the buildup toward war began, ACT UP/San Francisco, which had supported drawing connections between AIDS and other issues, quickly became involved in antiwar activity. ACT UP/Golden Gate, which had taken the opposite position, debated the issue for many weeks before eventually endorsing demonstrations against the war. Other gay and lesbian organizations that also played an important role in the antiwar movement were Queer Nation (in particular its antiwar committee, Queer Peace), LAGAI (Lesbians and Gays Against Intervention), formed in the early 1980s to oppose U.S. intervention in Central America, and DAGGER (Dykes' and Gay Guys' Emergency Response), formed in the fall of 1990 to oppose a U.S. military role in the Persian Gulf.

In spite of lingering tensions from the recent split in ACT UP, which had affected all wings of the movement, ACT UP/San Francisco, Queer Nation, LAGAI, and DAGGER worked together to see that there was a visible gay and lesbian presence at the demonstrations that took place immediately after the war began and also at the massive Coalition- and Campaign-sponsored demonstrations on January 19 and January 26. These organizations also held their own jointly sponsored gay and lesbian demonstrations against the war, and they worked together to educate the gay and lesbian community about the war and to draw gays and lesbians to demonstrations and other antiwar events. The homosexual organizations contributed their own flavor to these demonstrations. On the morning of January 15, in the demonstration at the San Francisco Federal Building, the gay and lesbian activists who led the protest on one side of the building set a considerably more provocative tone than prevailed on the other sides of the building. Arawn Eibhlyn, a member of ACT UP/San Francisco who helped plan the gay/lesbian sector of the demonstration, told me,

> We wanted to make sure that there was a strong homosexual tone. We did a queer fashion show; Queer Nation led a kiss-in; people laid out American flags and lay down on them and simulated fucking. Our intention was to show disrespect to the U.S. government, and to make connections between the war and censorship issues. There were straight people as well as gays and lesbians; they were welcome if they were willing to participate in gay chants.

One of those chants went as follows: "Fags suck dicks, dykes lick labia; U.S. out of Saudi Arabia" (Arawn Eibhlyn, personal communication, June 27, 1991, San Francisco). The gay and lesbian contingents in the January 17 and 26 demonstrations also had their own chants, including "The War: It's a Dick Thing," and "Cut It Out or We'll Cut It Off." Nancy Solomon, a member of San Francisco ACT UP, told me that the latter two chants were led by women; some men joined in, some couldn't bring themselves to say the words. "It was hilarious," she said,

> To watch straight people react [to the gay and lesbian chants]. Some laughed and joined in, some grimaced, some said, "Do you have to chant something as distasteful as that?" To me, it was great. I was part of a group, I was surrounded by friends. For me, gay identity has always gone hand-in-hand with being on the left, being pro-deviance, pro-opposition. (Nancy Solomon, personal communication, June 28, 1991, San Francisco)

There were some tensions in the relations between the homosexual community and the larger peace movement. Some homosexual activists expressed resentment over the fact that, while large numbers of gays and lesbians attended general antiwar demonstrations, few straight people attended the specifically gay and lesbian demonstrations and also over the fact that the Coalition showed only perfunctory interest in representation from the homosexual community, and the Campaign showed no interest at all. But relations with the locally based peace groups, especially the Pledge of Resistance, were much better. As both homosexual activists and Pledge staff pointed out to me, there are in fact no clear-cut lines between the homosexual community and the peace movement as a whole: Many leading activists in the peace movement (and in other progressive movements) are homosexuals; this is particularly true among women in the leadership of these movements. Ten or fifteen years ago the question of sexism was the focus of considerable discussion in these organizations; women staff members at the Pledge of Resistance told me that discussions of homophobia have now largely taken the place that was once occupied by attention to sexism (Judy Rohrer and Darla Rucker, personal communication, June 19, 1991).

The prominent role of gay and lesbian organizations helped to give the movement against the Gulf War a diversity that has often been lacking in protest movements in the United States. People, and groups, of color were also present in larger numbers than has often been the case in the peace movement. Black, Chicano, Asian American, Native American, and Arab American leaders spoke out against the war; polls showed that people of color, especially blacks, opposed the war in considerably higher proportions than whites. In the Bay Area the most visible antiwar organization of people of color was Roots Against War, or RAW, a group made up of people of a variety of racial backgrounds.[1]

RAW began at a forum held at San Francisco State University, in mid-December, featuring Tahan Jones, an African American conscientious objector to the war. After the speech, Abdi Jibril, a San Francisco State student, stood up and called for people of color to come together and form their own antiwar organization. About 10 people met in response to this call; by the time the war began, meetings were attracting 50 or 60 people. The majority of RAW members were in their twenties, though a few were in their teens, and a few in their forties and fifties. Some were students at San Francisco State or at the University of California, Berkeley; some were former students at those universities or others. Initially, RAW drew mainly African Americans and Latinos, but by the time the war began it also included Asians, Palestinians, Pacific Islanders. A considerable number of RAW members had backgrounds in other radical activities, mostly in the anarchist community or in the Revolutionary Communist party (RCP), a Maoist group that many independent activists in the Bay Area have looked upon with considerable suspicion. Many RAW members with backgrounds in leftist organizations were tired of being used as tokens, being constantly called upon to speak or perform other functions to demonstrate the group's commitment to opposing racism. RAW members with leftist backgrounds also brought with them a determination to oppose the war in a militant and uncompromising manner. While most of the antiwar movement was making public statements of support for the U.S. troops in the Middle East in an effort to avoid being labeled "anti-American," RAW took the position of supporting the troops that refused to go, and those that came home, but refusing to give its support to the troops carrying out the war.

RAW held antiwar forums, directed primarily at an audience of people of color, and put out leaflets urging people of color to attend antiwar demonstrations. RAW led a demonstration through San Francisco's largely Latino Mission District on the afternoon of January 15. RAW members spent a great deal of time in the streets, speaking to people about the war, urging them to join RAW in the antiwar demonstrations. In the demonstrations themselves, the RAW contingent provided a burst of energy. Some RAW members brought Congo drums; others danced. They carried posters with Malcolm X's portrait and antiwar signs and banners in Spanish as well as English. Many people of color joined the RAW contingent during the marches; some subsequently came to RAW meetings.

In spite of the fact that most RAW members were students, former students, or in some way connected to the universities, RAW considered itself a community organization rather than a university-based organization. During the war, RAW held marches through Latino and African American neighborhoods and held antiwar rallies in these communities. On the whole, they were not welcomed. On one of these marches, they entered the courtyard of Valencia Gardens, a housing project inhabited largely by poor African Americans and Latinos, holding banners with Malcolm X's portrait; speakers urged the residents to oppose the war and join them in demonstrating against it. People in the courtyard shouted at them, "Get out of here, leave us alone." The RAW contingent left; a few stayed behind and asked Valencia Gardens residents why they had been so hostile. "You're bringing the police into this neighborhood with your march," the RAW members were told. "Besides, what are you doing for this community? Don't come here and preach to us about the war; we have enough problems of our own." At evaluation meetings that RAW held after the war, some members raised questions about whether it had been appropriate for them to describe RAW as a community organization; most of its members were, after all, college students or college educated, from middle-class backgrounds; few actually had connections to the poor and working class that the term *community* was meant to suggest. RAW decided to redefine itself as a university-oriented organization.

Conflicts within RAW, in the weeks before and during the war, had to do with issues of identity in an organization that was quite heterogeneous, and not only in terms of race. In fact, there was little if any conflict between members of different races. What conflict emerged had to do with the difficulties of building an organization composed of men and women, gays, lesbians, and straight people and also conflicts between people whose parents were both of one race and those with mixed racial backgrounds. Women, who at one point made up about 75% of the organization, felt that men nevertheless were dominant. Speakers at RAW-sponsored forums were often contacted and invited in haste; some made remarks in their speeches that violated the political principles of at least some RAW members. In a discussion of rap music, at one forum, a speaker made what were taken to be sexist remarks; at another forum, remarks that were taken to be homophobic were made. These heightened tensions within RAW between homosexual and straight people. About a third of the African Americans in RAW had one white parent; at times such people were accused of being white, not really understanding the black experience. The rapidity of events and the pressure to respond quickly made it difficult for RAW to deal with any of these tensions; discussions of them were continually put off to the next meeting. For the most part, RAW members worked together well. But, if the antiwar movement had lasted longer, issues such as these would no doubt have become more pressing.

The issues of identity that emerged in RAW pervaded the Bay Area antiwar movement. While the established peace organizations, the churches, and to a lesser extent some of the Bay Area labor unions provided the institutional backbone of the movement, the more informal groups that did much of the campus and community organizing were frequently defined around sexual, racial, or gender identity. Groups of people of color opposing the war, in addition to RAW, included the African Americans for Peace and Justice, the Palestinian Solidarity Committee, the Chicano Moratorium, the Raza United Against the War. Furthermore, for many activists, issues of identity emerged, or became more salient, during the course of the war. Some activists, belonging to an organization defined in terms of one identity, found themselves caught up in issues posed by another aspect of their identity. Members of RAW found themselves in conflict over issues of homosexual/straight and male/female relations; many gay and lesbian activists found themselves confronting issues of Jewish identity and anti-Semitism. Kate Raphael, a member of DAGGER (Dykes' and Gay Guys' Emergency Response) told me that there was tension within the gay and lesbian community over the question of Israel. A group called Queer Jews for Peace was formed; some of its members felt that groups such as DAGGER, which were critical of Israel, were anti-Semitic. Kate pointed out that there have always been large numbers of Jews in the peace movement; in DAGGER, all of the lesbians, and some of the gay men, were Jews. All were critical of Israel's treatment of the Palestinians. Kate said that some DAGGER members questioned the right of Israel to exist as a Jewish state but that she did not agree. Kate and many of the other Jews in DAGGER became increasingly aware of expressions of anti-Semitism, outside the peace movement and also within it: It seemed as if the war somehow allowed people to say things that ordinarily they would refrain from saying. Kate said that, as the daughter of a holocaust survivor, with a vivid awareness of the history of Nazism in Germany, it made her very uneasy when antiwar speakers spoke of wealthy Jews supporting the war effort or blamed Bush's policies on the influence of the Israel lobby.

There was little acknowledgment, Kate said, of the role of Jews in the peace movement; instead, she saw non-Jews trying to distance themselves from the Jewish left or from Jews. She saw this most often, she said, on the part of white men associated with the sectarian left; she suspected that they were trying to impress people of color, believing (erroneously, Kate thought) that people of color in the antiwar movement were receptive to anti-Semitism. She mentioned signs that she saw at rallies reading, "No War for Jews," and statements in the left press to the effect that "once again the Israeli dog wags the American tail." She pointed out that, if a Jew supported the war or took an ambiguous position on it, someone was sure to point out that that person was a Jew; if a Jew opposed the war, the fact that he or she was a Jew was likely to go unmentioned; a Jewish opponent of the war seemed to not count as a Jew. Kate said that she heard a speech by Willamette Brown, a lesbian black activist, who mentioned her disappointment with "the Jewish perspective" on the war. "People wouldn't do that to any other group," Kate said. "No one would assume that one black speaks for the entire community" (Kate Raphael, personal communication, May 24, 1991, San Francisco).

For Jews who were opposed to the war, responding to the assumption that Jews supported the war was complicated by the fact that for at least the last three decades the organized Jewish community has been overwhelmingly associated with and identified with Israel and has distanced itself from the tradition of progressive politics that the Jewish left of the first part of this century represented. This legacy is continued by the large number of Jews who participate in progressive movements, but, because most of them do not do so explicitly as Jews, the tradition of Jewish radicalism has lost visibility. In recent years some of the divisions among Jews have begun to break down; it is no longer the case that those who organize themselves and speak as Jews are certain to be conservative or that radical Jews are sure to keep their Jewish identity separate from their politics. There are a number of progressive Jewish groups in the Bay Area; one of these, the International Jewish Peace Union, spoke out against U.S. military intervention in the Middle East from the moment it was put forward as an option. But the International Jewish Peace Union is small and has little in the way of resources.

It was *Tikkun*, the Jewish magazine based in the Bay Area, that was taken by activists and others in the Bay Area and beyond to be the voice of the progressive or, perhaps more accurate, liberal Jewish community. Michael Lerner, the editor of *Tikkun*, waffled on the question of the war. In an article in the November-December issue, he wrote that he was torn between the progressive within him that opposed U.S. intervention and the Jew who feared for the security of Israel and wanted Saddam destroyed. He called for a preemptive strike again Iraq. He accused those in the peace movement who publicly criticized Israel of anti-Semitism (Lerner, 1990). Perhaps in part because of the outraged response from many *Tikkun* subscribers and others to a call for a first strike, Lerner changed his position. Under the auspices of *Tikkun*, he held a Jewish teach-in against the war, at which he called for Jews to oppose Bush's war. He apologized for his earlier support of military intervention and called upon others who might also have supported the war at first to rethink their positions as he had. But he continued to identify criticisms of Israel with anti-Semitism.

In the Bay Area the role of identity politics in the antiwar movement was positive in many ways. The gay and lesbian organizations played a major role in the antiwar movement; the gay and lesbian community was probably more mobilized against the war than any other single community in the area. Gay and lesbian organizations, and organizations of people of color, gave the movement flair, creativity, energy. The prominent role of these organizations gave many gay activists, and activists of color, a sense that they were no longer simply supporting someone else's movement; this was their movement as well. Nancy Solomon argued that it was identity politics that gave the movement its sense of rootedness in community and also its streak of defiance. "What's good about the idea of queer identity," she said,

> is that it's trying to encompass any kind of outrageous thing that you can think of. It's pro-sex, pro-deviance, shave your head and dye it purple. A friend of mine is—what's the politically correct term for it? Well, overweight, a big, black dyke, with short black hair, and she wears a black leather jacket. There's no assimilation here. To me, that's what's vibrant and great about this new politics. Her identity is multilayered, and it's completely in-your-face, this is who I am and I don't care what you think.

Nancy Solomon, who like Kate Raphael had been disturbed by the indications of anti-Semitism that she saw during the war, pointed out that having a multilayered identity, in her case that of a lesbian and a Jew, often meant conflict with others in those communities. "I would be comfortable challenging homophobia in a Jewish organization, or challenging anti-Semitism in a queer organization," she said. "But I'd rather be challenging anti-Semitism in a queer organization because that's my community, that's where the social opportunities are for me. I'd hate to be a heterosexual these days," she said, "especially a heterosexual looking for a relationship, or for a community. There used to be a left community, but it just isn't there any more" (Nancy Solomon, personal communication, June 28, 1990, San Francisco).

The politics of identity worked better for some people than others; it drew upon communities defined by their oppression or marginalization in terms of sexual orientation or race. It was not nearly as helpful in fostering the development of other kinds of communities. Especially after the war began, there were many people who wanted someplace to go, some community to be part of. For those who did not fit into any of the identity-based groups, or who did not understand their opposition to the war in those terms, there was often no place to go. The Middle East Peace Action, an ad hoc committee that had come together to organize demonstrations and other events, was swamped with phone calls from people who wanted to come to meetings; unsure of how to incorporate all these people, and afraid that suddenly opening up our meetings would destroy our capacity to organize antiwar events, we simply told them to go away.

In Santa Cruz the Persian Gulf Peace Coalition, which played the same role of orchestrating antiwar events, faced the same problem: After the war broke out, they were swamped with people who wanted to attend meetings. It became difficult for the coalition to function; many key activists stopped attending meetings. Another closed committee of activists was formed; this brought charges of elitism (John Hunter, personal communication, June 13, Santa Cruz; Pete Shanks, personal communication, June 5, Santa Cruz). The politics of identity brought groups that have been all too marginal to the peace movement into its mainstream. But it did not provide a framework for incorporating everyone who might have wanted to do more than attend demonstrations.

The politics of identity were also a major factor in the antiwar movement in Santa Cruz, especially on the UCSC campus, where for several years undergraduate politics, and student government, has been dominated by a number of identity-based organizations: MECHA (an organization of Chicano/Chicana students), ABSA (the African-Black Student Alliance), APISA (Asian/Pacific Islanders' Student Alliance), and more recently the Progressive Jewish Student Union. MECHA, ABSA, APISA, and a large number of other organizations based on particular racial/ethnic identities make up the Third World Core, a coalition of organizations of students of color. These organizations have played an increasingly prominent role in the Student Union Assembly.

Early in the Fall Quarter, a small group of students came together to educate the campus about, and mobilize it against, what appeared to be an impending war in the Middle East. These students were white; their organization, which they called the SCSSR (Santa Cruz Students for Social Responsibility), attracted a few students of color but remained a largely white organization. Their first effort was to circulate a questionnaire asking students, faculty, and staff if they would support a shutdown of the campus in the event of a war; the responses showed widespread sympathy for a shutdown and also helped generate discussion about the war and other possible responses. SCSSR activists were meanwhile consulting with other student organizations about responses to the war; out of these discussions, SCSSR called a meeting to organize an undergraduate antiwar coalition. There was broad participation in the coalition; nevertheless, in the months leading up to the war, and during the war itself, it was SCSSR activists who did most of the work in mobilizing what turned out to be a very impressive campus antiwar movement, including a 2-day shutdown of the campus and many demonstrations, teach-ins, forums, and other events. SCSSR members essentially became the staff of the student coalition, doing antiwar work in the name of (and subject to the control of) the student antiwar coalition.

The solidarity of the coalition remained relatively intact until several weeks into the war when, in the wake of SCUD attacks on Israel, the Progressive Jewish Student Union, a coalition member, announced that it could no longer take the position of opposing the war. This set off several weeks of discussion on what the coalition should call itself and, by implication, what stand it should take on the war. Eventually the term *antiwar* was dropped and replaced by the words *peace and justice*. Meanwhile, the coalition was falling apart, partly because of internal dissension, partly as a result of the growing demoralization of the antiwar movement on campus and more broadly.

After the Progressive Jewish Student Union withdrew its opposition to the war and conflicts within the coalition intensified, Julie Martin, a member of SCSSR who had called the coalition together and continued to be its most active organizer, talked to several members of the faculty antiwar organization, who proposed holding a forum on problems of coalition building, with a majority of speakers of color. "I presented this idea at a coalition meeting," Julie later told me,

and I was told that this was an imperialist policy, that we didn't need a lot of people coming in from the outside. I was told that I was a racist. I said that white people can feel insulted too. One woman said that you can only be insulted if you're a person of color or a Jew. She read a passage from a book about how much people of color and Jews have been victimized. She said I didn't have a right to feel insulted. In fact I'm a Jew, and a lot of people in the room knew it. But I didn't put that out.

Julie said that chairing coalition meetings was extremely difficult, because everyone in the room was intent upon representing not just an organization but a conception: the African American perspective, the Jewish perspective, the gay/lesbian perspective. In fact, she said, the identities were not nearly as neatly parceled out as one would have thought from listening to people's remarks. Though the representative of the Progressive Jewish Student Union spoke in the name of Jews, in fact about a third of the members of the coalition were Jewish, and many often found themselves in disagreement with positions taken by the PJSU. "The PJSU representative would say, 'Jews think such-and-such,' and about a third of the room would squirm," Julie said. "Unfortunately none of us had the courage to say anything, except privately, among ourselves." There were also many lesbians in the coalition, not all of them representing lesbian or homosexual organizations; on the Santa Cruz campus, as elsewhere, women often play a leading role in political activism, and many women leaders in a range of progressive movements are lesbians.

There were lesbians representing organizations that did not describe themselves as homosexual; there were students of color representing particular racial groups who were themselves of mixed background. At some point during the course of the war, one of the MECHA representatives discovered that she had a Jewish grandfather and became interested in Jewish issues.

The crosshatched quality of identities within the coalition did not detract from the fervor with which coalition members put forward the views of particular constituencies or from their certainty that they knew what these constituencies thought. Jewish students who disagreed with the Progressive Jewish Student Union found its claims to represent Jews galling. At one point, the woman representing BALI (Bisexual and Lesbian Individuals), after a conflict with the PJSU representative, said in exasperation, "Look, both you and I are queer Jews, so stop giving me a hard time." Charges of racism and anti-Semitism were often uttered in the same breath and became a more or less routine part of political discourse. Many of the organizations of students of color were uneasy about civil disobedience, which members of SCSSR and some other white student radicals tended to push for; the students of color were afraid that arrests might lead to the loss of fellowships or other penalties that might jeopardize the careers of students with little resources to fall back upon. A civil disobedience demonstration, organized independently by members of SCSSR, brought on charges that the antiwar movement was racist and anti-Semitic (Julie Martin, personal communication, June 1, 1991, Santa Cruz).

SCSSR was treated with suspicion throughout the war by the other organizations in the student coalition, partly because it was predominantly white and partly because it was organized around opposition to the war rather than around an identity. Amy Cho, a leader of the Asian/Pacific Islanders' Association and also the chair of the Student Union, told me that the organizations of students of color were determined that white issues should not become the center of student politics and also that in their experience identity provided a solid basis for politics; organizations concerned with issues, rather than identity, tended to come and go and could not be trusted. Furthermore, she said, discussion, or alliance, with people who did not speak from an identity was difficult. "When some people speak from a location, and others don't, then you don't know where you are on any of these issues [of racism, sexism, homophobia, anti-Semitism]. If I locate myself as a Korean American woman, I can't talk to someone who doesn't locate themself [*sic*]." She said that she respected the work that SCSSR had done in bringing the student coalition together and in doing most of the work to mobilize the campus against the war, but the fact that the SCSSR had no location in identity was a problem (Amy Cho, personal communication, June 13, 1991, Santa Cruz).

Part of what was involved in the tensions between the SCSSR and other organizations in the student coalition was that the SCSSR was a new arrival on the scene of student politics and was nevertheless dominating the student antiwar movement. Another factor was the greater uneasiness of the existing student organizations about antiwar militance, partly because these organizations had not been formed to oppose the war and did not want to jeopardize their main aims. They also did not want to jeopardize their alliance: When the PJSU withdrew its opposition to the war, the other organizations were willing to modify their opposition to the war partly to avoid undermining an alliance that predated the war and would continue to be important after the war, an alliance that sustains the influence of all these organizations within student politics. Hesitation about a clear and perhaps militant opposition to the war also was reflected in the sense of the students of color that their foothold in the university might be precarious and the response of many Jewish students to the danger that the war posed to Israel.

The problems in the coalition also involved a clash between two different ways of understanding politics. The SCSSR was trying to introduce a politics that centered on an issue; this was discordant in a student movement dominated by the idea that politics was an expression of identity, in particular an identity based on oppression or marginalization. The virtue of identity politics is that it insists on the inclusion of groups that are marginalized within society and whose perspective has in the past not been given adequate recognition even within many progressive movements. The danger of identity politics is that it can reduce to a politics of the self, often revolving around a definition of the self as victimized. In the extreme, this can lead to power being allotted in proportion to claims of victimization; it can lead to an interest group politics in which there is little basis for groups working together and little connection to a progressive vision of overarching social change.

The experience of the antiwar movement on the Santa Cruz campus suggests that here at least the language of identity politics has largely taken over, that many student activists do not see any other basis for politics as legitimate. Identity politics seems to be the politics of the 1990s; few undergraduates have experience with any other sort of politics. Santa Cruz is a relatively progressive campus; it is also a center for the poststructuralist/postmodernist intellectual currents that promote particularity and renounce conceptions of universal value. These two influences intersect to encourage a conception of radicalism centered on the defense of particular, marginalized, or oppressed identities. UCSC is also a relatively elite campus. This may also have something to do with the fierceness with which such identities are defended. White and middle-class guilt are important components in the construction of radical politics, though usually unspoken. Identity is an uncertain and fragile matter for many people these days; this is especially true for young people, for whom many categories of identity are not yet fixed and who often come from backgrounds that are mixed in terms of race or ethnicity. The appeal to identity is one version of a politics of nationalism that in a variety of guises appears to be sweeping many areas of the world. In the wake of the collapse of the socialist world, it often seems difficult to imagine anything but nationalism, or identity, as a basis for politics. It also no doubt expresses the desire for some stable definition of the self, some reliable basis for community, in a society and world in which it often seems that everything is in flux.

Since the end of the war, there has been much discussion among activists about whether the antiwar movement could have prevented the war or ended it before so many Iraqis were killed. Some have argued that we made the mistake of opposing the last war, that is, believing that the Gulf War was a repeat of the Vietnam War and falling back on a strategy of opposition that was appropriate for that war but did not work this time. At a meeting of the UC Berkeley Peace Committee a month or so after the war ended (April 8, 1991), Peter Dale Scott, Professor of English and antiwar activist, argued that we relied too much on demonstrations.[2] He argued that it was as if we were trying to repeat the strategy of the movement against the Vietnam War: The massive demonstrations of 1971 were a major factor in turning the tide against that war. The difference, he pointed out, was that opposition to the war in Vietnam had by that time been building for 5 or 6 years, and those demonstrations helped to turn an antiwar minority into a majority. We faced a different situation: We were a small minority in a sea of popular support for the war. It was not enough to "go out and be ourselves on the streets." Demonstrations, Scott said, were appropriate as part of an antiwar strategy, but our main focus should have been on education, on convincing the public that the war was not in the interest of Americans or anyone else.

It is true that many of us thought, or hoped, that we were opposing the last war. Through the fall there was in fact substantial public reluctance to support U.S. military involvement in the Gulf. We hoped that the lessons of Vietnam had held, and that widespread public misgivings of the prewar months could be turned into a fierce majority opposition once war began. We were of course wrong: We were caught off guard by the quick and dramatic drop in opposition to war virtually the moment the bombing began. Many of us then found ourselves in the awkward and unhappy position of hoping that the war would last a long time, that the Iraqi opposition would be strong enough to impose substantial costs on the United States. We were afraid that, if the United States won a quick and overwhelming victory, the experience would serve to justify the use of force in other conflicts to come. We predicted that the war would be long because we had to make this argument to mobilize opposition. We believed it because our actions were premised on it and because we guiltily hoped that it would turn out to be true. We quickly learned that we were dealing with a very different kind of war.

As many activists argued after the war was over, it is not clear that the antiwar movement could have done better if we had been able to predict the shift in public opinion toward support of the war or if we had understood how quickly the United States could defeat Iraq. In spite of a shrinking base of support, we mobilized massive opposition, especially in the first 2 weeks after the war began. In spite of predictions that this would be a long war, many of us dropped everything else to oppose the war. For 10 days or so, San Francisco, Santa Cruz, and many other cities and towns were entirely caught up in antiwar activity. Max Elbaum, in "The Storm at Home" (1991), argues that the Bush administration's intention of winning a military victory over Iraq was determined by factors beyond the control of the antiwar movement. The administration saw its opportunity to greatly enhance U.S. power in the Middle East and believed that the United States had the military capacity to win an overwhelming victory; the Soviet Union no longer stood in the way of such plans; there was not sufficient opposition from Western European governments to pose a serious obstacle. U.S. public opinion swung over to support of the war once it seemed that the United States would win easily.

The movements, and constituencies, that made up the antiwar movement in the Bay Area and Santa Cruz mostly fall into the category that over the last 10 years or so has come to be called "new social movements." According to the terminology introduced by Alain Touraine,

Alberto Melucci, and other European social analysts, and now increasingly adopted by analysts in the United States as well, the "old social movements," the movements of the nineteenth century and the first several decades of the twentieth, were those organized around class, especially the movements of the working class; these movements, often defining themselves as socialist, regarded sustained organization as a necessity and tended toward hierarchy and bureaucracy. The "new social movements" are those of the 1960s and beyond, those organized around issues and identities not immediately related to class; these movements have often been infused with an anarchist sensibility, have often rejected institutional politics and attempted to work outside it.[3] The women's movement, the gay and lesbian movements, movements of color are all examples of movements concerned with the redefinition of social identity and the defense or creation of communities around those identities. The peace movement and the environmental movement are examples of movements concerned with issues that transcend or at least operate at a remove from issues of class. These have been among the most vital movements of the 1970s and 1980s in the United States; it was from these arenas that the antiwar movement emerged.

To the extent that "new social movement theory" recommends a strategy, or a direction, for the movements of this period, it is a focus on the defense or creation of communities and the articulation of new identities and cultures, or sets of values.[4] The movement against the Gulf War was in large part based on communities engaged in redefining identity, assigning new meaning to identities and social positions that are frequently devalued. In the Bay Area the gay and lesbian community was the strongest base for antiwar activism and gave the antiwar movement much of its vitality. Groups of people of color also played an important role. On the UC Santa Cruz campus, groups organized around sexual and racial identity made up much of the base of the antiwar movement. The women's movement had little organized presence in the antiwar movement in either city, but the movement included at least as many women as men, not only as participants but as leaders. Identity politics showed its most positive side off the campus, where small organized groups devoted themselves to mobilizing their constituencies against the war. It showed its most negative side in campus politics, where jockeying for power among various groups was more salient.

The main problem that the Bay Area antiwar movement faced was that it could not win alone. Ultimately it did not matter how many people in Santa Cruz, San Francisco, and the East Bay opposed the war; ending the war required a national movement and a national strategy. The movement in the larger Bay Area flourished as long as it was possible to believe that opposition to the war around the nation was developing. The movement in the Bay Area began to collapse 10 days or so after the war began, largely because it had become clear that in the nation as a whole support for the war was overwhelming.

In looking back over the experience of the antiwar movement in the larger Bay Area, I see two factors that caused serious problems: (a) a strain within identity politics that magnified internal divisions in the movement and (b) the absence of any forum for arriving at a national strategy. The latter seems to me to have been by far the more serious of the two problems. The strength of the Bay Area antiwar movement reflected the strength of a progressive culture and the fact that a few progressive institutions have survived the Reagan era. The weakness of the antiwar movement was that it expressed what amounted to a counterculture rather than a national political force. A war cannot be effectively opposed by a local counterculture or even a series of loosely linked countercultures in various parts of the country.

Such a judgment raised the question: What are the prospects for progressive politics in an era in which most social movements are organized around identity? I think the answer is that it is necessary to move beyond identity politics, and, if it is necessary, I hope it is also possible. This is not to argue against movements organized on the basis of particular social groups. The term *identity politics* does not refer to every movement with a particular social base. It refers to a politics in which the assertion or construction of identity is a salient concern. The civil rights movement was based in the southern black community, in particular the black church, but it was not an example of identity politics because it was not predominantly concerned with constructing black identity. Through the creation of community, and the experience of collective struggle, the civil rights movement did contribute greatly to black culture and to the reformulation of black identity. But at least for most of the history of the civil rights movement, neither the beloved community nor black pride were ends in themselves.

In many social movements that have emerged more recently, identity has become a more salient issue. This is probably largely because so many aspects of identity are undergoing rapid change and also because the assertion of identity appears to hold out a solid basis for community, which many people otherwise experience as thin and unreliable. Social movements cannot win people's loyalties, or provide people with a base for political activity, without addressing these issues. But there is a delicate balance between two dangers: the first, of ignoring these concerns, and the second, of getting lost in them. When the creation of community becomes an end in itself, conflict is driven underground; the community becomes static; and people begin to leave.

When the assertion of identity becomes an end in itself, differences—often including spurious distinctions—quickly take precedence over shared concerns; communication deteriorates; and the basis for a broad movement or effective political action evaporates. These are the problems of a movement in decline or in remission. If the movement against the Gulf War had grown, opposition to the war would have created a sense of unity; difference and particularity would probably not have overwhelmed that sense of unity but would have emerged within it and with luck would have prodded it forward. At moments, such as the current one, when there seems to be no basis for unity, it seems to me that it is important nevertheless to remember that the assertion of identity is only one side of an ongoing tension between the need for autonomy and the need for a more inclusive collectivity.

NOTES

1. This account of Roots Against War is based on a personal communication with Tanya Mayo (May 17, 1991).

2. Scott Kennedy of the Resource Center for Nonviolence made a similar argument at a conference to evaluate the antiwar movement in Santa Cruz (June 1, 1991).

3. For a description of what is meant by "new social movements," see Carl Boggs (1986). For discussions of construction of identity and meaning as elements in the politics of the new social movements, see Alberto Melucci (1985) and Claus Offe (1985).

4. For discussions of strategy, or direction, for the new social movements, see Ernesto Laclau and Chantal Mouffe (1985), Alberto Melucci (1989), and Alain Tourain (1988).

REFERENCES

Boggs, C. (1986). *Social movements and political power: Emerging forms of radicalism in the West.* Philadelphia: Temple University Press.

Elbaum, M. (1991, April). The war at home. *Crossroads*, pp. 21-22.

Laclau, E., & Mouffe, C. (1985). *Hegemony and socialist strategy: Toward a radical democratic politics.* London: Verso.

Lerner, M. (1990, November-December). My inner conflict about Iraq. *Tikkun*, pp. 48-57.

Melucci, A. (1985). The symbolic challenge of contemporary movements. *Social Research, 52*(4), 789-816.

Melucci, A. (1989). *Nomads of the present.* Philadelphia: Temple University Press.

Offe, C. (1985). New social movements: Challenging the boundaries of institutional politics. *Social Research, 52*(4), 817-867.

Tourain, A. (1988). *Return of the actor: Social theory in postindustrial society.* Minneapolis: University of Minnesota Press.

Conclusion: Prospects and Strategies for Mobilization in the Era of Global Cities

ROBERT FISHER
JOSEPH KLING

The chapters in this volume demonstrate that, at the least, social movements have not withered away, and, at best, contemporary grass-roots organizing represents the most significant current form of political opposition. People continue through community action to seek control of their lives and to give direction to their world. But no one knows the ultimate importance of the new citizen actions and the sorts of impacts they will have. It would be just as inappropriate, on the one hand, to give up on the possibilities for popularly directed social change, as it would, on the other, to suggest that contemporary forms of collective action will end the oppressions of our time or dislodge the entrenched elites who hold power. What we do assert, however, is that the community of activists and activist-scholars needs to rethink the very meanings and structures of collective action. The organizational dynamics of grass-roots efforts, the kinds of goals sought, the extent of the transformations achieved, the concepts defining the relation between the person and the state all require renegotiation and redefinition.

In this era of global transition, activists face a poorly charted terrain. But, as always, strategies and practices matter. Based on insights drawn from the chapters in the volume, in fact, we propose that community mobilization be informed by at least four value-based assumptions and practices: the acceptance of an identity politics that is polyvocal in outlook; the commitment to philosophies and programs that connect identity-based groups to cultural others; a focus on broadly formulated issues and programs, articulated through multicultural coalitions and alliances, as central instruments for the achievement of policy goals; and the engagement of the state as an arena for struggle and change.

While there are no guarantees as to what makes for effective social action, the presence of these practices and goals in contemporary grassroots formations and processes, we contend, is a necessary precondition to realize whatever potentials they do contain for the empowerment of subaltern groups. The first precondition for effective mobilization is the acceptance and support of identity politics. This is a politics grounded in communities of interest whose self-understandings have been molded by common histories, common experiences of exclusion, common traditions, and common language codes. In complex societies, cultural, racial, ethnic, and gender identities have generally displaced class as major sources of such collective feeling and political community, even though class structures continue to shape and define many of the oppressions and injustices that create the drive for identity-based organization in the first place. Practice will not be able to return to a discourse that treats the cultural self as in some sense derivative and secondary to class position. No movement can succeed in today's political milieux without giving particular voice to those who have been compelled by dominant cultures to experience themselves as different and marginalized.

Second, collective action must move beyond identity politics by affirming the importance of accountability to, and responsibility for, distant others. The contradictions between struggles for change based on culturally differentiated communities, and the need for members of these communities to "leave home" and join with different voices in larger goals and practices, has been one of the strongest threads running through this collection. Identity politics has much potential. But without a consciousness that transcends the fragmentation inherent in an overly deep commitment to the politics of the cultural self, the principle of identity becomes self-serving, parochial, and divisive.

The conditions of a postindustrial economy and postmodern culture may continually undermine the achievement of forums through which exchange and compromise across differences of identity can take place. In societies subject to fragmentation and the erosion of public philosophies, the experience of marginalized groups seems to lead almost inherently to the assertion of political needs and programs in particularist terms. To interpret identity in ways that directly confront state policies, and challenge repressive economic structures and cultural attitudes as a whole, is consistently read by constituency groupings as somehow surrendering integrity and giving up on autonomy and empowerment.

Because these responses dominate so much of the current discourse of political action, activists concerned with broad-based change have no alternative but to continue to fight for ideologies and organizational structures that look beyond community borders and that hold to larger, global readings of program and strategy. This means a willingness on the part of organizers, even as they recognize the deep historical sources of particularist sentiment and grant the legitimacy of the mistrust from which it is bred, to engage in conflict and open exchange with colleagues who insist exclusively on identity-based mobilization.

As the chapters of Epstein and Lehr demonstrate, unless there exist political and philosophical commitments that take collective action beyond identity politics, the points at which movements begin to be capable of broad social and political impact are the very points at which they begin to self-destruct.

There is an unavoidable contradiction here. For it is in the spaces where people confront each other and talk about their grievances that autonomous practices—as opposed to practices defined by professional experts and established by administrative apparatuses—come into play. There is a sense in which the term *agency* refers not to collective action per se but to the self-created activity and formulations that come out of the independent discussions, arguments, and choices of named constituencies. Boyte and Evans (1986) developed the notion of "free spaces" to give empirical meaning to those arenas where agency operates—arenas where oppressed groups find the voices to project programs, actions, and ends of their own. Allen translates the ideas of agency and free space into the language of Foucault with her observation that "resistance is born in the interplay between subjectivity and subjection." People come to their own sense of who they are and what they want and on that basis formulate demands and practices. The contradiction stems from the fact that free spaces alone do not guarantee the realization of humane voices and broad struggles for social justice. Organizers need to balance the claims of autonomy against the requirements for openness and acceptance of the other. In one sense, this has always been a central dilemma of activism. That, at least, has not changed. But in our decentered context where few experience class outside of racial, ethnic, or gendered identity, it is more pressing than before.

Third, the need for connection to the cultural other as ideological setting for agency and autonomy leads to another condition for effective practice: a constant focus on developing broadly formulated issues and building organizational forms that bring citizen action efforts together.

Such broadly formulated issues and organizational structures are the only instruments available for empirically moving beyond the voices of disparate identity. If the notion of the young Korean woman interviewed by Epstein prevails—that organizations concerned with issues rather than identity cannot be trusted—new social movement formations will never be able to realize their promise. They will remain extrapolitical cultural projects. As many chapters in the volume underscore, urban and national institutional politics still matter. Citizen action sometimes needs to challenge, other times to "coproduce" with, those holding formal political power, that is, helping make decisions and delivering services. But the ability to have impact on institutional political life turns on the willingness of social movements both to focus on broad issues, like the need for generalized, public health care within the confines of a capitalist society, and to form, and remain committed to, coalitions and alliances.

To do so, analysis must recognize the shared characteristics as well as the fragmentation inherent in contemporary efforts. These efforts do have a common structural form. They share comparable goals, tactics, a consciousness of oppositional politics, and a collective biography of oppression, even though the nature of that oppression and how it has been endured and confronted can be quite different. Given what they have in common as a basis for further unity, community-based efforts must make a priority of transcending local parochialisms of place and culture and building more inclusive structures like coalitions, alliances, political parties, even transnational organizations and networks. There is no getting around the dilemma, however, that, as a basis for such coalition work, community-based mobilizations must be willing to engage in conflict, both internal and external. This process includes being willing to work with other groups to reflect on, struggle over, and redefine organizing experiences.

Such alliance formation is no small challenge. Coalition work is among the hardest facing organizers, especially among organizations with scarce resources. Participants usually join so as to get more out of it than they put in. Nevertheless, as power and capital centralize locally and globally, so must resistance. It is the critical role of a common threat, shared ideological assumptions, leadership committed to the larger struggle as well as organization building, and the moral force of social movements that makes such cooperation possible. These, too, must become more of the focus of contemporary efforts. In addition, contemporary labor-community collaborative campaigns provide models for alliances that incorporate essential old and new social movement elements. They tie together, for example, campaigns to regulate corporate practices, which target capital directly or work through state intermediaries, with issues and constituencies focused on ecology, gender, and race. Finally, the broadly formulated issues and inclusive structures need to become more directly involved with the state and with the dynamics of public decision making. Labor-based social movements almost always sought to connect themselves to political parties. Community action groups have tended to remain mostly outside institutional politics. Their locus of activity and experience remains their community. There they win tangible improvements in people's lives. There they give constituents a sense of their own power. But rarely are they able to truly alter relations of power beyond the community. Urban and national politics, not to mention regional and more global formations, remain in the hands of "the other." The early neopopulist movements of the 1970s in the United States and the citizen initiatives of Western Europe made independence from political parties almost a principle of organization. This is becoming less true as the importance of the state and the struggle over public sites for public discourse become more apparent.

Still, under the politics of postindustrialism, retreat from institutionalized political action seems as endemic as does identity politics. While there is much to be suspicious of in the workings of parties and the state bureaucracies they allegedly oversee, the consequence of cutting loose from legislative and party politics is to turn control of public policy over to corporate power and the forces of cultural conservatism. In the United States the centrality of the state to social empowerment is perhaps becoming clearer as people experience the ways in which such issues as restriction of abortion and civil rights, lack of adequate health care, poverty, and the threat of AIDS begin to impede more and more directly on their lives. We suggest that the election of Bill Clinton in the United States reflects, obvious limits aside, the potential relegitimization of the public sector and the role of the state in addressing issues of national welfare.

The party system in the West as a whole is in crisis, though perhaps less so in Western Europe than in the United States, and there is no way of telling, at this moment, what will emerge from its metamorphosis. But executives and legislatures still act, and the decisions they make continue to have significant and direct impacts on the opportunities available to individuals and communities. This seems better understood in Third World nations than in industrially advanced ones. The disaffected constituencies of developed societies can begin to relearn through a citizen action that focuses on both the community and the state, on the political economy as well as on culture, that public policy matters, that the decline of public life ultimately undermines all popular resistance. It may not be clear what sorts of institutional and nationally oriented alternatives make sense. But it is certain that new forms will only develop through efforts that challenge, work with, and sometimes even support the elected and appointed leaders who have a disproportional share of power to influence the nature of our communities, cities, nation, and world.

Moreover, the lack of clear direction for institutional politics is all the more reason for organizers and activists to seek to invent solutions and discover new political structures. The alternatives are to surrender to the privatization of the political and to give in to the tides of withdrawal. Such solutions may offer the prospect of "going along with history" and present themselves therefore as smart and expedient. But other than the argument from convenience, what is the logic behind it? Community mobilization is the dominant form of resistance in complex society. It is a basis for restoring public life, empowering individuals and communities, and challenging the state and capital. The chapters in this book are evidence for that. But the chapters also show that the ability of social movements to empower people to challenge exploitative economic institutions and repressive cultural norms remains problematic. If, however, as we argued in the Introduction, agency and contingency, as well as structures, matter, then it follows that people will continually find ways to construct new movement forms and to assert control over their lives. People are shaped by structures. But they also act independently and seek innovative ways of resisting domination. That, too, is part of daily life.

REFERENCE

Evans, S. M., & Boyte, H. C. (1986). *Free spaces: The sources of democratic change in America.* New York: Harper and Row.

Index

325

About the Contributors

JUDITH ALLEN is Principal Lecturer and Director of the Housing Education Centre at the University of Westminster in London. Her main intellectual interest is how contemporary social theory can be used to understand contemporary urban housing politics. In the 1970's and 1980's, she organized private tenants in Paddington, and in the 1980's was involved in advising the Greater London Council on a variety of housing and planning issues in central London. After the death of community based urban politics in the City of Westminster in the late 1980's, she decided to pursue the same objectives by joining the Management Committee on a nonprofit landlord.

SONIA E. ALVAREZ is Associate Professor of Politics at the University of California, Santa Cruz. Her research has centered on social movements, especially women's movements, and the politics of democratization in South America. She has been involved in national and international feminist politics and in Latin American solidarity work since the late 1970s. She is the author of *Engendering Democracy in Brazil: Women's Movements in Transition Politics* (Princeton University Press, 1990) and is coeditor, with Arturo Escobar, of *The Making of Social Movements in Latin America: Identity, Strategy, and Democracy* (Westview Press, 1992). Her articles on Latin American social movements and on gender politics in contemporary Brazil and the Southern Cone have appeared in *Signs, Feminist Studies* and several collections. She is currently working on a book about popular movements, urban regimes and emergent democratic alternatives in postauthoritarian Brazil.

SOPHIE BODY-GENDROT, a comparatist political scientist, is Professor of American Civilization at the Sorbonne. She is the Editor-in-Chief of *Revue française d'etudes americaines*. Her most recent books are *The United States and its Immigrants, Diversified Modes of Incorporation* (1991) and *City and Violence, the Irruption of New Actors* (1990).

GARY DELGADO has over 20 years experience as a community organizer. He has been lead organizer with the New York City branch of the National Welfare Rights organization, one of the initial organizers of ACORN, and a cofounder of the Center for Third World Organizing. In addition, he has taught community organizing and action research courses at five universities. He is the author of *Organizing the Movement: The Roots and Growth of ACORN* (1986) and over 25 articles on community organizing and labor organizing efforts. He is currently the Director of the Applied Research Center in Oakland, California and a Scholar—in—Residence at the Institute for the Study of Social Change at University of California, Berkeley.

BARBARA EPSTEIN teaches in the History of Consciousness Board at the University of California, Santa Cruz. Her most recent book is *Political Protest and Cultural Revolution: Nonviolent Direct Action in the 1970s and 1980s* (University of California Press, 1991). She is currently working on a book on the political culture of the late forties and early fifties in the United States, which asks what made it possible for anti-Communism to take hold as easily as it did.

NORMAN FAINSTEIN teaches sociology at the City University of New York, where he is Dean of Arts and Sciences at Baruch College. He has published several books and numerous articles in the fields of urban studies, political economy, and race. He is currently working on a study of the politics of the ghetto and the underclass. Norman Fainstein was educated at MIT, where he holds a Ph.D. in political science, and has taught at Columbia University and the New School for Social Research.

SUSAN S. FAINSTEIN is Professor of Urban Planning and Policy Development at Rutgers University. She is coeditor of *Divided Cities: New York and London in the Contemporary World* and author of *The City Builders: Property, Politics, and Planning in London and New York*. The author of many articles on urban politics and policy, she has written extensively on neighborhood movements and is currently working on an evaluation of the Neighborhood Revitalization Program in Minneapolis.

ROBERT FISHER is Professor and Chair of Political Social Work at the University of Houston, Graduate School of Social Work. He received his Ph.D. in urban and social history from New York University and his B.A. in history from Rutgers University. He is the author of *Let* *the People Decide: Neighborhood Organizing in America* (Twayne, 1984—2nd, updated edition forthcoming in 1994). His primary interests are community organizing, urban studies, and social movements. He is currently working on a book about organizing in "private" cities like Houston, Texas. Since the late 1960s he has been active, on and off, in peace and justice efforts at the grass-roots level.

JOSEPH KLING teaches in the Government Department at St. Lawrence University. For many years, Kling worked in East New York, in Brooklyn, as a group worker and community organizer. Most recently he was coeditor, with Prudence Posner, of *Dilemma of Activism: Class, Community, and the Politics of Local Mobilization* (Temple University Press, 1990).

VALERIE LEHR is Assistant Professor of Government and the Coordinator of Gender Studies at St. Lawrence University. She received her Ph.D. in government and politics from the University of Maryland, College Park. Her research interests include the future of gay and lesbian political organizing, as well as theoretical work on political morality, psychoanalytic theory, and democracy.

BETTY REID MANDELL organized a welfare rights group in Iowa City in 1965. She has taught organizing and written about welfare issues. In 1986 she initiated *Survival News,* a newspaper written for, about, and partly by low-income people. In this role, she has worked with local welfare rights groups and national groups. *Survival News* is now the official paper of the National Welfare Rights Union.

SALLIE A. MARSTON is Associate Professor of Geography and Regional Development at the University of Arizona. She has published articles on nineteenth and twentieth century America neighborhood politics and is currently completing a book entitled *The People and the Public Sphere: The Space and Culture of Democracy in an American City,* which is to be published by the University of Arizona Press. Her research and teaching interests include women and politics, sociospatial constructions of citizenship, and the changing spaces of political activism.

MARGIT MAYER is Professor of Politics at the Free University of Berlin. She has written on urban social movements and state responses in the USA and West Germany (Habilitation), on the genesis of the

American nation state, and on the German Green Party. She is editing a book on *Theories of New Social Movements in Europe and the USA* (Routledge). Her current research interests include the significance and changes of local politics and the role of social movement institutionalization processes in local politics.

GEORGE TOWERS teaches Geography at Concord College. He has researched the intersection of economic restructuring, urban growth, and political activism along the U.S./Mexican border. He is currently investigating the regional expression of export promotion in Belize.

ANN WITHORN has worked with welfare rights groups since the late 1960s, has taught courses, and has written on welfare issues. The local welfare rights group at the University of Massachusetts, Boston—Advocacy for Resources for Modern Survival (ARMS)—grew out of a class she taught in 1980.

MATHEW ZACHARIAH is Professor on the Faculty of Education at the University of Calgary (U of C), Canada. He teaches courses on education's role in development and on international development problems at U of C and other universities. He is the author of several publications including *Revolution Through Reform* (New Delhi: Sage, 1988), which compares Mahatma Gandhi's philosophy of Sarvodaya with Conscientization, the Latin American philosophy of education associated with Paulo Freire. Another book, *Science for Social Revolution?* about the KSSP is in press (New Delhi, Sage.) In many of his professional service activities he works for changes in values and attitudes in the Western World that would help promote constructive change in the economically poorer but culturally rich countries of the South.